Praise for

QB

"Steve Young is a hero of mine, and his story is a source of inspiration for me. His perseverance, intelligence, and most of all, grace under pressure NFL-style, makes this book a fascinating read. Thanks, Steve, for sharing your story with one of your biggest fans!"
— **Tom Brady**

"All football fans know what a tremendously talented and successful quarterback Steve Young was in his NFL career. But what they don't know about are the challenges and personal obstacles Steve had to overcome to make his dreams come true. This is a most exciting and compelling story."
— **Roger Staubach**

"There has never been a QB like Steve Young, and there has never been a football memoir quite like *QB: My Life Behind the Spiral*. Young's battles with anxiety make you forget you are reading about a Hall of Famer, and make you root for him at every turn. This is a revealing, honest, compelling book that any fan will enjoy."
— **Michael Rosenberg, senior writer, *Sports Illustrated***

"Steve was not just another Hall of Fame QB — he was extraordinary in every facet of life. His passion, preparation, and attention to detail is so vivid you feel as though this *QB* has put you right in the middle of a huddle of life. I've never read a football book with more honesty and integrity — it's typical Steve. What a quarterback! What a man!"
— **Jim Nantz, CBS Sports**

"Steve Young's scrambling, pinpoint passing, and perseverance helped make him an NFL Hall of Fame quarterback. He wowed us every Sunday. Until reading *QB*, though, I had no idea about the personal mountains he had to climb to make his dreams come true. This is a most memorable story for all fans."
— **Chris Berman, ESPN**

"Steve Young's *QB: My Life Behind the Spiral* reads like he used to play: with fearlessness, creativity, and accomplishment. This is not a typical, self-serving athlete autobiography. Young is unflinchingly honest in detailing his battles with anxiety, serving as role model for far more than just staring down a fourth quarter blitz. It's a remarkable read."

— **Dan Wetzel, national columnist for Yahoo Sports**

QB

My Life Behind the Spiral

STEVE YOUNG

with Jeff Benedict

Mariner Books
Houghton Mifflin Harcourt
Boston   New York

First Mariner Books edition 2017

Copyright © 2016 by J. Steven Young

hmhco.com

Library of Congress Cataloging-in-Publication Data
Names: Young, Steve, date, author. | Benedict, Jeff, author.
Title: QB : my life behind the spiral / Steve Young with Jeff Benedict.
Description: Boston : Houghton Mifflin Harcourt, [2016] | Includes index.
Identifiers: LCCN 2016024863 (print) | LCCN 2016027360 (ebook)
ISBN 9780544845763 (hardcover) | ISBN 9780544845770 (ebook) |
ISBN 9781328745729 (pbk.)
Subjects: LCSH: Young, Steve, date. | Football players — United States —
Biography. | Quarterbacks (Football) — United States — Biography.
Classification: LCC GV939.Y69 A3 2016 (print) | LCC GV939.Y69 (ebook) |
DDC 796.332092 [B] — dc23
LC record available at https://lccn.loc.gov/2016024863

Book design by Chloe Foster

Printed in the United States of America
DOC 10 9 8 7 6 5 4 3 2 1

To Barb, my soul mate, my best friend, my everything.

To Braedon, Jackson, Summer, and Laila,
the most precious gifts of my life.

This is for you.

CONTENTS

viii · *Contents*

1

HEAD GAMES

I'M GRIPPING A football with my left hand, standing on a perfectly manicured grass field at the San Francisco 49ers training facility in Santa Clara, California. I'm wearing cleats, gray sweats, and a red jersey bearing my last name — YOUNG — and number — 8. No pads. No helmet. Practice starts in a few minutes. It's a walk-through, a final chance to go over tomorrow's game plan.

Deep in thought, I start spinning the football like a basketball on the tip of my left index finger. It looks geometrically challenging. But at this point in my life there isn't much I can't do with an oval-shaped ball made of leather sewn together by white strings. I'm thirty-three and I'm a professional quarterback. On weekend afternoons I run around a place called Candlestick Park pursued by eleven men who want to hammer me. I throw passes to Jerry Rice, the greatest receiver in the history of the game. I'm the MVP of the NFL and the highest-paid player in the league. I'm also a bachelor with a law degree.

People think I live a charmed life. Maybe I do. After all, I play a boys' game for a living. But it's not just a game to me. It's more like life or death. Standing here today, I feel as though I'm climbing Everest, nearing the summit. I've been this far twice before, yet never beyond. Today, though, I am determined to get to the top. Suddenly, threatening clouds gather and the sky darkens. There is a fierce headwind, and I have no ropes or safety harness. Fighting a building sense of nausea, I keep reaching, keep moving forward, like I always do. Almost there now. Then a familiar, heavy voice in my head says: *What if I can't get it done?*

I hear that same voice before every big game. But today that voice is louder than ever. It's Saturday, January 14, 1995. Tomorrow is the biggest game of my life. We face the Dallas Cowboys in the NFC Championship game for the third straight year. In '92 and '93 they beat us and went on to win back-to-back Super Bowls.

This year we are the two best teams in the league again. We are 14-3 and have the number-one offense. They are 13-4 and have the number-one defense. No AFC team can touch us. Whoever wins tomorrow will go on to win the Super Bowl. In short, San Francisco versus Dallas *is* the Super Bowl.

Our team owner, Eddie DeBartolo, hates losing to anyone. But he especially hates losing to Dallas. Around here, passing titles, MVP awards, and division titles are nice. But success is defined solely by winning the Super Bowl. Anything less is failure. That's the Joe Montana effect. He won four Super Bowls before I replaced him. And that's what I'm up against.

The team trainer is heading my way. He looks worried. I know what's on his mind. It's my neck. I jammed it a week ago in a playoff game against the Chicago Bears. After I ran for a touchdown that put the game away, safety Shaun Gayle drilled me. It was a late hit that sent me sprawling. I finished the game, but by the next day I had trouble turning my head. The medical staff has been working on me all week in preparation for tomorrow. Traction. Chiropractic adjustments. Electric stimulation.

"How does it feel?" the trainer says.

"Ready to go," I tell him.

To illustrate I turn my head from side to side, displaying nearly full range of motion.

Satisfied, he walks off.

This year my quarterback rating — 112.8 — is the highest in league history: over 4,000 yards passing, with 35 touchdown passes and just 10 interceptions. But I still run the ball more than any other quarterback. I have eight rushing touchdowns, and I average over five yards per carry.

All week the Cowboys have been promising the media that they will make me pay if I try to run against them. My biggest nemesis is future

Hall of Famer Charles Haley, the Cowboys' six-foot-six, 255-pound defensive end. He's one of the most disruptive forces in the NFL, and he used to play for us. Because of bad blood between him and our coaching staff, we traded him to Dallas two years ago. Big mistake. He helped them win two Super Bowls, and nothing motivates him more than knocking me down. His teammates say they are going to nail me, punish me the way Shaun Gayle did.

I'm mindful of Haley the way a surfer is mindful of a shark in the water. But once I take the field I fear nothing, especially not the hits. I might be the only quarterback who gets a thrill out of being chased. When I first joined the 49ers my teammates started calling me "Crash" because sometimes I initiate contact by lowering my shoulder and barreling into oncoming tacklers. I didn't become a football player to run out of bounds. I want to experience every aspect of the game, including the physicality.

But there's another reason I don't shy away from contact. The physical beating I take on the field every weekend is therapy for the mental beating I go through each week just to get myself on the field. I am the fastest quarterback in the NFL. I can hit the whiskers on a cat with a football from a distance of forty yards. I have a photographic memory that enables me to visualize what everyone in the huddle is supposed to do on each of the hundreds of plays in our playbook. Still, on game day, I don't want to get out of bed. It's the riddle of my anxiety:

I long to be the best quarterback in the NFL.

I dread being the best quarterback in the NFL.

It's hard to explain anxiety to those who don't experience it. Deion Sanders thinks I'm too serious, too uptight. He goes by the nickname "Prime Time," wears a red bandana on his head, and dances on the field. He tells me I need to learn to have fun.

Fun? That doesn't enter into it at all. For me, football is a quest. Quests entail overcoming hardship, trials of adversity in the pursuit of true joy. I'm now in my eleventh season in this league. I've had my share of hardships, adversity, and trials. I long for more of the joy part.

It's time for practice to begin. I bend over to tie my shoes. Suddenly, out of nowhere, something hits me with tremendous force. The point of contact is the crown of my head. I'm propelled backwards, landing on my back. Stunned, I look up. Defensive end Richard Dent is standing over me. He's six-five and weighs 270.

"Steve, are you okay? I'm sorry, man. I'm really sorry."

I grimace and reach for my forehead. *What just happened?*

Dent explains. He had been playing catch. A teammate threw him a long pass. He was running and looking back over his shoulder for the ball when he barreled into me. It was a freak accident.

Inside I laugh. Dent is third all-time in career quarterback sacks. He's one of the fiercest pass rushers in NFL history. Eddie and Carmen signed him specifically to help us beat Dallas. Yet on the eve of the Dallas game he takes out his own quarterback.

He extends a hand and helps me up. "I'm really sorry," he says again.

"I'll be all right."

But I'm not all right. My neck stiffens by the minute. By the end of the walk-through I know I've got a problem. A bump has formed on the side of my neck. Back in the locker room the trainer gives me ibuprofen for the inflammation and ice for the swelling. The muscles around my shoulder blades are tightening too. I don't want my teammates to see me hurt. The training room is empty. There the medical staff tries to break up the neck spasms with electric stimulation. That doesn't work. So they try traction. That doesn't work either. The entire area around my neck is too tight and too sore to manipulate.

The rest of the team leaves for our hotel. I stay behind to get examined by the team's physical medicine and rehabilitation specialist. Dr. Robert Gamburd starts by trying to test my range of motion. But I can't turn my head in either direction. I can't look up either. I can only look down. I feel like my head is in a vice grip.

"I have to play tomorrow," I tell him.

He goes through my options. I can wait and see if the ice and ibuprofen start to work. Or he can give me a steroid injection in my neck. Dexamethasone is a potent, fast-acting anti-inflammatory that will stop the spasms, reduce the swelling, and dull the pain for up to forty-eight hours. But there are risks:

Pain is protective. Masking it may lead to more serious damage.

Sometimes the injection causes more soreness than the injury.

The injection can lead to infection. Unlikely. But possible.

Finally, there's no guarantee the drug will produce the desired result. While he talks to me I talk to myself:

What if I can't play tomorrow?

I have to play tomorrow.

Can beating the Cowboys get any harder?

It's now 2:30. Less than two hours since Dent ran into me. My neck hasn't had much time to respond to the ibuprofen and ice. Maybe I should wait and see. In my fifteen-year career — eleven as a pro and four in college — I have played with plenty of pain. But I try to avoid putting chemicals in my body.

"I can always give you the injection later if things don't improve," he says.

I agree to check in with him in a few hours.

I duck into the San Francisco Airport Marriott. The team stays here before every home game. I go to room 9043. My name should be etched above the door. It's been my room since I joined the Niners in 1987. Tight end Brent Jones has been my roommate the entire time. We're the only two players who share a room, something I've never appreciated more than I do now. The last thing I need to do the night before the biggest game of my life is to sit alone in a room, staring at the walls. Brent knows all about my anxiety. He talks me through my fears. He gets me from the hotel to the stadium each week. He's more than a teammate. He's a brother.

Brent is six-four and weighs 240, with thick, broad shoulders and a gregarious smile. He's watching TV when I enter the room, holding my neck.

"Dude, what is wrong with you?" he says.

"Bro, my neck is messed up."

"What do you mean your neck is messed up?"

"Richard Dent ran into me."

He cracks up, thinking it's just my anxiety talking again. "What?" he says.

"He was messing around. It was an accident."

Brent shakes his head. "Dude," he says, "you're amazing."

I know what he's thinking. *This is just Steve getting himself worked up before the game.* I don't bother trying to convince him that this time my fears aren't all in my head, that the pain in my neck is real. I lie down on the bed and apply ice.

"What if I can't turn my head tomorrow?"

"You'll be all right."

"What if this throws off my timing?"

"Bro, c'mon," Brent says. "Brush it off. We have the NFC Championship game tomorrow."

A little while later he tries to get me to go to the team meal. But I'm in no mood for food. I don't want to see anyone either.

My absence at dinner prompts a visit from the trainer. He sees that my neck is getting worse and places another call to the doctor. Panic starts to set in. Team president Carmen Policy is briefed on the situation. Carmen wants to know the bottom line. The doctor tells him that even with the injection I might not regain enough range of motion to play effectively. But at this point, without the injection, it's a safe bet that I won't be able to play at all.

Carmen faces a series of decisions. Does he report my injury to the league? Does he tell Eddie? What about our players? He opts to say nothing. If he tells the NFL, then Dallas will find out, which will only motivate Charles Haley and company to really come after me. He doesn't want to tell Eddie; his mercurial temper will erupt. And there's no point in telling the team. The news will only shake players' confidence.

I have no choice. At 5:30, Dr. Gamburd enters my hotel room with his medical bag. No one else is in the room. I don't say much. Nor does he. I lie face down on my bed while he prepares a needle with four milliliters of dexamethasone and a small dose of Novocain. His fingers probe for the spot on the back of my neck between the third and fourth vertebrae. Then comes the pinprick, followed by a cold sensation that overtakes the inflamed area. I just breathe.

"Try and take it easy for the rest of the night," he says, and then he leaves.

I roll over and close my eyes. But I'm preoccupied. Too many thoughts: *Two straight losses to Dallas. Two missed Super Bowls. My neck. Pass protection. Charles Haley. Losing is not an option. My whole career has been building toward this moment. I have to play. I have to get it done this time.*

Before lights out I walk down the hall to Bart Oates's room. He's the starting center. In football a unique relationship of trust exists between a center and a quarterback. Every play on offense begins with me lining up behind Bart and barking out the snap count until he hikes the ball. The moment he delivers the ball into my hands his primary responsibility is my protection. If I get sacked, Bart takes it personally. If a defender goes after me, Bart goes after the defender. Sometimes he gets in fights for me.

He and I go way back. We were teammates in college at BYU. As a fellow Mormon, Bart is one guy who really appreciates the pressure I'm under. Not just to win football games, but to find my soul mate. Marriage and raising a family is at the core of our faith. I'm the most visible Mormon in the world, yet I'm alone. I've spent many a night at Bart's dinner table commiserating with him and his wife Michelle about my situation.

On the night before games we have a routine. I gather with Bart and three other Mormon players on our team. Since all five of us are ordained priests and we are never able to attend Sunday services during the season, we typically give each other the sacrament in these pregame gatherings.

This time Bart senses that I'm in crisis.

"What is it?" he asks.

I give him the abridged version of events.

"C'mon," he says. "Your neck is jammed. So what? It's no big deal."

Typical Bart. Whenever my fears surface he downplays them. He's always telling me not to worry so much.

I don't bother telling him about the injection. With the others looking on, Bart places his hands on my head and gives me a blessing. He says nothing about winning or playing well. He expresses gratitude for the life we live. And he prays for my protection and my safety. We're not in a church. But I feel peace for the first time all day.

I thank him and tell him that I don't know what I'd do without him.

"Hey, tomorrow we are going to beat the Cowboys," he says. "And you are going to lead us."

I wake up. It's morning, but still dark out. I sit up and turn my head. No stiffness. I have full range of motion. The steroid is working.

I look out the window at the lights on the runway jutting out into San

Francisco Bay. One jet lands, taxiing toward the terminal. Another takes off, slowly disappearing in the distance. One of the reasons I love this room is the view of the planes, especially around sunsets and sunrises. It's calming.

But at this moment I don't feel calm. One thought consumes me: We *cannot* — I cannot — go down three times in a row to the Cowboys. There can be no *great effort* that results in *tough loss*. That just won't do. It *CAN-NOT* happen!

I stare out the window for a long time. Eventually Brent wakes up. I tell him that I'm not going to breakfast. My stomach isn't feeling great. Plus, I don't want to talk to anyone. He says he'll bring me back my usual: two PowerBars and two bananas. That's what I eat before every game.

I meet Dr. Gamburd in the training room at the stadium two hours before kickoff.

"How do you feel?" he says.

"I'm going to play," I tell him.

I remove my shirt and he observes the muscle spasms in my shoulders. The twitching is uncontrollable. He tells me it's a result of the neck trauma. Then he injects Novocain into two trigger points above my left shoulder blade. I feel tingling, and then the spasms soon stop.

Offensive coordinator Mike Shanahan pulls me aside. He tells me that he's making a last-minute adjustment to our offensive scheme. He doesn't want to take a chance on Dallas getting to me. He's going to use Brent Jones in pass protection as an extra blocker. He'll be assigned to help out on Haley. That means Brent won't be available on most passing routes.

At 11:30, I take the field to stretch and loosen my arm. It's 65 degrees and sunny. But it has rained a record-setting sixteen straight days in San Francisco. The field is a mess. Groundskeepers wearing knee-high black rubber boots and yellow rain parkas work on the sod. Footing is going to be a problem.

Today is the first time the Fox Network will broadcast an NFC Championship game. John Madden is doing color. Pat Summerall has the play-by-play. They are on the field, chatting with players. I'm in no mood to chat. Not today.

I pick up a ball and start rotating my left arm like a windmill. The Eagles' "Life in the Fast Lane" is playing through the stadium sound system. I throw the ball to Brent Jones.

"This is our time," he says.

I nod.

"Today Dallas is going down," he says.

I nod again.

Deion Sanders walks up. "Steve, you gotta do what you do today," he says. "You gotta run it."

After warm-ups we head back to the locker room. Brent removes a copy of the magazine *Inside Sports* from his bag. I'm on the cover, along with the headline: "Dallas Is Dead." He hangs it on his locker. I feel sick to my stomach. Over 69,000 people are in the stadium. It's the largest football crowd in Candlestick history. Millions more will tune in at home. The pregame hype is unprecedented. If Dallas wins, they are positioned to be the first team in history to win three straight Super Bowls. If we win, we are positioned to be the first NFL team to win five Super Bowls.

I run to a bathroom stall and kneel over the toilet. The anti-inflammatory is making me nauseous. Suddenly my breakfast comes up.

Head coach George Seifert calls everybody in. The locker room is split-level. We pack into the lower part and take a knee. In a fiery speech, Jerry Rice reminds the team what's at stake if we lose to the Cowboys again. "There's no way!" he shouts, the veins pulsing in his neck and forehead. Fifty-two men respond with primal yells. Then we recite the Lord's Prayer. It's time.

I put on my helmet. The moment I look through the face mask a different voice speaks in my head: *This is not just a game. This is a defining moment in your life. You are built for this.*

This is the voice that propels me through the cramped locker room doorway into the tunnel. It's exactly sixty-seven steps to the dugout that leads to the field. I love this walk. Condensation drips from the low ceiling. Cleats — *click-clack, click-clack* — echo through the tunnel. The rumble of the fans pulses through the concrete ceiling. Security guards nod as I walk past. "Good luck, Steve," one of them says.

We stop when we reach the San Francisco Giants' dugout. Ushers in yellow jackets surround the entrance to the field. The cheerleaders are lined up, high-kicking and shaking pom-poms. The sulfurous odor from high tide wafts through the air. Fans scream deliriously. I take it all in. More than anything I want to give everyone in the stadium what they want — a victory.

I step to the ledge and the public address announcer thunders: "Steve Young!" I dart out.

There is no turning back.

I jog under the goalposts and through a gauntlet of teammates. The crowd noise is deafening, but I am silent. I show no emotion. I just want to get this thing started.

Dallas wins the coin toss and elects to receive. On the third play of the game, Eric Davis picks off Troy Aikman and returns the ball 44 yards for a touchdown. We lead 7–0.

We kick off again. Three plays later Michael Irvin fumbles and we recover on the Dallas 39-yard line. I huddle the offense. I tell them we're scoring again. On the fifth play from scrimmage I drop back. In a matter of two seconds I look left and pump-fake to Jerry Rice. He's covered. I look over the middle for John Taylor. Covered. Brent Jones is in pass protection. I bounce on my toes and look to the right for my last option — Ricky Watters out of the backfield. Before he looks back I let it fly down the right sideline. He catches it in stride and races 29 yards to the end zone. Candlestick erupts. We are up 14–0.

On the ensuing kickoff, Kevin Williams fumbles. We recover on the Dallas 35-yard line. A few plays later we face first-and-ten from the Dallas 10-yard line. I call a quarterback draw. On the snap I take three quick steps back, as if to pass. Haley comes like a crazed animal around one end, creating a brief opening up the middle. Taking advantage, I head for the end zone. At the 5-yard line a linebacker hits my legs. I bounce off, but he wraps up my feet as another linebacker goes for my head. I duck just in time and land hard on the 1-yard line as another Cowboy jumps on my back. Second-and-goal from the 1.

The crowd loves it. My teammates love it. On the next play William Floyd scores. Seven minutes into the game we are up 21–0. It's the first time in NFC Championship history that a team has scored three touchdowns in the first quarter.

I get on the phone with Coach Shanahan, who is up in the press box. He's not satisfied. "Don't let up!" he shouts in my ear. "The only way we're gonna beat the Cowboys is we gotta go for fifty."

He's right. We might need that much to beat these guys. I hang up and grab Jerry, Ricky Watters, and my offensive line. "We're going for fifty!" I yell at them.

Before the quarter ends, Dallas scores. They add another touchdown in the second quarter. We are up 24–14. But the momentum has shifted. With 1:02 remaining in the half, Dallas has the ball on its own 16-yard line. I expect them to run out the clock. Instead, Aikman throws three straight incomplete passes. Then the punter shanks it. We get the ball back on the Dallas 39. We still have time for a few plays.

Shanahan wants another touchdown. So do I. We advance to the Dallas 28 with thirteen seconds left. I approach the line of scrimmage and see that Cowboys defensive back Larry Brown is lined up opposite Rice. It's single coverage. I purposely avoid looking at Jerry because I don't want to alert the Cowboys. On the snap he breaks to the outside and streaks toward the goal line. I throw a perfectly arced spiral to the corner of the end zone. Jerry dives and catches it with eight seconds remaining. We go into the locker room up 31–14. Haley hasn't gotten to me once. The Cowboys have no sacks.

We start the second half with a turnover. Not good. Moments later Emmitt Smith scores. Less than four minutes into the third quarter and Dallas cuts our lead to ten: 31–21.

The Cowboys start taunting me. "You've got a monkey on your back," defensive back James Washington says. "Number sixteen. Joe Montana."

Joe's shadow has always been long, but at this stage I'm no longer looking over my shoulder. This is my team and my quest. I tell myself: *There is no better time than now to find out if I can do this.*

With just under seven minutes remaining in the third quarter, we face second-and-goal from the Dallas 3-yard line. Shanahan calls another quarterback draw. But instead of rushing around the end, Haley stunts to the inside. The other defensive end does the same thing. The middle is jammed, leaving me nowhere to run. I scramble, find some space to the right, and break for the end zone. Linebacker Robert Jones lunges for me at the 3-yard line. I barely elude his outstretched arms when James Washington lunges for my shoulders. I duck and his thigh slams into my head. He goes down. But I stay upright until defensive tackle Chad Hennings slams into my left side and falls at my feet. My body spirals over his, and I land atop Washington and Jones, which means I'm not down. My knee hasn't touched the ground. I make a final lunge and extend my arms. The ball crosses the goal line. Touchdown.

We're done! We're gonna win this game! I spring up and fire the ball into the ground, staking a flag atop Everest. I've finally reached the summit. I let out a guttural yell. Candlestick is deafening. I have never heard it this loud. Jerry Rice wraps his arms around me. Brent Jones and Ricky Watters surround us. Their lips are moving, but I can't hear what they're saying. Noise never sounded so soothing; exhaustion never felt so rejuvenating. With 6:53 left in the third quarter, we are up 38–21.

When I reach the sideline Richard Dent smacks my helmet. "Way to go, Steve! Way to go." I don't have the heart to tell him that I reaggravated my neck injury on the touchdown run.

The medical team is waiting for me when I reach the bench. I sit between two trainers and Dr. Gamburd stands, facing me. "How do you feel?"

"It hurts to look left," I tell him.

"Which side did you get hit?"

"On my right. But it hurts to look left."

I remove my helmet, and he starts to manipulate my neck with his hands. It's painful.

But no amount of pain can overcome the relief I feel.

The fourth quarter goes by in a flash. With 1:44 remaining, all that remains is for us to run out the clock. I break the huddle and follow Bart Oates to the line of scrimmage. I flash back to the first time I ever took a snap from Oates.

It is my freshman year of college and my first day of practice. Oates is a senior. I line up behind him, and he hikes me the ball. Backpedaling, I trip, fumble, and land on my butt. Everyone laughs.

"This guy sucks," Oates says.

The coach says, "Young, you'll never make it as a quarterback."

Now I line up behind Oates at Candlestick in the NFC Championship game. He snaps it. This time I don't stumble. I kneel. The mud at my feet feels like heaven. Dallas is out of timeouts. I wish time could stand still. My linemen — Steve Wallace, Jesse Sapolu, and Harris Barton — smack my helmet. Brent Jones, Jerry Rice, and John Taylor point at me. I love these men. For the first time all season Dallas has gone an entire game without registering a sack. And we are going to the Super Bowl. I have finally made it in San Francisco.

I huddle the team one more time. Every fan in the stadium is standing. Clapping. Cheering. I look up and see the scoreboard flashing that I am the Miller Lite Player of the Game. I smile. I've never had a beer in my life. I'm a thirty-three-year-old dry Mormon.

Oates looks at me in the huddle. "Enjoy this moment," he says.

The cheering reaches a crescendo.

"Release, man," Oates says. "Savor it."

I approach the line of scrimmage. I take the final snap of the game and take a knee. Time runs out. I bounce up and congratulate the Cowboys defense for a hard-fought contest. Then I find Aikman. He congratulates me. I thank him.

Echoes of "*Steve! Steve! Steve! Steve!*" pulse through Candlestick. I'm still holding the game ball. I raise my hands above my head. Candlestick is finally my house. I want to visit every room. I want to touch every fan. I run toward the back of the end zone and jump the guardrail. The fans mob me. I climb atop the Giants' dugout and thrust my fist in the air.

"*Steve! Steve! Steve! Steve! Steve!*"

I still have my helmet on. I still have the ball. I jump down from the dugout, tuck the ball under my arm, and start running. I don't know where I'm going. I'm just running. Television cameramen, photographers, and fans follow. I have never done a victory lap in my life. I'm always so buttoned up, so restrained. But today I am unleashed. I run all the way around the stadium, slapping hands with fans who line the route.

By the time I make it all the way around the stadium I'm running on pure adrenaline. Owner Eddie DeBartolo is waiting for me at the steps of the stage erected in the south end zone. He's wearing a white shirt and tie and he's holding a brand new 49ers championship baseball cap. He slaps my hand. "You did it, Steve. You did it!"

In the locker room I run into Carmen Policy. He hugs me as if I'm his son. I kiss his cheek as if he's my father.

"You deserve this," he says. "You earned it."

My eyes well up. All I ever wanted was to please these guys, my teammates, and the fans. My body is famished, dehydrated, fatigued, and bruised. But that's not why I'm crying. The joy that I feared would never come finally has. My uniform is drenched in sweat and caked in mud. But long after every one of my teammates has showered, I'm still in my pads. I want to take in the view from Everest.

2

GRIT

W HEN I WAS a little boy my mother vowed she would never let me play football. It was too violent and I was too shy. Besides, the games were on Sundays and we spent Sundays in church. My life would have turned out very differently if my father hadn't convinced my mother to go back on her vow.

My dad was born in Provo, Utah, in 1936. His parents named him Le-Grande, a popular name among Utah Mormons in those days. His great-great-grandfather was Brigham Young, who led the Mormons across the Plains, settled Utah, and established the Church of Jesus Christ of Latter-Day Saints in Salt Lake City.

Raised a few blocks from the Brigham Young University campus, my dad attended Joaquin Elementary School. In fifth grade a classmate nick-named him "Grit" for his toughness. The name stuck because it fit. He never backed down from a challenge. Never walked away from a fight. Never gave up. And never settled for second best.

His best friend Robert Oaks was the same way. They pushed each other and were rugged and adventurous. After high school they spent a summer working in a national forest in northern Idaho. They joined the National Guard together. Then they enrolled at BYU and tried out for the football team. Oaks didn't make the team and ended up joining the Air Force. He went on to become a four-star general and commander in chief of US Air Forces in Europe and NATO Central Europe. Dad made the team and played running back his freshman year. But partway through his sophomore season he sustained a season-ending knee injury.

Forced to sit out, Grit went off to Australia on a two-year Mormon mission at age twenty. After he returned to BYU he worked his way into the team's starting lineup. His senior year he led BYU in rushing, bruising his way to 423 yards and solidifying his nickname. That's when he met Sherry Steed. A lot of girls were after Grit. A lot of guys chased Sherry. But once Sherry and Grit got together it was game over. Her Mormon roots were as deep as his. Her ancestors were pioneers who had followed Brigham Young in handcarts and settled the town of Layton.

Grit and Sherry married in 1960. A little over a year later I was born at LDS Hospital in Salt Lake City, on October 11, 1961. They brought me home to a tiny two-room apartment in an old Army barracks on the University of Utah campus. The barracks had been converted to housing for married students. We lived on the top level of a three-story unit.

Dad was in his first year of law school. Mom had quit her job as a secretary to raise me. I was six months old when I got away from her in my walker. Before she could catch me I had tumbled down a steep set of wooden steps, my walker repeatedly flipping over before crashing to a stop on the second-floor landing. Mom trailed after me, screaming: "My baby! My baby!"

Our neighbors rushed out of their apartments. I was in a heap, wailing. Mom was sure I was severely injured. But I survived without any breaks or bruises. I didn't even end up seeing a doctor. By the afternoon I was back in my walker, tooling around as if nothing had happened. Even as a baby I had thick bones and was built to be durable like my dad. My quick recovery was a pretty accurate preview of my ability to take a big hit and bounce right back.

I was too young to know it at the time, but that single event helped shape my relationship with my mother. She blamed herself for my fall. And she shuddered at the thought of how easily things could have turned out differently. From that moment on she never let me out of her sight. We became inseparable. She was my protector, my guardian.

On my second birthday my mom had another baby — my little brother Mike. We were very close. Maybe it was because we shared the same birthday. Maybe it was just that my mom spent almost all of her time with us. Regardless, we were very close.

My dad, on the other hand, was my hero. While in law school he worked full-time as a janitor. During the day his face was buried in law books. At night he would sweep, mop, scrub, paint, and haul trash. Personal exercise was his only leisure activity. But there was nothing leisurely in his approach to working out. He was a fitness fanatic. He passed his energy on to me at a young age. By age two I could do ten push-ups. At age three I was up to twenty push-ups and I could dribble an adult-size basketball. If there is such a thing as an athleticism gene, I got mine from Grit.

Although my dad never pushed me to play sports, he did a lot to encourage me. My first toy was a miniature plastic football. Dad put my left hand behind my back and placed the football in my right hand. Then he took a few steps back and extended his hands. I switched the ball to my left hand and threw it. He put the ball back in my right hand and I switched it again. We repeated this routine again. And again. And again. Finally, Dad gave up. I was a lefty. Oddly, I shot baskets and played guitar with my right hand, and I kicked with my right foot. But when it came to everything else, I was a lefty.

I don't remember much prior to my seventh birthday. But I remember turning seven. My brother Mike turned five on the same day. His birthday party was held in the backyard while mine went on in the front yard. At one point, Dad had all of our friends gather in the backyard while he tossed tennis balls — "high pops" — over the house from the front yard. Every time someone caught one my dad gave out a quarter. When the game was over, Dad whistled and we ran to the front yard. Every kid in the neighborhood knew my dad's whistle. My siblings and I would be outside playing with our friends and Dad would step outside the house and whistle. I'd turn to my friends and say: "Gotta go. Time for dinner." It was a regular occurrence.

One of my birthday presents that year was a left-handed baseball mitt. The following spring, I joined my first team, a Little League baseball club. Dad was working as a labor lawyer in the Salt Lake City offices of Anaconda Company, one of the biggest copper mining outfits in the world.

Mom and Dad had a third child by this point—my sister Melissa. We lived on Lone Peak Drive in the Cottonwood section of Salt Lake City. I shared a room with Mike. Our neighborhood was filled with families like ours, young and Mormon. My elementary school was a few houses down. So was the baseball diamond. It was an idyllic place.

I liked school. But I didn't like being away from Mom and my little brother and sister. For the first few weeks Mom walked me to school each morning. Then she stayed with me in the classroom. To avoid embarrassment, we told my classmates that she was the class mother. That way kids wouldn't make fun of me. Eventually, my second-grade teacher made me class president, and something about the responsibility of leading my second-grade class enabled me to become more independent. At that point Mom started dropping me off at the front door and I could get by without her during the school day.

Nighttime was another story. I could not go to sleep if Mom and Dad were not home. One afternoon Dad picked me up early from school and told me he was taking Mike, Melissa, and me to spend the night at my aunt's house. Dad had plans to bring Mom along on an overnight business trip. When I got in the backseat of the car, "Big Girls Don't Cry" was playing on the radio. *Forget that,* I told myself. *Big boys do cry.* I cried all the way to my aunt's house. I loved my aunt, but I didn't want to be away from home. It was a brutal two days. I cried the entire time, prompting my parents to cut their trip short and return home.

A year later Mike got tonsillitis and had to have his tonsils removed. The doctor suggested to my mother that, out of convenience, I should get mine removed at the same time even though my tonsils were healthy. Deathly afraid of being away from home, I was more worried about the overnight stay at the hospital than the procedure. "I'm not sick!" I shouted at the hospital staff. "I'm not sick!" But I was forced to stay. It was a raw deal.

Dad didn't really understand my fears. I didn't either. I just knew I couldn't handle separation, especially at night. I had no idea why. So I kept my fears to myself.

3

GREENWICH

I WAS IN THIRD grade when I learned that we were moving to the East Coast. Dad came home from work one day and announced that he was being transferred to his company's corporate office in midtown Manhattan. My parents weren't pleased. They preferred Utah. But they didn't have much say in the matter. So they looked for a silver lining — their children would develop deeper religious convictions by growing up in an area of the country where Mormonism wasn't so prevalent.

That was an understatement. We went from one extreme to the other.

In the summer of 1970 we sold our home in Salt Lake City and settled thirty-five miles outside New York City in Greenwich, Connecticut, a town with 60,000 residents. There were a grand total of two Mormon families in the entire town. We made three. The nearest Mormon congregation was more than half an hour away, in Scarsdale, New York. That wasn't the only change. Greenwich was also far more affluent than Salt Lake City. The town had the wealthiest residents per capita in the United States. My parents didn't fit the profile. But they were told that Greenwich had the best public schools in the tristate area. That's why my dad chose to settle there. He needed a private loan from his employer to go along with a mortgage just to be able to afford a $69,500 two-story cape with brown cedar clapboard siding. I've always joked that I grew up on the mean streets of Greenwich.

My grammar school was at the end of my street. After my first day at my new school I didn't need my mother to walk me there. I instantly fell in love with my third-grade teacher, Ms. Wheelis. Roughly thirty, she was the most beautiful woman I had ever seen, a true belle with a Southern accent, big hair, and pretty eyes. She was my first crush. I was so eager to get to school every day that I sprinted from my front door to the school yard.

Kids in Greenwich grew up around sports that were completely foreign to me — squash, polo, sailing, tennis, and a crisp game of badminton. But Pop Warner football? Forget it. Not in Greenwich. Not in 1970. There was no such thing.

Fortunately, we lived in one of the few subdivisions in town. The homes were all on small lots with similar construction. Our neighborhood was a mix of professionals and craftsmen. All the dads got together and formed a neighborhood Pee Wee football league. When my dad announced he was signing me up, my mom objected on the grounds that football was too aggressive and violent. I was quiet and shy. Mom feared I'd get hurt. "There's no way I'm letting Steve play football, Grit," she said.

You can imagine the response of a man called Grit to the "getting hurt" bit. But Mom also disliked that Pee Wee football games were played on Sunday. In our home, Sunday was a day for church and family, not youth sports. Dad knew that if I was going to play sports, it would be on Sunday, but he saw no reason why I couldn't go to church and play football on the same day. Basically, he wanted me to have the same opportunities he had experienced through youth sports.

Mom finally gave in when I promised her I'd never compromise my beliefs if she let me play on Sundays.

My team was the North Mianus Cowboys. Our helmets came from Sears and resembled the ones worn by the Dallas Cowboys. That suited me just fine. Dallas had just won the Super Bowl, and my favorite player was Roger Staubach.

I told my coach I wanted to play quarterback and wear number 12, like Staubach. But the coach chose his son as the signal caller. Dad explained to me that the quarterback position usually goes to the coach's son. He offered to become a coach, but I told him no way. I didn't want to be known as the coach's son, and if I couldn't earn the quarterback position, I preferred to play a different position. I ended up playing running back and wearing number 36, my dad's number in college.

I took some pretty good licks. The harder the hits the more the fathers applauded. After the first few games my mother had seen enough. "Grit," she insisted, "I'd rather Steve didn't play football. Maybe he should learn to play a musical instrument."

"Sherry," my dad said, "was I a musician or a football player when you met me?"

That ended once and for all the "football is too rough" debate.

But Mom continued to struggle with me playing on Sunday. And it wasn't just for my sake. Mom felt uneasy about hauling my younger siblings to the ball field to watch me play football on the Sabbath.

But Grit took a practical approach. We no longer lived in Utah. "If Steve is going to play sports, we have to adapt," he told her. "It's the way you have to do it in Connecticut."

The North Mianus Cowboys went 6-0 and won the Pickwick Loop title. I led the team in touchdowns. But the thing I remember most about the season is a play that involved my mother. One day we were playing the Belhaven Buzzards, and a bigger kid collared me by the neck and threw me down. I hit the ground so hard I lost my wind. Even though neck tackling was forbidden in the league, no penalty was called. But the officials did stop the game. My father trotted onto the field, where I lay, choking back tears and gasping for air. "You'll be fine, son," he said. "Nothing serious." Typical Grit.

Then, out of the corner of my eye, I saw my mom storming in my direction. She had come out of the bleachers. *Holy smokes,* I thought. *Go back, Mom. Go back.* I was afraid she was coming to give me a kiss or something. But it was worse than that. She brushed past Grit and practically kicked me in the head in her rush to get to the player who had thrown me down. The poor kid had fear in his eyes. "Don't neck-tackle!" she pointed and yelled.

He was trembling by this point. "Okay, I promise," he blurted.

Coaches and players from both teams stood speechless as Mom marched off the field, her high heels aerating the grass turf.

Mortified, I got up and dusted myself off.

My dad expected me to take my licks and to endure. But Mom was my protector. She'd do battle with anyone.

The same year that I started playing Pee Wee football I learned a lasting lesson about hard work and perseverance that still stays with me. "Stingray" bikes were all the rage. A lot of kids in my neighborhood had one. I told my parents I wanted one. Dad could easily afford one. So it was a real disappointment when he said he wouldn't buy one for me.

But he made me a deal: if I earned half the cost of the bike, he'd pay the rest.

At first I got mad at him. But then I got to work. I got a paper route and saved every penny I earned. It took way longer than I wanted to wait for the bike. At times it felt like I'd never get there. But each week I got a little closer.

On the day I reached the halfway point, Dad patted me on the back and took me to the bike shop. I picked out a purple Schwinn Stingray. Lesson learned — *good things come to those who work hard and persevere.* I washed that bike every day. At night I brought it in the house, hauled it up the stairs, and parked it next to my bed. I did that for months.

Despite being the only Mormons in our part of Greenwich (the other two Mormon families lived across town), we felt right at home in our neighborhood. Most of the neighboring families were Italian and Irish Catholics. We all shared the same values. And sports were like a second religion, especially baseball. I got in with a group of guys who did everything together — Mike "Gas" Gasparino, Paul "Paulie" Perry, Eddie Sheehan, and Steve "Gebber" Gebhardt. They called me "Springy" because I walked on my toes. We collected baseball cards, played home run derby, and even devised our own neighborhood league using major league rosters. We were creating fantasy leagues way before the term was invented.

Eddie and Gebber and those guys were all about competition. Everything in our neighborhood had a score. Everything we did had a winner and a loser. If there had been a kick-the-can league, we would have joined it.

When we were thirteen we all played on the same Babe Ruth baseball team, called the Clam Box. I didn't start, but I got in most games. My confidence was shaky, though, especially at the plate. By midseason I was still hitless. It got to a point where I didn't want to bat. My batting average was actually zero. And I struck out more than anyone on the team.

I sat alone in my room after games, a stack of *Sports Illustrated* magazines beside my bed. It was 1974. Pete Rose was on one cover. Reggie Jackson was on another. *I'll never be like those guys. I can't even hit a pitch thrown by a thirteen-year-old.*

Discouraged, I told my dad that I was quitting.

That didn't go over well. We were at the kitchen table, just the two of us, sitting opposite each other in squeaky chairs. All serious conversations took place in our boxy kitchen. I stared at my baseball schedule. A magnet held it to the side of the refrigerator alongside a picture of Jesus.

"You have the talent," Dad told me. "You have the ability. You need to work this out."

My dad didn't envision me as a future pro baseball player. He never pushed me to play. But once I signed up, he certainly expected me to give it my all. He repeated his three rules:

Do what you say.

Finish what you start.

Don't cheat.

Needless to say, our conversation that day was short and I didn't quit.

But I kept striking out. Going into the final game of the season, I was 0-for-42 at the plate. My confidence was totally shot. But in my final at-bat I drag-bunted for a single. I finished the season with one hit.

The day after the season ended Dad took me to the park as soon as he got home from work. He brought a bucket of balls. He pitched to me until I had taken one hundred swings. We repeated this night after night. When winter came, we continued. Even in snow we put on winter gloves and took batting practice. Over a one-year period he threw me thousands of pitches. He wasn't trying to turn me into a major leaguer. He just had a very workmanlike approach to everything he did. Whether doing legal work in his office or teaching me how to hit, he relished a job well done.

"You gotta work at it," he kept telling me.

The next year in Babe Ruth I batted .380. Lesson learned — *if you want to be good at something, it takes practice, practice, and more practice.* Around this same time, I learned to ride a unicycle by using the same approach — practice, practice, practice. I got so good at it that I got paid $5 to perform with my friend Dave Hogan during halftime at Greenwich High basketball games.

I was now in my third year of Babe Ruth baseball. At fifteen, I was the best pitcher in Greenwich. I threw a no-hitter to start the season. We took baseball so seriously that we scheduled voluntary practices every Saturday. The coaches didn't attend — just the players. We didn't believe in days off.

When there were Sunday games, I was always the last one to show up. By the time I got home from church in Scarsdale, I had to sprint to the field just in time to get in some batting practice. None of my teammates gave me grief. But Mormonism was completely foreign to them. They had lots of questions. Eventually I invited them to attend service with me. That way they could see for themselves.

They took me up on the offer. One Sunday five of them tagged along. This gave me an opportunity at a young age to explain my beliefs. One in particular got their attention — the fact that Mormons don't smoke or drink. None of my friends smoked. But they had all tried beer. Not me. Mormons believe in something called The Word of Wisdom. It's essentially a health code that lists things that are bad for the body — tobacco, alcohol, and drugs — and prescribes healthy dietary habits, such as eating in season and in moderation. But I was more drawn to the promise at the end of the scripture, which says that those who abide by these rules will "run and not be weary, walk and not faint." As an athlete, I took that promise literally. I believed that if I didn't use alcohol or tobacco, I'd have great endurance and be protected from serious injury.

The bishop of my congregation in Scarsdale was Ted Simmons. He had a very practical approach to religion that I appreciated. Although many Mormon families were opposed to letting their kids play sports on Sunday, Bishop Simmons supported my decision to play on Sunday because he knew that I was committed to the faith. He believed that I had an obligation to my teammates as well as my church. He encouraged me to be loyal to both.

There was another thing I loved about Bishop Simmons — his daughter Tori. She was a year older than me and lived in Scarsdale. I only saw her on Sundays, but I did everything in my power to see her more often. In eighth grade I even asked Bishop Simmons for special permission to attend an early morning Bible study class at our Scarsdale meetinghouse. The class was for high school kids. But I told him I was ready and spiritually motivated. The real reason I wanted in was, of course, to see Tori. The bishop gave me the okay. That first year I got up at 5:30 on school days and traveled thirty minutes to the chapel. But I never complained. I rode with the Larkin sisters. The Larkins were another Mormon family in Greenwich, and their daughters were as cute at Tori. Church was great.

Most of my friends in Greenwich were jocks. But I also had a separate group of friends at Greenwich High through the honors program. We took Physics, French, AP English, Western Civ, and a bunch of other classes together. We were a tight-knit group. My best friend in the bunch was David van Blerkom, one of the smartest kids in town. David lived around the corner from my house. He and his mother moved into the neighborhood one year after we did. They arrived driving a car with Utah plates. My mom figured they had to be Mormons.

They weren't. But David's mother had a strong connection to the faith. She had grown up in Salt Lake City, but she was never baptized a Mormon. David was raised in New York City without any knowledge of Mormonism. The car with Utah plates belonged to David's grandmother.

My parents were thrilled to meet someone in Greenwich who had a connection to Utah. My mother invited them to attend church with us, and from time to time they did. But David and I never discussed religion much. We collected stamps, coins, and baseball cards. David didn't play football or baseball, but he was a gifted tennis player. He taught me to play.

Some kids at school mocked him as a "nerd." When we were in middle school a bully made him cry by calling him humiliating names. Normally, I talked my way out of fights, but in this instance I stepped in and shoved the bully against a locker. His ear started bleeding, and he left David alone.

David and I remained close in high school, and he began to take a gen-

In the Mormon faith boys are eligible to become priests at age sixteen. There are no vows of celibacy, but you are expected to refrain from swearing, drinking, or having sex before marriage. One of my primary responsibilities on Sundays was to bless and administer the sacrament, and David and I often did that together.

Another thing priests are authorized to do is baptize people. Right around the time David got baptized my younger brother Tom turned eight — the traditional age of baptism in the Mormon faith. Normally, fathers baptize sons, and when I was eight my dad had baptized me. Always looking to give me opportunities to live my religion, Dad invited me to baptize Tom. I was nervous, but I did it, and afterward I felt really good about myself. I felt I had done something meaningful. Mostly I liked the fact that my father trusted me with something sacred.

On March 19, 1978, I attended a Sunday school class where all teenagers were encouraged to keep a personal journal. That night I got started. I wrote:

I feel like the church is becoming a stronger influence every day. Yesterday in baseball I got to hit off the pitching machine and struck at ten balls. Missed them all. I hope it will be better tomorrow. I hope my parents know that I love them. I am very curious to see how everything is going to turn out with Tori. Utah got beat by Notre Dame last night.

That pretty much summed up my life at sixteen — church, sports, family, girl problems, and more sports. In one respect I had two lives: my school friends and my church friends.

I liked girls in both places. My girlfriend at church continued to be Tori, the bishop's daughter, until she left for college after my junior year of high school. But as far back as junior high I had a crush on Christy Fichtner. She was the first girl I ever kissed. It happened in seventh grade when a bunch of my friends dared me to go to her house and kiss her.

They waited around the corner for two hours while I hemmed and hawed at Christy's front door, talking to her about who knows what. Finally, I got up the courage to do it. Then I ran around the corner and my friends yelled: "It's about time!" From that moment forward I had a thing for Christy. So did every other boy at Greenwich High. I wondered if I'd ever win her over.

By the summer heading into my junior year I had a lot on my mind. I was sixteen and sad about turning seventeen. I'd be one step closer to adulthood, and I would have preferred to stay young forever. I had my eye on two girls, one at church and one at school. But my biggest worries were over football. I wanted desperately to be the varsity quarterback.

But there was no way. I could barely throw the ball twenty yards. My throws never spiraled. And in one game as the JV quarterback during my sophomore year I had thrown six interceptions. One I remember slipped out of my hand as I threw. It went straight up in the air and came down into the hands of a lineman. We lost big. Afterward the head varsity coach, Mike Ornato, came in the locker room and announced: "This is the worst group of athletes I've ever seen in my life!"

I spent the summer between my sophomore and junior years getting into better shape. Still, I knew I had no shot at starting at quarterback. A senior named Billy Barber had the position locked up. Billy had a good arm. I had speed. My dad told me to compete for the running back position.

Two-a-day football practices started on August 28.

I worried that I wouldn't have enough stamina. So I worked on it, even overcompensating by running a few miles a day and doing hundreds of push-ups on my own. Plus, I lifted weights every other day. I showed up at fall practice in the best shape of anyone on the team. By the end of two-a-days I was the starting running back.

Our last preseason scrimmage game was against New Canaan High on September 9, 1979. I remember the opponent and the date because the events on the field changed the course of my life. Partway through the game quarterback Billy Barber separated his shoulder. "Young!" Coach Ornato shouted. "You're playing quarterback."

I told myself: *Don't screw this up.*

I lined up behind the center and reached between his legs, and he snapped the ball. I was so nervous that I fumbled.

"Fall on it!" the coach screamed. "Fall on it!"

I know the rule — *never try picking up a fumble in traffic*. An oval-shaped ball takes unpredictable bounces. Better to secure it and lose yardage than turn it over by trying unsuccessfully to pick it up.

But I didn't want my first play as quarterback to be a fumble. I had to make a play. So I behaved like a running back. I scooped up the ball and started dodging tacklers. A couple of big guys hit me, but I shrugged them off. Then I saw an opening on the outside. I took off. I knew I was already the fastest guy on the field, but fear made me even faster. It's not that I was afraid of getting tackled. I feared failure and disappointing people.

Forty yards later I was in the end zone. Touchdown! Nobody was close to me.

We won the scrimmage game. That night I wrote in my journal:

I guess I will start a few games this year. Billy Barber hurt himself and now I am definitely going to play. I am going to need some confidence and exposure. It's a big step but I think I can handle it. It's going to be a real test. I'm sort of scared that I'm going to do bad, but I know I won't.

That's how it was for me. Scared, but confident. Hungry to play, determined not to disappoint.

We opened the regular season against heavily favored Ridgefield. I got my chance at starting quarterback, and I made the most of it. I ran wild, and we upset them, 27–0. After the game I found out that Christy Fichtner, my longtime crush, wanted to date me. Before going to bed I wrote about my prospects in my journal:

I really don't know what's going to happen. Only time will tell. Christy Fichtner — wow that would be something else. How lucky can you get?

I never returned to running back. Coach Ornato switched our offensive scheme to the wishbone to take advantage of my speed. Then we played one of the top-ranked high school teams in the state — Trumbull. They were supposed to kill us. Plus, I was still learning the wishbone. We all were. But it was homecoming weekend, and Christy Fichtner was my date. There was no way I was going home a loser with her looking on from the sideline. I busted loose for a 76-yard touchdown run and a 72-yard touchdown run. I finished with 202 yards rushing on 11 carries. We trounced Trumbull, 33–9.

A few weeks later I did it again, rushing for 175 yards and two touchdowns against Stamford. Coach Ornato liked my running ability so much that he almost never called pass plays. The offensive scheme consisted of my legs and feet. In rare instances when I did pass, I literally spun the ball out of my hand like a top. In other words, I wasn't very good at it.

Since we ran the wishbone, I was never shown how to correctly throw a football. It didn't matter. I was a running quarterback. I finished the season with 980 yards rushing on 102 carries. No running back in the conference had numbers like that, never mind a quarterback. The *Bridgeport Post* named me to the All-State team, and the *New York Daily News* named me one of the outstanding players in Fairfield County. Recruiting letters started coming in. My speed had turned me into the top quarterback in the state.

My junior year of high school was transformative. In addition to starting at quarterback, I was the point guard on the basketball team and the best pitcher on the baseball team. I was dating the head cheerleader. I had a perfect GPA and was a member of the Honor Society. I never missed a day of school. Plus, I had a bunch of responsibilities on Sundays as a young priest at my church.

But I didn't feel like I was doing enough with my life. On January 18, 1979, I wrote in my journal:

My whole life is passive. I've got to get moving.

This was the last time I wrote in my journal. Despite my worries about being too passive, by midway through my junior year I was way too busy. I just didn't realize it. My dad's habit of being super-focused had rubbed off on me. When I was not playing sports I was working out. When I was not training I was studying. If I wasn't tied up with athletics and academics, I was doing things for the church.

Even though I was very shy, my social life was picking up too. I got invited to lots of parties. I didn't care much for parties — too much standing around. I'm not one for making idle chatter.

Plus, I don't drink.

The first time I showed up at a party my teammates led me to the kitchen and opened the refrigerator. It contained a bottle of milk. Not a carton, a bottle. "That's for you, Young," one of them said.

I laughed. So did they. It became standard procedure for them to have milk on hand at every party I attended. They never pressured me to drink. When my buddies held a beer-guzzling contest, I guzzled milk. It's the one contest I always lost. Apparently, it's a lot easier to guzzle beer than milk.

My parents knew my friends drank alcohol. But they let me hang out with them because my buddies supplied me with milk. My father told me that it was a lot easier to be a Mormon in Greenwich than in Salt Lake City. He was on to something. My Catholic friends were very protective of me.

One night a bunch of guys from a rival school crashed our party. They taunted me, calling me a goodie-goodie. A few of them surrounded me. They were determined to force me to drink beer. I wasn't sure what to do. Then my buddy Gas stepped in.

"Hey," he said, pushing the ringleader in the chest. "He's Mormon. He doesn't drink. Leave him alone."

A few of my other teammates lined up behind Gas. The guys from the other school backed down. Then I went to the refrigerator to find my milk. This time my buddies drank milk right along with me.

In the summer of '79 my favorite movie was *Rocky II*. It inspired me to drink raw eggs and jog three to five miles each night to get in better shape. I would have punched sides of beef if I'd lived near a meatpacking plant.

When football practice started in August 1979 for my senior year, I was named co-captain of the team. The other co-captain was Mike Gasparino. I was the fastest guy on the team. Gas was the strongest. We dedicated the rest of the summer to becoming even faster and stronger. We practically lived in the high school weight room. I had read somewhere that when Dick Butkus played for the Chicago Bears he trained by pushing his car around his neighborhood. Gas and I were pretty fanatical. We decided to copy Butkus.

My dad had a '65 Oldsmobile he let me drive. It was a boat. Gas and I pushed it up and down Revere Road, a dead-end street near my house. We put my nine-year-old brother Tom behind the wheel and told him to keep us straight.

Our legs burned with pain. But the Butkus workout paid off. In our season opener I rushed for 129 yards and two touchdowns and threw for another. We won 48–21. Then we faced heavily favored Stamford High. They dominated us early and led 12–2 at the half. But in the second half I ran for one touchdown and passed for another. We won 16–14 and were dubbed "the Comeback Kids."

I could outrun anybody in the open field. Plus, I had the upper body strength to run over defenders when necessary. The offseason conditioning really made the game fun. But my dad let me know that if I didn't maintain solid grades he wouldn't hesitate to take me off the team. We had an ongoing dialogue that went like this:

DAD: What's your plan?
ME: Play quarterback in the NFL.
DAD: That's not a plan. That's a dream. What's your plan?

His philosophy was straightforward: football is a dream — getting a solid education is a plan. So I did him one better by maintaining a perfect 4.2 GPA.

A few weeks into my senior year I knew I had a problem. I was acing French, Physics, and Western Civ. But one afternoon my Calculus teacher, Terry Lowe, pulled me aside after class.

"I appreciate all that you have on your plate, but I don't care if it's football season," he told me. "For me, your focus is here. This comes before that. So good luck to you if you think you're getting an A in my class."

Nothing motivates me more than being told I can't do something. Calculus became like a football opponent. I had to beat it. Besides, I wanted to show Mr. Lowe that he had underestimated me.

My friend David va.. Blerkom was a math whiz. He came over to my house each night after I got home from football practice. We stayed up until midnight studying. I helped him with Western Civ, and he helped me with Calculus. By midseason I had an A average in Mr. Lowe's class. He became my favorite teacher. I loved the fact that he gave me no breaks.

On the field we rolled to a 6-1 start. I was getting a lot of press. College recruiting letters and scholarship offers were coming in too. Princeton, Cornell, Virginia, North Carolina, Army, and Syracuse showed the most interest. Each of the schools pursuing me featured an offense with a running quarterback. They were all strong academically too. It dawned on me that I had a big decision ahead of me. I don't like big decisions. The idea of getting an education at Princeton was pretty appealing. So was the prospect of playing quarterback at Syracuse. But it was a lot to consider. I preferred to just keep playing football.

A lawyer in my dad's office was a New York Giants season-ticket-holder. Once in a while he had a scheduling conflict and gave his tickets to my dad. Grit always took me. The games were usually on a Sunday. We went to church just long enough to take the sacrament — my dad never missed that. Then we were out the door and off to the Meadowlands.

I remember a fall afternoon during my senior year. I was sitting beside my dad in Giants Stadium and my mind started to wander. I pictured myself playing quarterback in Giants Stadium with him looking on. At seventeen, I couldn't imagine anything that would make him prouder.

Dad was a football fanatic. But he didn't fill my head with notions of playing pro ball. Quite the opposite. He was satisfied when I simply made the varsity team. He was pleasantly surprised when I became the starting quarterback. But the recruiting letters stunned him. The idea that football might be my ticket to an Ivy League education really impressed him.

But I had something bigger in mind. I still had a Roger Staubach poster hanging on the wall above my bed. It was the first thing I saw every morning and the last thing I looked at each night. My dream was to play in the NFL and be just like Roger. I'd stare at his hands and how he gripped the football. Initially, my hands were too small. But each year they got bigger and I got closer to replicating Roger's grip. Alongside my dad, Roger was my idol. He had won the Heisman and been MVP of the

Super Bowl. More important, he had served in the US Navy and done a tour in Vietnam. I idolized him.

I admired Staubach and his commitment to our country so much that I was truly considering West Point. On November 17, 1979, I took a recruiting trip there. The mood on the Army campus was somber. It was only two weeks after fifty-two Americans were taken hostage in Iran. I stood on the Army sideline during the game. My eyes were fixed on the opposing team's quarterback, Pitt freshman Dan Marino. He was six-four, and his passes were like guided missiles. He dismantled Army's defense. Watching Marino up close, I thought to myself: *How will I ever throw it like him? I'm never going to play quarterback in college, much less the NFL.*

A week later, on Thanksgiving, my team lost to Darien, 17–0. My high school football career was over. In two seasons I had carried the ball 267 times for 1,928 yards and 21 touchdowns. Ten of those scores came on runs of 30 yards or more. Five of them were on runs longer than 50 yards. I was named Offensive Player of the Year in Connecticut.

The time had come to pick a college.

4

TURNING POINT

WEST POINT WAS only about fifty miles from home, which made it attractive. But I was fooling myself to think I'd survive at West Point. The campus could have been across town and I'd still have struggled. Leaving home for any campus was going to be an enormous challenge.

The truth was, I was nearly eighteen and had never spent a single night away from family. No sleepovers with friends. No summer camps. Nothing other than one night in a hospital for a tonsil surgery I didn't need. The thought of being away made me anxious. Plus, I was self-conscious about my fear. So I always made up some excuse whenever I was invited to an overnight activity.

Despite being the captain of three sports teams, I had real fears and anxieties. During daylight I was confident enough, especially when I had a ball in my hand. But at night I just needed to be home.

No one seemed to understand this better than my mother's brother, Bob Steed. The best thing for a kid with anxiety is an adult who understands him no matter what. Uncle Bob was that way with me.

My uncle was an accountant in Utah. But he followed my high school football career in Connecticut as if he lived next door. My mother sent him newspaper clippings after every game. Uncle Bob told anyone in Utah who would listen that I was going to be the next great quarterback to play for BYU.

Of course, no one took him seriously. Not even my family. But that didn't stop Uncle Bob. During my junior year he started peppering BYU's head coach, LaVell Edwards, with letters, telling him that he should take a look at me. My grandmother even sent Coach Edwards a package of articles about my achievements.

At first LaVell showed no interest. Then Ted Simmons, my former bishop from Scarsdale, got into the act. He and Edwards had attended Utah State University together and were old fraternity brothers. Simmons called Edwards and told him that he had to check out the quarterback from Greenwich High.

It was 1979. At that time BYU didn't recruit much in the Northeast. But LaVell wanted to increase the program's profile in that part of the country. Simmons knew that. So he came up with a clever way to help LaVell and me. He arranged a speech for LaVell at a Mormon church in New York City. The audience was hundreds of Mormon teenagers and their parents from all over the tristate area. Simmons assigned me to introduce LaVell.

Afterward LaVell talked to me and requested some game film. Then I got a letter from BYU's offensive coordinator, Norm Chow, saying they were keeping an eye on me. But after that, I never heard much else from them. There was no in-home visit. No invitation to visit the school. Nothing.

On one level, I was okay with that. It's not like I had my heart set on BYU. My dad had played there. My parents had met there. And it is the flagship school for my faith. But I wanted to go where I was wanted. Syracuse and North Carolina brought me to their campuses. Both schools ran the option, and both schools promised me I'd be their next quarterback. BYU was much more lukewarm about my playing quarterback for them. But on another level, in the back of my mind I knew that BYU would be a safer bet when it came to dealing with my anxiety. At least we had lots of family in Utah, including my Uncle Bob. Plus, I'd have the familiar world of Mormonism around me.

As soon as my senior season ended I made my choice: North Carolina. One of the assistant coaches there was from Fairfield County. He knew my abilities as a running quarterback. I'd be the number-two guy as a freshman at UNC and then, as a sophomore, I'd start. Everything was set. There was just one problem — North Carolina's coaching staff had no idea I was afraid to leave home. And I was afraid to tell them. I didn't even want to admit it to myself.

Several renowned hospitals were within driving range of my home in Greenwich. People came to them from around the country for advanced surgeries and acute medical care. Occasionally my bishop asked me to check in on fellow Mormons who were out-of-town patients.

During football season my bishop called me one night at home and said he needed my help with a special case. A fourteen-year-old girl named Ann had come from Idaho for brain surgery. My bishop said she had a very serious disease. I dropped everything and drove to the hospital.

I was not prepared for what I saw when I arrived. Ann was strapped to her bed. She had a nervous disorder that caused her to shake uncontrollably, sometimes violently. She'd had the condition her whole life, and it had taken a toll on her family. In addition to being worn down from dealing with the situation, they couldn't afford to travel across country. So Ann was all alone and far from home.

Doctors hoped the brain surgery would correct the severe tremors. But first she had to undergo two minor operations to prepare her for the more extensive procedure. Ann was in for an extended stay.

Her spirits lifted when I was with her. We spent time talking about our beliefs. She told me about growing up in Idaho. I told her what I was doing in school. I also told her jokes and made her laugh. Afterward the doctor told me that Ann rarely smiled when I wasn't there. He encouraged me to continue to visit.

I made a point to come once a week. It gave her something to look forward to. I looked forward to it too. Being around Ann reminded me how lucky I was to have the opportunities I had in life. Ann's medical condition had forced her to miss out on so many things. I realized that when I was around Ann I didn't worry about my own struggles.

The first two minor surgeries went well. But two weeks before the major surgery the doctor told me that it would go better if Ann was upbeat and positive. "Try and lift her spirits," he told me.

Three days before the surgery we threw a party for Ann. The nurses decorated her room with balloons and streamers. We all had party whistles. There was a cake too. I was the only one in attendance who didn't work at the hospital.

After things wound down I was alone with Ann. She lay on her bed, looking subdued. I tried to think of something to say.

"Friday is the big day, Ann."

She was quiet. But I could tell she wanted to tell me something. I leaned closer.

"You're my best friend in the whole world," she whispered.

I paused. I had caring parents and four siblings. I had teammates. I had friends at school and friends at church. Ann had me.

"Ann, you are my best friend too."

"I love you," she whispered.

That's a word that doesn't flow easily from my mouth. But through bedside visits I had come to cherish her friendship. "I love you too," I told her.

Tears formed in her eyes. "I also know my Heavenly Father loves me," she said.

"You're right, Ann. He does."

"And I'm going back to my Heavenly Father."

It took me a minute to realize what she was saying. She didn't think she was going to make it. She thought she was going to die.

"Whoa, wait a minute," I said. "Don't think like that. You're going to pull through."

"I'm going back, Steve."

I noticed she didn't look scared. Her expression was peaceful. She was fourteen, and she thought she was going to die. And she was at peace with it.

I stayed with her for another fifteen minutes before the nurses said she needed to rest. It was the last time I saw Ann. She passed away shortly after the surgery. I cried when I found out. Through her I'd learned what friendship and love were all about. About 5 percent of love is romantic. The other 95 percent is something else. It's caring for another more than yourself. It's empathy and compassion and sacrifice. It's setting aside your own concerns to lift someone else. She did all those things for me.

I'm a big believer in little moments that become major turning points in life. In January 1980, I had one of those moments. National Signing Day was ten days away. I was all set to formalize my commitment to North Carolina when I received a call at home from LaVell Edwards. He was in New York City on business and asked if he could pay me a visit. A couple of hours later he was in my living room.

"You're a great athlete," he said. "Great speed."

I nodded.

"I'm not sure about your throwing abilities because you seldom threw the ball in high school," he continued. "But there's certainly a place for you in our program."

"I want a legitimate chance to play quarterback," I said.

"You bet, Steve."

A bunch of recruits were making visits to BYU the following weekend. LaVell invited me to join them. I looked at my parents. Dad looked at LaVell.

"Under the NCAA rules, Steve is eligible to make one more official visit for recruiting purposes," Dad said.

"What do you say, Steve?" Edwards asked.

"I'd like to think about it," I said.

"Sure."

Edwards left without a commitment. Suddenly I was indecisive about Carolina. BYU, after all, was a virtual quarterback factory — Virgil Carter, Gifford Nielsen, Marc Wilson. They all went on to play in the NFL, and Jim McMahon was in line to be next. Despite coming from the wishbone, I longed to be a throwing quarterback. So I couldn't ask for a better system than BYU's. But there was another factor in my thinking: *How will I survive being away from home?* Deep down, I feared I'd never last at North Carolina. Except for the assistant coach from Fairfield County, I didn't know a soul there. The more I thought about it the more I convinced myself that BYU was probably the only place where I had a chance of getting through four years of college.

When facing big decisions, Mormons are taught to take a day to fast and pray. After LaVell's visit, I was doing a lot of both. A few days later, I got on a plane to Provo. A dozen other recruits were there with me. During my visit BYU's running back coach pulled me aside. He told me that BYU didn't have a scholarship for me. The problem was that BYU preferred the pro-style, drop-back quarterback with a big arm, and I didn't fit the profile. I was a running quarterback.

"You have a real good shot at working your way into a position in the backfield," he said. "I strongly urge you to walk on."

I just looked at him. *Walk on?* That wasn't exactly what I had in mind. Neither was playing running back.

My mind was spinning. Just when I had set my heart on playing quarterback for BYU it sounded like BYU didn't want me to play quarterback. The coaches didn't think enough of me to offer me a scholarship. I was not happy.

At the end of the weekend all twelve recruits had an exit interview with LaVell. We were interviewed in alphabetical order. That meant I was last. Waiting my turn, I sat outside LaVell's office, stewing.

Should I walk on at BYU or accept a full ride at North Carolina? In truth, both options came with drawbacks.

Finally, LaVell called me in.

I took a seat across from his desk. Immediately I noticed the books on the shelf behind him. They were mainly religious titles. One was *Jesus the Christ* by Mormon author James E. Talmage. The same book was on the shelf at my home.

In Greenwich, football and church never merged. My football life and my church life were completely separate. All of a sudden football and religion had merged in LaVell's office. More than ever I wanted to play for him. But BYU didn't really want me.

"We really appreciate you coming out," LaVell said.

"I appreciate the opportunity."

"I remember the time you introduced me when I went out to speak in New York," he said. "I admired the way you handled that."

"Thank you."

"You're a natural leader," he continued. "We really think a lot of you as a person. And you're a terrific athlete. But truth be told, I didn't have a scholarship for you."

I noticed that he said "didn't," not "don't." I leaned forward. He pursed his lips and squinted.

"The guy that was in here just before you just told me he has decided to go elsewhere," Edwards said.

I was speechless.

"So I have one scholarship," he said.

"I'll take it."

Edwards grinned. "You will?"

I laughed. "I will."

The next day I flew home. My parents met me at LaGuardia. Dad was stoic. Mom was anxious. "So how was your flight?" she said.

I knew what she really wanted to ask.

"Mom, I'm going to BYU."

She wrapped her arms around me and kissed me. Grit shook my hand and patted my shoulder. I knew he was proud.

On February 2, 1980, I signed my letter of intent. My decision was official.

I took Christy to senior prom. We stayed out until two in the morning. Later that day I pitched a no-hitter to open the American Legion baseball season. We always joked that I was the only sober one in the game. A couple of weeks later I graduated and my days at Greenwich High were over.

I couldn't help thinking my days with Christy were numbered too. I adored her, but around the same time I committed to BYU she signed with an international modeling agency. Our lives were speeding in opposite directions. Right after graduation she headed to Europe for photo shoots. She was consumed with the start of her career. I was consumed with getting ready for college football. I lived in the gym, lifting weights and going through a daily regimen of push-ups, pull-ups, sit-ups, and jump rope exercises. At night I ran. I had three routes. The hardest one required running from my house up and down Palmer Hill, and back. I'd put on my Walkman, crank up the volume, and take off. I practically wore out my Bruce Springsteen and Earth, Wind & Fire cassettes.

I'd promise myself I'd do six laps up and down the hill. By the fourth lap I'd be dying — and talking to myself.

I need to walk for a minute.
Just keep running.
I need to catch my breath.
If you stop once, you'll stop again. Don't stop.

I always forced myself to go the distance without slowing down. My reward came when I got back to the house and collapsed on the front lawn. My heart racing, I'd lie on the grass and look at the sky, satisfied with the sense of accomplishment.

Before I left for college, a new Mormon church was built much closer to our home in nearby New Canaan, Connecticut, and my family started attending there. In late June I was ordained an elder in the New Canaan chapel. With members of the congregation looking on, I sat on a chair. My father stood behind me, placed his hands on my head, and offered a blessing. I don't remember any specifics of the prayer. I just remember feeling a tremendous sense of gratitude that I belonged to a church where my father could ordain me. It formed a bond between us. It also made me realize I now had a lifetime commitment to serve others.

I was already serious about living the tenets of my faith. But the experience of becoming an elder at eighteen reaffirmed in my mind the need to be vigilant in certain areas where college students tend to be more relaxed. One was the expectation to refrain from sexual relations until marriage. That wasn't a new concept. My parents had raised me on that value. But my ordination reaffirmed that message as I left home for school.

With a duffle bag strapped over my shoulder and a baseball cap on my head, I said good-bye to my parents at JFK. Mom cried. Dad pursed his lips and nodded. It was his way of saying, *Time to get to work.* Then we hugged. I didn't want to let go.

I kept a straight face until I got on the plane. Then I looked out the window and immediately wanted to get off.

But I knew I couldn't.

5

TEN THOUSAND SPIRALS

I LANDED IN UTAH a week before football camp opened at BYU. Uncle Bob met me at the airport and took me to his place to spend the night. I wished I could stay with him, but he lived too far from Provo. I was miserable. My anxiety was heavy.

"I'm not gonna make it here," I told him.

"You'll be fine."

"I just want to go home."

"Once you start playing ball you'll be fine."

"I don't know."

My mother had anticipated this. So before I left home she talked with a family in our congregation — Claire and Eugene Freedman — about finding a family in Provo for me to stay with until the start of football camp. Claire's sister, Carole Burr, lived in Provo. She and her husband had nine children. Carole said they'd make room for me.

When I felt anxious it was easier to be alone with my troubles. So the idea of staying with a family that had nine children was a little overwhelming. I mean, I didn't even know these people.

"You'll like them," Uncle Bob told me as we drove past the BYU campus, up toward the mountain. We continued to go up, up, up, snaking around a winding road leading farther and farther from campus and residential neighborhoods. Finally, we came to Mountain Ridge Road. It was an appropriate name. We were on the edge of a mountain. The road was a dead end with just two houses. I saw a white split-rail fence surrounding a property that looked like a child's paradise — leafy trees, lush green grass, a giant swing set, and a basketball hoop at the end of the driveway. The house was a big white colonial with black shutters. Part of the house had a stone facade. There was an attached garage with carriage doors and what looked like a second-story guest residence.

The place sort of reminded me of Greenwich, except the view was breathtaking. The property overlooked the entire city of Provo. I could see for miles. The only other house around was right next door. It was a beautifully constructed modern structure with lots of windows and trees. It looked like something I would have expected to see in Beverly Hills. Carole Burr greeted us at the doorstep. She wasn't what I expected for a mother of nine. She was trim, tanned, and wearing stylish clothing. And she was smiling.

"This is my nephew Steve," Bob told her.

"I've heard a lot about you," she said.

"Well, thank you for letting me stay with you," I said.

She gave me a hug and ushered us in. Kids were running through the house. First, Carole introduced me to her husband Jim, who owned a commercial helicopter company. He and Carole had three boys and six girls. The oldest child — Bryan — was twenty and off serving a Mormon mission. The next oldest — Brett — was my age. The other boy was twelve. The girls were seventeen, fourte, ten, eight, six, and four.

There was a tremendous amount of noise and commotion. But the house was clean and full of sunlight. The little girls started tugging on me right away, as if I were an older brother. Brett led me to a bedroom that was set up for me. For some reason I immediately felt a sense of security. Maybe it was all the kids. Maybe it was the swings and basketball hoop and white fence. I dropped my bags in the bedroom and said good-bye to my uncle.

I spent a week with the Burrs. A lot of that time was spent talking with Carole. She was a couple of years older than my mother. But like my mother, Carole had endless energy. I liked the way she treated me like a tenth child. She even stocked extra bottles of milk in the refrigerator when she discovered how much I liked it. And she got after me to make my bed every morning and keep my room tidy.

My week with the Burrs went by too fast. I wasn't ready for the next challenge. On the day I was supposed to report to campus to begin summer orientation and football practice, I wouldn't get out of bed. Carole had to practically drag me.

"Carole," I told her, "I'd rather just stay here with your family."

"C'mon, Steve," she said, escorting me to the car. "You're going to be fine. And we are right up the hill. You can always come home. You have a room here."

August 18, 1980. I entered the Smith Fieldhouse on BYU's campus to get my equipment and locker assignment. Close to one hundred players milled around in street clothes. I was the only guy from Connecticut. I didn't know anyone, and no one knew me. Depth charts for each position were taped on the wall. I ran my finger down the quarterbacks list:

> Jim McMahon
> Royce Bybee
> Eric Krzmarzick
> Gym Kimball
> Mark Haugo

I scanned all the way down to the eighth and final spot before I found the name I was looking for: Steve Young.

I spun around, leaned back against the wall, and dropped my head. I had never been eighth in anything.

What am I doing here?

There are two sides to me. There's the anxiety-ridden side, which often fills me with fear when I most need to be at my best. This is the part of me that I don't want anyone to know about. But there's also the ultracompetitive side. This side hates losing at anything and is evident every time I play sports. That's the paradox. I was lonely and I desperately wanted to catch the next flight back to Connecticut. But I also wanted to prove that I could be great here.

I was still staring at the floor when I noticed that someone was standing next to me. Actually, I noticed his sneakers. They were untied. Mine were too. Everyone else's were knotted. I looked up and made eye contact with the guy. He smiled and extended his hand.

"I'm Jim Herrmann."

"Steve Young."

"Where you from?"

"Greenwich, Connecticut."

"I'm from Hartland, Wisconsin."

Herrmann was six-foot-six, with massive square shoulders. I assumed he was Mormon. He assumed I was not. We were both wrong.

The only two things Herrmann knew about Mormons was that we don't drink and we reside in Utah. He figured my hometown disqualified me. I told him that I was practically the only Mormon in my high school.

He told me that he was the only guy in his school who didn't drink beer. Pretty impressive, given that his hometown was the beer capital of the state that brewed the most beer in the country. Virtually everyone in Hartland worked in the beer industry. Teenage boys in Hartland grew up on beer. "I just never had the urge," Herrmann said.

He was much more outgoing than me, and I immediately liked him. He introduced me to Lee Johnson, another freshman. Lee was a highly recruited kicker and punter out of Texas. He spoke with a drawl and wore Wrangler jeans and cowboy boots. And he was even more outgoing than Herrmann. He talked fast and acted like he was hyped up on caffeine. And man was he funny.

The three of us ended up on the same floor in the freshman dorms. We started hanging around together. Guys nicknamed us "the Three Amigos."

Doug Scovil coached the quarterbacks under LaVell Edwards. Before joining BYU's staff, Scovil had been the quarterback coach for the San Francisco 49ers, where he'd worked with John Brodie, Steve Spurrier, and Norm Snead. Edwards had total trust in him. But Scovil had no faith in me. Not as a quarterback anyway.

In our first official practice the team was split up by position. All the quarterbacks and centers followed Scovil. We had four centers. Two of them — Bart Oates and Trevor Matich — were headed to the NFL. One of the guards was Andy Reid, who would go on to become a very successful NFL head coach. They were giants compared to the guys I played with in high school.

The quarterbacks were impressive too. All of them were pro-style passers with big arms. Especially McMahon. He effortlessly hit targets fifty yards away. I was intimidated just standing near him.

"Three-step drops," Scovil barked.

One by one the quarterbacks got under center, took the snap, dropped back three steps, and let loose. I'd never done a three-step drop in my life. In fact, I had never dropped back to pass. Greenwich High ran the wishbone. I was used to throwing while rolling out. So all of this was totally new to me. My nerves were a mess. Worse, I hadn't been issued cleats yet. So I was wearing high-top sneakers.

I placed my hands under Bart Oates, and he snapped the ball. The moment I stepped back I slipped and landed flat on my butt. The ball hit the ground. Coach Scovil rolled his eyes. My teammates laughed. But it wasn't funny to me.

I felt so insecure. I knew I wasn't ready to throw it with the big boys. McMahon was the best passer in college football. I really didn't know how to throw a football. Not properly anyway. I had a strong arm. But no one had ever taught me the proper mechanics of throwing. My legs, not my arm, had earned me All-State honors. To make it here, though, I needed my arm. *How am I going to make it here?*

I was in way over my head. The centers had the same impression. After the first few days of camp Oates and Matich were standing around critiquing the quarterbacks. Oates pointed at me. "That guy sucks," he said.

"He can't throw," Matich said.

"He's a lefty," Oates said.

More laughter.

Unfortunately, Scovil thought I was a joke too. He was convinced that lefties didn't make great drop-back passers. His proof was the Hall of Fame. Every modern-era quarterback inducted into the Hall of Fame had been right-handed. After one week of camp Scovil told me bluntly: "You'll never play quarterback at BYU. I don't coach lefties."

That statement actually motivated me. Despite all of my insecurities, I was attracted to the impossible.

Meantime, Scovil assigned me to the practice team, otherwise known as the meat squad. Basically, my job was to play quarterback against BYU's starting defense.

After a couple of weeks I was tired of being a tackling dummy. I telephoned my dad back home.

"I should have gone to North Carolina."

"What's wrong?"

"This is miserable. I hate it."

"Calm down, Steve."

"They don't even know my name here!"

"Give it some time."

"I don't want to give it time. I want to come home."

I went on and on for half an hour. Finally, he gave me his advice: "Steve, you have to suck it up."

I had a room in the dorm, but I didn't unpack my bags. Every chance I got I slept over at the Burrs' house. There I'd play with the kids and nobody cared that I was a football player. I had no expectations to fulfill. It was the one place I could just relax and let my guard down. Plus, Carole was my sounding board for all of my frustrations and insecurities. She and I would stay up at night and talk. Then in the morning she'd encourage me to keep going and send me back to campus in time for practice.

But what motivated me the most was Coach Scovil. I went to practice every day determined to prove him wrong. I strapped on my helmet and remembered his words: "You'll never play quarterback at BYU."

I decided to take out my frustrations on BYU's defense. I did everything possible to make them look bad. It was my way of letting Scovil and everybody else know that they were making a big mistake by relegating me to the practice squad. One way or another, people were going to know my name.

BYU's first game was on the road against New Mexico. They ran the wishbone, so the practice squad was assigned to simulate New Mexico's offense. I was the only one who knew how to run the option, and I ran wild in the scrimmages. No one on our defense could catch me. The defensive coaches screamed at the linebackers. "Contain him! Contain him!"

But I was too fast and no one was used to a running quarterback. Kyle Whittingham, the captain of the defense, hated me because I was making him look bad. He could never get a clean hit on me. Fed up, one day he chased me out of bounds and hit me so hard I went airborne and landed on my head.

He stood over me and yelled, "Now just sit there!"

I popped right up and hustled back to the huddle. The next play I ran to the outside and blew past Whittingham. I scored so many touchdowns so easily in scrimmage it was ridiculous. BYU never solved the wishbone. Despite being heavily favored, we lost the season opener on the road to New Mexico, 25–21.

It was 1980, and college football programs still had JV teams. That's where I ended up. Some JV players also got to dress for home varsity games. If a jersey was hanging in front of your locker on the day before game day, you were dressing. No jersey meant you were not.

Our home opener was against San Diego State on September 13.

My buddy Lee Johnson found out that he was kicking off, and my other buddy, Jim Herrmann, was told he'd see action in third-down situations. I was not dressing. Instead, I received two tickets to the game. I would get to watch from the stands.

But I wasn't about to be a spectator at my own team's game. I went to my Uncle Bob's house, and we watched it together on TV.

"Your day is coming," he said.

"Not with Scovil," I told him. "There's no way."

To make things worse, I couldn't stop thinking about the fact that North Carolina's starting quarterback had gone down with an injury. If I had gone there, I'd have been the starting quarterback as a freshman.

After the game I called my dad. It was midnight back east when Grit picked up. He was groggy, and I was depressed.

"I blew it," I told him.

"What are you talking about?" he said.

"I should have gone to North Carolina."

"Steve, you've barely been there a month," he said. "You've got to hang in there."

"I'm done. I'm quitting. I'm coming home." My bags were already packed.

Dad cleared his throat. "You can certainly quit. But you can't come home. I'm not living with a quitter. So you can decide for yourself."

I hung up mad. But I stayed at BYU.

A few weeks later I was in the locker room after practice, trying to bum a ride to Carole Burr's place.

"Hey, Young," someone yelled. "I'll take you."

I turned around. It was Jim McMahon. Shirtless, he had on blue jeans and shades, a wad of gum in his cheek. Up to this point he'd never spoken to me. Suddenly I was trailing him to his car.

"Hop in," he said.

I didn't say a word. This was Mr. Cool, the top passer in the nation, a Heisman candidate. I was the JV quarterback, the lefty who couldn't throw, the guy who sucked.

The first thing I noticed was his stereo and the giant set of speakers in the backseat. He was so famous that I figured he listened to a station that only famous people knew about. He keyed the ignition, and the radio came on. It was tuned to the same rock station I liked. I was shocked as we cruised off campus listening to Van Halen.

I told myself: *This is big-time.*

He pulled up in front of the Burrs' and I hopped out. As McMahon sped off I watched his taillights disappear in the darkness and wondered, *How in the world will I ever get to where he is?*

Jim Herrmann and Lee Johnson made the team and got to travel for road games. Relegated to JV, I'd go up to Carole Burr's place and listen to the games on the radio. It was unbearable. One night I turned off the game and we went for a walk in the yard and talked about Mormon missions. I told her that, even though there was no requirement to serve a mission, I had always wanted to go on one. I was fully prepared to go too. I just wasn't sure I could survive being away from my home and my family for two years. I had never admitted that to anyone until I told Carole. She told me not to worry and reminded me that God knows our hearts.

She knew, like my folks knew, that a kid who struggled so mightily with leaving home at all would certainly struggle leaving for two years.

That was such a relief to me.

While we were walking and talking I noticed some activity at the house next door, and I finally got around to asking who lived there. The Osmonds, she said. That got my attention — I had grown up watching Donny and Marie on television. Carole explained that the house next door had been built for Carole's mother, who lived in it until she died. Then the Osmonds bought it and moved the family from LA to Provo. By that point Donny and Marie had become famous. The location afforded them a great deal of privacy. And Carole had become a close friend to them, in much the same way she was becoming a best friend to me.

But celebrity did not impress Carole. The fact that she never mentioned that the Osmonds were her neighbors until I asked about the house next door made a lasting impression on me.

November 1, 1980. BYU is playing the University of Texas at El Paso (UTEP) at home. My dorm is one block from the stadium. I decide to use my complimentary ticket and go to the game. I blend in with the fans as I approach the gate. I'm so lost in my own misery that I don't notice the marching band coming behind me. "Get out of the way!" the drum major yells as he pushes me aside, saving me from being run over. Then I pass unrecognized through the turnstile. Nobody knows that I'm on the team. Feeling as alone as I have ever felt in my life, I wipe a tear from my cheek and find my seat.

McMahon has a huge game, leading BYU to an 83–7 win. I leave before it's over.

Somehow, some way, I am going to get on that field, I tell myself.

I was the first one to show up for the next practice. And I hung around when the practice squad players were dismissed at the end of practice. Some of the varsity players noticed me and snickered. I didn't care. I was determined to outwork everyone else, and I figured I might also learn something by watching McMahon.

I followed this routine for the rest of the season — first to arrive, last to leave. And I studied everything McMahon did. His footwork. The way he maneuvered in the pocket. His arm motion. I even studied his grip. I noticed that he held the ball with his index finger above the strings, pointing toward the tip. When he released the ball his index finger guided the direction of the pass. His accuracy was superb.

Working out by myself, I started imitating him. Instead of spinning the ball out of my hand, I learned to push the ball out of my hand as if throwing a screwball. When I released the ball my thumb ended up pointing down instead of up. Overnight, I discovered that I could throw the ball with pinpoint accuracy and a lot of power. Suddenly, throwing became thrilling. I hit the bull's eye every time. I wish someone had taught me how to throw much earlier.

BYU finished the regular season 11-1. McMahon led the team to eleven straight wins. We were ranked in the top twenty and headed to a bowl game against Southern Methodist University. Thanks to a strong second half of the season, I was named MVP of the JV team.

I was beginning to feel a lot better about my chances. In fact, when LaVell Edwards called me into his office just before the end of the semester, I figured he was going to invite me to travel with the team for the Holiday Bowl game.

"Steve, we're going to move you to defense."

I was stunned.

"But I can be a quarterback here," I said.

"You shouldn't be a quarterback. You're our fastest guy."

I'd been clocked at 4:41 in the 40. But at this moment I felt like my speed was actually working against me.

"You could play any position," he continued. "Besides, we've got too many quarterbacks."

It wasn't the conversation I had anticipated. Especially given that my throwing had just improved dramatically.

He went on to explain that after the Christmas break he wanted me to start working out with Tom Holmoe, the best defensive back on the team. "He'll help teach you the position," Edwards said. "Teach you the basic pass coverage techniques."

I didn't bother arguing. His mind was made up.

Dejected, I watched the Holiday Bowl from the sidelines as McMahon led BYU in a miraculous, come-from-behind, one-point victory over SMU by throwing a Hail Mary touchdown pass on the last play of the game. There was nothing I wanted more than to lead BYU to a last-second, come-from-behind victory in a bowl game. That was my dream. But McMahon was living my dream, and the dream was dead for me. Scovil had gotten his wish — BYU would not have a lefty quarterback. I was destined for defense.

The Christmas break gave me time to think about my future. I decided to step away from football and serve a two-year mission. It wasn't a snap decision. I'd been mulling it over all semester. My father had served a mission after his freshman year at BYU, and I had always aspired to do the same. LaVell's decision to make me into a defensive back spurred me to go sooner rather than later.

I completed the necessary paperwork and notified my bishop. The plan was set. I would leave in the spring, right after I completed my freshman year.

My parents were pleased. But as soon as I committed I started to feel anxious. A mission is a great opportunity. But I knew myself too well. There was no way I'd survive being away for two years. Mormon missionaries don't come home on holidays. Family can't visit them either. Even telephone calls are restricted to just Mother's Day and Christmas. The thought of total separation overwhelmed me. I didn't understand the source of my fears. But I knew they were real.

There's no way, I told myself. *I'll never make it.*

I was barely hanging on at BYU. I was calling home a few times a week. The dresser drawers in my dorm room were empty because I never bothered to unpack for the entire fall semester. I often retreated to the Burrs' place.

The more I thought about a mission the sicker I became. I decided to talk to my dad. I knew he didn't relate to my anxiety. He and I are wired differently. But I knew he'd give me sound advice.

Still home for the holidays, I sat opposite my dad at the kitchen table and told him my dilemma.

"It just doesn't feel right," I said. "I think the best thing is for me to just go back to school."

He'd been on enough late-night phone calls from Provo. He knew my struggle with separation. He also knew that I was finally getting used to Provo. It wasn't home, but I could survive there. A two-year mission in a faraway place was another story.

"Well," he said, "you better go talk to the bishop."

Our congregation had just gotten a new bishop, Kay Rasmussen. He was a vice president at Harcourt Brace Jovanovich, a big publishing house in New York City. Bishop Rasmussen didn't know me particularly well, but he had previously interviewed me and determined that I was qualified to serve a mission. I felt terribly guilty as I drove to the church to tell him that I wasn't going to go through with it.

Rasmussen was from Idaho, and he spoke slowly and softly. He had a way of putting people at ease. Still, I struggled to get the words out. "I really think the right thing for me to do is continue going to school at BYU," I said.

He leaned forward. "Can I tell you something?" he said.

I tensed up. *Here it comes.*

"A couple of weeks before you came home for Christmas break I was sitting in church, looking out over the congregation," he said. "And I got the impression that you were going to come see me at some point to tell me that you felt the right thing to do was return to BYU."

"You're kidding."

"That's not all," he continued. "I also got the impression that I should tell you that you should return to BYU."

He wasn't kidding. He was dead serious. I was speechless.

I had fully expected him to try to talk me into going on my mission. Instead, he gave me three simple pieces of advice:

Serve Jesus Christ.

Live your religion.

Be a great example.

Then, without elaborating or trying to explain his impressions, he simply reiterated that it felt right to him that I return to school.

"Bishop Rasmussen, I've always wanted to serve a mission. I want to do the right thing."

"Steve, your mission might be to do what you were born to do in terms of playing football."

He put his arms around me and wished me well. The meeting was over.

I felt a tremendous sense of relief as I left his office. But I was also confused. The last thing he said to me — the part about being born to play football — made no sense. I wasn't even the eighth-string quarterback anymore. I had been demoted to defense. My dream of playing quarterback at BYU was all but over, and if I couldn't play quarterback I had no interest in playing football. So I wasn't sure what to make of my bishop's comment.

Before I returned to Provo for spring semester Dad sat me down at the kitchen table for a pep talk.

"What do you want to do?" he said.

"I still want to play quarterback."

He dropped his head and took a deep breath. I sensed that he was as frustrated as I was.

"Look," he said, "all those other guys ahead of you on the depth chart have gone through years of spring practice. You're just a freshman. You'll get your chance this spring."

"But Coach Edwards is moving me to defense."

"Give it one more shot," he said. "If it doesn't work out, we'll figure something out at the end of the semester."

Tom Holmoe was a junior safety and a legitimate NFL prospect. He was also a Lutheran from Los Angeles, another supremely talented non-Mormon athlete LaVell had managed to recruit. When I got back to Provo, Holmoe started working out with me every day, teaching me backpedaling drills and coverage techniques.

I liked Holmoe. But I hated defense. I didn't want to backpedal. I wanted to run the offense. It killed me to be doing pass coverage drills while the quarterbacks were in the same facility working out with the receivers. I should have been with them.

I was barely back in school a few days when I heard on the news that Doug Scovil had been hired as the new head coach at San Diego State.

"No way!" I shouted.

I pumped my fist in the air. The quarterback coach who hated lefties was gone. It was midnight back east. I called my dad anyway.

"I've got my shot!" I said.

"What are you talking about?"

"Scovil is gone."

"What do you mean he's gone?"

"He took the head job at San Diego State. I'm going to get my shot."

I couldn't sleep. The next day I asked Holmoe if he'd throw with me after we finished our defensive drills. I also stepped up my private workouts. I had an oversized duffle bag stuffed with footballs. There was a huge net hanging at the far end of the fieldhouse. I lined up behind an imaginary center, did the three-step drop, and threw into the net. From the beginning of January to the end of February, I threw more than 10,000 spirals. Over and over again. And then some. My arm hurt. But I wanted to be a quarterback.

When I wasn't working out I worked as a towel boy at BYU basketball games. I got the job through BYU's equipment manager, Floyd Johnson. During the fall we had become close. Among other duties, Johnson was in charge of assigning BYU football players to speak to youth groups in and around Provo. He made sure I spoke somewhere almost every week.

I liked Johnson so much that I started hanging out with him in the equipment room. I went there to study and do homework. And we talked. I told him that I had been captain of the basketball team at Greenwich High and that I was a huge Danny Ainge fan. Ainge was the only guy on campus who was on par with Jim McMahon. A two-sport star, he was drafted in high school by the Toronto Blue Jays in 1977. During his summers at BYU he played pro baseball. Plus, he was a two-time All-American in basketball. I watched every home game from the visiting team's bench, where I provided towels and water for the players. After games I'd pick up the dirty towels and clean the visiting team's locker room, where I'd hear a lot of postgame tirades from losing coaches. I didn't get paid, but I didn't care. I wanted the courtside seat. After the games I ran all the way back to my dorm, dribbling an imaginary ball, hitting buzzer beaters, pretending I was Danny Ainge. Like McMahon, he inspired me.

Shortly after Doug Scovil left, LaVell hired San Diego State's former offensive coordinator, Ted Tollner, as our new quarterback coach. LaVell spent the winter months recruiting and was seldom around. But Coach Tollner spent a lot of time in the fieldhouse. He saw me throwing, day after day. Eventually he stopped me.

"What are you doing?" he said.

"Well, they've got me at DB. But I want to play quarterback."

He didn't say much more. I continued throwing. A few days before the start of spring practice Tollner had a talk with LaVell. He asked if LaVell was still determined to move me to defense. When LaVell said that he was, Tollner asked if he'd seen me throw lately. LaVell hadn't. So Tollner convinced him to watch me before finalizing his decision.

I was working out by myself when I noticed LaVell trailing Tollner as they walked toward me. Tollner put up some targets and said, "Let's show Coach Edwards what you can do."

On Tollner's signal, I dropped back and hit the target. He kept moving the targets farther back. I kept nailing them. My spiral was tight, my arm motion fluid, and my footwork clean.

LaVell turned to Tollner. "Well, so much for that idea," he said. "He's staying at quarterback."

Tollner motioned me over with his index finger. LaVell looked at me. "I'll give you two weeks of spring ball," Edwards said. "Then we'll see where you're at."

March 15, 1981. It was the first day of spring ball, and when McMahon hurt his throwing arm he was forced to sit out the entire two weeks. I ended up taking the majority of the snaps. In a few months' time I had jumped from eighth to second on the quarterback depth chart. A number of factors went into this. One guy ahead of me graduated. Another transferred. Some of the guys I just outworked. When we played our annual blue-white scrimmage on April 3 at Cougar Stadium, the fans and the media expected to see McMahon. But LaVell rested him and started me in his place. I threw with accuracy and velocity. Plus, I ran all over the place.

After the game one football writer declared me the best athlete on the roster. Ted Tollner told me it was official — I would not be switching to defense. LaVell named me Jim McMahon's backup heading into the 1981 season. Ted saw something in me, and he believed in me enough to lobby LaVell on my behalf. Without Ted, I probably would have never played quarterback at BYU.

The irony is that Coach Tollner left after just one year at BYU. But that one year changed the direction of my life.

When my neighbor David van Blerkom converted to Mormonism during our sophomore year of high school, he said there were two things he would never do — attend BYU and serve a Mormon mission. He ended up doing both. Owing to my workouts and practice schedule, I didn't see much of him during our freshman year. But when spring semester ended we drove back to Connecticut together. It was 2,000 miles from Provo to Greenwich. We spent much of the journey discussing his decision to serve a Mormon mission. Right after we got home he began packing for France. His last day in Greenwich was June 1, 1981. That night he came over to say good-bye to my parents. Then he and I sat in his car until two in the morning, talking. I struggled with the fact that he was going and I was staying. I felt guilty. He reminded me of what our bishop had told me about having a different mission.

Then he asked me to do him a favor. Through much of high school David had worked at the Old Greenwich Tennis Academy. He often played there with a kid from Argentina named Rich Fogth. Thanks to David, Rich wanted to become a Mormon. David asked me to teach Rich about our faith. I gave him my word that I would, and later that summer I baptized Rich Fogth.

I also caught up with my old girlfriend, Christy. Her modeling career had really taken off. She would eventually beat out Halle Berry as Miss USA and finish as a runner-up in the Miss Universe competition. But by this point we had gone our separate ways and I was dating some great girls at BYU. I was totally focused on the challenge of succeeding Jim McMahon as BYU's next quarterback.

6

JUST RELAX

I COULDN'T WAIT FOR summer practice to start. As soon as I arrived in Provo I went to the Burrs' house. I walked in and went straight to the refrigerator. Carole had extra bottles of milk waiting for me. When I drank from the bottle the little kids started laughing and making fun of me. It was like coming home.

I wasted no time linking up with Jim Herrmann and Lee Johnson. Lee found out he was being redshirted: he wouldn't play that season. But Jim would see a lot of time. I was backing up McMahon. The three of us moved into an off-campus apartment with three other guys, and somehow I ended up rooming with a complete stranger. He was a nuclear physicist who kept to himself.

Herm and LJ wanted to go out every night. There were girls to meet and pranks to play. We even took tubing from a science lab and constructed a contraption that enabled us to launch water balloons like cannonballs. LJ bragged that he could hit students coming out of the library from 300 feet away.

I missed out on some fun as the responsibility of backing up McMahon sunk in. He was the top quarterback in the country and a front-runner to win the Heisman, and if he went down I would go in. The prospect excited and overwhelmed me. We had one of the most complex passing schemes in the nation, and I had a lot to learn. Not surprisingly, my worries began to creep in.

. . .

At the start of the regular season, I was assigned to be Jim McMahon's roommate when we traveled for away games. Jim and I are different in a lot of ways. He is a Catholic from Utah who likes beer. I am a Mormon from Connecticut who prefers milk. He chafed against BYU's strict honor code. The rules were second nature to me; I had grown up under similar ones. He prided himself on being a rebel. I was shy and kept a low profile.

But we got along well, and Jim was a great mentor. When we were alone he taught me all sorts of things about throwing a football. But the most important thing he taught me was confidence. "You could be a great one, Steve," he told me. Coming from him that meant a lot.

Our first three games were blowouts. We beat Cal State 31–8, Air Force 45–21, and UTEP 65–8. McMahon was unstoppable. He racked up 1,000 yards passing in three games. I was in awe. We were beating teams so badly that LaVell stuck me in games late in the fourth quarter just to mop up and get some experience.

By the time we traveled to Boulder to face Colorado on September 26, 1981, I had thrown a grand total of 17 passes, completing nine, including one touchdown. Colorado was the biggest game on our schedule that year. We were now ranked eleventh in the country. We were also riding a fifteen-game winning streak, the longest in the nation.

McMahon lit up the Buffaloes early, building a 24–0 lead. But one minute and nineteen seconds into the third quarter, his knee buckled on the turf. He ended up on his back. Writhing, he removed his helmet and grabbed his head. LaVell ran onto the field. McMahon was helped off.

While doctors tended to McMahon, we punted and Colorado drove the length of the field and scored a touchdown. The crowd was energized. LaVell told me McMahon was done. His knee was hyperextended. Nearly two full quarters of football remained. I had never been in a game with that much time on the clock.

"Just relax," LaVell told me. "Be patient out there."

Patience is not in my DNA. I run to the huddle. Our center is Bart Oates, the same guy who declared that I sucked on the first day of camp the prior year. First play call is a pass. I complete it for a 26-yard gain.

Second play is a rollout. I am supposed to throw. But I see a running lane. So I take off. I go for 29 yards before two linebackers meet me at the Colorado 10-yard line. They expect me to head for the sideline. Instead, I put my head down like a fullback and barrel into them — first-and-goal.

The offensive linemen love it. Moments later I throw a touchdown pass to Gordon Hudson, putting us up 31–6.

Nobody expects this out of me.

Bart Oates slaps my helmet.

LaVell nods.

"I knew you could do it, kid," McMahon says.

Jim is never jealous. He always encourages me.

But Colorado responds with 14 points. Their defense steps up the pass rush too. Anytime they get close to me I take off running. On a broken pass play in the fourth quarter I scramble for 37 yards before Colorado drags me down. Then I throw a 22-yard touchdown pass to cement the victory. We win 41–20. I finish with more yards rushing than passing, and our winning streak reaches sixteen games.

My father is in the stands. He has flown into Boulder on the way back from a West Coast business trip, and Uncle Bob is with him. They hadn't expected me to play. I meet them at the edge of the field. Uncle Bob is bouncing up and down, yelling, "I knew you could do it. I knew you could do it."

Dad is more reserved. He doesn't express approval with words. He does it with his expressions and demeanor. So when he utters the word "Wow!" I am elated. He is pleased.

The Denver media surrounded me afterward. It was my first press conference. I didn't know what to expect. Somehow word got out that I was Brigham Young's great-great-great-grandson.

The next day the headline in the *Denver Post* was: "Brigham Young Would Have Been Very Proud of a Kin Named Steve." My connection to the early Mormon prophet quickly eclipsed my performance. By Monday the *New York Times* reported: "Brigham Young's great-great-grandson, Steve Young, is the backup quarterback at the university named after his ancestor."

It was pretty surreal. One year earlier I was nearly run over by the marching band as I entered the stadium as a JV player to watch a game from the stands. Then I was relegated to defense. Yet here I was quarterbacking the team to a win with my dad looking on. I felt so grateful to Ted Tollner and LaVell for believing in me. I was determined not to let them down.

Our next game was at home against Utah State. McMahon didn't practice all week. But he planned on playing in the game. I planned on him playing too. Twenty-four hours before kickoff LaVell informed me that Jim had undergone an MRI and the doctor hadn't cleared him to play. I was starting.

Starting? At home? Whoa! Wait a minute.

I panicked. The Utah State game was a quirk in the schedule. It was slated for Friday because that Saturday was the Mormon Church's annual conference in Salt Lake City. Mormons from around the world converged in Utah for the conference. Many would tune in to the game the night before. In Greenwich I had never played in front of Mormons. At BYU everyone is a Mormon and our team was like an extension of the faith for many people. I didn't want to let them down. Plus, our sixteen-game winning streak was on the line.

I started to worry. I started talking to myself: *I can't do this. There's no way.* BYU fans were accustomed to 400-yard passing games and big-margin victories. The team hadn't lost since the first game of McMahon's junior season. *What if we lose?*

Anxiety for people who don't have anxiety is simply fear. But fear is much more complex for people who live with anxiety. For starters, anxiety is genetic. I didn't learn that until much, much later in life. Anxiety comes from deep within your body, and when it flows out it's almost impossible to control on your own. I was a nineteen-year-old college student who didn't understand how anxiety worked. All I knew was that I couldn't gain control of my worries. And nothing worried me more than disappointing people. The thought of letting our fans down overwhelmed me leading up to game day.

An hour before the game I was in the locker room throwing up. Mc-

Mahon limped in wearing blue jeans, a giant sheepskin coat, and a wide-rimmed cowboy hat. He reminded me of Clint Eastwood in *A Fistful of Dollars*.

"Don't panic, kid," he said. "Just let the passes fly."

That was easy for him to say. He was always so cool, so relaxed.

My first pass soars ten feet over the head of the intended receiver. Ten feet! The next play I get sacked. We go three and out.

On our next possession I settle down and find my rhythm. But Utah State puts heat on me all day. They sack me five times and flush me from the pocket so often that I end up running the ball 21 times, for 102 yards. I rush for more yardage than our entire backfield of running backs.

I throw the ball well too, completing 21 of 40 passes for over 300 yards. After trailing the entire game, I orchestrate a long drive in the final minutes to tie the score at 26–26.

A minute later my roommate Jim Herrmann pressures Utah State's quarterback, forcing him to throw a bad pass, which is intercepted and returned for a touchdown. Game over. We win 32–26 and improve to 5-0.

The win streak extends to seventeen games. My legs are so sore from being hit that I can barely walk. But I feel nothing but joy. My first college start is in the books and it's a *W*.

Afterward I went out with Herm and LJ to celebrate. On the way back to our apartment, Herm said he'd buy LJ a pizza if he streaked naked down the main drag near campus. LJ stripped down and took off running. Students milling around the streets couldn't believe it. Herm fell down laughing. These were my two best friends.

That kind of stuff was outside my comfort zone. But there was a part of me that envied the way LJ and Herm were able to let themselves run free. For me, I couldn't help focusing on the next hurdle. Our winning streak was at seventeen. It was homecoming week. The University of Nevada at Las Vegas was in town. McMahon was still out. That meant I would start again. I fretted about it all week.

· · ·

In the game, despite throwing four interceptions, I complete 27 of 40 passes for 269 yards and we have a 41–24 lead midway through the third quarter. But then our defense falls apart. UNLV scores three touchdowns after long drives and upsets us 45–41. The longest winning streak in college football is over.

Even though we lose, I feel good about my performance. I feel good because my body hurts so badly. I get some satisfaction from knowing that I left everything on the field.

Days after the game I go with Herm and LJ to see Christopher Cross perform at the Marriott Center. I limp in with a box of popcorn in one arm and a pretty girl on the other. Then it hits me. *I can't believe it!* I think to myself. *I have survived. I made it. I'm here.*

McMahon returned to action the following week, and I went back on the sideline. I have to admit, it was a bit of a relief. Being the starting quarterback at BYU was much more pressure than I had imagined. With McMahon healthy, I figured I could finally chill a bit.

I was wrong. A few days after the UNLV loss I was leaving the locker room when LaVell's secretary, Shirley Johnson, informed me that a producer from ABC's *Good Morning America* had called and wanted to fly me to New York to be interviewed.

"Me? Why me?"

Shirley grinned. She told me that co-anchor David Hartman had gotten wind that I was Brigham Young's descendant. He wanted to talk to me about playing quarterback at my ancestor's university.

Oh, boy.

Shirley congratulated me. No BYU athlete had ever been on *Good Morning America*. Not even Danny Ainge or Jim McMahon.

I was not thrilled about this. I hated the idea of missing practice.

But Shirley said LaVell didn't mind. My appearance would be great exposure for the football program and the school.

Reluctantly, I agreed to do it. But I didn't tell anyone I was going to New York. Not even my parents, who lived forty-five minutes outside the city. I know that probably sounds strange. But whenever big things were happening to me I would always try to make them seem smaller so I could manage them better. For instance, I didn't tell my dad when I got promoted to be McMahon's backup. It was my way of telling myself it was no big deal. By not telling my folks that I was going to be on national television, I was telling myself: *You can do this. It's not that big of a deal.* It was my way of coping.

A few hours later I was on a nonstop flight from Salt Lake City to JFK. It dawned on me that millions of people watch *Good Morning America.* I had never been on national television. No one had given me media training. I had no idea what to expect. There would probably be questions about Mormonism. My answers would be a direct reflection on my faith and my school. There are no do-overs on live television.

I tried to anticipate the questions. But David Hartman's first one caught me completely off guard.

"Are you a celebrity at BYU?" he said.

"No. My great-great-great-grandfather had fifty-two children, so when you get down to the third generation, there are a lot of us around."

Hartman grinned. So did I. The edge was off.

"Still," I added, "I'm proud of my heritage."

The interview went smoothly. I didn't say anything embarrassing. Afterward I flew back to Utah. I figured the national media interest was finally behind me. But then a week later my picture and a story about me being interviewed on *Good Morning America* appeared in *People* magazine. The publicity was getting out of hand.

The one place I could always go to get away was Carole Burr's. A couple of nights a week I went up there and stayed in the bedroom she maintained for me. One day while I was there I was out in the yard playing with her kids. Jimmy Osmond came over from next door. He's a year and a half younger than me. He introduced me to his sister Marie. She's two years older than me. I told her how much I enjoyed watching her on television in the mid-'70s. She asked how I liked playing football for BYU. I told her I was still learning.

Marie and I enjoyed each other's company and ended up going on a date. It was my first real exposure to the burden of celebrity. This was 1981, and Marie and her brother Donny were the two most visible Mormons in the world. She preferred to avoid crowded public places — movie theaters, popular restaurants, and shopping malls. So we ended up going bowling. Mostly we just talked. It was a low-key evening. It was clear to both of us that we were better off as friends.

After taking Marie home I went next door and talked with Carole. As usual, her insight gave me great perspective. It seemed like only yesterday that I was a high school kid struggling to leave home. Now I was at a huge college, where I was excelling in the classroom and playing quarterback. Life was good. Before going to sleep I knelt beside my bed and let God know I was grateful.

McMahon didn't miss another start. Despite sitting out two and a half games, he became the first player in NCAA history to pass for over 4,000 yards in a single season. He set seventy NCAA passing records. He was, hands down, the best quarterback to ever play for BYU.

As soon as his senior season ended people looked to me as his successor. I immediately felt the pressure. McMahon wasn't just the greatest quarterback in school history: according to the record book he might have been the greatest quarterback in the history of college football. He left very big shoes to fill.

LaVell called me into his office. I expected a pep talk. Instead, he told me that quarterback coach Ted Tollner had taken a job at the University of Southern California.

I felt an allegiance to Tollner. Without him, I would have been on defense at that point.

"I have a replacement candidate in mind," LaVell said. "But before reaching a final decision I'd like you to talk to him."

"Who is it?"

"His name is Mike Holmgren."

I didn't know the name.

LaVell said he was a young assistant at San Francisco State and had played ball at USC.

"The only thing I want to know is how he feels about coaching a lefty."

"Don't worry, Steve. Just talk to him."

The minute I met Holmgren I wanted him as my coach. He was gregarious with a great sense of humor. He was way younger than anyone else on

Edwards's staff. But it was immediately apparent that he knew his stuff. In a way he was actually a lot like me — hyperfocused and out to prove himself. He almost felt like the older brother I never had.

LaVell called me back in after my session with Holmgren. "So what do you think of him?" he said.

"I don't want to play for anybody else."

Edwards hired Holmgren.

7

COMPARISONS

STEVE YOUNG VS. JIM MCMAHON. The comparisons began the moment I arrived in Provo for football camp in July 1982. Even after Jim was drafted by the Chicago Bears the comparisons only increased. It was a burden, but I tried to keep it light.

One reporter asked if I could fill McMahon's shoes. No, I told him. McMahon is a size 10. I'm a 13.

It wasn't just the Utah media. The national press hounded me about being McMahon's successor. "I am not Jim McMahon," I told *Sports Illustrated* for the '82 college football preview issue. "Nor do I want to be Jim McMahon."

But the truth was that I thought about McMahon's legacy every day. The pressure to measure up gnawed at me constantly. Holmgren finally pulled me aside during training camp. "Stop trying to be Jim," he told me. "Just be Steve."

We opened the '82 season on the road against UNLV and blew them out 27–0. The real test came the following week against Georgia. The Bulldogs were nationally ranked and led by All-America running back Herschel Walker.

The night before the game we had a team meeting. It was pouring out. The forecast called for similar weather at game time. My experience throwing the football was pretty limited. I had a grand total of three starts under my belt. None were in the rain, and rain changes everything in football. Footing is slippery. Vision is impaired. Most importantly, the ball is heavier and slick, making it harder to throw and catch. Grip is a real problem.

Looking out the window at the rain coming down in sheets, I started talking to myself. *The game will be on national television. There are over 80,000 seats in Sanford Stadium in Athens, Georgia — 80,207 to be exact. I have never played in front of that many people. Plus, my parents have driven down from Connecticut.*

I was a bundle of nerves.

Georgia scores first. Then my friend Tom Holmoe intercepts a Georgia pass and returns it 63 yards for a touchdown, tying the game at 7–7. For my efforts, all I do is throw interception after interception. By halftime I've thrown five, including one in the end zone to end the half.

As I jog off the field toward the locker room, LaVell grabs me.

"Now, Steve, when something like that happens —"

"I know. I know. I know."

"Listen to me."

"I've got it figured out, Coach."

"You don't have it figured out, Steve."

"No, no, I'm fine."

"You're not fine."

"Coach, there is no problem. We're gonna win the game."

He looks at me like I'm nuts. I've just thrown five interceptions in one half. That has to be an all-time BYU record. Yet I'm telling the head coach that I have it all under control.

Bewildered, LaVell just shakes his head.

The truth is that I'm saying those things out of fear that he's going to bench me. And I can't live with that.

I enter the second half with one goal — no more interceptions. But in our third possession I attempt a simple 15-yard pass toward our sideline. Georgia's strong side linebacker deflects the ball, sending it straight up into the air. I take off in a dead sprint. The linebacker never sees me coming. Just as the ball is coming into his hands I tattoo him, separating him from the ball and driving him out of bounds. No interception. I've delivered one of the hardest hits of the day.

On our next possession I throw a 21-yard touchdown pass to put us up 14-7. In all I attempt 46 passes and complete 22 for 285 yards. But we still lose, 17–14.

The next week we lost 39–38 to Air Force. We were 1-2. In two weeks I had lost as many games as McMahon had lost in two years. Clearly this was not good.

Holmgren was the only guy around who hated losing as much as I did. He was also the only guy who screamed at me when I made mistakes. He was a hard-charging guy trying to make a name for himself as a coach. I was a hard-charging kid trying to make a name for myself as a quarterback. That's why we got along so well. After the loss to Air Force, Mike and I made a pact: no more losses.

We first identified a series of things I was doing wrong. My biggest problem was impatience. I had a tendency to flee the pocket at the first sign of pressure. Another problem was my tendency to force passes into double coverage. And I wasn't giving my receivers long enough to get open on the deep routes.

"By the time your receivers finally make the turn, they look back and see you running it," Holmgren told me. "They will quit if you keep doing that. Stay in the pocket. Be patient."

The following week I stayed in the pocket and we blasted UTEP 51–3. More importantly, Holmgren and I were bonding. We got so close that he started using me as a babysitter for his kids. Mike wasn't a Mormon, but he knew that Mormons were encouraged to marry early and start a family, which many of my teammates had done. Mike constantly joked that I needed to find a wife and settle down.

It seemed like everyone felt the urge to give me marital advice. I got all kinds of letters from Mormons throughout the country who were convinced I was supposed to marry their daughter. My bishop at the time, Scott Runia, said that he received over 200 letters per year from women who claimed they'd had a revelation that they were supposed to be with me. Parents were sending photo album résumés of their daughters to my parents and other members of my family. It was bizarre.

I always loved the idea of getting married, but I was all about finding the right girl. That effort was always made more difficult because playing quarterback at BYU consumed me. It was more than a full-time job. Plus, I was trying to maintain a 4.0 GPA. My dad still cared more about grades than football. In his mind, football was a great way to pay for college, but it was a very unreliable way to make a long-term living. He wanted me to get a real job. He kept reminding me: playing football is a dream, not a plan. Getting an education that leads to a profession is a plan. In his book, college was about making sure I landed a good job.

When it came to grades I didn't need much external motivation. I had a double major — finance and international relations — and I minored in French. I didn't have as much time as I preferred for studying. Fortunately, I have a photographic memory. If I read something once and then write it down, I can close my eyes and see it in my mind. In a testing situation I can visualize — word for word — what I've written out. My near-perfect recall helped me ace tests and master the playbook.

With all that was going on, I figured it was time I got a car. I was always bumming rides somewhere — practice, school, speeches. I called home and asked my dad to arrange a car loan. I wanted to buy a vehicle in Provo.

He had other plans.

"I'll bring you the Olds," he said.

His '65 Olds had over 200,000 miles on it. It was the same car I had pushed around the neighborhood when trying to imitate Dick Butkus. Not exactly what I had in mind for the college scene.

"Oh, c'mon, Dad. No way!"

He was serious.

"I'll drive it out," he told me.

"It'll never make it," I said.

"It'll make it."

There was no arguing with him.

He drove the car nearly 2,000 miles to Provo. The minute Dad rolled into town, Herm and LJ nicknamed my car the "Tuna Boat." The glove box was filled with my Bruce Springsteen cassette tapes. I became the designated chauffeur to and from practice.

The problem was fuel. The Tuna Boat was a gas hog. And I was broke. Between school and football, I had no time for a part-time job. But my father didn't believe in spoiling me. Most days I was lucky if I had $3 in my pocket. I'd put $2 in the tank and use the other dollar to buy three hot dogs at 7-Eleven.

November 20, 1982. The sky is gray. Snow is in the forecast. And I am sick to my stomach. It's nerves. The Western Athletic Conference championship is on the line. We're 7-1 in our conference. If we beat Utah, we win the WAC and go to the Holiday Bowl. It's expected. But beating Utah is not a given. Our rivalry with them is called "the Holy War" for a reason. Our games are grudge matches. It's personal. They have a losing record in the conference, but beating us would be like winning a championship for the Utes.

I look out the window as our team bus pulls up outside Rice Stadium. Utah fans are shouting and hurling things. Suddenly, they surround the bus and start rocking it. It gets hairy before the police intervene and escort us to the locker room. The ugliness continues on the field. During pregame warm-ups, a Utah fan in the stands throws a frozen banana and hits our assistant coach, Fred Whittingham, in the head, momentarily knocking him unconscious.

We have to win this game. I run back to the locker room and throw up. Holmgren assures me we're ready. We average 34 points a game. They can't stop us, he tells me.

But the weather is against us. Wind and freezing temperatures slow down our passing game, forcing us to improvise. Fortunately, improvisation is what I do best. I scramble. I run. We convert on critical third downs. It's an ugly game, but we win, 17–12. Over 36,000 fans are silent as the final seconds tick off the clock.

I'm silent too. Leaving the field, I glance up at the scoreboard at the south end of the stadium. Giant snowflakes land on my face mask. All afternoon I've had to blow on my hands to keep them from freezing, but suddenly I'm warm. We are 8-1 in the WAC. The conference title is ours. I have accomplished something that has always eluded me before: I have led my team to a championship.

I was on great teams in high school, but we never won a championship.

At BYU I've always wondered whether I had it in me to do this. I don't have to wonder anymore.

I CAN DO THIS.

A barrier is broken. This is bigger than football. I have proven to myself that I am actually good enough to lead. I've never felt so satisfied.

December 17, 1982. We face Ohio State in the Holiday Bowl. The Buckeyes manhandle us from the start, and by the fourth quarter the outcome is a foregone conclusion. But I still want to score. With less than five minutes to play, I drop back to pass from our 40-yard line. No one is open and the pocket is collapsing. So I take off, running 25 yards before cutting back to avoid a couple of oncoming tacklers. Suddenly, a linebacker trailing the play blindsides me and I am airborne. He hits me so hard that my helmet breaks and I have the wind knocked out of me.

Defenders rarely land a clean hit on me. I have a sixth sense about oncoming tacklers. But this guy nails me. I have never been hit so hard in my life. I am literally gasping for air.

After examining me on the sideline, the team doctor tells me I'm done. LaVell congratulates me on a good season.

I'm furious. Ohio State is mauling us. We are losing by 30, and I have sustained the worst physical punishment of my college career. There is no way I'm staying out.

I strap on my helmet and approach LaVell.

"Coach, I gotta go back in."

"It's okay, Steve. We had a good year."

"Coach, I gotta go back in!"

He waves me off. Less than a minute remains. The game is over.

The moment LaVell turns his head, I run back on the field. The second-string quarterback flashes a confused look when I reach the huddle. "You're out," I tell him.

Confused, my linemen look at me. There's time for one play.

"Let's go," I say. "C'mon. Let's score."

I hit a receiver on a crossing pattern. He breaks for the end zone but is tackled on Ohio State's 2-yard line. Time expires. Final score: 47–17.

My junior season is over. I've completed 62 percent of my passes for

3,100 yards. I've also rushed for 407 yards. But we finish 8-4. That, to me, is disappointing.

It was Christmastime, and I was in a chapel in New Canaan, Connecticut. Mormons from all over western Connecticut and eastern New York packed the pews. I looked out at all the teenagers in the audience. They had come to hear me tell football stories. But I had something else on my mind. Just three years earlier, I'd been one of two Mormon boys in a high school with 3,000 students. That was where I'd learned the importance of staying true to one's convictions.

I began by telling the youth that I was the eighth-string quarterback when I got to BYU. They were surprised. People had this notion that everything had come easily for me. It hadn't. I talked about the fact that no one had believed in me and no one had known my name when I arrived in Provo. I talked about what it took to go from eighth string to first string. I assured them that during that time there was always one person — the Savior — who knew my name and my struggles. And having a brother in Jesus was better than being the starting quarterback for BYU.

I discovered that one of my favorite things to do was talk to kids.

Spring semester flew by, and then my junior year was over and I had a ticket to fly home from Salt Lake City. Two days before my flight, I got a call from back east. It was April 22, 1983, and my former bishop's wife, Bonne Simmons from Scarsdale, was on the line. Her nineteen-year-old daughter Jill was a freshman at BYU. Jill was like a little sister to me. She was a great athlete, and we'd been close friends ever since I dated her older sister Tori during high school.

Bonne told me that Jill was planning to drive home from Provo. Concerned about Jill making the journey alone, she asked if I'd be willing to accompany her. I really wanted to fly. But the Simmonses were practically family, so I agreed.

Jill and I left Utah on a Friday night around 10:00 PM. A third friend, a BYU student from Idaho, decided to ride along at the last minute. He hopped in the back. Jill took the passenger seat. I drove.

We took I-80 and I drove through the night while the two of them slept. At around 7:00 AM, we stopped for breakfast at McDonald's in North Platte, Nebraska. Even after breakfast, I was beat, so Jill said she'd drive for a while. I moved into the front passenger's seat and fell asleep immediately.

About thirty minutes later I awoke to the sensation of bumping. Jill was slumped over, her head against the driver's side window, and the car was speeding across the wide highway median. I grabbed the wheel, but the front of the car dug into the wet ground and the car flipped. I was not wearing a seat belt, and I bounced from side to side as the car rolled four times. There were no airbags. Even so, I felt like something was shielding me.

The car finally came to a stop on its wheels. The student in the back was badly hurt, but conscious. Jill wasn't moving, and she was hanging out the driver's side window. I had no injuries. Not even a scratch. But I did cut my wrist climbing through the broken window. Then I pulled Jill out and laid her on the grass. She wasn't breathing.

I gave her mouth-to-mouth. "C'mon, Jill. You gotta breathe," I said in between breaths. "C'mon, Jill. Don't leave me. Stay with me, Jill."

Few cars were on the highway that morning. But some stopped and people got out to help. "What's happening?" one guy yelled.

"Call an ambulance!" I shouted. I tried frantically to revive Jill. "Please, Heavenly Father, let her live."

It seemed like she was starting to breathe, but she remained unconscious. I cleared her long, dark hair away from her eyes. "Jill, you can't go!" I yelled. "Come back."

I wanted so badly to hold her, but I had to keep performing mouth-to-mouth. I feared she'd die if I stopped. My tears flowed.

It took almost thirty minutes for the ambulance to arrive. It felt like forever. While I was waiting for the ambulance, it dawned on me that I was an ordained elder. Desperate, I placed my hands on Jill's head and administered a blessing. I believe fiercely in miracles and angels, and I called for every available one to bring her back right at that moment.

Finally, the ambulance arrived. The paramedics placed her on a stretcher and loaded her into the ambulance. I hopped in a police cruiser and followed the ambulance to the emergency room.

· · ·

When we reached Good Samaritan Hospital in Kearney, an officer pulled me aside. "She didn't make it," he said solemnly. Jill was gone.

I went into shock. "What do you mean she didn't make it? She can't be gone! She can't be!" I just couldn't believe it.

This was the first time I experienced the sudden death of a loved one and it completely overwhelmed me. I felt so alone. And so responsible.

How am I going to face her parents? They trusted me to get Jill home and I didn't make it. That awful feeling of responsibility tormented me. *I was there! I was sitting right next to her!*

The next day I caught a flight out of Omaha. I cried the whole way home. I told myself I should not be alive. I'd been in the front seat too. I hadn't even been wearing a seat belt.

Anxiety distorts reality, creating a false sense of loneliness, but the loneliness I felt on the plane was real. I was supposed to be driving Jill home; instead I was flying home without her. It was the heaviest feeling I had experienced in my life.

I never wanted to be closer to God than at that moment. *Please, Heavenly Father, help me get through this. What do I say to her parents?* These thoughts went through my head the whole way home.

My mom and dad were waiting when I landed at LaGuardia. There was nothing they could say to console me. We drove directly to Scarsdale, and the moment Ted and Bonne saw me they wept. So did my parents. So did I. The reality of the tragedy hit all of us at once.

After the funeral, I spent much of my summer at the Simmonses' home. The hardest part for me was having Bonne say to me over and over again: "Tell me what happened." I understood why Bonne needed to go over it. She had trouble believing that it had happened, and I was the connection to the reality. Yet talking about it felt like a constant reminder to me that I had messed up. If only I had stayed awake. If only I had just kept driving. I couldn't see past these thoughts.

The family suspected that Jill had fallen asleep at the wheel. They also wondered if she had had a seizure. But no explanation could make things any easier. Her parents weren't the same as they had been. Neither was I.

Prior to the accident I had thought often about God's power to heal, but it wasn't until after the crash that I learned what that really means. As time went on, I started to accept that I had done all I could. I also got a peaceful reassurance in my mind that Jill was doing very well in heaven. It was a spiritual confirmation that she was okay.

At that point, I asked myself: *How are you going to live the rest of your life?* I thought about that car repeatedly flipping over, and how I felt like I was floating in a pocket of air. And how, miraculously, I was unscathed.

I took it this way, as a message — *You've been spared and you'd better figure out why.* I felt obligated to live my life in a way that would never dishonor that experience.

From that day forward I would hear Jill's voice whenever I was doing something — or about to do something — I might regret. I don't mean I'd literally hear her voice. But in my mind I could picture her saying, *Steve, what are you doing?* And I'd say to myself: *You're right. I need to fix this.* This helped me make last-minute adjustments at critical junctures of my life when I was about to do something that felt wrong.

I don't want to come across as some moralist or someone who doesn't make mistakes. I'm neither. The point is that I floated in air for a reason. For me, walking away from that accident became a defining moment. The experience committed me to living my life in a more meaningful, Christ-like way.

Jill became my North Star and guardian angel.

8

ALL-AMERICAN

THREE MONTHS AFTER the accident I returned to Provo for my senior year. I moved into an apartment complex called Old Mill with LJ and Herm. Academically, we were all seniors. But in terms of football eligibility, LJ and Herm were classified as juniors because both of them had redshirted for a year. They would play two more years, but the '83 season was my last chance to play with them.

The hype and expectations for my senior year were over the top. BYU was a preseason top-twenty team. We were being projected as potentially the best team in BYU history. My name was in the preseason Heisman conversation. The expectations motivated me and tormented me at the same time.

Our first game was at Baylor. Our offense put up huge numbers. But our special teams couldn't stop Baylor's punt returner Gerald McNeil. He returned two punts for touchdowns. He was so fast that our defense couldn't catch him either. As a receiver, he ran past our defensive backs all night. His speed was the difference. We lost 40–36. So much for going undefeated.

Furious, I vowed we wouldn't lose another game.

We started destroying teams. We scored 63 against Bowling Green. We put up 46 against Air Force. Then we headed to Pasadena to play UCLA in a nationally televised game at the Rose Bowl. For BYU, this was about as big as it got. Our program was always looking for ways to convince the national media that we were playing great football. We had never faced UCLA before.

It was sunny and 68 degrees at kickoff, but the field was soggy. UCLA's starting quarterback, Rick Neuheisel, was injured. His backup was Steve Bono. He had a great receiving corps, led by Mike Sherrard. We jumped out front early and scored 14 first-quarter points. Bono then hit Sherrard on a 33-yard touchdown pass. The game was a see-saw battle from there, but we never trailed. I completed 25 of 36 passes for 270 yards and two touchdowns. I also ran for 67 yards on 14 carries. We won 37–35.

UCLA was our third straight win, and it was another big step forward for me and the program. We kept on winning, and our margins of victory got bigger and bigger: 41 against Wyoming, 66 against New Mexico, 47 against San Diego State. The last one felt particularly good, given that San Diego State was coached by BYU's former quarterback coach Doug Scovil, who told me I'd never play quarterback at BYU.

Our team was rolling, and I was enjoying life off the field with LJ and Herm. All three of us were starting. We lived off pizza and ice cream. We always argued over who was paying. Every night just before midnight we walked a few blocks to a place that sold gigantic homemade chocolate chip cookies. Life was good.

October 29, 1983. We've won six straight, and now we face Utah State. Late in the first half I sustain a blow to the head. I'm woozy, but I insist on staying in the game. On our next possession I run onto the field and call a play in the huddle. But by the time I take my position under the center I can't remember the play. My mind is blank. No recall whatsoever.

I go to the sideline and tell LaVell that something's wrong.

He sends in backup quarterback Robbie Bosco while the medical staff examine me and determine I have a concussion.

The trainer says it's not too serious. But he wants to hold me out.

By halftime I feel better, and they allow me to return to the field. I play the entire second half. After Utah State scores late to go up 34–31, I lead us on a drive deep into Utah State territory. With eleven seconds remaining, I barrel into the end zone for the game-winning touchdown. We win

38–34. It is one of the greatest feelings I have ever experienced. It's also our seventh straight win since losing to Baylor.

The Heisman race was on. A bunch of quarterbacks were in the running — Doug Flutie, Jeff Hostetler, Boomer Esiason. But it was really a two-man race between Nebraska running back Mike Rozier and me. I was getting so much attention from the national media that it was like a circus around our football program. In the second week of November I appeared on *Good Morning America* again. The day after that I taped a television special with Bob Hope.

The television gigs forced me to miss two days of practice leading up to the Colorado State game, and Mike Holmgren didn't like it. We had to beat Colorado State to win the WAC in order to qualify for a bowl game. When I got off to an uncharacteristically slow start against Colorado State, Holmgren exploded on the sideline and threatened to bench me. But I turned it on in the second half, and we ended up winning, 24–6.

After the game, LaVell's secretary Shirley motioned me into her office. Whenever Shirley said she needed to see me, I knew it was a national media request. But in this instance it was bigger than that. She told me that one of the senior leaders of the Mormon Church, Elder Neal A. Maxwell, had called and wanted to see me.

Mormons consider Maxwell an apostle. So this was a bit like getting invited to meet with a cardinal in Vatican City. It was a big deal.

"Why does he want to see me?"

She shrugged and smiled. "No idea."

"Where do I go?"

"His home."

"I'm going to his home?"

She nodded and handed me a piece of paper with directions.

I couldn't fathom what someone so important wanted with me. I was just a twenty-one-year-old college kid trying to make it from day to day.

I showered and put on a pair of blue jeans and a polo shirt. I even tied my sneakers, something I never did.

I jumped in my vehicle and headed north. I was too nervous to listen to Springsteen. I was going to see an apostle. I fretted the whole way.

Did I do something wrong?

Is this because I haven't served a mission for the church?
Why else would he want to talk to me?

I pulled up to a very modest home on a residential street below the University of Utah campus. I parked and rang the doorbell. He answered wearing dress slacks and a white shirt and tie.

"Hello, Steve," he said, extending his hand. "Please come in."

I took a seat on the sofa.

"How are you holding up?" he said.

I immediately started explaining why I hadn't served a Mormon mission. He politely listened, then changed the subject. It was apparent that he had something else on his mind. He asked about my family. He asked about school. He asked about football. He made me feel safe, safe enough to tell him that certain things scared me. For one thing, thanks to football I was fast becoming the most public Mormon in America. As it turned out, that was why he asked to see me. He wanted to make sure I was holding up under so much scrutiny.

After visiting for an hour, he offered me a blessing. With his hands on my head, he told me God was pleased with me. I felt an enormous sense of relief. Before I left, he patted me on the back. "I'm not worried about you," he said. "You have tremendous timidity."

I left reassured. But I had no idea what he meant. I had never heard the word "timidity." I looked it up as soon as I got back to my apartment. It meant lacking confidence, fearful, hesitant. I wasn't sure what to make of his word choice. It didn't sound like a compliment. But the more I thought about it, I realized he was very perceptive. He not only understood me. He pointed out that my diffidence kept me grounded. It's hard to be cocky and arrogant when you are always unsure about yourself. I told myself there was an upside to anxiety after all.

The week before Thanksgiving we finished the regular season by pounding Utah 55–7. We were 10-1 and ranked number nine in the nation. In early December I flew back east and visited the Associated Press office in New York. I was there when the AP announced its All-America team. The names came over the wire service. I watched as a machine spit out the paper. Then I tore it off. My name was listed. That week the awards kept coming:

College Football Player of the Year.

The Davey O'Brien Award.

Sports Illustrated said I was better than NFL rookie quarterback John Elway. Gil Brandt, the president of player personnel for the Dallas Cowboys, predicted I would be the number-one pick in the NFL draft. "If you could somehow measure what one player means to a team, Steve Young would be the most valuable player in college football today," Brandt said. "I don't know whether LaVell Edwards would ever say this, but I think he's better than any other quarterback they've had. And he's the most accurate passer I've ever seen. Period."

LaVell Edwards informed me that I had been invited to attend the Heisman ceremony, along with Doug Flutie from Boston College and Mike Rozier from Nebraska. Rozier was the clear favorite to win the award, particularly since Nebraska was 12-0 and ranked number one in the nation. We were supposed to stay at the Downtown Athletic Club in New York City, but I preferred my own bedroom in Greenwich. The night before the ceremony I stayed up late talking with my dad. He was more excited than I was.

"Don't get your hopes up," I told him. "Rozier's got this."

"But it's great to even be considered for the Heisman," he said. "It's a big honor."

The next morning my parents drove me into the city for the big announcement. The voting was a lot closer than I expected. Rozier got 1,801 votes. I received 1,172. I was surprised that so many sportswriters went for a kid from BYU. Flutie finished a distant third with 253 votes. All three of us received old-fashioned gold-and-blue sweatpants and sweatshirts. Then Rozier was awarded the trophy. Afterward I thought to myself, *Mike's going home with the trophy, and I'm going home with a sweat suit.* I laughed to myself: *Finishing second sucks.*

On the way out of the Downtown Athletic Club I turned to my mom. "You know," I said with a grin, "I would have liked to have won that thing."

December 23, 1983. The Holiday Bowl against Missouri is my last chance to put on a BYU uniform. On the first play of the game, linebacker Bobby Bell sacks me. On the third play of the game, Bell pressures me and I throw an interception. Missouri goes up 7–0.

In our second series I shrug off a possible sack and throw a pass that bounces off my receiver and into the hands of a Missouri defensive back.

Two possessions. Two interceptions.

We finally score in the second quarter when I scamper 10 yards for a touchdown to tie the game. But our offense never really gets on track in the first half. We go to the locker room down 10–7.

In the third quarter I lead us on a 94-yard scoring drive that ends with a 33-yard touchdown pass to running back Eddie Stinnett to put us up 14–10. I sense that we have momentum. But Missouri scores in the fourth quarter to go up 17–14. We fail to counter. The game appears to be lost when Missouri gets the ball back and chews up the clock while mounting another drive deep inside our territory. All I can do is watch as Missouri inches closer to our end zone while the game clock runs down. It's killing me.

On a critical fourth down from our 6-yard line, Missouri fails to convert. We get the ball back with 3:57 remaining. We have 94 yards to go to reach Missouri's end zone. But a field goal will tie the game.

I love these situations. "We're gonna win this," I tell everyone in the huddle. "It's ours."

We mount our best drive of the game. It takes us just over three minutes to reach the Tigers' 15-yard line, where we call our final time-out. Thirty-one seconds remain. I run to the sideline and huddle with offensive coordinator Norm Chow. We are within field goal range. But we have time to take one shot at the end zone.

"Run the flea flicker," Chow says.

"You mean the play we used to run in practice for fun?"

"Yeah. Fake right, twenty-eight quarterback screen left."

More than a little surprised, I say to Chow: "Ah, remind me. How do we do it?"

Chow walks me through the play. I am supposed to hand the ball to the running back, and he follows the offensive line to the right like it's a sweep. Then the running back pulls up and passes back across the field to me, the quarterback.

It's incredibly risky putting the ball in a halfback's hands to throw a pass inside the red zone with just seconds left on the clock. Plus, we have never run this play in a game situation. And our running back has never thrown a pass. There is no way LaVell Edwards would call this play in this situation. But Mike Holmgren is up in the box. He agrees with Chow. It's such a risky call that Missouri will never expect it.

I run back to the huddle and grab running back Eddie Stinnett.

"Eddie, remember that dumb play we used to practice all the time for fun?"

"What play?"

"You know, the flea flicker."

"Oh, yeah. Yeah. The flea flicker."

"Well, we're gonna run it."

Eddie is just as surprised as I am. "Now?"

"Eddie, just throw it! I don't care what happens. Just turn and throw it to me."

Our linemen are freaking out.

On the snap I hand off to Eddie. Our entire offensive line sweeps right. Eddie follows. And Missouri's entire defense goes after him. All except linebacker Bobby Bell. He hangs back on the weak side. When Eddie turns to throw, Bell sees the play and steps into the passing lane. As he leaps, I am sure he will intercept the ball and go all the way for a touchdown. But Eddie's throw floats in the air and Bell leaps too soon. He's on his way down when the wobbly pass barely nicks his outstretched hands. I fully extend my body and barely get the tips of my two middle fingers on the back half of the ball. Somehow I hold on and don't lose my balance. At about the 20-yard line, I tuck the ball under my arm and break for the end zone. The Missouri defense is in pursuit. I pick up a couple blocks, dodge a tackle, and get hammered at the 2-yard line. But I keep my feet and my momentum carries me across the goal line. Touchdown!

My dream has come true: a last-second, come-from-behind victory in a bowl game. I've imagined this moment a thousand times over the previous four years. I am so ecstatic that I hold the ball above my head and high-step around the end zone like I'm dancing on hot coals. My teammates mob me. BYU fans are going crazy. People run on the field. Fireworks go off in the stadium. It is the most exhilarating thing I have ever experienced.

Coach Edwards is as stunned as everyone else. "That was one of the dumbest calls I've ever seen," he later tells Chow and Holmgren. "But it was brilliant because it worked."

We win 21–17, and I become the first player to throw a touchdown, run for a touchdown, and catch a touchdown pass in the same game. We finish 11-1 and are ranked number seven in the nation.

My college career was over. In two seasons as a starter I threw for 7,733 yards and rushed for 1,084 while generating 74 touchdowns. In my senior season I completed 71.3 percent of my passes — the best passing season in NCAA history. I was certainly satisfied and amazed. On the one hand, the anxious side of me thought: *You've done enough.* But the bigger, competitive side of me said: *You can go further.*

After the Holiday Bowl, I flew home to Connecticut for Christmas to deal with the inevitable next step. For months my dad had been bombarded with calls from sports agents. They all wanted to represent me. But Dad didn't trust any of them. Most weren't even lawyers. The ones who were didn't appear credible. Dad had been practicing labor law in New York for more than a decade. When one agent claimed he was a labor lawyer, Dad put the screws to him. The agent buckled and admitted he wasn't actually a labor lawyer. Dad told him to get lost.

During the season Dad shielded me from all of the agents. Throughout my senior year I kept telling myself to never go pro because the anxiety would cripple me. But as usual, the desire to compete and to win beat down my fears. I knew it was time to act. With the bowl game behind me, I had a big decision to make — whether to play in the NFL or the start-up United States Football League. Playing quarterback in the NFL was my boyhood dream. But the USFL was new, brash, and coming on strong as a challenger. Some of the best young talent — Reggie White, Herschel Walker, Jim Kelly — were accepting much larger contract offers from USFL teams.

For the new league to succeed it had to have a successful franchise in Los Angeles — the second-biggest television market in the country. So the Los Angeles Express was looking for a franchise player to build a team around.

The USFL held its draft on January 4, 1984. On the eve of the draft I was asleep in my bedroom at home when my parents' phone rang. It was 3:00 AM. My dad took the call. Then he got me up.

"It's for you," he said.

It was Don Klosterman, the general manager of the Los Angeles Express.

"You are the franchise player we want," he told me. "We plan to draft you tomorrow. But we don't want to waste the pick if you aren't going to play here."

I listened as Klosterman made a persuasive pitch. But I didn't commit.

"As long as you don't say forget it, we're drafting you," he said.

"I wouldn't say forget it."

After hanging up, I couldn't sleep. The next day the Express drafted me in the first round. One thing was clear: I really needed an agent. Dad promised to get on it.

9

THE $40 MILLION MAN

Leigh Steinberg was the most powerful sports agent in America. His clients commanded the highest salaries, and he represented many of the top quarterbacks. During my senior year, Steinberg negotiated a five-year, $6 million contract for Warren Moon, making him the highest-paid player in the history of the NFL. Steinberg was the agent my father wanted to represent me.

But Steinberg was the only agent who hadn't reached out to me. After the LA Express drafted me, my father got tired of waiting. He picked up the phone and called Steinberg.

"Why haven't you called us?"

"I didn't see the need," Steinberg said. "I knew you'd eventually call me."

My dad liked him right away. Days later Steinberg flew from California to Connecticut to meet my parents. The session went so well that my mother invited him to sleep at our place rather than at a hotel. I was still in Provo going to college. So they put Leigh in my room. He slept in my bed.

The next day Leigh flew to Salt Lake City. We planned to meet at the airport, but I couldn't find him. Then I heard my name being called on loudspeakers all over the airport, paging me to the information desk. So much for trying to be inconspicuous.

As I approached I spotted a man in blue jeans, a polo shirt, and flip-flops. He looked like a college kid. I was wearing exactly the same thing. When our eyes met he grinned. It was Leigh. He was thirty-five, but he had the face of a twenty-year-old. And he wasn't all buttoned up, which was a good thing. Because I prefer people who are down to earth, people I can talk to and confide in.

We took a booth in an airport restaurant. For the first hour we didn't mention football. We started by talking politics. I liked Ronald Reagan. He didn't. I was a conservative Republican. He was a liberal Democrat. I was from ultraconservative Greenwich. He was from ultraliberal Berkeley. So the back-and-forth was pretty spirited.

Then we got to religion. Leigh was Jewish. He had no Mormon clients, but he knew a lot about the faith because he had grown up next door to the Mormon temple in Los Angeles. He admired the fact that I had never tasted alcohol, never experimented with drugs, never had sex. I told him that my reputation was more important to me than money or anything else. We talked about that for a long time.

Eventually we got to football, contracts, and the NFL. After two hours we shook hands and said good-bye. I had an agent.

That February was a strange time in my life. The Los Angeles Express had drafted me, and the team was already in training camp preparing for the season, which started in March. But I hadn't signed with the Express. Nor did I plan to report for camp. I was in Provo, trying to finish my degree. I was writing outlines for a Microeconomics exam on utility and demand. I was also writing a case study on a Japanese chemical conglomerate — Mitsui — doing business in Iran.

Meantime, the Cincinnati Bengals held the first pick in the 1984 NFL draft. Bengals head coach Sam Wyche flew to Utah to work me out at BYU.

I'm driving down University Avenue toward the stadium to meet Wyche when it hits me:

I arrived in this town as an eighth-string lefty. Nobody knew my name. The players thought I was a joke, and the quarterback coach said I'd never make it here. Anxious and discouraged, I wanted to quit and go home. But I never stopped battling. I never stopped believing in myself. Look at me now. I not only made it — I'm an All-American, and I nearly won the Heisman. I've never felt better.

Turning into the stadium parking lot, I look through the windshield at the snow-capped mountains.

I love this place. I'm so comfortable here. Provo is my town. I'm king of the hill. I'm at peace here. And an easy path awaits me. I can go to law school, become a lawyer, and start a family. It would be a wonderful life.

I turn off the engine and step out of the car.

I can't go pro. What I went through when I first got here, which felt hellish at times, is nothing compared to what awaits me at the next level. I know it's irrational, but this anxiety can eat me up. It's real and powerful. Going pro will only make my anxiety worse because I'll be on a much bigger stage and I'll be playing for money. Don't do it.

I enter the stadium and see Wyche.

Of course I'm going to do it.

Wyche put me through an extensive workout and liked what he saw. Afterward he turned to me and said: "We have the first pick, and we're going to draft you."

So much for my conversation with myself on the drive down. So much for going off to law school and taking the easier path. As usual, I was attracted to the steep climb. Playing in the NFL, after all, had long been my dream.

But did I really want to go to Cincinnati?

Leigh didn't want me in Cincinnati either. Bengals owner Mike Brown was notoriously cheap. Plus, Cincinnati already had a solid starter in Ken Anderson. I'd be a backup again.

Leigh suggested that I sign with the Express. He said they were ready to make an offer we couldn't refuse. But the USFL felt like a big step down from the NFL.

Leigh countered that many of the top players coming out of college were going to the USFL. Plenty of coaches and general managers in the USFL were coming from the NFL. Don Klosterman was a perfect example. He had been the GM of the Los Angeles Rams before joining the

Express. He had brought a lot of NFL brass with him, including quarterback coach Sid Gillman, the father of the modern passing game, and head coach John Hadl, the former quarterback for the Los Angeles Rams and San Diego Chargers.

February 19, 1984, was a Sunday. That afternoon Herm and LJ drove me to a tiny airstrip, near a cow pasture just past the outskirts of Provo, that mainly serviced small single-engine planes. As we approached we were dazzled by the shiny new Gulfstream that sat on the tarmac.

"Is that for you?" Herm marveled.

"Yeah."

"Sweet!" LJ said.

It was the first time that any of us had seen a private jet. The G-5 looked so out of place in rural Utah. It belonged to the owner of the Los Angeles Express, William Oldenburg.

I said good-bye to Herm and LJ and hopped aboard. I was in LA an hour later. Leigh met me and took me to the Bel Air Country Club, where I played nine holes of golf with Klosterman. As a teenager, I had caddied at one of the private country clubs in Greenwich, but I had never done much more than fool around on a golf course. Yet here I was on one of the nicest courses in the country. Famous actors and other celebrities were also playing on the course, which made me a little self-conscious. Afterward we had dinner in the clubhouse restaurant, and every few minutes somebody famous dropped by our table to say hello —former California governor Pat Brown, Los Angeles Olympic Organizing Committee chairman Peter Ueberroth, more actors. I kept telling myself: *This is big-time.*

I was very intrigued by the city. But what I really liked was Don's personal touch.

"There are three hundred thousand Mormons in the LA area," Don said.

That got my attention.

"And lots of Mormon churches."

Leigh smiled. Don had done his homework.

The next day we visited the team's training facility in Manhattan Beach.

Don wore a BYU pin on his lapel. He introduced me to Sid Gillman, whom the Express had hired specifically to mentor me. Another plus.

Then I met Coach Hadl and sat in on a quarterbacks meeting with him and Gillman. The chance to be coached and taught by them was certainly a draw.

I also met the players. Gordon Hudson, my favorite receiver at BYU, was on the team. He had been drafted specifically to help lure me there. And the offensive line had three All-Americans — Mike Ruether from Texas; Baylor's Mark Adickes; and Oregon's Gary Zimmerman, a future NFL Hall of Famer. That trio of linemen was as good as any in the NFL, and they had all been signed to protect me.

After practice, Don took Leigh and me to his house for dinner. His back patio overlooked the entire city of Los Angeles. I had never seen such a view. As the sun dipped behind the horizon the city stretched out below us in a carpet of lights.

Joe Namath was Don's neighbor. After dinner we went next door, and Joe invited me to his basement to play pool. I was much more comfortable around a pool table than on a golf course. My childhood home had a pool table in the basement, and I used to play all the time.

I grabbed a cue stick and Joe racked the balls.

"Joe, tell Steve your story," Don said.

While we played, Joe recounted that after his All-American season at Alabama, the NFL and the AFL drafted him on the same day. He bucked conventional wisdom and signed a contract with the AFL's New York Jets that made him the highest-paid player in pro football history.

I knew the rest of the story. A few years later Namath led the Jets to an upset Super Bowl victory over the NFL's Baltimore Colts. I remembered watching Super Bowl III in my living room as a nine-year-old boy.

And there I was playing pool with Joe.

"Don't be afraid to join the USFL," Namath told me.

The following morning Leigh and I flew on Oldenburg's plane to San Francisco. A driver in a Stutz Bearcat met us on the runway. It was another one of Oldenburg's toys. The steering wheel was on the right side. The driver delivered us to the Transamerica Pyramid Building, which was the San Francisco headquarters of Investment Mortgage International, the company Oldenburg had founded. Scrolling above the front entrance ran an electric ticker message board. It flashed the words: WELCOME STEVE YOUNG, QUARTERBACK EXTRAORDINAIRE ... WELCOME LEIGH STEINBERG, LAWYER PAR EXCELLENCE.

We entered through gigantic gold doors, and IMI's chief corporate counsel, Martin Mandel, greeted us in the lobby with a smile and a handshake. He led us to the penthouse suite, where we met Oldenburg, a short, pugnacious, bullish-looking man who knew nothing about football but had purchased the Express for $7 million and trusted Don to run the organization for him.

Leigh and Mandel headed off to a private room to work on the contract offer while I had lunch with Oldenburg. First he showed me his trophy room, which included pictures of him with everyone from Henry Kissinger to Captain Kangaroo to Wayne Newton. Then he took me to his office. It was more like a luxury suite. There was leather furniture, a fully stocked bar with a marble countertop, and big windows that offered a stunning view of the city. Over dinner he promised me a series of incentives if I signed with the Express: an endorsement deal with a bank he owned in Salt Lake City; a guaranteed job with his investment company in the offseason and after I retired; and an endowed scholarship program for BYU students who wanted to serve Mormon missions.

By the time dinner ended, Leigh had a general agreement with the Express — a guaranteed $5.9 million over four years. An additional $34.1 million in deferred payments would be available through an annuity over the ensuing forty-three years. The deferred payment — $200,000 — would come in 1990. Then each subsequent year the payment would escalate until the final payout of $3 million in the final year. By then I'd be in my late sixties. The combined total of the guaranteed money and the annuity was $40 million.

I trusted Leigh with the details. I was too overwhelmed by the prospect of receiving over $1 million per year to play football. The burden to earn that kind of money only drove up my anxiety levels.

I had one week to accept the offer.

As soon as we left Oldenburg's offices I turned to Leigh. "That's way too much money," I told him.

Leigh laughed.

But I was serious. I wasn't comfortable with being paid so much before I had proven myself.

"All I need is enough to buy four new tires for my '65 Olds," I said.

"You'll certainly be able to do that," he told me.

I returned to Provo on Oldenburg's jet. Herm and LJ met me at the airstrip.

LJ was talking a mile a minute. Herm was joking around. I said nothing.

"Dude, what's wrong?" Herm said.

"You guys won't believe what they're offering," I told him.

"How much?" LJ asked.

I was too embarrassed to say the number.

"C'mon, Steve," Herm said.

"Yeah, what's the number? Let's hear it," LJ said.

They were whooping and hollering on the car ride back.

"Forty million dollars," I finally said.

"Whoa!" LJ said.

"Look, most of that is deferred," I said. "But it's still one of the all-time biggest sports contracts."

It was the first time I had ever known LJ to be speechless. No one said another word the rest of the way back to our apartment. I went to bed but couldn't sleep. It was well after midnight when I headed for my car. I started the engine, popped in Springsteen's "Born to Run," and cruised aimlessly up and down the deserted streets of Provo. I should have been elated at that offer. But I was conflicted. The thought of LA overwhelmed me. The real problem was that I didn't want to say good-bye to BYU. It had taken a few years for Provo to feel like home, and I didn't want to have to go make a new home in LA.

I should have been on top of the world. I had the choice of being the number-one pick in the NFL draft or going to LA to earn millions playing for the LA Express. But instead of celebrating with friends, I was alone in my car, listening to Bruce, talking to myself.

Don't keep doing this.

You did it in high school, and it was kind of death-defying.

You tried it in college, and it got really death-defying.

Don't keep this up.

It's time to get off the track and just settle things down. Don't think you can roll into LA and just make it happen at the professional level. Not with your background. Not with your anxieties.

A tornado whirled inside me. I was a private person by nature. Yet I was on the cusp of being the highest-paid player in the history of pro sports. That meant unprecedented scrutiny. It meant that people would expect me to be the best quarterback in either league.

You can't do that!

But I also wanted to see how far I could go. I wanted the challenge. I was a wishbone quarterback in high school, and I figured out how to make it at the biggest quarterback school in America. I couldn't help wondering how far I could go in the pros. But I was terrified that I'd fail.

While I was in Provo, talking myself in and out of playing pro football, my father got an unexpected call at home in Greenwich.

"This is Howard Cosell."

The voice sounded just like the most recognizable television sports broadcaster in the country. But my dad was skeptical.

"This isn't Howard Cosell," he said.

Howard got indignant. "Yes, it is!"

Dad was stunned. "What can I do for you, Howard?"

"I want to speak to your son."

"Well, he's still out at school."

The next thing I knew I was on the phone with Cosell. He told me I'd be a star in the USFL and that the NFL was a crumbling giant.

Leigh continued to discourage me from the NFL too. I started calling other guys for advice. Reggie White, an All-American defensive lineman at Tennessee, had already opted for the USFL. He encouraged me to do the same. The other All-Americans I called were all spurning the NFL.

Roger Staubach — my childhood hero — called me. It felt surreal. Unlike everyone else, he encouraged me to avoid the USFL. "You'll never really make it until you make it in the NFL," he told me.

Staubach's words definitely caused me to think. Deep down I preferred the NFL. But there was no way I was going to sit the bench in Cincinnati, a city where I didn't know anyone. On the other hand, I could go to LA and learn from Sid Gillman and John Hadl while playing with the best collection of young talent anywhere. The average age on the roster was twenty-three. They were loaded with All-Americans. NFL GMs would have killed for a lineup like this. I knew I'd be on a great team.

With my dad's support, I flew back to San Francisco to sign the contract with the Express at the IMI offices. When I arrived, Leigh and Don were working through the final details. They parked me in a conference room, where I studied for an upcoming exam in Microeconomics. Every once in a while Leigh ducked in to update me on the negotiations. It was taking longer than I expected. One of the sticking points was how much money the Express would guarantee up front. Leigh was looking for $2.5 million. They were offering $500,000. I could not have cared less.

Meantime, Dad was back in New York, and he insisted on vetting the contract. He made Leigh read every word of it over the phone. Dad took copious notes. The back-and-forth took hours. Eventually, Oldenburg burst into the room, clutching a wad of $100 bills.

"What?" he shouted. "My money's not good enough for you?"

"Hold on," Leigh said, trying to calm him down.

"You want guarantees?" Oldenburg bellowed. "You can have the whole damn thing in cash."

He threw the fistful of bills at me. At least $5,000 in cash landed all over the floor. All I could see was Ben Franklin looking up at me.

Oldenburg then stormed out.

Chuckling at the craziness, I scooped up the money and said to Leigh: "I guess this is mine?"

He laughed.

We couldn't figure out why Oldenburg was so wound up, but we soon learned that it was his birthday and a big party had been planned for him downtown. He wanted my contract done before he left for the celebration.

I went back to my schoolwork while Leigh and Don resumed negotiations. It was about 2:30 in the morning when they finally came to terms on the up-front guarantee.

But before Klosterman got word to Oldenburg, Leigh and I were summoned to Oldenburg's office. By this time he was pretty loaded. The moment we entered his suite he got in my face. "I want to know why this thing isn't getting done," he shouted.

Leigh stepped between us. "Mr. Oldenburg, we have a deal in principle. We're trying to paper it out."

"I don't f   ing care. It's my birthday!"

He pushed Leigh aside and repeatedly jammed his finger in my chest. "You f——n' Mormon! I want to know why you don't want to play for me."

I held my ground. "If you touch me again, I'm going to deck you," I told him firmly, even though he was in his midforties.

Furious, he spun and cleared all the glasses from the bar top with his arm. Glass shattered all over the floor. Then he picked up a chair. I lunged at him before he could throw it through the window.

"Whoa! Mr. Oldenburg, don't do that," I said, restraining him from behind. "You need to relax."

He dropped the chair. "You're not playing for me! Get your asses out of here."

Leigh and I looked at each other. Suddenly we understood why Oldenburg's nickname was "Mr. Dynamite."

"Security!" Oldenburg shouted. "Security!"

"We're going," Leigh said.

Two guards rushed in. They escorted us out of the building and deposited us on the street. It was 3:30 in the morning. We had no wheels, and there were no taxis in sight. Leigh was laughing. I was fed up.

"There's no way I'm playing for that guy," I told Leigh. "The man is a lunatic."

Leigh grimaced. "Welcome to pro football."

We stood in the street, trying to figure out what to do next, when Klosterman emerged from the building. He was hyperventilating. Beads of sweat covered his face. I feared that he was on the verge of having a heart attack. He apologized for Oldenburg's behavior, put us in his limo, and directed the driver to take us to Leigh's apartment in Berkeley.

Word traveled fast that the deal with the LA Express had fallen apart. Leigh's phone started ringing. NFL commissioner Pete Rozelle called to talk me into entering the NFL draft. We heard again from Staubach and Namath and Cosell. I even got a call from Donald Trump, owner of the New Jersey Generals. He assured me that the USFL would one day be bigger than the NFL.

Then, back in Provo, I got a call from Oldenburg. He was sober, and he apologized profusely. He told me about the birthday celebration. He also agreed to the up-front money Leigh had been seeking. I accepted Oldenburg's apology.

Leigh went over the deal with me one more time: $40 million over forty-three years. But most of the money was deferred. Under the terms, I was obligated to play for the Express for four years for a guaranteed $5.9 million. The rest of the payments — $34.1 million — were deferred. The first deferred payment — $200,000 — would come in 1990, then would escalate each year until the final payout of $3 million in the final year.

The numbers were, of course, staggering to me. I never equated playing football with money. I played for the competition. I played for the thrill. Sudden wealth made the game feel like a job, an obligation, a harness.

I called my dad.

"Accept the offer," he said.

Dad had finally come to grips with the idea that I could make a handsome living playing football. But I was the one who was losing my grip. The size of the contract was overwhelming.

I drove over to campus and entered the Smith Fieldhouse. It was late. No one was around. I sat in the bleachers and buried my face in my hands. After a while I heard someone enter. It was Herm. "Dude," he said, "why are you so bummed?"

"It's the money," I told him. "It's too much. Way too much."

"Dude, I don't get it," he said. "Two nights ago we were trying to decide whether to get sausage or pepperoni as an extra topping on our pizza. We were moaning and groaning because we didn't have the extra thirty-five cents to get both. And now you don't want to take the money?"

March 6, 1984. More than 100 journalists packed a ballroom at the Beverly Hills Hotel. Reporters had come from as far away as Japan. A sea of television cameras and microphones surrounded the lectern. I was backstage in the green room, dressed in a pair of wool pants, a white shirt and tie, and a blazer. I was sweating. And pacing.

I didn't want the whole world to know how much the Express was paying me. I had $20 in my wallet. I didn't even have a credit card. I had yet to graduate from college. But I was about to become an instant millionaire. And I felt like I was making the biggest mistake of my life. I couldn't do it.

Leigh told me everyone was waiting. The top brass from the LA Express were seated at the table. The media had been in place for an hour.

"I'm not going out there," I told him.

"Come on. We've been through this a million times."

"Sorry, but I'm not going through with it."

"Just sit tight," he said. "Don't go anywhere."

Leigh entered the press conference and assured everyone that everything was fine and that I'd be right out. Then he came back to me and walked me through all the reasons why I was going to go through with the contract, all the same arguments we'd covered again and again. It boiled down to the fact that the LA Express was a better option — in terms of both my development as a player and my finances — than the Cincinnati Bengals.

But I was entertaining a third option. I would walk away from football altogether. Just give it up. Go to law school. Get married. Settle down. I told him so.

"Steve, you'd never be satisfied with that life," he said. "You are a competitor. You've always dreamed of playing on the big stage. Pro football is the biggest stage. You have to prove yourself there."

But I didn't want the burden that would come with $40 million.

Leigh held out his hand. "C'mon."

Something made me get off the couch and follow him into the press conference. Cameras started clicking and flashing. I smiled. The rest is a blur.

After the press conference, Leigh handed me two checks outside the Beverly Hills Hotel. One was for $1 million, the other for $1.5 million. I stuffed them in my sport coat pocket. Then I boarded a private plane bound for Salt Lake City, knowing that I had to return to LA and start playing in a couple of days. The checks felt like a ball and chain. I never asked to be the highest-paid player in sports. In fact, I didn't want to be paid at all. Not to play football. At least not yet. I hadn't proven myself. I hadn't earned it.

As soon as my plane was airborne I was overcome with a flood of anxiety. I felt like I was going to vomit. I got up and approached the pilot.

"I know this sounds crazy. But can you radio ahead?"

"Sure. Who do you want me to contact?"

"The Mormon Church headquarters."

The pilot looked over his shoulder at me like I was nuts.

"I need to see one of the apostles."

Now he really thought I was nuts.

"Just tell them it is an emergency and Steve Young needs to see someone as soon as we land."

About thirty minutes later the pilot told me that a man by the name of Neal Maxwell would see me at his home after we landed.

Neal Maxwell was the one apostle I had met. I figured that there was some divine intervention involved.

"I have directions for you," the pilot said.

"Never mind," I told him. "I know where he lives."

The local media was waiting for me at the airport. I put on a smile and said all the right things. Then I went straight to Maxwell's home. As soon as he opened his door he sensed that I was in a state of complete panic.

"Steve, what's wrong?"

"I just signed a contract to join the USFL."

"I heard about that."

"I can't do this for money. I can't do it."

"Can't do what for money?"

"Play football."

I pulled the folded checks from my pocket and handed them to him. "I want you to have these."

He looked at them and raised his eyebrows.

"I'm going on *Good Morning America* in the morning. And I'm planning to say that all of my earnings will go to the church."

"Steve, wait a minute."

He tried handing the checks back to me.

I put up my hands. "I can't take all that money. No way. It can't happen."

He encouraged me to settle down. "I don't believe that you handing me these checks today and announcing that you've done so in the morning is the Lord's plan."

"I promise you it's the way the Lord wants me to do it," I said.

He led me into his private study and we prayed together. Then he counseled me that many challenges in life can't be avoided and must be experienced. He reminded me that one of the oldest lessons in the Bible is that it's easier for a camel to go through the eye of a needle than for a rich man to enter the kingdom of God. "Simply giving away the money in some ways might be avoiding the very experience that God intends for you to have," he told me. "Sometimes the most rigorous experiences of this life should not be avoided."

Then he handed back the checks. "These belong to you," he said.

Deep down, despite all the turmoil, I knew he was right.

Looking back, I am forever grateful for Elder Maxwell's wisdom.

That night, Dan Rather opened the *CBS Evening News* broadcast by talking about my contract. At that time in pro sports, the numbers on my contract were staggering. The next morning my contract made headlines across the world. I was dubbed "The Man with the Golden Arm" and "The 40 Million Dollar Quarterback." The contract prompted a huge backlash. The media called it "ludicrous," "obscene," and "insane."

I agreed. But I also knew that most of my money was deferred and it wasn't guaranteed. So I never expected that aspect of the contract to be emphasized, never mind publicized. The truth was that I had not signed for $40 million. But the details no longer mattered. It was all about perception. And I'd just been run over by the perception of being the $40 million man.

I was compared to the highest-paid players in other sports. Magic Johnson had a $25 million contract over twenty-five years. Wayne Gretzky received $21 million over twenty-one years. Dave Winfield had $21 million over ten years. Nobody in the NFL made anything close to what I'd be getting paid.

What hurt the most was the backlash from the local media in Utah.

Columnist Lee Benson at the *Deseret News* took me to task on the front page of the sports section. Suddenly I represented everything that was wrong with professional sports. Overnight I had become a symbol for greed, excess, and self-importance. I was afraid to show my face in public, especially in Provo.

Benson's story crushed me. This was essentially my hometown paper. I felt like I'd let everyone down. Gripped by anxiety, I was frozen. For a couple of days I struggled to do simple things like eat and sleep.

Uncle Bob dropped in to check on me. He was my accountant, and he'd worked on the deal with Leigh.

"Steve, where are the checks?" he said.

"I've got 'em."

"We need to deposit them in the bank."

I reached into my pocket. "Here," I said. "I don't want anything to do with these."

He reminded me that my contract required me to report to the LA Express within seventy-two hours of signing.

"I'm not going," I said.

Uncle Bob turned to Herm and LJ. They didn't know what to do with me either. Herm called Carole Burr. She came to the apartment. Then she called my dad. "Grit, you'd better get out here," she told him.

The following morning Dad showed up in my bedroom in Provo. I was disheveled and anxious.

"What's the problem?" he said.

"I can't do this."

"You can do this."

"No, I can't."

"You can. You can play football."

"I don't want to do this anymore."

"You really don't have a choice. You signed a contract."

10

THE EXPRESS

I BELIEVE IN ANGELS. Not ones with wings. I mean individuals that God places in our path to help get us through life's rough spots. Carole Burr was the angel who got me through the BYU years. Every time I needed an ear, she listened. When I needed a place to hide, she let me use the bedroom in her basement. Mostly she just gave me encouragement.

Herm and LJ were like angels too. They always had my back.

But I was not close to anybody in LA. On the flight to LA, I sat in the window seat beside my dad. Staring out at the clouds, I felt lost and lonely. When we landed, a short, muscular guy in an LA Express sweat suit met us outside baggage claim.

"Steve, I'm George Curtis. I'm the team trainer. I'll bring you to the practice facility."

Curtis had been a personal trainer for some of the top pro athletes on the Los Angeles Lakers and Los Angeles Rams before joining the Express.

"George, I can't do this," I said.

His eyes widened. He didn't know what to say.

I explained my situation. "I just can't pull this off," I told him.

"Steve, I know you can do this," he said. "Everyone's behind you."

I looked at him, and he stared into my eyes with a serious, penetrating look, as if he knew me. Yet he was a total stranger. Or so I thought.

"Steve, I'm a Mormon," he said.

"You are?"

"I am. And I'll be with you every step of the way. We'll do this day to day."

Dad couldn't believe it. Neither could I.

At a critical moment, another stranger emerged to be with me every step of the way.

The USFL season ran from March through July. So the Express had already played a few games when I arrived. Coach John Hadl gave me three weeks to learn the offense. While I got acclimated, the NFL and the players' union conspired to hold a supplemental draft for those of us who had joined the USFL. My decision to join the USFL was made easier by the fact that I thought one of two things would happen. Either the success of the USFL would force the NFL to fold us into the league or, if the USFL failed, I'd be able to enter the NFL as an undrafted player and essentially pick the team that I wanted to play for. This supplemental draft dashed those hopes. Now players like me who would have been eligible for the regular 1984 college draft but chose instead to join the USFL were bound to NFL teams. The Tampa Bay Buccaneers had the number-one overall pick. They selected me. That meant the Buccaneers would control the rights to negotiate with me if I ever decided to jump to the NFL. So much for my backup plan of entering the NFL as a free agent.

I got my first start for the Express at home against the New Jersey Generals on April 1, 1984. The game drew the largest crowd — nearly 20,000 — in the team's short history. The offense was still very new to me, so I improvised a lot. I ran the ball more than the running backs. I completed 19 of 29 passes for 163 yards. We lost 26–10. But I was encouraged. It felt so good to be on the field. Playing took my mind off all the controversy about my salary.

Two weeks later I became the first player in pro football history to rush for 100 yards and throw for 300 yards in one game. I did it against the Chicago Blitz, and we won the game, 49–29. In the shower after the game, I let my emotions go. With water splashing on my face, my teammates couldn't tell that tears were running down my face. I loved playing for the Express, but it was so hard to live up to the expectations. Yet I had just done something on the field that had never been done in the NFL or the USFL. That was pretty exhilarating.

At this point I was practically living in the film room with quarterback coach Sid Gillman. Sid was the architect of many key aspects of the modern game. In the 1960s he became the first coach to use motion to counter blitzing defenses. He also introduced the deep passing game. And he was an early proponent for a Super Bowl. Having him as a quarterback coach was like being an aspiring physicist learning from Einstein.

Some nights Sid kept me in the film room until midnight going over reads. Back then, we watched film on a projector. I would know it was time to call it a night when the reel would end and I'd look over and see Sid sleeping as the tape clicked and clicked and clicked. Other days we worked out together after the rest of the team went home. Sid was ornery and really hard on me. But he constantly told me that he loved coaching me. Once, when we were alone, he looked over the practice field and said: "Steve, this is not a game. It's a canvas and you are Michelangelo."

I had never heard anyone talk about football in these terms. It is a game of brute force, an unforgiving contest of wills that leaves men bloodied, bruised, and broken. The concept of a quarterback as an artist changed my approach to passing. Sid also increased my vision of what was possible. Halfway through the season he put a football in my hand during warm-ups before a game. "There's no rubber band on that ball, Steve," he said. "Just let it go. It's not coming back."

Letting go wasn't generally easy for me, but the one place where I was comfortable letting go was on the football field. Sid wanted to see me loosen up even more. One day in practice he even tied my feet with a rope so I couldn't leave the pocket. "You can be one of the greatest throwers in football," he said. "But you can't do it with the ball under your arm."

Everyone laughed, including me.

The guy used more four-letter words in a day than I typically heard in a year. I rarely swear, so Sid apologized whenever he let go with a particularly colorful riff. "Sorry, Young," he'd say. Ten minutes later he was back at it. That was just Sid. I didn't mind. I loved the guy. He made the game fun and me better.

• • •

My parents came to see me play live for the first time when we had a road game at RFK Stadium in Washington. This wasn't like going to a BYU game — they weren't prepared for drunken fans who used foul language to brutalize me. As usual, plenty of banners inside the stadium referred to $40 million and that I was a waste of money.

Dad took the abuse in stride, but Mom didn't.

By the fourth quarter it was raining pretty hard. While attempting to throw a pass, I lost my grip on the wet ball, and it slipped out of my hand and rolled down my back. A defensive player scooped it up and ran for a touchdown. The sparse crowd chanted: "Forty million down the drain! Forty million down the drain!"

Fed up, Mom rose to her feet and shouted: "That's my son! He's a good boy. And by the way, it's . . . an . . . annuity! It's not $40 million."

The stadium was pretty empty, so her voice carried. My dad told me later that a bunch of drunken Washington fans a few rows in front of them reacted to my mother by raining f-bombs down on me.

Then the drunks turned their attention to my mother. "No wonder he sucks," one of them shouted. "Look at you. You're an ugly woman." (She's actually very beautiful.)

The entire section broke out in laughter. It was a nightmare. Dad buried his head. Mom sat down and gave up.

After the game my mother told me she would never attend another USFL game. I told her that was probably a good idea.

I wanted to throttle Leigh Steinberg. I loved him, but he put me in a no-win situation when he branded me "the $40 million man." I was so consumed with trying to live up to those lofty expectations that I spent the first month living out of a duffle bag in the same airport hotel room that I had checked into the day I arrived in town. Every night I ate dinner alone in the same hotel restaurant. I got to know one waitress very well. I always sat at her table and ordered the same meal.

The routine suited me fine. It wasn't like I had any place to go after practice. Besides, I didn't even own a car. George Curtis picked me up each morning and dropped me off each night. That was my life until I finally rented a car and a seaside condo in Redondo Beach at 111 Yacht Club Way. As soon as my buddies Herm and LJ finished the spring semester at BYU they drove to LA and moved in with me. My place was sparsely furnished with rental beds and a living room set. That was all we needed. We were bachelors. My big purchase was a new television. The best thing about my place was that it was literally right on the water. I had to close the sliding-glass door at high tide or the spray from the surf would soak my couch.

Having my two best friends around helped me play better. While I practiced every day, Herm and LJ hung back at my condo. They spent their days at the pool. Basically, they had fun while I worked, but it was great having them around.

One day George Curtis said he wanted to talk to me.

"The GM wants you to wear a rib protector," he said.

"I'm not wearing a rib protector."

"They'll fine you if you don't."

"I don't care. They can fine me all they want."

"Steve, if you don't wear the rib protector, they'll hold you out of the starting lineup."

I couldn't let that happen. I agreed to wear the rib protector. Curtis outfitted me. He insisted that my chances of injuring my ribs would go way down. He also said he wanted me to start sliding to avoid taking hits.

I never slid because I felt that it exposed me to late hits and being speared. I preferred to find my way to the ground in ways that put me more in control. Knowing when and how to get to the ground was one of my talents.

"George, I have never slid. I'm not about to start."

"Look, if you don't take care of your body, you won't play."

Our next game was at home. I wore the rib protector, and the first time I ran the ball I slid before getting hit. The defender speared me in the ribs with his helmet after I was down. I could barely breathe, and it felt like all my ribs were broken.

George ran onto the field to treat me. As soon as he knelt over me I grabbed him by the collar. "I am never . . . sliding . . . again! Ever!"

He didn't say a word. For the rest of the season I refused to wear a rib protector and I refused to slide.

• • •

We finished the regular season 10-8, and we won our division. We also secured home-field advantage for the playoffs. We were young and getting better by the week. I figured we had a real shot at winning the league championship.

June 30, 1984. We're facing the Michigan Panthers in the playoffs. It's a home game for us, but fewer than 8,000 fans show. Down 21–13 with just under nine minutes remaining in the game, we get the ball on our own 20-yard line. On the first play of the drive I take off running after finding no open receivers. Panther linebacker Kyle Borland has a clean shot at me. Instead of sliding or heading out of bounds, I lower my shoulder. He hits me so hard I nearly lose consciousness. I land out of bounds, right near Coach Hadl's feet. I wobble when I try to stand up.

"Come out," Hadl says.

"No way," I say.

A few plays later we face fourth-and-one from the Michigan 47. I scramble for the first down. But the safety drills me. My right arm goes numb. I hold it up with my left hand.

"Come out, Steve," Hadl shouts.

I'm pretty sure my right hand is broken. But I wave Hadl off and stay in the game. With fifty-two seconds remaining, we face third-and-goal from the Michigan 12-yard line. I drop back, pump-fake, and take off for the end zone. Inches from the goal line I get hammered out of bounds. We score on the next play. Down 21–19, we go for two. Coach Hadl calls a pass play. But I keep the ball and rumble in for the score. Tie game.

We remain tied through two overtime periods. At the 3:33 mark of the third overtime period, we finally score to win the game, 27–21. It is the longest game in the history of professional football. Afterward *Sports Illustrated* dubs me "Little Stevie Wanderlust." Fortunately, my hand isn't broken.

It was the summer of 1984. *Footloose, Karate Kid,* and *Beverly Hills Cop* were in theaters. I saw all three. The Celtics beat the Lakers in seven to win the NBA Finals. I watched every game. Springsteen's "Born in the USA" was out. I owned it. And Bob Woodward's book on John Belushi was a best-seller. I owned that too. I was settling into my new life in LA.

One of the things that made my first pro season so enjoyable was the friendships I formed with my teammates. My offensive linemen, led by ex-NFL veteran Jeff Hart, met every Wednesday after practice for burgers and beers at a bar in Manhattan Beach. I always joined them, and they'd order a pitcher of milk for me because they had heard the stories about my high school days. My linemen were a great bunch of guys.

Meanwhile, Herm and LJ were back in Provo getting ready for the '84 season. Since they had both redshirted, they had one year of eligibility remaining. I wished I could go back. I wished I could play with them one more time. But I couldn't. The best I could do was join them when my season ended a few weeks later.

The conference championship should have been a home game for the Express, but the US Olympic Committee wouldn't let us use the Coliseum because they were preparing it for the 1984 Olympics. So our game was played in Phoenix. It was over 100 degrees on game day. Our guys simply ran out of gas and we lost, bringing an end to my first pro season. I had passed for 2,361 yards in just nine games.

It had been an exceptional season, but I was tired. I had gone from playing my senior season at BYU right into the USFL season, which ran from February to June. It was like playing two football seasons in one year. My body was beat up, and I was looking forward to some time off.

I caught the first flight to Provo and moved in with Herm, LJ, and Tyde Tanner. Tyde had taken a few classes with me, and we had become good friends in my final two years at BYU. He had a distinctive laugh and a great sense of humor, which enabled him to fit right in with Herm and LJ. We were in a four-bedroom apartment a few blocks from campus. I still had a few classes to complete for graduation. Herm and LJ were consumed with football. Each night after practice we went out for dinner. Tyde usually joined us. LJ insisted that since I was the one with a job, I should pay for everything. "Put it on the Gold card," he'd say.

Word got around that I was back in town. With BYU's regular season about to start, the play-by-play announcer who called the games for KSL Radio offered me a job as a color commentator. I had never done on-air analysis, but it would give me something to do, so I accepted.

A couple of games into the season I ran into Jim Nantz. He was a twenty-five-year-old television anchor and sportscaster for KSL in Salt

Lake City. After hearing me on the radio a couple of times, he invited me to join him in the booth to do color commentary on television at home games. I learned a lot working with Jim. I also enjoyed following my old team through the '84 season. But I had mixed emotions. BYU finished the '84 season 13-0 and won the National Championship. The year before we had won eleven straight after barely losing our first game to Baylor owing to a couple of punt returns. We should have been 12-0 and won back-to-back National Championships.

I was happy for LJ and Herm. After being voted a first-team All-American punter, Johnson was drafted by the Houston Oilers. And the Dallas Cowboys drafted Herrmann. I just regretted not winning the National Championship with them. As they trained for the NFL, I headed back to LA for my second season with the Express.

Training camp opened under a cloud. Federal regulators had accused our owner of conspiring to defraud a savings and loan association of $26 million. Oldenburg denied the charges. But with a criminal probe under way, the USFL forced Oldenburg to step down as owner. For a while we didn't have an owner. Every day was an adventure.

The team stayed at a hotel near our training camp facility. One afternoon we were in meetings when Coach Hadl stepped out to take a call. A few minutes later he returned. "Fellas," he said, "they've kicked us out of the hotel because we haven't paid our bill."

We went over the roster to identify players who lived in the LA area. Receiver Jo-Jo Townsell was from LA. "Jo-Jo, how many can you take?" He placed a call to his mother. She said she could house three guys.

On it went. I started calling our team "the LA Orphans."

Just a few days before our season opener a helicopter hovered above our practice field. I was in the huddle calling a play when the chopper touched down right on the field. A television crew hopped out. The reporter approached me. "You've just folded," he said. "What's your reaction?"

I wasn't really surprised, but I was disappointed. All of us were. After my rookie season there was talk that some of the better USFL teams might be folded into the NFL. Since the Express was one of the best teams, we figured we'd be chosen. Now, all of that was in jeopardy.

When the Express went bust, the USFL stepped in and bailed out the organization. But the '85 season was a disaster from the start. The team's finances were such a mess that some players didn't get paid. Nearly twenty guys walked off the team midway through the season. Fans stopped showing up for home games too. The Los Angeles Memorial Coliseum held 92,000. The Express officially reported having 5,800 season-ticket-holders, but even that was a stretch. We had the worst attendance in the league. It was so quiet in the Coliseum that I literally had to whisper in the huddle. Otherwise, the defense would have heard the play calling. Often I moved the huddle farther back from the defense.

By week 14, we were 3-11. With no owner, our team had been largely dismantled. By this time, I was personally paying someone to cut the grass at our practice field. Many coaches weren't being paid, and I had to draw up our game plans. It was a shame to see such a promising team fall apart.

The following week we faced Denver at home. I was supposed to be in Provo for my college graduation. I skipped it to play in a game that drew the smallest crowd in league history — only 1,500 people showed up. And we lost again.

The next week we played in San Antonio. The temperature at game time topped 100 degrees, making it clear once again that the NFL had the right idea by scheduling games in the fall and winter. By the end of the San Antonio game we had eighteen players on IVs for dehydration. I was one of them.

Eager to get home, we were sitting on the runway in San Antonio when an equipment truck plowed into our plane, damaging the engine. Our GM had flown in World War II and insisted that we could still fly with a less than perfect engine. The players revolted. There was nearly a riot on the plane. Eight hours later the engine had been repaired and we took off. I couldn't wait for the season to end.

Our home attendance was so embarrassing that our final game was moved to Pierce College in Woodland Hills. Only thirty-three guys remained on our roster. The others had quit after not being paid, including two of our running backs. I volunteered to play running back for the final game.

On the way to the college the bus driver pulled over and refused to continue. "This bus isn't moving until I get paid," he said.

Turned out he hadn't been paid either.

Players started chanting: "Don't pay him! Let's get off!"

"Whoa, guys," I said. "We have to pay him."

One of the guys said he had a check.

"I'm not taking a check," the driver said. "Only cash."

One of the trainers rounded up $500 in cash, and we were off. At the field two of the game officials were tearing up cardboard boxes to create makeshift scoreboards. They wrote EXPRESS on one piece and WRANGLERS on the other. Then they taped them over the HOME and VISITOR signs on the scoreboard.

Doug Williams, who had been a Super Bowl MVP, quarterbacked the Arizona Wranglers, our opponent. "What have we gotten ourselves into?" he said sarcastically to me before the game. We both shook our heads and laughed.

The Express lost the game, 21–10. I did my postgame press conference from a sand hill next to the field. I was the last one to shower. Leigh Steinberg met me in the locker room after everyone else had left.

"You gotta get me out of my contract," I told him.

He nodded.

I cleaned out my locker and headed for the door.

"You left behind a pair of socks," Leigh said.

"They are not a high priority right now," I said.

11

RUNNING FOR
MY LIFE

DAYS AFTER MY second season in the USFL ended, I was back in
Provo. While I was there, Leigh worked on getting me out of LA.
Tampa Bay held the rights to negotiate with me if I chose to join the
NFL. But with two years remaining on my contract, USFL commissioner
Harry Usher wanted $2 million before he'd let me go. That was nearly
half of the $4.7 million the Express had paid me for my two seasons.
Leigh balked and called Usher's demand a king's ransom.

My other option was to simply sit until the USFL went belly up. But
Tampa Bay wanted me in uniform to start the '85 season. Leigh negotiated the price of my buyout down to $1.2 million. Then he spent the sum-
mer negotiating with the Buccaneers' owner, Hugh Culverhouse. *Forbes*
listed Culverhouse as one of the richest men in America. He was a powerful lawyer who had been general counsel for the IRS and a personal ad-
viser to President Gerald Ford, but he had made his fortune in real estate.
After a lengthy, difficult negotiation, he and Leigh agreed to a six-year
contract that would pay me approximately $1 million per year. I signed
the contract on September 10, 1985. That night I dined with Culverhouse
in Tampa. By this time I knew his reputation: Everyone feared him. The
players. The staff. Everyone. But I liked him and he liked me. Over the
course of a couple of hours we discussed everything from politics to law
to our families. I did have considerable angst about moving to Tampa, a

city where I knew no one. But I was eager to get my shot in the NFL, and I figured I was going to like playing for Culverhouse.

Switching to the NFL meant that for the second year in a row I had to play two football seasons in one calendar year. But I was so relieved to be out of the USFL that I didn't care. Itching to prove myself, I showed up ready to play, but I had missed all of training camp as well as the first game of the season. Head coach Leeman Bennett said he wanted to give me time to learn the offense. Until then, I would be backing up longtime veteran quarterback Steve DeBerg.

The conditions were a far cry from luxurious. The team put me up in a motel next to our practice facility, and my room was infested with cockroaches. The practice facility was even worse. It was next to the airport, and planes constantly took off, making it impossible to hear anything.

But the worst part was watching from the sidelines. DeBerg did a great job integrating me into the offense, but backup quarterbacks have too much time on their hands, which was a particularly bad thing for me. I didn't know people in Tampa. After practice I often got in my rental car and drove around by myself. Many nights I ate dinner alone at Wendy's. I kept telling Coach Bennett I was ready to play, but he kept saying he didn't want to rush me into the starting role too soon.

Five weeks into the season we were 0-5 and I was restless. Our team stunk. We got booed every time we took the field at home. Our own fans showered us with obscenities. I couldn't blame them. They were sick of our losing. I had only been in town for five weeks, and I was already sick of it too. And I believed I could help turn things around. DeBerg was a smart guy, and he was doing everything he could to help the team win. But at thirty-one years of age, he took a beating because he wasn't all that mobile and our offensive line struggled to protect him.

In our sixth game DeBerg went down with an injury. I ran to the bench and grabbed my helmet. But Bennett sent in third-string quarterback Alan Risher. The fans booed Bennett for not putting me in. But that didn't change his mind. I took my helmet off and retrieved the clipboard. We lost again.

The following week DeBerg returned to the lineup. We kept losing, and the fans and the media clamored for me to play. On November 17, the team suffered its worst defeat in the organization's history — a 62–28 loss to the Jets that dropped us to 1-10. The next day Bennett announced that I would start my first game the following week at home against the Lions.

November 24, 1985. I walk out of the tunnel at Tampa Stadium to an overwhelming ovation. More than 41,000 fans have shown up, our largest crowd of the year. Everyone is standing. I look up at them. They are clapping, shouting, dancing. All eyes are on me. My adrenaline rushes as I run onto the field, clapping my hands and pumping my fists. The crowd gets louder, and I feed off the energy. I never felt anything like this in the USFL.

I'm so eager that I'm soaked in sweat before kickoff. I'm about to take my first snap in the NFL. Finally. I tell myself this is really happening.

My teammates are pumped up too. Offensive lineman Ron Heller has put a sticker on the back of his helmet. It's an eye. "I put this eyeball on the back of my helmet," he tells me with a smile, "so I can keep an eye on you because I don't know where the hell you're going."

Our first play call is a pass. I drop back and Detroit blitzes. It feels like guys are coming from every direction. I scramble out of the pocket and take off. I break a tackle and elude another before being knocked down. I gain only four yards, but the crowd cheers wildly.

Two plays later I drop back again. Again Detroit blitzes. And again I take off for another gain and sustain a big hit. But I pop right up. It feels great to be playing.

On our second possession I complete my first pass in the NFL, a 9-yard throw to tight end Jimmie Giles. On my next pass attempt Detroit blitzes again. I shake off a sack attempt and run 15 yards downfield. As I cut back to avoid a tackle, linebacker Jimmy Williams hits me with a forearm shiver to the head, knocking me down. He is penalized for unnecessary roughness. It's a frustration play on his part. I already have almost 30 yards rushing, and none of my runs have been designed plays.

The penalty advances the ball all the way to the Lions' 12-yard line. Moments later we kick a field goal to go up 3–0. By halftime I have 33 yards rushing and 33 yards passing. We're down 7–6.

In the second half, Detroit adds to its lead with three field goals to go up 16–6. But in the fourth quarter I huddle up the offense and tell them we are going to win this thing. The temperature on the field is well over 90 degrees, and it's taking its toll on Detroit's defense.

We start a long drive from deep in our own territory. It ends with James Wilder crashing into the end zone. With 3:38 to play, we are down 16–13. The Lions can run out the clock with a couple of first downs, so we need a stop. Our fans get so loud that the Lions can't hear their quarterback. They fail to make a first down and have to punt. We return it all the way to the Lions' 37-yard line. With 2:35 to go, I start the drive with a 22-yard pass completion to Kevin House. Then I run the ball on two consecutive plays. With one minute left, Donald Igwebuike kicks a field goal and sends the game into overtime. Our fans go crazy.

I'm exhausted, and my legs are killing me. I have run the ball ten times for 60 yards. But in overtime I drive us into field goal range and Igwebuike hits one from 24 yards out to win the game, 19–16. I run onto the field, thrusting my fist in the air. Our fans are elated. "Celebration" by Kool and the Gang plays over the stadium sound system. It's only our second win of the season. For me it's a huge relief. The fans love the outcome.

I'm so happy that I don't realize how sore I am until I reach the locker room. Every muscle in my body aches. I wince when I pull off my pants. After talking to the press, I spend over an hour in the training room receiving treatment. But winning makes the pain worth it. The numbers for my first start in the NFL aren't bad: 16 completions on 27 attempts for 167 yards. No interceptions. Ten rushes for 60 yards. I am the first quarterback in team history to win my debut game.

I could barely walk when I left the stadium wearing a sweat suit. But I was energized by the victory. A white shirt, a tie, and dress slacks hung from the hook in the backseat of my rental car. Still aching, I eased behind the wheel and sped off to a Mormon church in St. Petersburg for a Sunday night speech to teens and their parents. I hadn't had time to prepare remarks, so I winged it. I talked about the story of my life: overcoming adversity.

December 1, 1985. We're in Green Bay. A foot of snow has already fallen. A foot more is expected before game time. A severe weather warning is in effect, and people have been urged not to travel unless absolutely necessary. The roads are so bad that a snowplow has to lead our bus from the hotel to Lambeau Field. The game is sold out, but there are 36,000 no-shows, the most in Packer history.

There is so much snow on the field that we don't bother going out to warm up. Inexplicably, our equipment manager has left most of our winter gear back in Florida. None of us has thermal underwear. Fortunately, we travel in business attire. Desperate to keep warm, I wear my suit jacket and dress slacks under my uniform. A lot of guys do the same.

The league should cancel this game. Thirty-five-mile-per-hour winds drop the wind chill temperature to minus 5 degrees. When the grounds crew tries removing the tarp at game time, it is frozen to the turf. There are no photographers or cheerleaders on the sidelines, only snowplows and guys with shovels.

I am absolutely frozen before the opening kickoff. My first pass sails in the wind, landing way beyond the intended receiver. I take a little off my next pass, and the wind knocks it down five yards in front of the intended receiver. We try to run the ball but can't get any traction in the snow. We punt, and the visibility is so bad that the Packers' punt returner never sees the ball. It lands behind him.

Midway through the second quarter I don't have a single pass completion. My fingers are numb. Worse, I can't see. The snow is coming in horizontally. Plus, we are wearing white uniforms, so my receivers blend in with the snow.

There is no way I am going the entire first half without a pass completion. In the huddle I turn to running back James Wilder. "Just cut in front of me," I tell him. "I'll shuffle you the ball so I can get a completion."

It works. I finally complete a pass. But we end the half down 7–0. I spend halftime draped over a heater. The feeling returns to my fingers. But it never stops snowing, and playing conditions in the second half are downright dangerous. The huddle around the sideline heaters resembles scenes from the film *March of the Penguins.* When Coach yells, "Punt team," eleven groans can be heard as guys leave the hard-earned inner circle.

In the third quarter I scramble out of the pocket. Packers defensive end Tim Harris chases me. I lose my footing and Harris pile-drives me face down into about a foot of wet snow. It packs my face mask. I can't see or breathe. Harris is lying on me. I claw desperately at my face mask, clearing an airhole. Harris finally rolls off, and I get up. I emerge from the snow pile looking like Frosty the Snowman. It's only my second start, and I'm starring in a blooper clip that will play on NFL highlights for decades.

We lose the game, 21–0. I complete eight of 17 passes for 53 yards. I run the ball seven times for 31 yards. I have ice on my eyebrows. My lips are purple. My feet and hands are numb. And I'm fed up. I can't wait to get back to sunny Florida.

I get bombarded with fan mail. Some of it comes from kids. But a lot of it comes from women who insist they want to be with me. Letters come with lipstick imprints and are signed by women using ridiculous pen names.

I answer the letters from kids, but I ignore the letters from women because most of them seem a little crazy. Even on the field, I can't escape the craziness. Two weeks after the Snow Bowl in Green Bay, we play the Colts at home. Partway through the second quarter I'm in the huddle when the head referee taps me on the shoulder. "Can I talk to you for a second?" he says.

I step away from the huddle.

"Hey, listen, my daughter's going to BYU," he whispers. Next thing I know, he starts trying to convince me that I should meet his daughter. "I'd like you to take her out," he says.

I cannot believe this. We're in the middle of a game!

"Uh, okay," I say. "What's her name?"

He tells me and I return to the huddle.

"What was that all about?" one of my linemen asks.

"Oh, our last timeout was too long," I tell him.

Late in the game we are down 31–23, and I'm trying to mount a comeback. I scramble out of the pocket and take a brutal hit that causes me to fumble just before the whistle blows to stop the play. I am lying on the ground when the defense recovers the loose ball, all but sealing our defeat. Suddenly, out of nowhere, a yellow flag lands next to me. The referee whose daughter is headed to BYU calls a personal foul on the defense. First down, Tampa Bay.

I get up and brush myself off. Then the ref walks past me and whispers: "She likes Italian food."

We finished the season 2-14. It was one of the worst seasons in franchise history, and we had the worst record in the league. But Hugh Culverhouse was looking for positives. I met with him after the season. "I love the way you fight," he told me over dinner. "I love the way you play. You are my quarterback for life. You're going to be here forever, and we're going to build this thing together."

I finally got the sense that things might work out in Tampa Bay. Plus, we held the first overall pick in the upcoming NFL draft. The team selected Auburn running back Bo Jackson. Bo was the Heisman winner. More important, he was a big back with sprinter speed. He was such a great athlete that he was also being pursued by the Kansas City Royals to play professional baseball. In hopes of convincing Bo to choose football over baseball, Culverhouse flew him to Tampa after the draft. He asked me to join them for dinner. My job was to help convince Jackson that together we could turn around the franchise.

Bo and I hit it off immediately. I loved the prospect of handing off to him. But right after we finished our salads, Culverhouse stepped away from the table to take a call. Bo turned to me and said: "I'm never coming here."

"But they drafted you," I said.

"I'm going to play baseball," he said.

I knew then that I was in the wrong place too. I was glad to be in the NFL, but Tampa Bay was a dead end. It was depressing. The problem was that I didn't see any way out. I left the dinner deflated.

Two weeks later Bo signed with the Kansas City Royals. Tampa had wasted the number-one pick.

I spent the off-season in Utah with Herm and LJ. All three of us had just finished our first season in the NFL. We moved back in with our friend Tyde Tanner. Virtually all of our other friends were married, but we were four twenty-four-year-old bachelors living the dream. Three of us were playing pro football, and Tyde was along for the ride. It's not that we didn't want to marry. We did. And we knew plenty of women.

But none of us had pulled the trigger. In my case the dating scene had gotten more and more complicated with each year of my career. Fame and money posed a challenge in sorting out people's true motivations. But my biggest problem was finding the time to cultivate a meaningful relationship. The burden I felt to train and perform and meet expectations as a pro quarterback left me little opportunity for other aspects of my life.

During the summer of '86 I finally met someone I thought I wanted to be with long-term. She was from Salt Lake City and came from a prominent Mormon family. Just before I headed back to Florida for training camp, we got engaged. We planned the wedding to take place in the Salt Lake temple as soon as the '86 season ended.

During the preseason I sustained my first "official" concussion as a pro, in an exhibition game against the St. Louis Cardinals. But I returned to practice the next day, and I finished camp strong. So I was disappointed when Leeman Bennett named DeBerg the starter heading into the regular season. On the one hand, I was happy for DeBerg. He and I were great friends and we carpooled together every day. I learned a great deal from him and considered him a mentor. At the same time, I wondered what was going on. Tampa Bay had drafted me to be the starter. And I had become the starter midway through the '85 season. Then, at the end of the season, the owner had said I was his quarterback for life and he wanted to build the franchise around me. Despite my strong preseason performance, the organization appeared content to pay me $1 million a year to hold a clipboard.

We opened the '86 season at home against the 49ers. DeBerg threw seven interceptions, one short of the NFL record. I kept thinking Bennett would put me in, but he never did. Meantime, on the other side of the ball, Joe Montana took a major blow to his back and had to leave the game. It was a tough break that required season-ending back surgery.

We lost, 31–7. I never saw action. It felt like 1985 all over again.

DeBerg started the next game as well, throwing two more interceptions. We lost again, and Bennett named me the starter for the third game of the season on the road against the Lions.

· · ·

Age two. Padded up with my dad's old gear and ready to go on Halloween.

Courtesy of the Young family

My first football team was the North Mianus Cowboys in Greenwich, Connecticut. I wore my dad's old number.

Courtesy of the Young family

I'm about eleven years old here. From left to right: Mike, holding his dog JJ, Melissa, Mom and Dad, Tommy, and me. To bug Mike, I would tell him JJ liked me better.

Courtesy of the Young family

My wife loves this picture so she insisted I include it. Tori Simmons and me at a church dance, age sixteen.

Courtesy of the Simmons family / Photo © Richard Olson

Jill Simmons was like a little sister to me. Her tragic death following a car accident on our way home from college in April 1983 was a defining moment that prompted me to ask myself: *How are you going to live the rest of your life?*

Courtesy of the Simmons family

The mean streets of Greenwich. My gang who made up the Clam Box baseball team, including Randy Caravella, Will Saleeby, Kevin Bedford, Eddie Sheehan, and my brother Mike. Steve Gebhardt and Paul Perry played for our rival. *Courtesy of the Young family*

I was captain of our football, basketball, and baseball teams my senior year, as well as All-State in each. Number 83 is Greg Campbell, my favorite receiver.

My dad drove this beauty, a '65 Oldsmobile Dynamic 88, across the country so that I had some wheels at BYU. Friends named it the "Tuna Boat." *Andy Hayt / Sports Illustrated / Getty Images*

With my quarterback coach Mike Holmgren (center) and head coach LaVell Edwards (right) at BYU in 1982. *Mark A. Philbrick / BYU Photo*

Responding to BYU fans after leading our team to a 37–35 victory over UCLA at the Pasadena Rose Bowl on October 1, 1983. *AP Photo / Doug Pizac*

With my family at our home in Greenwich in the summer of '84. From left to right: Tom, Mike, Dad, Mom, Jim, me, and Melissa. I always loved coming home and being with my family.   *Courtesy of the Young family*

With my three best friends in college, Lee Johnson (left), Tyde Tanner (center), and Jim Herrmann (right). These guys kept me laughing twenty-four hours a day. We always had each other's backs.   *Courtesy of Jim Herrmann*

Celebrating in the end zone after scoring the game-winning touchdown, on a crazy flea flicker, to defeat Missouri in the Holiday Bowl on December 23, 1983.

Mark A. Philbrick/BYU Photo

With Leigh Steinberg at the Beverly Hills Hotel on March 6, 1984, for a press conference announcing my $40 million contract with the LA Express. I may look calm, cool, and collected, but I was really about to throw up. *AP Photo / Doug Pizac*

The USFL was crazy, but I would never trade it. I played with some of the best and was coached by the great Sid Gillman.
Focus on Sport / Getty Images

I was in Tampa for 1½ seasons. It was the first time I ever saw players smoke at halftime. But I also witnessed some of the toughest guys on the field. *Focus on Sport / Getty Images*

The best protection in the league, my boys Jesse Sapolu (left) and Harris Barton (right).
© Michael Zagaris

This is the Kirtland, Ohio, T-shirt that literally helped pave the roads in Kirtland after this photo appeared in *Sports Illustrated.*
Mickey Pfleger / Sports Illustrated / *Getty Images*

Despite the quarterback controversy, I always had a good relationship with Joe. Our lockers were next to each other for six years.
© Michael Zagaris

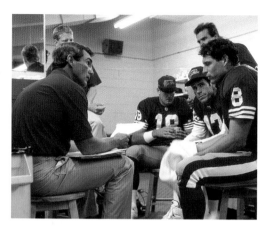

At halftime with one of the greatest offensive minds ever, Mike Shanahan. From left to right is Bill Musgrave, Elvis Grbac, Steve Bono, and coach Brian Pariani.
© Michael Zagaris

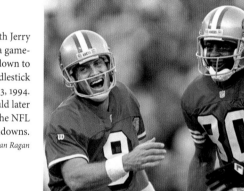

Celebrating with Jerry Rice after scoring a game-clinching touchdown to defeat Dallas at Candlestick on November 13, 1994. Jerry and I would later go on to set the NFL record for touchdowns.
AP Photo / Susan Ragan

Brent Jones was more than a teammate. We were like brothers.
Monica Davey / AFP / Getty Images

September 21, 1986. We have a nineteen-game losing streak on the road, the longest in the NFL. But in the first quarter I rush for one touchdown and Nathan Wonsley rushes for another to put us up 14–0 against Detroit. We never trail and go on to win 24–20, snapping our road losing streak. We are 1-2. And the starting job is mine for keeps.

Playing quarterback in Tampa Bay week in and week out was risky business. While I made my share of dumb mistakes, I knew from my USFL days that this team was not as put together as the Express. In my opinion, the Buccaneers would have lost to the Express nine times out of ten. The Buccaneers had a couple of veteran offensive linemen, like Ron Heller, but we had a lot of holes in our line too, which meant I literally ran for my life every Sunday. In New Orleans in the seventh game of the season, my luck ran out. I left the stadium on crutches, and the Saints beat us, 38–7, dropping us to 1-6.

I had never felt so beat up in my life. Every muscle ached. My neck was sore. I had a headache. I couldn't walk on my own. It even hurt to sit down. I had been knocked on my butt so many times that my tailbone was bruised.

While I was out with the injury I had more time with my fiancée. But the more we were together the more I was having second thoughts about tying the knot. I wasn't sure we were right for each other. As the season wore on I sensed I had a problem on my hands. I thought of my North Star, Jill. And I could hear her voice asking me: *Steve, what are you doing?*

But I told myself I couldn't deal with all this right now. It was the middle of the season. So I ignored the situation.

Two weeks after leaving the field on crutches I returned to action, rushing for two touchdowns and throwing for 193 yards while completing 14 out of 24 passes. Still, we lost again. The problem was that Tampa Bay had a losing culture. Some of the most fiercely competitive guys I ever played with — guys like James Wilder and Ron Heller — were on the Buccaneers. But winning takes accountability from all of the players. Our locker room had a culture of finger-pointing.

In the end, management sets the tone. The longer I was in Tampa the more I saw how poorly the team was managed and coached. We wound down the season on a losing streak that put us at 2-13 with one game remaining. Our final opponent was the St. Louis Cardinals. They were also 2-13. We were the two worst teams in the league. The loser of our game would secure the number-one pick in the upcoming draft.

I wanted desperately to go out on a winning note. If we lost, though, we'd have a better chance of improving the team for the next season, and the team certainly needed improvement. At one point in the second half one of our starting defensive players actually fell asleep in the middle of the game. The coaches were yelling his name, and he was knocked out on the bench. Guys thought it was funny, but I was furious. I still wanted to win.

We lost, 21–17, securing the worst record in the league for the second season in a row.

12

CHANGING PLACES

On JANUARY 5, 1987, I was in Utah, fretting over my upcoming wedding while the San Francisco 49ers were facing the New York Giants in the NFC playoffs. Joe Montana had returned after his back surgery. But Giants defensive tackle Jim Burt knocked Montana unconscious. He left Giants Stadium in an ambulance, and the Giants won, 49–3, en route to winning the Super Bowl.

At the time it never occurred to me that Joe Montana's health situation would have any impact on my future. I had my own problems. I was supposed to get married. The cake was ordered. I had my tux. My fiancée had her gown. But after the season ended, tensions grew between us over fundamental things, and it made me realize that I definitely didn't know my fiancée as well as I thought I did.

My parents had flown in from Connecticut. Leigh Steinberg had flown in from San Francisco. My fiancée's family and friends were all in town too.

But I knew there was no way I could go through with marrying my fiancée. On the eve of the wedding I drove to her parents' home and called it off. Her family was furious. It was an absolute mess.

I knew people wouldn't understand. But I also knew, deep down, that I had done the right thing for me and for her. We just weren't the right fit. My sense of relief was immediate, and I never looked back.

• • •

Tampa Bay fired Leeman Bennett and replaced him with Alabama head coach Ray Perkins. For the second year in a row the Buccaneers held the number-one pick in the NFL draft. With the draft still a month away, Tampa Bay signed University of Miami quarterback Vinny Testaverde to a six-year, $8.2 million contract on April 2, 1987.

A couple of days later I got a call from Perkins. He said, "Congratulations, you're a St. Louis Cardinal."

I called Leigh. He told me the Cardinals had offered the Buccaneers their first-round pick for me. That meant Tampa would have the first and second picks overall. Perkins had his eye on Alabama's All-American linebacker Cornelius Bennett.

I told Leigh there was no way I was going to St. Louis. The Cardinals were another team that was going nowhere. I saw no point in making a lateral move from one bad team to another. Leigh promised to do what he could to break up the trade.

But I didn't sit back and wait. I immediately called Hugh Culverhouse. I didn't even give him a chance to say hello.

"You traded me to the *Cardinals?* You tell me I'm your quarterback for life and you send me to the *Cardinals?* You can't do that to me."

He tried to explain, but I cut him off. "If we're going to do this together, then let's do this together," I told him. "But if we're not going to do this together, then you've got to help me."

"Steve, listen."

"'Quarterback for life.' That's what you said."

"Well, I did say that."

"You can't send me to St. Louis."

"Let me see what I can do."

After I talked to Culverhouse, Leigh called him and issued a threat. He told him I would retire rather than go to St. Louis.

Two hours later Culverhouse called me back and told me he had called off the trade. I had two weeks to figure out where I wanted to go.

Leigh and the 49ers' vice president, Carmen Policy, were friends. Formerly a lawyer in Youngstown, Ohio, the NFL executive was sharp, warm, effusive, and bright. Leigh called him "Charmin' Carmen." Leigh was also

close to 49ers head coach Bill Walsh. Given that Joe Montana had undergone back surgery at the start of the '86 season and then got knocked
out of the '86 playoffs when he took a hit that knocked him unconscious,
Leigh thought the 49ers might be in the market for a new quarterback.
He called them.

Bill Walsh was an old friend of LaVell Edwards's at BYU. Walsh called
Edwards and told him he would be coming to Provo to put me through a
workout.

Under the NFL rules, I still belonged to Tampa Bay. That meant I
couldn't work out for another team. But owing to the unusual situation I
was in with Culverhouse, Leigh said it was okay.

I met Bill at the BYU practice field. The first thing I noticed was his
white hair. He looked like a professor. He acted like one too. He used big
words, cited phrases from literature, and rattled off numbers like a math-
ematician. I threw for him. I did drills. I ran wind sprints. I did whatever
he wanted. Then we walked the field. It dawned on me that I was talking
with the San Francisco 49ers' head coach on the BYU football field while
under contract with the Tampa Bay Buccaneers.

Bill got to the point. He told me he wanted me to be the 49ers' next
quarterback.

"What about Joe Montana?" I said.

"Steve, you don't come back from a second back surgery," he said. "Joe
might wander around a little bit. But there's no way he's going to be able
to do it anymore."

That night Leigh talked to Bill by phone. Leigh wanted assurances that
I would not be stepping into a quarterback controversy with Joe Mon-
tana. In clear language, Bill told Leigh that Joe wasn't going to play again.
He was done.

Leigh was giddy when he called me. Bill had said he would develop
me into the best quarterback in football. I would be reunited with Mike
Holmgren, who was now the Niners' quarterback coach and offensive
coordinator. The Niners had the best organization in football. A veteran
offensive line stacked with All-Pros would protect me. I'd be throwing
to the best receiving corps in the league. San Francisco was only a short
flight from Salt Lake City. The list of positives went on and on.

"Are you kidding me? I'm in," I told Leigh. "This is a dream come true."

"Sold to the man with the white hair," he said, laughing.

The next step was to get the 49ers' owner, Eddie DeBartolo, to go along with the idea. Leigh talked to Carmen Policy and Carmen talked to Eddie. But it was a call from Culverhouse that convinced DeBartolo. "He's the best athlete I've ever seen on a football field," Culverhouse told him. "More importantly, you'd want your daughter to marry him."

DeBartolo rejected Culverhouse's demand for a top player in return for me. Instead, he countered with an offer of $1 million. It was a novel approach. Trades were not done that way in 1987. But Carmen researched the league rules governing trades. Although there was an unspoken understanding that teams didn't trade money for players, there was nothing prohibiting the 49ers from including cash in a trade for me. Besides, Culverhouse oversaw the league's finance committee. If he was part of the trade, the league was not likely to question it.

Culverhouse liked the idea. The Buccaneers needed money to pay Testaverde, and Culverhouse loved cash. He asked San Francisco to include a couple of draft picks to go along with the money. DeBartolo agreed.

On April 23, 1987, Leigh called and told me a deal had been struck. I was heading to San Francisco.

That night I went to see *The Mission* with Robert De Niro. The theme — the power of every human being to reconcile with his past — was one that resonated with me in a big way. I still struggled with the fact that I hadn't served a mission for the Mormon Church at age nineteen. Outside my faith, no one cared. But within the Mormon community I knew people still talked about it, especially now that I was in the NFL. People thought my status as a football player had influenced my decision not to serve a mission, unaware that I was an eighth-string nobody when I made that decision. It was only the fear and anxiety that had held me back. But now that I was a successful quarterback, I worried that kids would think I had shirked my responsibilities. I tried to make up for that by quietly living a personal code I had established for myself: never to do anything as a professional athlete — on the field or in private — that would set a poor example for kids.

· · ·

I arrived in San Francisco wearing cowboy boots. I wanted to look tall the first time I met the San Francisco media. One of the reporters asked how I would handle a quarterback controversy.

"You guys handle that," I said. "I've learned that you take care of what you can take care of."

I should not have said more. But I did.

"It's hard to replace a legend," I added. "I've played everywhere I've been. I want to play. To sit on the bench . . . I'll probably go crazy."

13

JOE MONTANA'S SHOES

A MONTH LATER I was in San Francisco for a three-day minicamp. A couple of nights beforehand Leigh had thrown a welcome party for me with about 200 people. I didn't care much for parties, so I hung out with Leigh's little boy. I asked him: "So who is your favorite quarterback?" He looked up at me. "Joe Montana."

I was so eager to get to minicamp that I arrived without my cleats. The equipment manager told me not to worry. I gave him my shoe size, and he found me a pair. The personnel in the locker room were a little intimidating. Everywhere I looked I saw elite NFL talent. Jerry Rice—the best receiver in the game. Dwight Clark—the guy who made "The Catch." Roger Craig—the high-stepping running back. John Taylor—another receiver with speed to burn. Ronnie Lott—the best safety in the league. Charles Haley—one of the best pass rushers in football.

This team was loaded. There was no free agency in the league at this point, so these guys had been together for years. They had won two Super Bowls together. I was the newcomer, the outsider.

Guys started stretching. Then Joe jogged onto the field. I couldn't help staring. I hadn't expected him to show. The veterans greeted him. After a few minutes I approached Joe and said hello. He was cordial, and so was I. But it was awkward.

I gravitated over toward the rookies and the guys trying to make the team. I met Harris Barton, a rookie first-round draft pick out of North Carolina. He was expected to compete for a starting position on the offensive line. I met Brent Jones. Cut by the Steelers, he hoped to catch on with the Niners. I started throwing a ball with Jones.

The minute drills began I felt the eyes on me. But my eyes were on Joe. His throwing motion was effortless. Every pass was a spiral. But the main thing I noticed was his movement. He looked healthy.

During a water break I cornered Bill Walsh. "Joe doesn't really look hurt."

He shrugged his shoulders. "Well, we'll see," he said. Then he turned and walked away.

A pit formed in my stomach. I had some experience replacing a legend. Jim McMahon was the king of college football and the prince of Provo when I arrived at BYU in 1980. I nearly went over the edge trying to fill his shoes. This was bigger than that. Way bigger! Joe Montana was the king of San Francisco. He brought the city its first Super Bowl. He was a two-time Super Bowl MVP.

I jumped in and took my snaps and made my throws. I put a little extra zip on the ball, and I went all out on every play and in every drill. It was a good first day. Toward the end of the session I took a knee. I felt good. Then I noticed the number on the back of my cleats: 16. *No way!*

I was wearing Joe's shoes.

I felt like an idiot. I wanted to kill the equipment manager, Ted Walsh. This was the first of many practical jokes he pulled over the years.

As soon as practice ended I hustled off the field in hopes of returning Joe's shoes before he entered the locker room. While I undressed, he walked up behind me.

"Nice shoes, Steve," he said, grinning.

I rolled my eyes and smiled.

"When you're finished, just throw them back in my locker."

The other thing that was different about the 49ers' minicamp was the number of reporters on hand to cover it. In Tampa only a few would show up. In San Francisco it was more like a herd. They immediately sensed that Bill had brought me in to replace Joe. The headline after the final day of camp read: "If Steve Starts, Will Joe Go?"

The question gave me indigestion. The last thing I wanted was a contest with Joe Montana. That was a no-win situation.

On the flight back to Utah I second-guessed my decision to sign with the 49ers. *What have I gotten myself into?*

I called Leigh. He tried to calm me down. He assured me that Bill Walsh had told him in clear language that Joe wasn't going to play again.

"It sure doesn't look that way to me," I told him.

He reminded me that minicamp was very different from the regular season. It's one thing to run around in shorts and do noncontact drills. It's another thing to survive the relentless pounding of a sixteen-game season.

"Let's see how it plays out, Steve."

My roommate at training camp was Randy Cross, the eleven-year veteran offensive lineman. An All-Pro, Cross had spent his entire career protecting Montana. Yet he bunked with me. I was unsure of myself and I still worried about everything, so I didn't say much. And few players said much to me. But one day I was in the buffet line, and a guy in his fifties started talking to me. His name was Jack Lambert, and he worked for the DeBartolo Corporation back in Cleveland. Lambert was Eddie DeBartolo Sr.'s right-hand man, and he oversaw many of the family's assets.

For some reason, Jack took a liking to me. He started eating lunch with me nearly every day during training camp. Every time he'd see me he'd put his arms around me and kiss me on the cheek. That kind of affection was typical within the DeBartolo family. Jack treated me like a son. I always kidded him by saying he was the Jewish mother I never had.

In contrast, I became defensive end Charles Haley's favorite target. Nobody escaped Haley's antics. But he said all kind of crazy things in an attempt to rattle me. One day he challenged me to a foot race in front of all the guys. Despite his size, Charles could outrun everyone on the team, and he had beaten everyone he had challenged to a race.

I really didn't want to race him, but I didn't have much choice. With everyone looking on, we lined up. Then I beat him. I wasn't sure that was a good idea, though. He hated losing to anyone, especially me.

I was hyperfocused on living up to the expectations that came with being a Niner. Winning the division wouldn't be good enough. Making the playoffs wouldn't be good enough. Even making it to the Super Bowl wouldn't suffice. We had to win the Super Bowl. Anything short of that would be a failure. It was a different world than Tampa Bay.

My main task was to learn the 49ers' vaunted "West Coast offense." Giants head coach Bill Parcells coined the term after his team knocked the 49ers out of the playoffs in '85. It was a shot at Bill Walsh's complex offensive scheme that spreads defenses out with an array of short, horizontal passes. Unlike Tampa Bay, where I was discouraged from running, Bill encouraged me to turn upfield when I saw openings. He said my ability to run added a new dimension to his West Coast scheme. I was eager to play under Bill's system.

In the preseason we play the Los Angeles Raiders. Joe plays the first half. Bill sends me out to start the second half. The first time I approach the line of scrimmage, Raiders linebacker Matt Millen starts yelling: "Mormon in the backfield! Mormon in the backfield!"

It throws off my concentration. *What? What did he say?*

The next play I come up under center. Same thing. "Alert! Alert! Mormon in the backfield!" Millen shouts. "Mormon in the backfield."

Millen jokingly harasses me for the rest of the game. I could only imagine how much ribbing Raiders quarterback Marc Wilson, also a Mormon, got from Millen every day in practice.

After the game, Wilson and tight end Todd Christensen, another Mormon, meet me at midfield. Christensen is coming off the best season of his career with a league-leading 95 receptions for 1,153 yards. They are among the small fraternity of Mormons in the league. "Hang in there, Steve," Todd tells me. "We're in this together."

The 1987 NFL season opened in conflict and uncertainty. The players' union was pushing for free agency. The owners wanted to maintain the status quo. The players threatened to walk after the second week of the season if the owners didn't budge.

We opened on the road at Pittsburgh. I had an excellent preseason. But despite what Bill and Leigh had been telling me, Joe was healthy, and naturally, he started. He put up big numbers against the Steelers. But he also threw three interceptions and we lost 30–17. I didn't see any action.

A week later we traveled to Cincinnati. Joe threw three more interceptions. But with two seconds remaining in the game, he threw a touch-down pass to Jerry Rice to give us a 27–26 victory. The Riverfront Stadium crowd was dumbfounded. Bill Walsh was so elated that he started skipping like a child. He skipped all the way off the field. Eddie DeBartolo met us in the locker room and patted every player on the back. Then he hugged Joe.

We flew back to San Francisco and went on strike. I joined my teammates and carried a picket sign outside team headquarters. My dad was furious with me. He spent his career fighting unions as a labor lawyer, so he did not want me on a picket line.

But I fundamentally believed in our position. The union wanted free agency rights for veteran players. As a guy who had spent two years wallowing in Tampa Bay, I supported players having the chance to seek employment elsewhere. It just didn't seem fair that some guys were stuck in places like Tampa Bay their entire career.

The NFL canceled the third week of the season while teams brought in replacement players. The union referred to them as scabs. A week later play resumed with the replacement players and the games counted in the standings. The "Niners" played the "Giants" at Giants Stadium, but only 16,000 fans showed up. Throughout the league 300,000 tickets were returned.

During the strike coaches were barred from communicating with players. But a group of players met privately with Bill Walsh and helped him with game plans. Joe was the leader of the group, and I also participated. None of us expected to be on strike long, and the replacement-player games would count, so we wanted Bill to succeed.

Three days after the 49ers' replacement players beat the Giants' replacement players, Joe Montana crossed the picket line. Dwight Clark, Roger Craig, and thirteen other players joined him. It was big news. The union didn't like it. But Joe was Joe.

The rest of us couldn't stay out when Joe was back, so the strike effectively ended when Joe returned. During the walkout the Niners won both games, so we were 3-1 when Joe returned to the lineup. In his first two games back he played superbly and we beat St. Louis and New Orleans to improve our record to 5-1.

I still hadn't seen any action. Not a single snap. I felt misled by Walsh. I didn't come to San Francisco to be a backup. I had come to play. But when I confronted Walsh, he changed the subject. So I talked to offensive coordinator and quarterback coach Mike Holmgren. I told him I wanted more reps in practice. I just wanted a fair shot.

It was awkward for Mike. Joe knew Mike and I were close from our BYU days, so Mike bent over backwards to avoid any impression of favoritism toward me. It reached a point where I thought Mike was actually favoring Joe. During game weeks Mike introduced the plays for the upcoming game on Wednesdays. He would post the plays on a chalkboard in a meeting room at our practice facility. The quarterbacks would review the play list, and Mike would quiz us. Joe would already know all the answers even though the game plan had just been posted. This routine went on for a few weeks.

I suspected Mike was meeting privately with Joe in advance. Finally, I brought it up with him. "Mike, how is it that Joe knows all of these answers?"

"Oh," Mike said, "he asks me to fax him the game plan when it is finished late Tuesday night."

I think to myself: *So Joe must memorize it sometime between midnight on Tuesday and seven AM on Wednesday.*

"Well, Mike, would you mind faxing it to me as well?"

"Sure," he said.

"I know it's hard on everybody," I said. "But I didn't come here to watch."

14

AWKWARD

NOVEMBER 1, 1987. We're leading the Rams in Los Angeles 31–7, and Joe has had a big day. Late in the fourth quarter Bill sends me in to mop up. Finally, I see action as a 49er. I hand the ball off twice and get sacked once. Then we punt. I don't even have a chance to break a sweat because moments later the game ends. We've improved to 6-1, but I'm frustrated. I skip the shower, change out of my uniform, and head straight for the team bus.

We were back in San Francisco by early evening. I went home to an empty house in Menlo Park. It belonged to Miami Dolphins tight end Greg Baty, who had bought the place while playing college ball at Stanford. He still lived in it during the off-season, but he let me stay there for the fall. I lived out of a duffle bag and ordered takeout every night.

Alone, I sat and assessed my situation. Through seven games I had been on the field for a grand total of three plays. I had thrown zero passes.

The next morning I didn't want to leave the house. I didn't even want to get out of bed. I felt like I lacked purpose. I called my dad. He told me to get up and go to work.

One of the things I learned from my dad was that self-pity will get you nowhere. It's counterproductive. But my situation had me in a rut.

My former BYU teammate Tom Holmoe saw how frustrated I was playing behind Joe. One day he took me to a Bay Area hospital to meet a ten-year-old boy he had gotten to know. The boy's name was Danny Jackson and he was battling brain cancer. And he was a huge 49ers fan.

Tom introduced us, and I asked Danny how he was doing.

"I'm doing great," he told me.

But his situation wasn't great. Extensive chemotherapy had compromised his spine and left him with severe scoliosis. The poor kid was constantly bent over. And the doctors said his cancer was incurable.

Still, Danny told me: "Aw, it's nothing. I'm going to have some surgery to straighten me up, and then I'm going to play for the Forty-Niners. No problem. This ain't nothin'."

Danny's outlook changed my perspective. *Just stop it with the self-pity,* I told myself. After visiting Danny, I got on my knees and thanked God for everything he had given me. I thanked him for my health. I thanked him for the opportunity to play pro football. I asked for forgiveness. I prayed for Danny.

The next morning I took a new approach. Even though I was not playing, I prepared for every game as if I would start. My nights were consumed with studying the playbook.

Two weeks later Joe sprained a knuckle on his throwing hand during practice. It was a freak accident. Nothing too serious, but as a precautionary measure, Bill told me I would start against the Saints at home on November 15.

The Saints had an extremely fast, aggressive group of linebackers: veteran Rickey Jackson and rookies Sam Mills, Pat Swilling, and Vaughan Johnson. Bill thought my speed and mobility would pose problems for them.

It's 54 degrees at game time, but I'm drenched in sweat. I'm so pumped up to be on a great team and finally be starting. Nervous, but ready, I take the field and Bill pulls me aside. "Steve, like I told you, you're going to be one of the greats," he said. "Let's go do this."

In our first possession I move us to midfield. Walsh calls a running play. I'm at the line of scrimmage. My center Randy Cross yells: "Get out of it! Get out of it!"

I think: *Oh crap! It must be a bad play.* I call an audible, changing the play to a pass to tight end John Frank.

I overthrow Frank by a mile. Out of nowhere Jerry Rice streaks in and makes a fingertip catch. He goes all the way for a 46-yard touchdown. The place erupts.

I jog to the sideline, and Bill Walsh is all smiles. He pats me on the shoulder. "How did you know?" he says. "How did you know to get to the pass play and get it to Jerry?"

I have a split second to decide whether to tell him what really happened. *No,* I tell myself. *Just go with it.*

I look at Walsh and shrug. "Coach, I just felt it."

Then I go find Randy Cross on the bench. "Why did we have to get out of that run play?" I say.

He looks up at me. "I wasn't talking to you," he says. "I was talking to Fahnhorst."

I laugh. Keith Fahnhorst is our offensive tackle. Cross had been yelling at him to change his blocking assignment. My first touchdown pass as a San Francisco 49er comes on a running play that I mistakenly changed to a pass play, only to miss the intended receiver and have Jerry Rice catch it. Crazy.

In our second possession I start moving us downfield again. I complete five of six passes. I also run the ball three times. I feel so liberated to be on the field. I love this offense.

With a minute left in the first quarter, I am flushed from the pocket. I take off running. Two linebackers converge on me. One takes out my legs. I'm airborne when the second backer hits me helmet to helmet, sending me into a 180-degree spin.

That's the last thing I remember.

I've landed on my head. I'm momentarily dazed and confused. I don't know where I am. For a moment I have trouble hearing.

The trainer and doctor run out, but I don't want help. After a few minutes, I get up and walk off the field on my own. Joe takes my place while the medical staff evaluate me. They tell me I have a concussion. I insist I'm fine. But Joe plays the rest of the game. It bugs me that I've finally gotten a chance to start and the medical staff won't clear me to return to the field.

My neck was stiff for days, and I had some tenderness in my upper spine, but I was cleared to play the following week. Nonetheless, I resumed my role as Joe's backup. We won three straight, knocking off Tampa Bay, Cleveland, and Green Bay. During that stretch I took a grand total of three snaps, against Cleveland. I threw an incomplete pass and ran the ball twice for minus-three yards.

With three games remaining in the regular season, I was eager to get back on the field. We were scheduled to face the Chicago Bears at Candlestick on *Monday Night Football*. Both teams were 10-2. We had the number-one offense. They had the number-one defense. The winner would have a leg up on home-field advantage for the playoffs.

December 14, 1987. On our first possession, Joe drops back to pass, trips over Roger Craig, and is sacked by Dave Duerson. Joe lands awkwardly and hobbles off the field. I strap on my helmet and go in.

Facing second-and-17 from the Bears' 19-yard line, I drop back to pass. The Bears blitz. I see it and take off running. I get to the sideline, turn up field, and go for 15 yards before cornerback Vestee Jackson closes in on me. I can step out of bounds and avoid the hit. But that's not my style. I lower my shoulder and barrel over Jackson. He lands on his back, and my momentum carries me to the Bears' 1-yard line.

The crowd roars. The referee signals first down. Linemen smack my helmet. There is no better feeling.

On the next play I throw the ball to Jerry Rice for a touchdown to put us up 7–0. More cheers. When I reach the sideline Bill pats me on the back and tells me Joe is done for the night. He has a twisted knee and a slightly pulled hamstring. I will have to go the rest of the game.

I have taken fewer than thirty snaps all season. Finally I get to go the distance in a game. And it's the Bears. It's William "The Refrigerator" Perry. It's Mike Singletary and Wilber Marshall. It's Richard Dent and Dan Hampton. I can't wait to get back on the field.

On our next possession I drive us down the field. We get a field goal to go up 10–0. In the second quarter I throw a 13-yard touchdown pass to Dwight Clark, his last as a 49er, putting us up 20–0 at the half. We build the lead to 34–0 by the fourth quarter. We are embarrassing the top defense in the NFL.

But I don't pay attention to the scoreboard. I have built up so much frustration from standing around watching Joe all season that I just want to keep going. On our next possession Bill calls for a reverse handoff to Jerry Rice. But Bears defensive end Dan Hampton isn't fooled. He's waiting for Jerry. So I throw my body at Hampton. It's not a fair fight. Hampton is twice my size and three times as strong. He destroys me on the play. But my block clears the way for Jerry, who runs for 12 yards and another first down.

I am slow getting up. My left shoulder feels jammed. Not good. From the ground I see William Perry. He seems pleased that I'm down. I flash back to looking up at that kid who collared me in Pee Wee football. I imagine *Monday Night Football* broadcaster Al Michaels saying on national television: "We are not sure what's going on, but there is a mother on the field and she's shaking The Refrigerator."

I get up smiling. My linemen start calling me "Crash." Walsh thinks I'm hurt and wants me to come out. I tell him no way. Not at home on Monday night. Not against the Bears. Not after I've waited all season to play. I want to experience every bit of the game, even the hits. Six plays later I throw another touchdown pass to Rice. It's my third one to Jerry on the night and my fourth one overall.

We beat Chicago on national television 41–0. Bill loves it. Our fans love it. But Bears coach Mike Ditka isn't pleased. On his way off the field he hurls his gum into the stands and hits a 49ers fan.

The win put us in the driver's seat heading into the playoffs. It also put me in an awkward position in the locker room. All season I'd been itching for an opportunity to prove that I could cut it in San Francisco, and I'd finally gotten my opportunity, against the toughest defense in the NFL. We didn't just beat the Bears; we destroyed them. Usually the press surrounded Joe after a game. This time they surrounded me.

In truth, the competition between Joe and me was awkward for me. And it was awkward for my teammates too. They felt an allegiance to Joe. He had led them to Super Bowl victories, and I was unproven. But two veterans went out of their way to make me feel accepted — Dwight Clark and Ronnie Lott. I don't know why. But they saw me working hard. They saw me coming early, staying late. I never complained. I never criticized. Ronnie, in particular, appreciated my approach to the game. He didn't say anything, but he talked with glances and nods. When I popped back up after taking a big hit, he nodded his approval. That kind of acceptance gave me the confidence to keep going.

With two games remaining, victories over our two division rivals — Atlanta and Los Angeles — assure us the best record in the NFC and home-field advantage throughout the playoffs. Bill tells me that Joe is too banged up to play. I'm starting against Atlanta.

I run with reckless abandon in the Falcons game. I don't care. Every time they flush me out of the pocket I take off — 12 yards on one carry, 23 yards on another. At one point I run 29 yards for a touchdown. I finish the game with nearly 100 yards rushing and over 200 yards passing, including a pair of touchdown passes to Jerry Rice. We crush the Falcons, 35–7.

In the final regular-season game I start against the Rams. In the first half I throw two more touchdown passes to Rice, including a 50-yard bomb. I throw another one to Mike Wilson. By halftime I have nearly 200 yards passing and we are up 27–0.

In the locker room Bill tells me that he plans to play Joe in the second half. He wants to give him some work before the playoffs start. I don't want to come out. I want to play. But I lose the argument. Joe finishes the game. We finish the season 13-2.

Heading into the playoffs, the only question was who would start at quarterback — Joe or me. With Joe on the sideline during the final three regular-season games, we outscored our opponents 124–7. During that stretch I threw 10 touchdown passes and zero interceptions. My performance in those three games had done wonders for my confidence and fueled the quarterback controversy. Quarterback controversies typically begin when the starter is struggling. But Joe was coming off the best year of his career, throwing 31 touchdown passes and finishing as the highest-rated passer in a single season in NFL history. Yet Bill had brought me to San Francisco to be the starter, and when he gave me the ball I played like one. The situation was unprecedented. One thing was clear — I could do great things in this league, but I needed the ball in my hands.

We had a bye in the first round of the playoffs, and Bill held off on announcing who would start at quarterback. I figured it was out of my hands. All I could do was prepare in case Bill decided to go with me.

Bill scheduled a practice on Christmas. Afterward the players who were single were offered dinner at the homes of the married players. Joe invited me to dinner at his place.

It was my first visit to Joe's house. The meal was magnificent. His beautiful wife was gracious. While we were at the dinner table, Joe and I were talking when Joe's daughter, who was probably around three years old, raised her hand. "Dad," she said. "Dad."

Joe kept talking to me.

"Dad," she repeated. "Dad."

"What?" Joe said sweetly.

"Is this the guy we hate?" she said innocently.

It was all I could do not to burst out laughing.

"No," Joe tells her. "That was someone else."

January 9, 1988. We're at Candlestick to play the Vikings. I'm disappointed but not surprised that I'm not starting. Joe has the best record in playoff history. And he's led us to the best record in the league during the '87 season. We are heavily favored to beat Minnesota. I figure I'm lucky to be part of this.

Minnesota scores on three of its first four possessions. Vikings wide receiver Anthony Carter makes circus catches and runs wild. Meantime, Joe can't find his rhythm. Minnesota's pass rush is all over him. Almost every time he releases the ball he gets hit. Then, with 7:36 left in the first half, Joe throws a floater toward the sideline that is intercepted and returned 45 yards for a touchdown. Minnesota leads 20–3.

At this point Joe has completed just five of 12 passes for 58 yards.

We should be killing these guys. We are favored to win the Super Bowl, not lose in the first round to the lowly Vikings. In the locker room at halftime Bill rants. Then he pulls me aside and says, "Be ready."

Be ready? I think. *I've been memorizing plays and preparing in every way possible since joining the team. I've been ready for the past sixteen weeks!*

It starts raining at the start of the third quarter, and Jeff Fuller picks off a Viking pass and returns it 48 yards for a touchdown to cut Minnesota's lead to 20–10. But our offense continues to struggle. Trailing 27–10, we stall again and have to punt. Joe jogs to the sideline, and Bill tells him: "I'm going with Steve."

Joe puts on his raincoat and I remove mine. Behind the bench I start throwing. The fans see me and start yelling obscenities at Walsh. I try to block it out. Bill's decision makes me the villain. But my job is to help the team win.

After the Vikings punt, I trot onto the field with 6:29 remaining in the third quarter. I hear booing. I get the sense that even the guys in the huddle prefer Joe. It's not like I blame them. He's the man in these situations. Me? I've never even attended an NFL playoff game, much less played in one. But all I can do is go to work. And the moment I feel the ball in my hands I am itching to see what I can do.

On my first snap I fake the handoff to Tom Rathman and complete a 35-yard pass to Roger Craig out of the backfield. Two plays later I run the bootleg and race 10 yards for a touchdown. The crowd goes crazy, but the play is called back for a holding penalty. Two plays later I roll left on third-and-goal. I pump-fake and take off for the end zone again. At the goal line I dive to avoid an oncoming tackler, crossing the goal line. This time there are no flags. The fans are delirious. Minnesota's lead is cut to 10. It's foggy, wet, and cold. But my adrenaline is so high that I'm sweating. I come off the field, and Bill tells me to keep it going.

Minnesota is forced to punt on its next possession. We get the ball right back. After a pass completion on first down, I fake a handoff and bootleg around the left side. Once I get past Chris Doleman it is wide-open space. I sprint 42 yards before being belted out of bounds. First down on Minnesota's 31-yard line. I already have 55 yards rushing in just two carries. Until I came in the team had just 32 yards rushing on the day. My legs have ignited the crowd.

Just before the end of the third quarter we attempt a field goal. But it comes up short. The Vikings mount another long drive, chewing up the clock and boosting the lead to 33–17. Then, after a long drive into Minnesota territory, I throw an interception inside the 20-yard line.

We get the ball back with 5:55 to play. I drive us 68 yards on eight plays before throwing a touchdown pass to John Frank to cut Minnesota's lead to 33–24, but time is our enemy.

Minnesota kicks one more field goal with 3:42 remaining to put the game out of reach. I am frustrated. I can't help wondering where we'd be if Bill had turned me loose sooner. In twenty-two minutes I have completed 12 of 17 passes and carried the ball six times for 72 yards. But we're out of time. Minnesota upsets us, 36–24.

This one hurts. We are hands down the best team in the NFL. Yet we are eliminated in the first round of the playoffs. For the third year in a row the Niners have not made it out of the first round. Our locker room is devoid of sound.

15

QUARTERBACK CONTROVERSY

Hungry to play, I spent the off-season working out in Provo. I had about six months until training camp, and I dedicated my time to lifting, running, and throwing. But I couldn't spend all my time training, and the question was, what would I do when I wasn't training?

Since college I had toyed with the idea of law school. I figured it was time I took the next step.

During the spring of 1988 I went to see Reese Hansen, the associate dean of BYU's law school. I told him that I realized the NFL schedule wasn't exactly conducive to being a full-time law student — I would be unavailable to take fall classes because I'd be playing football — but I wanted to enroll.

He explained that the situation was even more complicated than I realized. First-year law courses lasted all year. By missing fall semester, I would miss half the lectures and half the readings for all of the first-year courses. And since the 49ers were always in the playoffs, I would also miss the start of winter semester classes, putting me at an even further disadvantage. Under the attendance policy I'd never make it, and missing so much in-class material, I would be highly unlikely to pass the exams anyway.

I told him I wanted no special treatment. No favors. I was not looking for an easy path. I just wanted an opportunity to seek a law degree at my alma mater.

Hansen said he was willing to explore options, and we agreed to keep talking.

Back in San Francisco, the fallout from our first-round loss to the Vikings continued. Eddie DeBartolo stripped Bill Walsh of his title as team president. But Walsh stayed on as head coach. At the NFL owners' meeting, rumors circulated that Montana might be traded. The 49ers even confirmed that the team had had discussions with various teams about Joe. My name surfaced in trade talks too. And the Niners used all their draft picks to load up on defense. We selected linebackers Pierce Holt and Bill Romanowski.

Heading into training camp, I wanted to play down the competition between Joe and me. But on July 31, 1988, Bill Walsh said this to the media: "Well, our strength is at quarterback. But our problem is we have two. There's a quarterback controversy developing. We're going to have to select between Steve Young and Joe Montana."

A quarterback controversy developing? No kidding. Walsh had created it. And now he was fueling it. The national media was all over it. *The Sporting News* put us on the cover of its football preview issue under the headline: "Quarterback Controversy: How Long Will Montana Maintain Edge in Young Rivalry?"

The tension was palpable.

Training camp opened in Rocklin, and I needed a roommate who would be a friend and a confidant. The teammate I had in mind was Brent Jones. I'd gotten to know him a little during the previous season, and we shared some things in common. He had played college ball at Santa Clara and was drafted by the Pittsburgh Steelers in '86. They cut him after he was in a car accident. He was married and had two little girls. He was a Christian. He didn't party. And like me, he was a backup who was fighting for a starting spot.

Mike Holmgren was in charge of room assignments. I told him I wanted to be paired with Brent. Mike told me that Brent already had chosen a roommate for camp — running back Tom Rathman. But Mike knew my style, and he knew the pressure and uncertainty I was dealing with. He said he'd talk to Brent.

The next day Brent and I moved into a dorm room together at Sierra

College. We hit it off instantly. Other than the married-with-kids part, we were pretty similar. Each night after practice we would sit in our room going over everything we had done in camp that day. We broke down each play. I compared myself to Joe. He compared himself to the other tight ends. Then we went to bed.

But we didn't go to sleep. We lay awake for hours talking about the day when I would be the starting quarterback and he would be the starting tight end. We talked about winning the Super Bowl.

We talked about other things too. Religion. Politics. Women. We were both Republicans, and we were both Christians. So we lined up there. On the female front, he had the one thing I wanted — a wife.

"Why aren't you married?" he said.

I laughed. "It's complicated," I told him.

"Break it down for me."

"It would take too long."

"I have all night," he said.

"Just know there are lots of choices, but I'm looking for the one."

We ended up talking until 3:00 AM.

When the alarm went off a few hours later we groaned. When practice started we died. Luckily I was in the best shape of my life.

Unfortunately, Joe Montana looked to be in the best shape of his life too. The competition between us in camp was fierce. He saw me as a threat. I saw him as an obstacle. But despite being super-competitive, neither of us liked conflict. He never said anything derogatory to me. I never said anything negative about him. But it was clear we were both gunning for the same thing. And everyone was watching.

At the end of July, we flew to London, England, to face the Miami Dolphins in an exhibition game. It was part of the NFL's effort to expand the brand. We were overseas for almost a week. I ended up spending a lot of time traveling around London with Harris Barton and veteran tight end John Frank. Both were Jewish. They joked about hanging out with a Mormon. But while we walked around Piccadilly Circus and went to theater performances, we discovered that our religions shared some common elements.

Harris and John were two of the smartest players I'd ever been around.

Harris graduated from North Carolina with a degree in finance. John had a degree in chemistry and was enrolled in medical school. He attended classes in the off-season at Ohio State University, much as I planned to do with law classes at BYU. John's goal was to become a surgeon. I was particularly interested in the research he had published on diseases of the head and neck. He was intrigued by my interest in law.

The game itself was a big success. We played in front of 70,000 fans at Wembley Stadium. I relieved Joe in the second quarter and threw a touchdown pass and actually ended up playing most of the game.

By the time we got back to the Bay Area only two weeks remained until the start of the regular season. At the end of camp all the guys left our hotel and returned to their homes. John and I had no places of our own, so the team extended our stay while we searched for housing.

I would have been content to spend the entire season living at the hotel — my possessions were confined to a backpack and a duffle bag. But John wanted more space, so he found a ranch house in the foothills of the Santa Cruz Mountains in Saratoga. It was too big and too expensive for one guy, so I decided to join him.

The sprawling one-story home had a huge galley kitchen and a suite of bedrooms off the main part of the house. Each bedroom had a private entrance that opened to a patio. The views of the valley were spectacular. There was also a pool and a pool house with guest quarters in a secluded wooded area on the property. We nicknamed the main house "The Ponderosa" and called it "The Rosa" for short.

September 4, 1988. We are in New Orleans for the season opener. The Saints are coming off their first winning season in franchise history and their first playoff appearance. They are projected to challenge us for the division title. Joe is starting. But prior to pregame warm-ups, Bill pulls Joe and me into the coaches' room beneath the Superdome.

"Joe, Steve is going to play sometime today," he says. "So be ready for him to come into the game."

Joe says nothing and walks off.

Bill turns to me. "I don't know when it's going to happen," he says. "But it's going to happen."

The Saints jump out to a 17–10 first-half lead. Their young, aggressive defense is beating us off the ball. But we have a huge third quarter to go up 31–17. After the Saints open the fourth quarter with a touchdown to cut our lead to seven, Bill turns to Joe on the sideline and tells him he's putting me in. Then he turns to me and says: "Let's go, Steve."

A penalty on the ensuing kickoff pushes us all the way back to our own goal line. We run three plays and punt. Then New Orleans chews up six minutes and drives inside our 10-yard line before Michael Carter picks off Bobby Hebert on the 6. For the second consecutive series, we're starting inside our own 10-yard line.

On first down I hand off to Roger Craig, and he's stuffed at the line of scrimmage. The Saints linebackers are too fast, and they are anticipating the plays. To exploit this and take advantage of my speed, Bill calls a bootleg left. It is designed to get the defense going to the right by faking a handoff in that direction before I pivot and run in the opposite direction. I'm supposed to bring tight end John Frank in motion from the right to the left to block for me. I'm so eager to run the play that I forget to send John in motion. So when I bootleg left, Pat Swilling is closing in on me. Scrambling in the end zone, I spot Tom Rathman near the sideline. As Swilling tries to bring me down, I throw off balance and the ball lands a few feet from Rathman. Referee Jerry Markbreit flags me for intentional grounding. Worse, intentional grounding from the end zone is a safety. Our lead is cut to 31–26, and we have to punt.

I'm mad at Markbreit — my pass was very close to Rathman. But I'm mad at myself too. I jog off the field, yelling at myself. Then Walsh yells at me for screwing up the play. Brutal.

We kick off. New Orleans runs it all the way back to our 39-yard line. The momentum has turned. We desperately need a stop. Nose tackle Michael Carter sacks Saints quarterback Bobby Hebert. The ball pops out, and Kevin Fagan recovers it at midfield. Our ball. I breathe a sigh of relief.

Joe wants back in, but his elbow is bruised. Bill sends me back out. I put together a solid drive. Unable to get in the end zone, we kick a field goal to go up 34–26 with 1:40 remaining. It's enough to secure the win.

The amazing thing here is that Joe had twice been the Super Bowl MVP at this point. Yet Bill had pulled him out of a key divisional game and put me in. Moreover, he left me in even after one of my biggest bone-head plays. It seemed to me that he was genuinely trying to make good on his promise to give me a chance to play.

Despite Bill's efforts, I am mad at myself and frustrated by the quarterback situation. As soon as our locker room opens, the press surrounds me.

"Steve, are you satisfied with this kind of role? Do you expect this all year, like a relief pitcher? You kind of get called out of the bullpen."

I bite my tongue. "I'm satisfied to play for the 49ers. And, ah, we'll take it from there."

One of the reporters from the Bay Area asks me about playing time.

"If you want to talk to someone who wants to play, come talk to me," I tell him.

"Is it hard to keep your intensity up during the week?"

I'm so sick of these questions. But I smile. "No," I say. "We basically split time. I get a lot of repetitions during the week. So I feel like I'm preparing just as well."

The next day John was worried that he had suffered a lacerated kidney or a ruptured spleen in the Saints game. On his own, he got a CT scan at a Palo Alto clinic. It revealed three broken ribs. Furious, he told me he was unwilling to risk more serious internal injuries. He planned to take himself out of the lineup.

I had issues too. Coach Walsh named me the starter for week two. He told the media that Joe's elbow was bruised. But the team knew better. We all knew that Joe was the ultimate competitor. He played hurt a lot, and a bruised elbow wasn't going to be enough to sideline him. But our next opponent was the New York Giants. The last time San Francisco had played New York, Joe left the field in an ambulance. Plus, Bill thought my mobility would pose problems for the Giants' defense, which was the fiercest in the league.

The Giants-49ers rivalry was the hottest in pro football. But it was new to me. The two teams had squared off in the playoffs in '84, '85, and '86. During that span each team won a Super Bowl. The Giants established supremacy through a smash-mouth defense led by linebacker Lawrence

Taylor. The Niners overwhelmed teams with a passing attack that spread defenses thin and put a lot of points on the board. The two teams' style of play was as far apart as their homes on opposite coasts. Even geography figured into the rivalry. After soundly defeating San Francisco in the '85 playoffs, Parcells had told the press: "What do you think of that West Coast offense now?"

I was about to get my first taste of the rivalry.

September 10, 1988. It's the night before the game and I am in my hotel room, watching Ivan Lendl beat Andre Agassi to advance to the US Open final. Afterward I keep Brent Jones up half the night going over the game plan. Our first twenty-five plays are scripted. I have them memorized. But I insist on reviewing them again and again. I am obsessed with preparation. Brent finally tells me to relax.

But I don't relax when I'm starting. I think of reasons to worry. And then worry some more. We are playing a Super Bowl team. The guys in the other locker room — Lawrence Taylor, Harry Carson, Phil Simms, Mark Bavaro — are champions. This isn't some random game in Atlanta. It's the CBS game of the week. The whole country will be tuning in. John Madden and Pat Summerall are calling it. It feels really big.

The atmosphere at Giants Stadium is enough to make the hair stand up on the back of my neck. As a boy, I came here with my dad and dreamed of playing in front of him. Now it's happening. Nearly 76,000 people are on their feet when the Giants kick off. Confetti swirls in the air and speckles the field. It's Labor Day weekend, but it feels like the playoffs.

The Giants score first to go up 7–0. But I find my rhythm and we score the next 10 points. I complete 11 of 18 passes for 115 yards. I also run the ball five times for 48 yards. The Giants add a late first-half field goal. The score is tied 10–10 at the half. I am confident that we will win this thing.

But in the locker room Bill decides to make a switch and go with Joe in the second half. I am beside myself. I don't want to come out. But turnaround is fair play.

As hard as it is, I always make sure that I'm clear about my job. If I'm starting, I'm starting. If I'm on the sideline, I'm helping. The goal is to win whether I'm playing or signaling plays in from the sideline. So at the start of the second half in New York I go from the huddle to the sideline and my role switches.

The Giants' defense stiffens in the third quarter. We manage just a field goal. On the sideline I huddle with Joe, and he asks me if he is seeing everything that I see. We process pictures of the Giants' defense and look for ways to exploit it. With under two minutes to play, the Giants score and go up 17–13. We get the ball back deep in our own territory with 1:14 remaining. The Giants haven't allowed a single long drive the entire half. The crowd is on its feet. After Joe throws an incomplete pass to Rice and a fumbled snap, we face third-and-long from our own 22-yard line with forty-two seconds remaining. Bill Walsh gives me the play, and before I can signal it in to Joe, he reads Bill's lips and calls the play. On the snap Jerry Rice streaks down the right sideline into double coverage. Joe throws a perfect spiral that hits Jerry in stride. He runs by everyone and races 78 yards for a touchdown. I am jumping up and down on the sideline. We beat the Giants 20–17. We are 2-0.

Starting in San Francisco, I tell myself, is going to be tough.

Bill names Joe the starter for our home opener against Atlanta. He throws for 343 yards and a pair of touchdowns. He also throws three interceptions. I don't play. Atlanta upsets us 34–17.

Bill sticks with Joe the following week against Seattle, where he throws four more touchdowns and we blow them out 38–7. I see action in the fourth quarter and complete four of six passes, including a touchdown pass. We are 3-1.

But I am miserable. I wonder what it will take to get back in the lineup.

At night I shared my frustrations with John back at The Rosa. Because of his injury, he hadn't played in three weeks. We talked about our problems until John headed to bed around 8:00 PM. I was alone in the living room watching TV when there was a knock on the outside door to John's bedroom. John was a little spooked. Our place was out in the country. It was dark, and no one lived nearby. But he got up to answer the door. He peeked through the keyhole and saw two middle-aged men in dark suits. They looked like FBI agents. John opened the door.

"Can I help you?"

"We're here to see Steve Young," one of them said.

John was pretty protective of me. "What's going on here?" he asked them. "Is he in trouble?"

"No, no, no," one of them said. "I'm the bishop of Steve's congregation, and we've come by to say hello."

John, wearing only his boxers, let them in and ushered them into the living room. I looked up from the television and started cracking up. I had yet to meet the bishop, but the moment I saw him I knew he was from the church. I also knew they were dropping by because I didn't have family around and they wanted to make me feel welcome in the local congregation. That's what Mormons do.

And here was John trying to figure it all out. As soon as he saw me laughing, he started laughing. So did my visitors.

I was the first Mormon John had ever met. The more he learned about Mormonism the more he liked it. He loved the fact that two strangers dropped by to check on me. He also liked our emphasis on family values and clean living. "It reminds me a lot of Judaism," he said.

I admired John's religious commitment and welcomed the chance to learn about Judaism from him. The more time we spent together the closer we became as friends.

Our fifth game of the '88 season is against Detroit. John Frank returns to action, but in the first half he hits the ground hard after making a block. A pile of guys land on him, crushing his left hand. At halftime an X-ray reveals a break. The medical staff tell him he can play the second half with a cast. John looks at the X-ray and refuses. We get by the Lions 20–13 to improve to 4-1.

Later in the week John had surgery. His hand was pretty busted up. We talked to each other about our dilemmas. He was worried that football might jeopardize his dream of becoming a surgeon. I worried that I was destined to go another year as Joe's backup, and I was losing my patience. I prepared for every game as if I was going to be the starter. Even if Joe was healthy, I prepared to start. That way, if something happened to him,

I was ready. If nothing happened, I signaled in the plays. I did my part. But man, it was brutal to do all that work every week and have it be for nothing. Some games I would run a bunch of sprints after the final gun just to work off some of the steam.

My other responsibility was to quarterback the scout team in practice each week. Basically, I went against our defense to help prepare them for upcoming opponents. Charles Haley made a habit of trying to intimidate me by hitting me and saying crazy stuff to me. I ignored him. That sort of thing got old fast. Everyone knew that my presence created tension for Joe, which affected the whole team. In one respect, this made life unpleasant for me, but at the same time this creative tension brought out the best in both of us on the field. But not necessarily in everyone else.

The more I talked to John the more I thought I had to go to law school. I figured if he could work his way through med school while in the NFL, I could certainly work my way through law school.

I checked back in with the dean at BYU and was happy to learn that they had come up with a plan that would enable me to enroll. He called it "the Steve Young Plan." It required me to start classes as soon as the season ended, probably in late January or early February, depending on how deep the Niners went in the playoffs. I would audit classes for the winter semester. At the end of the semester I would take the exams. If I passed them, I would be eligible to then take the exams covering the fall semester classes that I had missed. If I passed the fall exams, I would become eligible to enroll the following year — in 1990 — as a first-year law student, at which point I could start accumulating credits.

In other words, BYU Law School would give me a trial run to see if I could pass the first-year exams. If I didn't, I was out. If I did, I could enroll a year later and retake the first-year classes for credit. Either way I had to pay tuition for the first year of audited classes. That's why it was dubbed the Steve Young Plan — it was so unappealing that no one else would agree to it. That was the idea.

I agreed to the plan.

On October 9, we play at home against Denver. We are 4-1. The Broncos are 2-4. But Joe struggles. Denver knocks him out of the game twice. Both times he returns. In the fourth quarter John Elway throws a touchdown pass to tie the game at 13.

Meantime, the wind gusts at Candlestick reach 40 miles per hour, making it nearly impossible to throw the ball. Bill tells me he's pulling Joe. I run onto the field and get booed. The game goes into overtime. I throw an interception and get booed even louder. Denver kicks a field goal and wins 16–13, dropping us to 4-2.

The next week Joe gets painkiller injections to his ribs and elbow before our game against the Rams. It's frustrating. I'm perfectly healthy. I want to start. I put my pads on every Sunday believing I will. But I don't. Joe does. We win by a field goal to improve to 5-2.

October 24, 1988. We're playing the Bears on *Monday Night Football*. The question is whether Joe is well enough to start. He is still ailing from injuries to his ribs and elbow. The Bears game is critical. They are 6-1. We are 5-2. Once again we look like the two best teams in the NFC. And the Bears haven't forgotten that we drubbed them 41–0 on Monday night last season when I had the best game of my pro career.

With Joe less than 100 percent, I figure I might start. But he says he can play. The Bears shut down our offense, and they give Joe a beating. I'm on the sideline, itching to get in the game. Bill sticks with Joe, and the Bears control the tempo. It's very late in the fourth quarter and we are losing 10–9 when Bill tells me something is wrong with Joe's elbow. He sends me in for the final series. There isn't enough time, and the Bears know we have to pass. So they send everyone. I throw a 1-yard pass completion and scramble twice for a total of three yards. We go three and out. The Bears run out the clock. Game over. We fall to 5-3.

I was now beside myself. The musical chairs approach at the starting quarterback position was driving me nuts. I resented Bill for putting me into games when we were behind and it was too late to catch up. Joe resented Bill every time he got pulled and I went in. The only thing we shared was mutual frustration toward Bill.

I called Leigh after the Bears game and told him I couldn't take this. I wanted either to play or to get traded. I loved being on the 49ers. But I wanted to play.

Leigh got it. He said he'd call Carmen Policy.

That night Leigh called me back and told me that Carmen begged me to be patient.

Later in the week Bill told me Joe wasn't going to be able to go against the Vikings. I was starting.

16

THE RUN

EVERY PLAYER RECEIVED two complimentary tickets for each home game. I rarely used mine. I had been in San Francisco for a year and a half, but I didn't really know many people outside the team. I didn't get out much and pretty much kept to myself. I didn't have family coming to the games either. My parents were way back in Connecticut, and my siblings were in college or med school.

A couple of days before the Vikings game I gave my tickets to Jim Herrmann, who had recently moved into The Ponderosa with John Frank and me. He called our college friend Greg "Mad Dog" Madsen, a huge supporter of mine who lived in the Bay Area. *Well,* I figured, *at least I'll have two people rooting for me.*

The Vikings had embarrassed us in the playoffs eight months earlier. The entire 49ers organization wanted to avenge the loss. Plus, we trailed the Rams and the Saints in the NFC West. At 5-3, we'd do grave damage to our playoff chances if we lost to Minnesota.

October 30, 1988. I get booed the first time I take the field. The booing gets louder when our first couple of drives stall. Late in the first quarter I get hit just as I release the ball and land on my back. A Vikings defender lands on top of me. He says: "You a Mormon?"

"Yeah."

"You're not Mormon."

"Yeah, I'm Mormon. Now get off me."

A few plays later I scramble toward the sideline, and the same guy shoves me out of bounds. I turn to head back to the huddle. But he's in my way.

"Are Mormons Christians?"

"Yeah."

"No, they're not."

"Yeah, we are."

I'm trying to win a football game, and this guy is all over me with questions about my religion.

The Vikings take a 7–0 lead in the second quarter, and the catcalls from the stands are relentless. Then the guy who has been hounding me about my religion sacks me. He won't let me up. "What's this about the Book of Mormon?" he says.

Typically, I don't mind being asked about my religion. But I don't want to discuss it during a game.

"I'll catch you after the game to chat," I tell him. "I don't want to see you again until then."

We end the first half down 7–3, and our fans are all over me.

I'm afraid that if I don't turn it around I'll get pulled.

In the third quarter I lead us on a 97-yard drive that ends with a 1-yard touchdown run by Roger Craig to finally put us up, 10–7.

But Minnesota counters with a 67-yard touchdown pass to Anthony Carter.

On the first play of our next possession I throw a 73-yard touchdown to John Taylor to put us back up 17–14. The crowd is now energized. Our offense is clicking for the first time all day.

At the start of the fourth quarter we get the ball back on our own 20. I hand off to Roger Craig, but the ball is stripped from his hands and Minnesota recovers. Moments later they score to go up 21–17.

For the remainder of the fourth quarter we can't move the ball. The game is slipping away. Minnesota sacks me four times, and I overthrow a couple of open receivers. I am getting booed again.

After our defense forces Minnesota to punt, we get the ball back on our own 33-yard line with a few minutes remaining. Bill sticks with me. If

I don't make something happen, the loss will rest squarely on my shoulders.

We run three plays and advance to the Minnesota 49-yard line. It's third-and-short. One minute and fifty-eight seconds remain.

Walsh calls a pass play. My first option is an in-route to wide receiver Mike Wilson.

I take a five-step drop and bring my arm back to throw. Wilson isn't open, and Minnesota's front four are pouring down on me like an avalanche. I pull the ball down, duck, and spin to my right. Three Vikings defenders and four of my linemen land in a heap. Still on my feet, somehow I stumble out of the pile and take off.

Tom Rathman sees me and turns upfield in front of me. Three Vikings defenders are coming at us. Rathman lunges to block the one in the middle, taking him out. The other two go airborne and hit me simultaneously. They both land on the ground. But I keep my feet. As a fourth tackler dives for my ankles, I break left toward the Vikings' sideline. The ball slips out of my hand, but I snatch it out of the air and sidestep another tackler.

At this point every other quarterback in the league would have headed out of bounds, avoiding the hit and stopping the clock. But as another defender approaches, I cut back toward the middle of the field, causing another Viking to fall down. Then I change directions again, heading downfield.

At the 30-yard line I pick up another block and change direction yet again. I burst between two linebackers before they can get a hand on me. At the 20 another linebacker reaches for me and misses. Then Jerry Rice delivers a block.

All that remains are two defensive backs pursuing me from the left and right. They are fast, and I'm out of breath. There is no way I'm going down. I split the defenders, stiff-arming one as I streak to the 10.

Still running, I look over my shoulder, lose my balance, and stumble at the 5. As Joey Browner closes in, I dive for the end zone. Frustrated, Browner jumps on my teammate Mike Wilson's back and pile-drives him down on me.

Touchdown!

The Stick erupts. I have never heard anything this loud. I rise to my feet, lungs burning. I desperately need oxygen. My teammate Guy McIntyre pounds me on the back. More players surround me. The crowd noise is deafening. I can't even hear my own teammates. Our fans are delirious. They are cheering for me. I have run 49 yards to put us up 24–21 with just over a minute remaining in the game.

My legs feel like jelly. I have nothing left in the tank. I am completely drained. Physically. Emotionally. Mentally. Pure adrenaline gets me to the sideline.

Bill has a big smile on his face. "Pretty good job," he says, wryly. "Glad you know what you're doing." That's pretty high praise coming from a guy who rarely gives compliments. I'm grateful Bill values the combination of my legs and my arm.

With the final seconds ticking down at The Stick, I stand and gaze at the fans through my face mask. I look at the upper decks. A sea of people in red and gold are shouting their approval. The noise gives me an inner sense of satisfaction. Savoring the moment, I wish time would stand still. I long for moments like this.

As soon as the game ends I find the Vikings defender who was badgering me about Mormonism. I compliment him on his play. He congratulates me on the run, and we both laugh about the dialogue between us during the game.

Eddie DeBartolo is standing outside the locker room, smacking and hugging players. He throws his arms around me and tells me he wants to see me in the owner's box after I've showered. Reporters are stacked up at my locker. I remove my shoulder pads and start fielding questions.

An hour passes, and I meet up with Leigh. I have never been to the owner's box before. Leigh says he'll lead the way. On the way up he can't stop talking about the run. He's convinced that it will force Walsh to start me again.

"Steve, trust me. It's going to go down as one of the greatest runs in NFL history!"

"That was just chaos," I tell him.

Leigh is laughing about all the crazy cutbacks, the way I made guys dive and miss, the way I stumbled and dove into the end zone. At that

moment in the Vikings game I was desperate. I had to make a play. I had
to do something great. The result was a long, frenetic run. It was all by
instinct.

Eddie's suite is directly above the corner of the end zone where I scored.
It's packed with Eddie's buddies from Youngstown, Ohio. The moment I
enter everyone stands and applauds. It gives me goose bumps.

"Steve, that was amazing," Eddie says.

"Truly amazing," Carmen adds.

Jack Lambert kisses my cheek and gives me a bear hug. He, more than
anyone in the room, knows how important this moment is to me. Up to
this point, Eddie DeBartolo has always treated me very well. But now I
feel like part of the family. I'm in the inner sanctum. I have the sense that
things are finally changing for me.

By the time Leigh and I left the suite the stadium was long empty. While
we made our way down to the player parking lot, Leigh got pretty animated. He told me that getting invited to Eddie's box was a rite of passage.
He even started quoting the Bible.

I laughed at how carried away he was getting.

But he was serious. He reminded me that Eddie loved Joe like an
adopted son. Eddie's heart bled Montana. "But today," he said, "everyone
in that owner's box saw something they have never seen before on a football field. Something so stunning and exciting that it made their hearts
stop."

"Bro, you need to calm down," I told him.

"Steve, quarterbacks don't do what you did today."

"I'm not the first scrambler," I said.

Leigh said there was a big difference between scrambling laterally in
order to get free to make a pass and scrambling down the field to advance
the ball on the ground. "Today they realized that they are witnessing a
very, very special talent that can win games in a way that no quarterback
has in the past."

"I was just running."

"That's the point, Steve."

"But I want to be known as a passing quarterback, not a running one."

"Geez, Steve, you are like a pretty girl who wants to be known for her brains."

In the parking lot outside the stadium, I met up with Jim Herrmann and Greg Madsen. My Jeep was the only vehicle remaining. We hopped in and headed to Max's for a big meal. "It's on me," I told them. Of course, with those guys it was always on me.

17

MISSED OPPORTUNITY

AFTER WE BEAT MINNESOTA, Bill wanted to make me the perma-nent starter. Our next opponent was the Cardinals. Joe was healthy enough to play, but I got the ball. Joe wasn't happy. He didn't say anything to me. Nobody did. But everybody realized that the quarterback contro-versy had now entered uncharted territory.

The night before the Cardinals game, Brent and I talked until well past midnight. With John Frank still sidelined with a broken hand, Brent was starting at tight end. We broke down the defense. We reviewed our plays. We each downed a gallon of ice cream. It was well after midnight before we finally crashed.

November 6, 1988. It is scorching hot at game time in Phoenix. Bill pulls me aside. "If you play well today, I think you can keep the job," he says.

We roll to a 16–0 halftime lead. At the start of the third quarter I throw a touchdown pass to Brent. I run to the end zone to congratulate him, and he hoists me in the air. We are up 23–0. When I get to the sideline, Walsh says, "I think we can keep this going." I know what that means — we win this game and I'll start again next week.

The Cardinals finally get on the board with 10:51 remaining in the fourth quarter. We're still up 23–7. But we start committing stupid pen-alties, and our defense is withering in the heat. Phoenix adds another touchdown and a field goal. Suddenly we are clinging to a six-point lead with two minutes to play. On a critical third-and-long situation, I fake a handoff right and bootleg to my left. I'm sprinting for the first-down marker on the sideline. With defenders closing in, I can either keep running for the first-down marker on the sideline or I can remain in bounds and get tackled short of the first down, which would keep the clock running. I lunge for the marker and go crashing out of bounds.

The ref spots the ball just shy of the first down. From my knees, I scream at him and jam my index finger into the turf, showing him where he should have marked the ball. He ignores me. I jump up and grab his arm. "I know I was past the marker," I shout.

The official doesn't like me grabbing his arm. The Cardinals start complaining, and I argue with them too. There are so many ramifications to that mark, especially for me. If we get the first down, we win and I keep playing. If we don't get the first down, we lose and I don't get to keep playing.

The ref sticks to his original mark, inches shy of the first down. We punt, giving the ball back to Phoenix with 1:06 remaining. Neil Lomax drives his team the length of the field. With three seconds left, he throws a touchdown pass to Roy Green. The extra point is good. We lose 24–23.

Eddie DeBartolo went off in the locker room afterward. We squandered a 23-point lead in just fifteen minutes. He tried to throw a locker, but it was too heavy. So he punched it and broke his hand. Walsh was livid too. It looked like we would miss the playoffs.

Whenever we lost, no one was more upset than Eddie. He was the kind of owner who would have suited up and put on a helmet if he'd had the size. There was no one I would have rather played for. Before he came along, the relationship between player and owner was at best a hello and a handshake. In many cases, owners treated players like chattel. Not Eddie. He treated players like we were part of his family. And he wasn't just a friend when the lights were on. He was there for us night and day. That's why everybody wanted to play for him. He transformed the NFL.

At the same time, his expectations were steep. The day after the loss to Phoenix, Bill had a breakdown of sorts. The pressure was apparently just too much. The team found out when Joe and Ronnie Lott called a team meeting. They told us that Bill was going through a rough spot. We had to step up for him.

Days later Joe resumed his place as the starter. I blamed myself. I was on the best team with the best quarterback job in the league. I wanted it and I wanted it badly. Yet I knew I had blown a chance, by inches, to take it.

I vowed to do everything possible to ensure I didn't miss my next opportunity.

Our next game was against the Raiders. Joe struggled the entire game. He threw for just 160 yards. His longest completion was 28 yards. He never found the end zone. But Bill never put me in. We lost 9–3, dropping our record to 6-5. The headline the following morning in the *San Francisco Chronicle* read: "The 49ers Are Dead, Gone, and Buried."

The loss to the Raiders marked the low point of the season. Leading up to the Redskins game, Ronnie Lott called another players-only meeting and delivered one of the best speeches I ever heard. He told us we were in a position to do something that had never been done — come back from the dead to win a Super Bowl.

Coming from anyone else, that kind of talk would have been dismissed as crazy. But everyone believed in Ronnie. He kept saying: "One heartbeat. One heartbeat."

"Put aside the petty bickering and personal agendas," he told us. "It's for the good of the team."

"One heartbeat" became our theme. The Redskins were the defending Super Bowl champions. We routed them, 37–21, and Joe had his best game of the season. From there he went on a roll. The team followed, winning four straight to clinch a playoff spot. During that stretch I was returned to signaling in plays from the sideline.

One afternoon I left practice with John Frank. On the way home he stopped for gas. While he pumped, my dad called. He tried to encourage me to remain positive. But I was way too frustrated for a pep talk. I hopped back in the car.

"Who was that?" John said.

"My dad," I said.

"I can tell you're really bummed. What did he say?"

"He said to realize how lucky I am to be in the position I'm in as a quarterback," I told him. "He reminded me how many people would be so envious to be in my position."

"He's right, Steve," John said. "Your dad's right."

I knew that, but I just didn't want to hear it.

It would be years before I could get that kind of perspective on my situation. At that moment, though, I really would have rather been a lawyer than a backup quarterback. I never would have gone to San Francisco if I'd known I'd be a backup. It had now been two years, and I was done with backing up.

We won our division and earned a bye week during the wild-card round of the playoffs. With two weeks to prepare for our playoff opponent, Bill Walsh gave us Christmas Eve off. My parents and all my siblings were spending the holidays in Park City. They wanted me to join them at the Utah ski resort for Christmas Eve dinner. John Frank didn't celebrate Christmas. But I convinced him to come with me. Our flight from San Francisco had a two-hour layover in Las Vegas.

John insisted that we to go the Strip. I had never gambled in my life. The last place on earth I wanted to be on Christmas Eve was in a casino. It just felt sacrilegious.

"It's all right, Steve," John told me. "Tonight you can be an honorary Jew."

He dragged me there. We ended up at a craps table at Caesar's Palace. The table was bathtub-shaped with a green felt surface. There were stacks of betting chips along the back side. Someone called a boxman controlled the chips and the money being put down by the players standing around the table. Another guy with a long wooden stick pushed chips to two dealers, who interacted with the players. A bunch of people were standing around the table, taking turns throwing dice. It was all very foreign to me.

John told me I had to try it.

I told him I didn't know anything about the game.

He said it was easy. He'd help me.

I told him I would not spend any money gambling.

He slapped down some money, and a dealer handed me the dice. I rolled and everyone at the table cheered. One of the dealers flipped on a light, and the other dealer gave me another set of dice and told me to roll again. I did and everyone at the table cheered again.

"You're on a roll," John said.

I really didn't know what I was doing. I just kept rolling and people kept cheering. The dealers were pushing chips my way. A crowd began to gather around the craps table. Pretty soon people were lined up three and four deep.

"Who is this guy?" one guy said.

"He looks like Steve Young," another guy said.

I said nothing.

"Whoever he is he's got a hot hand."

I rolled again. Everyone roared.

"Hey, look, he's throwing the dice lefty too," someone said. "He must be Steve Young."

"No," I said with a smile.

"You're a lefty," the guy said. "Are you sure you're not Steve Young?"

"*Steve Young* throwing dice on Christmas Eve in Vegas?" I said. "No, no, no."

John Frank was cracking up. "You're like Rain Man," he said.

Now I was laughing. The scene where Tom Cruise takes Dustin Hoffman to a casino in Vegas was among my favorites. I got into it and called for the dice. I started to have fun. It was a new experience. I had a pile of money. When I got up from the table, people were applauding me.

I waved them off and turned to leave.

"What about your money?" one of the dealers said.

"Oh, you guys keep it," I told him. "Merry Christmas."

That caused a stir. We scooted out during the chaos.

A couple of hours later we were in Park City. We arrived just in time for Christmas Eve dinner. My parents and my siblings treated John like family. We prayed before the meal and expressed gratitude for the birth of the Savior. We shared memories of Christmases past. We exchanged gifts. I even dressed up as Santa Claus for my nieces and nephews. John had never been to a Christmas celebration. But he felt right at home.

On the flight back to San Francisco, John thanked me.

"There are a lot of things I like that are unique to Mormonism," he told me. "It's a really nice religion. I really love the family values."

I thanked him for spending Christmas with my family.

"Steve, every Mormon girl I meet is beautiful, especially your sister. And every Mormon I meet is kind. I'd be a Mormon if it wasn't for that Jesus thing."

I cracked up.

We breezed through the playoffs. We torched Minnesota 34–9 in the first round. A week later we went to Chicago and routed the heavily favored Bears in a game that featured 30-mile-per-hour winds and temperatures that reached 26 degrees below zero. It was one of the coldest playoff games in NFL history. After the game the press asked Joe about the season-long quarterback controversy and the fact that I had started games while he was hurt.

"I didn't feel I was ever hurt," Joe said. "Bill felt I was, and he has the right to make that decision."

January 22, 1989. It's the Super Bowl, and I am on the sideline at Joe Robbie Stadium in Miami. I am ready to play. But my job today is to do everything I can to help Joe lead us to victory. One heartbeat. The game begins as a contest of field goals. Neither team has much success moving the ball. The first touchdown is not scored until the third quarter, when Cincinnati's Stanford Jennings returns a kickoff 93 yards to put the Bengals up 13–6. Joe ties it with a 14-yard touchdown pass to Rice in the fourth quarter. But Cincinnati kicks a late field goal to go up 16–13.

With three minutes to play, we get the ball back on our own 8-yard line. I can't help noticing as I huddle with Joe and Bill on the sideline that Joe looks completely relaxed. It's as if he feels no pressure. I signal in the plays, and he calmly orchestrates a flawless drive, managing the clock and moving the offense within field goal range. But Joe isn't looking to tie it. He wants to win it. With thirty-four seconds remaining, he throws a game-winning touchdown pass to John Taylor. We win 20–16. It is the greatest comeback in Super Bowl history.

In the locker room after the game we all kneel and say the Lord's

Prayer. Forty-five tired, emotionally drained men, holding hands in the bowels of the stadium. We all remember what Ronnie Lott said at the low point of the season — we are a team with one heartbeat. The victory gives the 49ers three Super Bowl wins in the 1980s. We go from being declared dead and buried to being branded the team of the decade.

Forty-eight hours after the Super Bowl I landed in Provo. I was twenty-seven and about to start law school. I needed a place to stay, and my kid sister Melissa was a junior at BYU. She lived with another girl from Connecticut in a two-bedroom apartment near campus. It had a walk-in closet under the basement steps. The space was just big enough for a cot, a makeshift desk, and a little shelf to hold my law books. That was good enough for me. As always, I kept my clothes in a duffle bag.

I was way behind my law school peers. I studied in my little room. I strung a light over my cot and immersed myself in Civil Procedure and Torts. After two seasons playing behind Joe, studying law books was therapeutic. To master the material I created my own handwritten outlines by spending my nights going through law books. Then I memorized them and my notes. This process enabled me to ace the exams.

A few weeks into law school John Frank visited me. I picked him up at the airport and drove him to my sister's place.

"Where's your apartment?" he said.

"I just share space with my sister."

We went down to the basement. I threw my law books in the walk-in closet. John saw the cot and a copy of *Black's Law Dictionary* next to it.

"What is this?" John said. "It looks like the inside of a submarine."

"It's my apartment," I told him.

He laughed. "What?"

"This is where I stay."

"Are you serious?"

"Yeah. I'm going to law school. I need a place to stay while I'm here. So this is where I stay."

Later in the day we went skiing in Park City. We were on the chairlift when John turned to me and said: "Steve, I'm done."

"What do you mean you're done?"

"I'm going to retire."

I couldn't believe it. He was only twenty-six. He was a starter on a winning Super Bowl team.

"Why are you going to do that?" I said. "You are at the top of your game."

He gave me his reasons. His body took a pounding in '88. The hand fracture in particular made him realize that being a surgeon meant more to him than being a football player.

"Well," I said, "make sure you think about this. Give it a lot of thought."

John spent a few days in Provo. Before he left, he challenged me to hike to the big white *Y* on the side of the mountain overlooking the BYU campus. In all my years in Provo I had never been to the Y. It took us a couple of hours. We were winded when we reached the spot. A couple of maintenance workers were using industrial paint guns to give it a fresh coat of paint. John thought we should commemorate our accomplishment by painting the Y.

"Can we help you?" I said to the workers.

They had no idea who we were. But they saw that we were serious. They handed us the equipment, and we painted the Y. I wished John wasn't retiring, but I admired him. His dedication to medical school was partly responsible for my decision to press forward with law school. Plus, I had my dad telling me that I was only one hit away from being out of a job. A law degree, he insisted, would give me job security when football was over.

I knew my dad was right—no matter how long I played, I needed an advanced degree to do something else important. I always wanted my tombstone to read: HERE LIES STEVE YOUNG. HE DID THIS, THIS, AND THIS. AND, OH BY THE WAY, HE PLAYED SOME FOOTBALL AS WELL.

At the end of the semester I took the exams and passed all of them. Then I took the exams for the fall semester classes that I had been unable to attend. Thanks to my detailed and memorized outlines, I passed those too. The dean told me I had qualified to enroll the following year as a full-time law student.

18

UNCASHED CHECKS

I RETURNED TO THE Bay Area just in time for training camp. For the third year in a row I needed a place to live. My good friend Harris Barton invited me to move in with him. He lived alone in a house he rented in Palo Alto. He offered me a room, with a bed and a nightstand. We hired a chef too. Her name was Iola, and she prepared some of the best down-home Southern food I ever tasted. Harris and I had as many as ten teammates over each night for dinner.

Training camp felt different this time around. The biggest change was the absence of Bill Walsh. He retired right after the Super Bowl. His long-time defensive coordinator, George Seifert, was the new head coach. Seifert made clear that the musical chairs approach to the quarterback position was history. It was a foregone conclusion that Joe was the starter and I was the backup.

I began to tell Leigh incessantly that I needed out.

"These are my peak years," I told him. "I have to play now. I need to get out of here."

The quarterback situation under Bill drove everybody crazy. But at least he believed in me and wanted me to play. George, on the other hand, was a defensive guy, and he wanted to make the quarterback situation simple. So he did.

Under George's approach, I knew it was going to be a long season. The one thing that took the edge off was the arrival of third-string quarterback Steve Bono. The Niners had signed him during the offseason. I immediately got along with him. So did Joe. The three of us started golfing together in training camp. We also played a lot of pranks. For instance, the entire team had bicycles at camp to get from place to place. Joe and Steve and I would hide certain players' bikes. One time we chained all fifty bikes together so no one could go anywhere.

At the end of camp, we signed All-Pro linebacker Matt Millen, the former Raider who heckled me as the Mormon in the backfield. He was a great addition to the team. During the week he regularly invited Harris and me to have dinner with his wife Pat and the rest of his family. There was only one caveat. He wanted us there at 6:30 sharp, and he wanted us out the door by 6:45. "Pat wants to feed you," he'd say with a smile. "But I've been around you guys all day long and I don't want to be around you anymore."

On the field Matt was as tough as they come. But he had a great sense of humor, and he had a way of making me feel like part of the family the minute I stepped inside his home.

We finally played our first home game on October 1 against the Los Angeles Rams. The night before we checked into the Marriott by the San Francisco Airport. We stayed there before every home game. Most of the players got individual rooms. Brent Jones and I were an exception. We shared room 9043.

As noted earlier, we always stayed in the same room and followed the same routine. After check-in we raced to order room service before the rest of the team got settled. We each ordered multiple entrees and devoured our food. Then we discussed our opponent. In this case it was the Rams. They were 3-0 like us, and they posed some challenges.

In fact, the next day LA upset us at home, 13–12. But Brent was Joe's favorite receiver on the day. He caught five passes for 51 yards. For the fourth consecutive week I didn't see action.

After the Rams game Jim Herrmann flew out to visit. I was depressed. The season was a quarter of the way over, and I hadn't taken a snap. Herm tried to cheer me up. He spent the week on Harris Barton's couch. During the day he rode with me to practice. I leased a new Jeep. In checking out the interior of the car, Herm opened the lid over the storage compartment between the front seats. He reached in and pulled out a handful of 49ers paychecks.

"Steve, are these checks?"

"Yeah."

"Dude, there are three or four of them in here."

"I know."

He did the math. "Whoa! There is a quarter of a million dollars here," he said.

I said nothing.

"Bro, don't you think you should cash these?"

"I can't cash those things."

"What? Why not?"

"I don't feel like I'm earning the money."

"What are you talking about?"

"I just don't feel good about cashing them. I'm not even playing. I'm not earning the money."

That night I moved the checks to a drawer in my nightstand, where I left them for the rest of the season.

October 15, 1989. We're 4-1, and we're in Dallas to face the winless Cowboys. Joe is out with a leg injury, so I'm starting. Dallas is starting rookie quarterback Troy Aikman, the number-one pick in the draft. The Cowboys were sold to Jerry Jones in the off-season, and he promptly fired legendary coach Tom Landry and replaced him with former University of Miami head coach Jimmy Johnson.

I can't wait to get going. In the first quarter I throw a 36-yard touchdown pass to Brent Jones. But Dallas's defense stiffens, and the first half ends with the score tied at 7.

Eager to make something happen, I run more in the third quarter. I'm making big gains, but I sprain my left shoulder. It hurts, but I'm not about to come out. I tell the team doctor I'm fine. George sticks with me, and we score 17 straight points, including an 8-yard touchdown pass to Jerry Rice. I throw just five incompletions all afternoon and rush for 79 yards on 11 carries. We win 31-14 to improve to 5-1.

• • •

Two nights later, on October 17, I went to the World Series with Harris Barton. The quarterback rivalry was hard on everybody, but particularly on Harris because we were roommates. That made things awkward in the locker room. At home we simply ignored the topic.

We settled into our seats behind home plate at Candlestick Park. It was Game 3 between the Giants and A's in what had been dubbed "The Battle of the Bay." It was late afternoon and the sun was shining. Jose Canseco and Mark McGwire hit bombs in batting practice. Stevie Wonder was about to perform the National Anthem when we heard something like the rush of a jet flying low overhead. The stadium shook and the light towers were swaying. Harris and I looked at each other.

"Holy crap!" I said.

"Wow, what was that?" he said.

It felt like an earthquake. The entire stadium erupted in cheers, as if to say, *Welcome to San Francisco!*

At that moment, no one inside the stadium was aware of the devastation in other parts of the city. The fans expected the game to start. But Candlestick had lost power, and some of the concrete on the upper deck had shaken loose. When the game was canceled, Harris and I made our way out of Candlestick. It was a mob scene. By the time we reached the car, there were reports of collapsed highways and bridges, power outages, and fires.

The drive back to our place was surreal. The Bay Area was frighteningly dark. The enormity of the situation settled in over the next forty-eight hours. A magnitude 6.9 earthquake had struck, and the damage to the city was catastrophic. Sixty people died. People were homeless. Businesses were destroyed. Roadways and bridges were upended. The structural safety of Candlestick Park was now in question, causing Major League Baseball to indefinitely postpone the World Series. We were not even sure if we could play our next game.

When we returned to practice days after the quake, I didn't feel like playing. A lot of guys didn't. It just felt trivial and wrong to be playing a game when so many people were homeless and families were burying loved ones. But 49ers vice president John McVay reminded us that people in the Bay Area needed a diversion from the tragedy. They also needed to feel a sense of normalcy. The games would go on.

· · ·

October 22, 1989. With Candlestick closed, the NFL has considered shifting our game against the Patriots to New England. But Eddie DeBartolo has insisted on keeping the game in the Bay Area. We end up playing at Stanford Stadium in Palo Alto. Over 86,000 people turn out. That's 15,000 more than Candlestick can hold.

On the second play of the game Patriots running back Johnny Stephens collides with our safety Jeff Fuller. Stephens pops right up. Fuller is motionless. Doctors and trainers run to him. They have to unscrew his face mask to enable him to breathe easier. But he never stands up. Eventually they lift him onto a gurney, and he leaves the stadium in an ambulance. At Stanford Hospital doctors determine that he has fractured two vertebrae and sustained severe nerve damage. The use of his right arm is permanently lost. His football career is over.

My father was right. Professional football players are always one hit away from being out of the game. But I don't think about that. None of us do. Football players feel indestructible. Once you get used to the speed and physicality of the game, it becomes normal. You actually feel like you're above getting hurt. So when a teammate sustains a career-ending injury, it is more than shocking.

That probably doesn't sound right to anyone outside the NFL. But when playing is what you do, you feel invincible. You don't see the dangers, and you don't consider that something horrible could be right around the corner. The minute you worry about getting hit you lose your edge.

In the second quarter Joe throws a touchdown pass to Jerry to tie the game at 7. But later in the quarter Joe takes a big hit that knocks him out of the game. At that point the score is tied 10–10. I take over and complete all but one of my passes, including three touchdown passes. We win 37–20.

Joe's injury forces him to miss his next start against the Jets. I lead us to a 23–10 win on the road, improving our record to 7-1.

I had just led the team to three straight wins. During that stretch, I completed 74 percent of my passes (37 of 50) with only one interception, while racking up 544 yards and six touchdown throws. I also rushed for over

100 yards, averaging almost six yards per carry. That's what drove me crazy — when I played I put up big numbers and we won.

The following week Joe started, and we beat the Giants 34–24 on *Monday Night Football*, establishing us as the best team in the league and giving us a leg up on home-field advantage for the playoffs. But Joe took a beating, and I ended up starting the following week in Atlanta.

December 3, 1989. It's unusually cold at Atlanta-Fulton County Stadium. We have the best record in the league; the Falcons have one of the worst. Yet we trail 10–6 at the half. I begin the second half by throwing a 38-yard touchdown pass to John Taylor. In the fourth quarter, I run for a touchdown to put the game away. I end up completing 91 percent of my passes for 175 yards. It's my best game of the season, and we improve to 11-2.

But the musical chairs approach continues. A week later Joe starts and leads the team to a dramatic come-from-behind victory over the Rams in Anaheim on *Monday Night Football*.

I was happy for the team. But I absolutely loathed my situation. The prospect of replacing Joe was ridiculous. *What was I thinking? It's never going to happen. Just forget it. Forget the whole thing.*

In the locker room a crowd of reporters surrounded Joe's locker. I tossed my shoulder pads on the floor. Nobody noticed me exit the locker room and return to the field. The lights were still on. A couple of television reporters were stationed in one corner of the stadium. Otherwise it was just the Anaheim Stadium grounds crew and the people who picked up trash in the stands. I sprinted from one end zone to the other. I sprinted back. I did it again. I felt the eyes of the stadium workers on me. But I didn't return their gaze. I just kept running 100-yard wind sprints. I had to. I couldn't take just standing around anymore. If I couldn't run up and down the field in game situations, I figured I would at least imagine it.

Thirty minutes later I left the field. I was drenched in sweat. My legs and lungs burned. It was close to 10:00 PM. I felt better. A little.

After the Rams game I went to see my little friend Danny Jackson, the cancer patient. He had turned thirteen. He had also undergone an operation to correct his scoliosis. But during the procedure his spinal cord had been accidentally severed. The result was that he would be a paraplegic for life.

We arranged for him to visit our practice facility. He used his chin to operate a lever that enabled him to get around in his motorized wheelchair. "As soon as I get my legs back I'm going to take Jerry Rice's place," he said.

I started to think he didn't understand the extreme difficulty of his personal circumstances. I was sure he didn't realize how tough it was for the rest of us to watch him struggle. Our team wished we could do more.

"Don't worry," he told me. "I'm doing great."

I didn't know how much I was helping Danny. But I knew he was a major inspiration to me. I was drawing strength from a kid who was hanging on by a thread. I decided to make his words my motto: *Don't worry. I'm doing great.*

December 17, 1989. We're at home against Buffalo, and I'm starting while Joe recovers from a rib injury from the week before. I'm out of sync, and Buffalo leads 3–0 at the half. We've lost only two games all season. I simply can't afford to lose when I start. I have to be perfect. In the second half I rush for one touchdown and throw one to Rice. We score 21 second-half points to win 21–10 and improve to a league-best 13-2.

A week later we blank the Bears 24–0 to finish the regular season with the best record in the league at 14-2. Joe has the best season of his career, passing for 3,512 yards and 26 touchdowns. He's named MVP of the league for the first time in his career.

In five games I throw for over 1,000 yards passing, including eight touchdowns. Combined, Joe and I have thrown for close to 5,000 yards and 34 touchdowns. We are heavily favored to repeat as Super Bowl champions.

For Christmas I went to see Danny Jackson at his home. His father told me Danny was fading fast. I had to bend over to hear Danny. "Great game," he whispered out of the corner of his mouth. His head and face were all twisted and distorted from the cancer.

It was all I could do not to cry. But I tried to be strong for him.

"You guys are the greatest," Danny told me.

In the first round of the NFC playoffs we crushed the Vikings, 41–13. We expected to face the Giants in the NFC Championship, but Los Angeles upset them in the Meadowlands. So we ended up going against our division rival, the Rams. We beat LA 30–3.

We faced Denver in Super Bowl XXIV at the Superdome in New Orleans. A couple of days before the game I got a call in my hotel room. It was Danny Jackson's father. He told me Danny had passed away. This time I cried. Danny's father did too. But through his tears he shared what Danny had told him just before he passed. He had told his father that dying was okay because he was looking forward to watching the Super Bowl from above.

"If you guys feel someone on the sidelines," his dad told me, "it's probably just Danny, looking for the best seat in the house."

Denver was no match for us. Joe threw five touchdown passes. Rice caught three. We won 55–10. I played in the final four minutes, and I loved the experience. But it was bittersweet. I loved that we had won, but whenever I didn't make a contribution I was disappointed, especially in the Super Bowl. I knew I wasn't supposed to play. But emotionally, I had prepared myself to play. I was disciplined about that. I had to be ready to play in case I was called on. It wasn't easy to prepare and prepare for big games, only to end up watching.

It was the 49ers' fourth Super Bowl championship of the decade. Joe was named Super Bowl MVP for the third time in his career, and we were crowned the team of the decade.

Days after the Super Bowl I was back in law school in Provo. About a week later I got a phone call from Eddie DeBartolo.

"Steve, what the hell is going on?"

"What?"

"Your whole salary last year has not been paid. What's going on?"

Oh, boy. He was furious, and I knew why. "Yeah," I said, "I didn't cash my checks."

"C'mon, Steve! What the hell is this?"

"But I have them."

"Well, will you please cash them? It's the end of the year. We've got books to balance. Can you do that?"

"Yeah."

"You're an important part of this team," he told me.

I hung up and called Harris Barton back in San Francisco. A season's worth of checks were still in my nightstand where I had left them.

"Can you go in my bedroom?" I told him. "In the drawer next to my bed there are some checks."

He laughed. "Yeah, I know where they are."

"Well, could you send them to me? I've got to get them in the bank."

The next day I received a FedEx envelope containing $4 million in checks.

Winning Super Bowls was great. But at twenty-eight years old, I couldn't help wondering if joining the 49ers had been a mistake. Joe looked like he might play another five years. By that time I'd be thirty-three and my best years would be behind me.

One year remained on my contract. It seemed absurd to ask to be traded from the best team in the league. But it would be no more absurd than spending my career as a backup. I spent hours on the phone with Leigh. Every call ended the same way, with me saying, "Get me out of here. I'm sick of this."

He agreed that I should go elsewhere. He called Carmen and told him I wanted out. Carmen said what he'd been saying for three years. Tell Steve to hang on just a little bit longer.

I told Leigh to tell Carmen I was tired of holding on. I didn't want to win Super Bowls holding a clipboard on the sidelines. I wanted to win one on the field, and that was never going to happen in San Francisco. Not as long as Joe was around.

Leigh insisted that it wasn't healthy for my career or my self-confidence to stay in San Francisco. But the 49ers refused to trade me. I would have to endure at least one more season before I could become a restricted free agent.

19

TIMES ARE CHANGING

MY DAD WAS a man of routines. He started every workday with an early morning trip to the Greenwich YMCA, where he swam, jogged, and went through a regimen of push-ups and sit-ups. My dad was also insanely competitive. One morning a guy said to him: "How many full sit-ups can you do?" My dad said, "One hundred." The guy said: "I'll take your hundred and do two-fifty." My dad said: "You're on."

For the next six months Grit and this guy had a daily morning duel to see who could do more sit-ups. They got to a point where they were each doing 1,100 sit-ups when the other guy finally said: "You win. I've had it."

But my dad didn't quit. Nope. Not Grit. He decided to see how far he could push himself, and every week he pushed harder. This went on for a few years. By the time I got to training camp in 1990, he was up to 8,000 sit-ups in one session.

I called him at home and told him he was nuts. He told me it was a good workout. It had become a personal challenge to see how far he could go. The desk manager at the Greenwich Y was arriving at 3:30 in the morning to let him in. It took him three hours to go through his sit-up routine every morning. I pictured him alone on his exercise mat: 7,451. 7,452. 7,453. 7,454.

If my dad could do that, I figured I could step up my conditioning too. While I wasn't playing I might as well train. I could get faster. I could get stronger. At some point I would get my chance to start. And I would be ready.

Attempting to become the first team in NFL history to win three straight Super Bowls, we started the '90 season by going 10-0. Joe started every game and was well on his way to another MVP season. I made cameo appearances in the closing minutes of a couple of games. But I felt like a player without a purpose.

On December 3, 1990, we faced the Giants on *Monday Night Football* at Candlestick. We were both 10-1. The outcome of the game was likely to determine which one of us played at home in the NFC Championship game.

In pregame warm-ups, Giants nose tackle Jim Burt walked up to Ronnie Lott and said: "Hey, man, Phil Simms said you're washed up."

"What?" Lott said.

"Yeah. Not only that," Burt continued, "but he says you can't run ... you can't do it anymore."

Those were fighting words. And the game was played like a street fight. It featured some of the hardest hitting I'd ever witnessed. Even the coaches went at it. Bill Parcells and George Seifert shouted profanities across the field at each other. We won, 7–3, but tempers continued to flair. The first-ever postgame prayer was supposed to take place at midfield. Before the two teams knelt, Ronnie Lott and Phil Simms got into a face mask–to–face mask shoving match on the 50-yard line. The prayer got moved to the end zone. It was that kind of night. Both teams fully expected to see each other in the playoffs.

With two games remaining, we were 13-1. Over the course of the season I had stepped on the field in the closing minutes of four games. I'd thrown one pass the entire season. One pass in fourteen games! The prime years of my career were being wasted. I was dying in San Francisco.

On the night before our game against New Orleans on December 23, George Seifert told me that Joe had a strained lower abdominal muscle and couldn't play. I was starting.

The Saints were 6-8, and we had already secured home-field advantage throughout the playoffs. So we were basically playing for pride. Still, I felt the pressure to get us to 14-1.

December 23, 1990. The Stick is a sea of red and white because so many fans are dressed up like Santa Claus. It's a festive atmosphere. Besides being two days before Christmas, we are on a fast track to our third consecutive Super Bowl.

I play one of the best games of my career, completing 22 of 37 pass attempts with no interceptions. I also rush for over 102 yards on just eight carries. But turnovers hurt us. Late in the fourth quarter we trail 13–10. I drive us into field goal range. With fifty-three seconds left, I hand the ball off to Dexter Carter. He fumbles on the Saints' 20-yard line. We lose and fall to 13-2.

The loss has no bearing on the standings. But it matters a lot to me. The team is 13-1 in Joe's starts. We've lost in my only start. I feel fully responsible.

I didn't want to see anybody. I just wanted to go home and go to bed. But a group of Mormons had planned to go caroling that night. Before the game I'd said I'd go. So I did.

Exhausted, frustrated, and downright mad, I was in no mood to sing. Two hours after losing to the Saints, I was on the doorstep of a Bay Area family that had adopted eleven severely disabled children. I had 49ers T-shirts for each child.

The family invited us into their home. The adopted children were in wheelchairs. Some were paraplegics. Some were quadriplegics. A few had muscular disorders. All of them wore 49ers hats and sweatshirts. Hours earlier they had watched the game. When they saw me they lit up.

One child had no arms or legs. He was literally reduced to a head and chest. To move he rolled like a ball. He was totally dependent on others. But when he sat in his electric wheelchair, he became remarkably mobile.

I couldn't control my emotions while singing "Silent Night." Tears streamed down my face. As he looked up at me I was overwhelmed by this boy's courage. Professional sports have a way of creating a false sense of self-importance. Suddenly, the suffering I'd experienced over our loss to the Saints seemed utterly insignificant.

After we sang, all the kids wanted to meet me. I stepped forward. One little boy was mute. He flashed a smile when I handed him a T-shirt. The boy next to him was also unable to speak, but he had a computer monitor on his lap. He wrote messages on it using a light held to his head by a Velcro strap. I could tell he wanted to write me a message. I knelt down. Using the light, he wrote: YOU BLEW IT.

He grinned.

I laughed.

Seven days later we close out the season at Minnesota. Joe starts, but our offense is uninspired. We're down 10–0 when Joe takes a big hit just before the half. George sends me out to start the second half. Eager to redeem myself after the loss to the Saints, I complete 15 of 24 passes for 205 yards. In the fourth quarter I throw touchdown passes to Jerry Rice and John Taylor to give us a come-from-behind 20–17 win.

For the second year in a row we finished 14-2, and also for the second year in a row Joe Montana was voted MVP of the league. He was getting better with age.

Meantime, in 1990 I started just one game and only played in six. I threw a total of 62 passes. Each statistical category marked a low point for my four years in San Francisco. At least under Bill Walsh I had hope. Bill and Carmen Policy treated me like a starting quarterback in waiting, and I got plenty of chances to play. But with George Seifert, I was just a pedestrian backup. That had a real negative effect on my psyche. I was actually starting to see myself as a backup. My career was wasting away, and I was losing my edge.

January 20, 1991. It is the NFC Championship game against the Giants at Candlestick. Two days earlier Joe came down with the flu. He is too weak to practice. He can't even get out of bed, so I prepare to start. But by this point, I know Joe. They'd have to put him in a straitjacket to keep him from playing.

I'm right. Joe starts. The game is tight the whole way. It's a lot like our Monday night game a month earlier. Defense dominates. The only touchdown of the day comes in the third quarter. With ten minutes remaining in the game, we lead 13–9 and we've got the ball. On third-and-long, Joe drops back to pass. No one is open. He rolls right. Lawrence Taylor gives chase. Joe stops and LT runs past him. Joe winds up. He doesn't see 280-pound Leonard Marshall bearing down on him from behind. Just as Joe starts to throw, Marshall plants his helmet in the center of his back. Joe's head snaps back, and both of his feet come off the ground. Players from both teams scramble for the loose ball. We get it. But Joe isn't moving. He's on all fours, his head facing down.

Players are forbidden to touch or help injured players. But I run onto the field. I'm the first one to get to him. I drop down on one knee and speak into the ear hole of his helmet.

"Joe, are you okay?"

No response.

"Are you all right, Joe?"

"I'll be all right," he whispers.

Then he groans. I notice his helmet is cracked — not a good sign. I fear his back is broken.

The doctor kneels beside Joe's left side. The internist taps my shoulder and asks me to step back. For four frustrating years we've battled like rival siblings. But I don't like seeing him battered and hurt. He's my teammate, and I revere him. I never admit that to him, but it's true.

More medical staff surround him. They rotate him onto his back. He keeps his helmet on. He's the toughest player I know. But he suddenly looks frail and vulnerable. This time he's not coming back. Not after a hit like that.

I head to our sideline, pick up a ball, and start warming up. Over 60,000 fans taunt LT. "Tayyy-lor. Tayyy-lor. Tayyy-lor." John Madden and Pat Summerall are calling the game for CBS. A sideline television camera is on me as I throw.

Finally, Joe is on his feet. Barely. The stadium roars with approval. But he can barely walk. The medical staff steadies him all the way to our bench. When they ask him where he hurts, he tells them: "Everywhere." He isn't trying to be funny.

I look up at the clock. Nine minutes remain. We are nine minutes away from our third straight Super Bowl. We have a four-point lead. It's up to me to finish it.

After we punt, our defense stops the Giants' offense on three plays, forcing them to punt. I buckle my chinstrap and huddle with George Seifert on the sideline. But the Giants fake the punt and snap the ball to linebacker Gary Reasons. We aren't ready. Reasons lumbers 30 yards for a first down deep in our territory. The Giants run three more plays before Matt Bahr kicks a field goal. Our lead is cut to 13–12. Five minutes and forty-seven seconds remain. We are on our own 20-yard line.

My turn. *It's go-time,* I tell myself. *This is it.*

On the first play I hand off to Roger Craig. He fumbles. My heart skips a beat. There's a pig pile. I can't see the ball. The refs separate players. We have it.

I huddle everyone up and tell Craig to forget about the fumble. We've got this. I call a pass play: 23 Texas.

My primary receiver is fullback Tom Rathman on an angle route. My second option is Brent Jones. He runs down the seam. If it's two-deep coverage, I take a shot at Jones.

We get to the line of scrimmage, and LT is lined up over Jones.

"Nine!" Jones yells. "Cover nine! Cover nine!"

I look at Jones.

"Watch Jones," LT shouts. "Watch Jones!"

Taylor can't stay with Jones. I hit him with a 25-yard completion. He barrels all the way to midfield before he's dragged down. Jones pops up, spikes the ball, and shouts: "It's over!" Then he walks by Taylor. "LT, I'm going back to the Super Bowl, baby."

Our fans are on their feet. My adrenaline is racing. I tell the team in the huddle: "We got this. We got this."

Next play I hand off to Roger again. Six-yard gain.

Seifert wants to chew up the clock. He calls another run for Roger. I hand off. It's a sweep to the right. He gets inside the Giants' 40-yard line. First down. Two and a half minutes remain. One more play and we will be at the two-minute warning. One more first down and the Giants won't be able to stop the clock.

George wants to run "90-O." It's an inside trap, meaning the linemen won't be doing straight man-to-man blocking. I hand it to Roger, and he gets hit at the line of scrimmage. The ball pops out, and Lawrence Taylor catches it and falls at my feet. Giants' ball.

"No!" I shout. I put my hands on my head. Taylor jumps up celebrating. Candlestick goes quiet. The Giants have the football. I can't believe it. The fans can't believe it.

It's now up to our defense. The Giants have all three of their time-outs left. Hostetler drives them into field goal range. With four seconds remaining, Matt Bahr comes out for a 30-yard kick. He hits it. Giants win 15–13. Our quest for a third consecutive Super Bowl win is over.

I still think about how different things would have been for the 49ers franchise and for me if that ball hadn't popped out of Roger Craig's hands and landed in Lawrence Taylor's. In the huddle before that play, everyone knew we were going to the Super Bowl. All we had to do was run one more play and punt, and the Giants would have had to go the length of the field with a little over a minute to play. We would have gone to our third consecutive Super Bowl. And with Joe injured, I would have started.

20

MORE THAN A FEELING

THE LOSS TO the Giants was hard to get over. And when they won the Super Bowl, it only got harder. Luckily I had law school to take my mind off of football. But I couldn't escape the fact that I had to figure out my future. I was at a crossroads. My contract with the Niners was up. Leigh felt that it was time for a change and pointed to my statistics as evidence:

1987	69 attempts/37 completions/10 TDs/0 interceptions
1988	101 attempts/54 completions/3 TDs/3 interceptions
1989	92 attempts/64 completions/8 TDs/3 interceptions
1990	62 attempts/38 completions/2 TDs/0 interceptions
Total	324-193-23-6

On paper it was pretty clear: I was trending in the wrong direction. In 1990 I had played less than in any of my first three years in San Francisco. Meanwhile, Joe was coming off the two best years of his career and was the back-to-back MVP of the league. He showed no signs of slowing down. It was as if my presence had been the catalyst for making the greatest quarterback in NFL history even greater.

I knew that I was good enough to start in the NFL. But I wouldn't start in San Francisco. Not before I was thirty years old.

"It's time to go elsewhere," Leigh told me.

My father agreed. Both felt that the situation had gotten so bad that it was unhealthy for me to stay. As a restricted free agent, I had the right to talk to other teams, and the 49ers had the right to match any offers that came my way. I authorized Leigh to test the waters.

There was no shortage of interest. The Seahawks wanted me. So I met with head coach Chuck Knox. The Chargers wanted me. So I met with GM Bobby Beathard. But the biggest push came from Raiders owner Al Davis. He told Leigh he had been watching me for years. He loved my approach. He personally guaranteed that I would be the starter the moment I signed with them. I would be joining a very good team. In 1990 the Raiders had finished 12-4 and gone all the way to the AFC Championship game. And Ronnie Lott and Roger Craig had already signed with the Raiders as free agents in the off-season.

Leigh told me to pack my bags for LA.

It seemed like the smart thing to do. Everybody I respected told me to leave San Francisco. I spent a few weeks mulling it over. When facing big decisions, I spend a lot of time on my knees. The more I prayed about this one, the more impressed I felt to stay in San Francisco. I truly believed I was going to become the starter. I had no basis for thinking that, nothing I could point to. It was just an inspired feeling. And there was no other organization I preferred to play for.

While trying to sort it all out, I ran into my former Niner teammate Tom Holmoe.

"I have a chance to go to the Raiders as a free agent," I told him.

"Go."

"Wait a second. Hear me out."

"Okay."

"I have a feeling that I'm going to become the starting quarterback in San Francisco."

"You're not going to play as long as Montana is the quarterback."

"I'm telling you I just have this feeling I should stay."

"The Forty-Niners aren't going to let you play over Joe. The Raiders are going to make you their quarterback."

"I think I should stay."

"What does Leigh say?"

"Leigh says go to Los Angeles."

"What does your family say?"

"Go to Los Angeles."

"And Al Davis wants you?"

"Yeah."

"Steve, go to the Raiders."

Every person whose opinion I trusted told me I would be crazy to re-sign with the Niners. If I stayed in San Francisco, I would continue as Joe Montana's backup.

But I was convinced that the 49ers' system was built for me — it was the ideal offense for a quarterback who could throw and run. I couldn't help thinking that people who moved on whenever things got hard ended up missing some of the greatest opportunities life had to offer. I told my-self I'd come too far to give up now.

I called Leigh and told him to forget the Raiders' offer. I was ignoring everyone's advice. I was staying put.

Leigh thought I was making a mistake. But he went to work on a new contract with the 49ers.

In May I signed a two-year, $4.5 million contract extension.

21

LOSING IT

B Y THE TIME training camp opened in July 1991, Joe had recovered from the hit that had knocked him out of the NFC Championship game six months earlier. He resumed his place as the starter, and I resumed my place as his backup. But that didn't last long. Our second preseason game was against the Chicago Bears in Berlin, Germany. Afterward some tendonitis flared up in the elbow of Joe's throwing arm. It was no big deal. But as a precautionary measure, I started taking most of the snaps in practice.

Joe sat out the next two preseason games. I played well. Our final preseason game was in Seattle on a Friday night. About an hour before kickoff, George Seifert cornered me in the tunnel beneath the Kingdome. "Joe's not playing," he said. "He's out."

"For how long?"

"Who knows?"

Energized, I put on my helmet and played flawlessly against the Seahawks, completing 10 of 11 passes. Everything clicked. We won easily to cap off a 5-0 preseason.

I barely had time to drop off my things in California before the team flew back east. Our season opener would be on *Monday Night Football* against the Giants, our perennial rivals. It had gotten to a point where just about every season it came down to a fight between them and us. Dating back to 1984, our two teams had won five of the seven Super Bowls. Most experts predicted that the road to Super Bowl XXVI would once again go through New York or San Francisco. And we had waited eight months to avenge our loss to them in the NFC Championship game.

Sunday was opening day around the NFL. Brent wanted to watch games in our hotel room. But I refused. I couldn't stand to watch football games before I played. I didn't want to know anything about how well Troy Aikman or Mark Rypien or Jim Kelly did. That would just put more pressure on me. I opted for movies instead. *City Slickers* had just come out on video. I rented it and watched it three times on Sunday.

I also hated leaving my room. The only time I left it was to tape a pregame interview with ABC on Sunday afternoon. When I returned Brent was watching a game. "Shut it off," I told him.

"Oh, c'mon, bro."

"Off!"

He left and watched the game in another room. I went back to *City Slickers*.

By Sunday night, I've got tunnel vision and just want to get on the field. For four years I've been chomping at the bit to be the starter. Now I'm starting. It's week one. It's *Monday Night Football*. It's LT and the New York Giants. The whole country will be tuning in. The worst part is the wait. Let's get this thing started.

September 2, 1991. It's Monday morning, and I telephone my dad.

"How do you feel?" my dad says.

"Ready to face the Giants," I tell him.

He chuckles. "You just love third-and-ten," he says. "There's just something sick about you. Everyone else likes third-and-one. Not you. You like third-and-ten."

He's right. I do like third-and-ten. I perform best when the stakes are highest. I hang up determined to beat New York.

The bus ride to the stadium is a short one, but it feels like forever. Stuck in traffic on the New Jersey Turnpike, I stare out the window. The tip of the Empire State Building is visible across the Hudson. I start thinking more about what my dad said. Even though I have always had inner fears and insecurities, I thrive on the pressure to earn the starting spot. It pushes me to new heights. I feel like a guy climbing up the side of the Empire State Building without a safety harness. I'm afraid, but I'm drawn to the thrill. I have to meet the challenge. I won't back down.

The Giants win the toss, and Jeff Hostetler leads them on a methodical drive, ending in a Matt Bahr field goal to open the scoring. 3–0 Giants.

The sold-out stadium crowd is on its feet as the Giants' defense takes the field. I trot toward our huddle. Lawrence Taylor is waving his arms in the air and yelling. He is such a disruptive force that we've altered our entire offensive scheme to account for him.

But I'm prepared. The moment I have a ball in my hands I feel in control. In the first quarter I throw a 73-yard touchdown pass to Jerry Rice to put us up 7–3.

That's the way it works with me, and always has. My need for relief from my mental anguish pushes me to excel on the field. Fear of failure enables me to look past superstars like LT. He may be the most intimidating defensive player in the league, but no player — not even LT — comes close to the threat I feel from the anxiety that bubbles up inside me before the game. But once I'm on the field I have no fear.

In the second half the Giants take the lead and in the fourth quarter we are down 13–7. We get the ball back on the Giants' 42-yard line late in the game. It's our final chance to score. I hit John Taylor with a 13-yard pass. First down. I hit Brent Jones with another 13-yard pass. Another first down. With less than five minutes to play, we are on the Giants' 5-yard line. I take the snap and roll left. Lawrence Taylor gives chase. I hear him coming. Guy McIntyre knocks him down as I turn the corner and go into the end zone. I spike the ball into the Meadowlands turf, and 76,000 Giants fans go silent. With the extra point we go up 14–13.

All that remains is for our defense to hold them. Jeff Hostetler starts a drive. He picks apart our defense with short sideline routes. He works the clock perfectly. It looks like a repeat of the way we lost the NFC Championship game. With ten seconds to play, Hostetler has the Giants in field goal range. Out trots Matt Bahr. As time expires he kicks a 35-yard field goal to beat us 16–14.

No way! Not again, I tell myself. For the second time in eight months, a Matt Bahr field goal gives the Giants a two-point victory over us. We start the season 0-1.

It is one game, but perspective and anxiety are not friends. One runs over the other when I start the season with a loss. Half the league is 0-1, yet I already feel under the gun.

Five days later we checked into the San Francisco Marriott on the night before our home opener against the San Diego Chargers. Brent and I went to room 9043. It was our fourth year as roommates. We settled in like we owned the place. And we resorted to our traditional pregame routine. We had a huge dinner. We ate a gallon of ice cream in the room. And I cued up *City Slickers.* After the movie I fretted about the San Diego Chargers. If we lost, we would start the season 0-2.

Brent talked me through my anxiety. I found reasons to be nervous. He found reasons not to be. We finally dozed off. But in the morning once again I didn't want to get out of bed. And once again Brent returned from breakfast with two bananas and two PowerBars.

Weather conditions at The Stick were ideal — 62 degrees and sunny. But I was weak and sick to my stomach. Joe was standing on the sideline in street clothes. I had to win this game. Had to.

Brent found me during warm-ups. "You got this, bro," he assured me. "You got this."

Again, the minute I take the field my anxiety vanishes. In the first half I throw touchdown passes to Jerry Rice and John Taylor. Then I throw a 70-yard touchdown to Rice in the second half. As long as I'm on the field I feel completely comfortable. It's my safe haven. I finish the day with 26 completions on 36 attempts for 348 yards and three touchdowns. I throw no interceptions. We crush the Chargers 34-14.

But late in the game Brent Jones tears a ligament in his knee. Days later he undergoes arthroscopic surgery. He will be out for at least eight weeks. Losing personnel is part of football. But without Brent, I'm really going to be on my own.

· · ·

September 14, 1991. We are in Minnesota to face the Vikings. It's the night before the game, and I'm alone in my hotel room. Brent is back home, recuperating from surgery. I watch *City Slickers* three times. I don't come out for meals. Finally, I call Brent and keep the poor guy on the phone for over an hour. He reminds me that we're 1-1. He's right. *Why am I so wound up?*

But the next morning I don't have Brent around to bring me bananas and PowerBars, so I go to the stadium on a completely empty stomach. Things begin well when I throw a 15-yard touchdown pass to Rice in the first quarter. But later in the first half Jerry gets open deep and I don't see him. I end up running the ball. He's furious. When I get to the sideline I put on the headset and Mike Holmgren rips into me too.

"Jerry was open!" he booms.

"I know. I know."

"Then why in the hell didn't you throw it to him?"

"I couldn't see him."

"Well, you better start seeing him."

He slams down the phone.

I mumble to myself: "I'll be sure to start seeing what I can't see as soon as I see it."

Minnesota scores 17 second-quarter points. We never recover. We're 1-2.

The next day I went over the game film with Holmgren. There are few occupations where your every move is videotaped, but in football it's the norm. It's intrusive, but it's also a great learning tool. Watching film is a great way to develop what I refer to as reflexive recall. Great quarterbacking doesn't happen until reactions and decisions are more a result of reflex and less a result of thinking.

The play where I missed Jerry Rice came up. "How did you miss him?" Holmgren said.

The problem was that my offensive line was so much bigger than me. I often couldn't see over them on the deep routes.

Holmgren told me that Jerry was always where he was supposed to be. I needed to trust Jerry. Even when I couldn't see him, I needed to throw to the spot where he was supposed to be.

That was a new concept. *Throw to a guy I can't see?*

"You better find a way to see him better or you will never be a great player," Mike told me. His words stung.

My situation with Jerry wasn't great either. We didn't click the way he and Joe did. Joe and Jerry had an unspoken language between them. I was not there yet with Jerry. He never knew when I was going to pull the ball down and take off running. Half the time I didn't even know when I was going to run it. That drove Jerry nuts. But the hardest adjustment for him was the different spin that comes from a ball thrown by a lefty. He hadn't gotten used to it.

After practice I couldn't go back to my apartment and spend another night alone. I felt that I needed to be around people. I needed company. So I drove to Palo Alto and had dinner with Mimi and Richard "Dick" Peery and their children. Dick was the leading real estate developer in Silicon Valley and a self-made billionaire, but you would never have known that based on how he lived his life. He was humble, generous, and unassuming. I knew him through church. He was a Mormon, and he had strong ties to BYU. When I arrived for dinner, I couldn't hide my depression. Part of my problem was that I was lonely. I was almost thirty years old, and despite how much I was dating, I still hadn't found "the one."

When dinner ended I still hung around, even though it got late. I didn't want to go back to my apartment. Dick said I was welcome to spend the night. So I did. The next day he extended the offer even further. He said he had plenty of room, and I was welcome to live with his family in the guest quarters.

One night turned into one week. Then a month. Mimi made me dinner night after night and treated me like a son. Being around a family was so much better than being alone.

I couldn't stop thinking about Mike Holmgren's words: *You better find a way to see him better or you will never be a great player.*

In my religion I take a lot of things on faith. I believe in things I can't see. If I could also learn to believe in the unseen on the football field, it might be a solution to my predicament. I needed to start throwing the ball to where I believed Jerry Rice would be even when I couldn't actually see him. That sounded risky, if not impossible. But if I didn't get comfortable with that concept, my starting job would be in jeopardy. So I started working on it in practice.

At first it was awkward. I simply wasn't comfortable throwing the ball blind. But in time I got more used to it. I had to grow into it. If I'd been six-five, things would have been different. But I was six-one, so I had to do a lot of throwing by faith. There is a lot of art in quarterbacking at six-one.

A week later I threw a 62-yard touchdown pass to Jerry without seeing him. It was my first taste of throwing blind. Holmgren's tip was really going to make a difference. We beat the Rams, and I had a big game, completing 21 of 31 attempts with no interceptions. After four weeks, I led the league in passing efficiency. But it sure didn't feel like it. My sense of self-worth was completely tied to wins and losses at that point. Although we just won one, we were only 2-2. I had no perspective on how well I was doing as a quarterback.

After the Rams game, George informed me that Joe's elbow was a lot worse than previously realized. He was undergoing surgery and would probably be out for the season. The starting job was mine.

Finally, the chance to go full-time. I was ecstatic. But of course I couldn't help worrying about all the implications of each win or loss and about the inevitable comparisons to Joe. I had to win or face the music.

September 29, 1991. We are in Los Angeles to face the Raiders and our old teammates Ronnie Lott and Roger Craig. Brent Jones is still back home recuperating, and my routine is off without him.

On the third play of the game I overthrow John Taylor and get intercepted. On our next possession we are on the Raiders' 1-yard line when I attempt a quarterback sneak. Winston Moss practically rips my head off. We end up settling for a field goal to go up 3–0.

The game is sloppy throughout. With 2:51 to play, we trail 12–6 when we get the ball back on our own 25-yard line. We have one time-out left. On the first snap I complete an 18-yard pass to Rice. First down. Then I hit Sherrard, who runs all the way to the Raiders' 34-yard line before getting out of bounds. My third pass is a completion to Rathman for another first down. In less than thirty seconds we've advanced to LA's 22-yard line. It's our best drive of the day. We're finally going to get in the end zone.

But our next three plays go nowhere. On fourth-and-seven, I drop back. The Raiders blitz, and I scramble and throw off my back foot. The pass falls incomplete. Game over. We are 2-3.

Tempers flare in the locker room. Charles Haley gets into an altercation with George Seifert. Then Charles singles me out for the loss. The scene quickly escalates into chaos. A set of swinging metal doors separates our locker area from the showers. The doors have glass panels with wire mesh. While shouting at me, Charles puts his fist through the glass. There's glass everywhere and shards of glass in his wrist and arm. It's a bloody mess.

The situation is so out of control that a couple of players run next door to the Raiders' locker room for help. Moments later, Ronnie Lott enters our locker room. He is the only one capable of getting Charles under control. Then the doctors step in.

I just want to dive into a hole.

Statistically, I was playing very well, but the comparisons and expectations were crushing me. When we landed in San Francisco, my teammates' wives or girlfriends were waiting. More than ever I longed for my wife to meet me at the airport. At that moment I would have given anything to have someone to hold me close. But I had no one. No wife. No girlfriend. I didn't even have a home. I drove to Dick Peery's house in Palo Alto, but I didn't go in. I sat in my car in the driveway and called Brent Jones.

"Haley went off," I told him. "Screaming and yelling."

"Dude, it's Charles. He does that all the time."

"No, bro. This time he went crazy. You have no idea."

Then I called Greg Madsen. The minute he heard my voice he knew I was in the depths of despair. I unloaded on him for two hours about my situation. Finally, he said, "Steve, this didn't *happen* to you. Your whole life you've been clearing hurdles that have brought you to this place. As hard as it seems right now, you have to own this experience."

Next I called Leigh. Then I called Jim Herrmann. Eventually I ran out of people to call. I buried my head in my hands and sobbed.

I stayed in my car until three in the morning.

Years later, after being diagnosed with bipolar disorder, Haley reflected on that time. "I'm not going to lie to you, man," he said. "I was a big Joe Montana fan. And anything that went against Joe, I didn't particularly like. As a man, I didn't give Steve what he deserved as an opportunity because I saw Steve as a threat to Joe."

That was what I was up against. Joe was hurt, and I was trying to lead the team in his absence. It felt like an impossible situation. Joe had certainly done things that no other quarterback had done. But people tended to forget that he had also lost some games and actually thrown interceptions.

The day after the loss to the Raiders was an off day. Eager to get away, I hopped a flight to Salt Lake City and went to see Carole Burr. She still didn't understand football, but she understood me. I told her what had happened in the locker room. I told her that the pressure of replacing Joe Montana was crushing me. I told her that I didn't want to go back to San Francisco. She said she had a close friend who was a psychologist and wanted to make an appointment for me.

I told her I'd think about it.

Before returning to the airport, I went to see my brother Mike. He was in medical school at the University of Utah. I waited for him to get out of class. It was nighttime when we walked the streets of Salt Lake City. I unloaded on him. We were losing games! The pressure to replace Joe Montana was unbearable. The weight of the expectations was crushing me. My anxiety was overwhelming me. But none of it made sense to him.

"I'm not going to make it to Thanksgiving," I told him.

"You'll be fine, Steve."

"No, I really don't think I'm going to make it."

He stopped walking and looked directly at me. "I'm in medical school," he said. "I have a wife and three kids. I'm the one who might not make it to Thanksgiving. But I'm pretty sure you're going to be okay."

I hugged my brother, thanked him for the perspective, and said good-bye.

Late that night I landed back in San Francisco.

Brent Jones couldn't practice, but he called and woke me up early Tuesday morning. "Let's go back to work," he said. "Let's focus. Let's get with the game plan."

We had a bye week, which afforded us two weeks to prepare for the Atlanta Falcons. I arrived at the practice facility ready to go, but the day soured. Dwight Clark, who had joined the Niners' front office, was quoted in the press talking about our loss to the Raiders: "These are the kinds of games Joe Montana wins in his sleep." That hurt. Mike Holmgren was so angry about the comment that he called Clark into his office and let him have it. I didn't say a word to Clark. Instead, I told myself he was right. I had to do better.

In the middle of the week I got a call from Bill Walsh. He wasn't with the organization anymore, but he said he wanted to see me. So I drove to his office on Sand Hill Road in Menlo Park.

When I arrived I could tell he was upset. He scolded me for taking all the bullets. "All you do is take the blame!" he said.

I hung my head. "Joe wouldn't have missed the receiver in the end zone," I said.

"I can tell you right now that if Joe was playing and these guys were playing the way they're playing, things wouldn't be any better."

"What am I supposed to say? It's not my fault?"

"There's no better quality than being accountable," Walsh said. "But there's such a thing as being over-accountable. You actually steal other people's accountability."

Football, he explained, is not a one-man game. The quarterback is the leader. But it takes all eleven men to succeed.

"You are not letting other people down," he said. "You are being let down, left and right."

I left his office feeling a better. But only a little.

22

BLESSING IN DISGUISE

TRADITIONALLY WE OWNED the Falcons. But they had a new head coach, Jerry Glanville, who had his team playing over their heads. And they had Deion Sanders, one of the best all-around athletes in the league.

During preparation week, Montana underwent season-ending surgery. That erased all doubt: the team was in my hands, a burden that fully settled on my shoulders. I wished it wasn't a bye week. The only way to redeem myself from the Raiders game fiasco was to get back on the field as soon as possible. But the closer the Falcons game got, the more anxious I became. The game was at Candlestick. We checked into the Marriott the night before. Brent Jones was still on crutches, but he stayed with me. As usual, I had *City Slickers* playing on the TV. And as usual I was fretting.

There was no way we could lose to the Falcons. We couldn't end up 2-4. Haley would erupt again. He'd blame me.

Brent tried to calm me down.

"Steve, I've known other people who have had anxiety issues," he said. "There are medications you can take."

But I was always leery of the addictive nature of medication. "I'll be fine," I told him.

"Seriously. You should see a specialist. You gotta do it before it eats you up and controls you," Brent said.

• • •

October 13, 1991. In the morning we stick to our routine. I sleep in and skip breakfast. He brings me the traditional bananas and a couple of PowerBars. "Am I a friend or what?" he says with a smile.

Atlanta jumps out to a quick 17–0 lead. Our fans are not happy. Deion Sanders is trash-talking. On our first possession of the second quarter I run a bootleg left from the Falcons' 6-yard line and outrun Sanders for a touchdown to put us on the board. Then, with forty-nine seconds left in the half, I throw a 54-yard touchdown pass to John Taylor to cut Atlanta's lead to 20–14.

During halftime the doctors want to make sure I'm all right. I've taken some vicious hits. But I insist I'm fine. I can take the hits. What I can't take is the fact that Joe Montana is sitting up in the owner's box with Eddie DeBartolo, watching us play from behind again. A year ago at this juncture Joe had led the team to a 5-0 start. We lose today and we'll be 2-4.

On the second play of the second half I get flushed from the pocket and head downfield. As I cut back to avoid a tackler I get hammered from behind and my helmet pops off. Still on my feet, I catch my helmet with my right hand while cradling the ball with my left. A pack of defenders knocks me to the turf.

On the next play 285-pound defensive tackle Tory Epps hits me as I throw and drives me into the turf, pulling one side of my jersey down beneath my shoulder pads. The pass is caught, but the play is negated by a penalty. Fed up, I push Epps off of me and pull my jersey back over my pads. On the next snap I throw a 57-yard touchdown pass to Rice to tie the score at 20.

I'm on the sideline, catching my breath and getting treated by the trainer, when we kick off to Atlanta. Deion Sanders runs it back 101 yards for a touchdown. Just like that, we are back down 27–20.

At the start of the fourth quarter I run the ball and Jessie Tuggle hits me square in the right shoulder. For a second it feels like I broke something. But I don't want to give Tuggle the satisfaction of knowing he hurt me. I'm angry. A few plays later we are inside the Atlanta 20-yard line. Seeking a first down, I run the bootleg left. Safety Scott Case gives chase. Just as I pass the first-down marker along the sideline he slams his forearm across my neck and hits my head before riding me out of bounds and driving me to the ground. The blow to my head draws an unnecessary roughness penalty, giving us first-and-goal from inside the 10-yard line.

On the next play I sidestep a blitz and take off for the end zone. Just inside the goal line, I encounter a flock of Falcons. There is nowhere to go. Running full speed, I go airborne at the 4-yard line. A defender hits my thighs, propelling me higher and forcing my body to go perpendicular. Scott Case is coming at me from the left, and Jessie Tuggle is approaching me from the right. They lower their helmets as I come down in the end zone. They miss me and go head to head with each other. I hop up. But they don't. Both of them are hurt on the play. With the extra point, we are back up 34–33.

Dazed and about to collapse, I find the doctor on the sideline. He administers smelling salts and checks my vision. It's a little blurry, but I don't tell him that. I say I'm fine. He says I'm getting the hell beat out of me. But I'll take the beating. It gives me the sense that I'm doing my part.

I finish with 350 yards passing and nearly 70 yards rushing, including two touchdowns. I play one of the best games of my career, yet we lose 36–34 and fall to 2–4. It's brutal.

After the game I limp to the training room. I have a splitting headache. My shoulder is throbbing. And something is wrong with my knee. It feels like I have torn a ligament or something. It is excruciating to put weight on it. But there is no way I'm saying a word about my knee to the medical team. I fear I'll lose my starting job.

Holmgren enters the trainer's room. "Steve," he says, "that was a courageous effort. I'm really proud of you."

I can't take it in. I crawl up on the training table and close my eyes. I don't want to see anyone. I feel like I am sinking. Maybe Brent was right. Maybe I need to see a sports psychologist.

Desperate, I stay in the training room until the locker room empties. Then I talk to Dr. James Klint. He is in charge of internal medicine for the team. He is also the one person on the medical staff with whom I feel a personal connection. We are friends. I call him Reggie. He is an oncologist and hematologist, and he also taught at Stanford. When he enters the training room I tell him that something isn't right. In every other area of my life — law school, dating, friendships, public speaking — I never get anxious. I can get up in front of a thousand strangers and give a speech without my heart rate changing. But during football season something happens to me.

Dr. Klint says that one of the best psychologists in the Bay Area is a close friend of his — Dr. Stanley Fischman. He specializes in child psychiatry. But Fischman sees adult patients on a referral basis. Reggie says he's going to call Fischman and make an appointment for me.

"I don't know, Reggie."

"Look, Steve, you can trust this guy," he says.

Five days later I pulled up outside a small medical office in Mountain View, a few blocks from El Camino Hospital. But I didn't get out of the car. I didn't want to go in. My mind-set was to resist help. All my life I had believed that going to talk to a psychiatrist was a sign of weakness.

I should be able to get through this on my own, I told myself.

I was about to drive off. But something propelled me out of the car and into the empty waiting area. A short, gray-haired man in his fifties met me and escorted me to his office. He asked me my age. I told him thirty. He told me the ground rules. "I don't talk to anybody without your permission," he said. "So everything you say in here stays in here."

I nodded.

"Now, how can I help you?"

Not sure where to begin, I told him about my situation with the 49ers and what it had been like trying to start in place of Joe Montana. The pressure had pushed me to a breaking point. I told him I started every day utterly exhausted — mentally, physically, and emotionally — and that I had never been this miserable.

Dr. Fischman didn't follow the 49ers. He didn't care much for football in general. But even he had some appreciation for the pressure of replacing Joe Montana.

"I don't like getting up in the morning during football season," I told him.

"Do you like to get up in the morning when it isn't football season?"

"I love to get up in the morning the rest of the year."

He jotted down a few notes and then asked about my family. I didn't go into much detail.

He asked if I was married.

No, I told him, adding that I desperately wanted a family, but that was on hold because of football. But I told him that not being married was another source of pressure and anxiety because of my religion. I explained that Mormons are expected to marry young. I felt like I was not measuring up.

He asked more questions about my occupation.

I told him that I beat myself up a lot, that when the team lost I felt personally responsible because I was the quarterback.

After a while he stopped me. He said that his sense was that my anxiety was situational and related to my occupation, since it appeared that it spiked during football season and then disappeared in the off-season.

This wasn't exactly a revelation.

"A lot of guys who have it relieve the pressure with alcohol or drugs," he told me.

"I've never had a drink," I told him. "And I've never taken drugs. Not even prescription drugs."

Stunned, he hesitated. "How have you been coping with all of this anxiety?"

"By strapping on my helmet each day," I explained. "By getting back on the field."

He was speechless.

After ninety minutes we finished the session and agreed to meet again in three days.

October 20, 1991. We face the Lions at home. Aside from the undefeated Washington Redskins, the Lions are the hottest team in the league. They've won five straight, and they run a new offense called "Run-and-Shoot." It's a system that relies on one running back and four receivers. It works for the Lions because they have Barry Sanders.

The day before the game deadly brushfires break out in Oakland's Berkeley Hills. On game day the winds out of the mountains reach 65 miles per hour. Humidity is almost zero. Close to 2,000 homes have been destroyed by the time we take the field for warm-ups. There have been twenty-five fatalities, mainly people trapped in automobiles on winding mountain roads.

But the game goes on. We kick off at 1:00 PM. The temperature on the field is a rare 100 degrees in San Francisco. A wall of smoke is visible in the distance. Ash drifts out of the sky and blankets Candlestick Park.

I know that if we lose to the Lions, we won't make the playoffs. On top of everything else I'm dealing with, I feel an added burden to win this one due to the fires. The Bay Area could really use a win.

I've got Charles Haley yelling at me. The fans are furious that we are 2-4 and it's as if it's my fault. Jerry is frustrated because he's still not used to the spin on my left-handed throws. Even my own teammates are staring at me as if to say: *What's going on?*

In the first half I complete 13 out of 13 pass attempts, including two touchdown passes, and we go up 21–3. Midway through the third quarter I still haven't thrown an incompletion. I perform best when my back is really against the wall. It's almost as if I'm attracted to extreme pressure. I finish the day by completing 18 of 20 passes for nearly 250 yards and a pair of touchdowns. I also rush for more yards than Barry Sanders. We crush Detroit 35–3. Strictly from a throwing standpoint, it's the finest game of my career. And our playoff hopes remain alive.

I was supposed to see Dr. Fischman for a follow-up the next day, but I didn't see the point. I liked him, but I wasn't convinced that talking about my problems was going to help them go away. I broke the appointment.

A week later we went on to Philadelphia and another do-or-die game. Brent was still on crutches, but he flew with the team for my sake. Guys thought he was crazy to travel when he couldn't walk. They didn't realize that he was along solely to help me get through the twenty-four hours leading up to game time.

Veterans Stadium is the worst facility in football, with its patchy field and huge gaps in the turf. It's also one of the most hostile environments in the NFL. Fortunately, the fans couldn't reach the opposing team. But the Eagles could. Led by Reggie White, Jerome Brown, Seth Joyner, and Andre Waters, the Eagles had one of the great defenses of all time, and they came after me all day.

Despite all of this, we controlled the game from the start and won our first road game, 23–7. I had clawed my way back, and we evened our record at 4-4. I told myself that maybe our team had turned a corner.

· · ·

November 3, 1991. We are in Atlanta for a rematch with the Falcons. We're both 4-4, tied for second place in the division, behind the Saints. In the first half I throw a 97-yard touchdown pass to John Taylor. It's the longest TD pass in team history. We lead 7-0. I want another score before the half. On our next possession I scramble and two Falcons hit me, whip-sawing my leg. My knee goes sideways. I never let a defensive player think he's hurt me. So I always get up and leave the field on my own. But this is different. My lower leg is flopping around like a wet noodle. I know I am in trouble.

The medical staff runs out. The doctor touches my knee, and I writhe in pain. "I'm done," I tell him. "I'm done."

They send for a golf cart.

Third-string quarterback Steve Bono replaces me. He plays well, but we lose 17–14 and drop to 4-5.

On the plane ride home I figured I was headed for surgery. An MRI the following morning at Stanford Hospital confirmed it. The 49ers' team physician, Dr. Michael Dillingham, reviewed the damage with me. All four major ligaments connecting my knee to my femur and tibia were torn. My ACL and my PCL were in very bad shape. Plus, my meniscus — the crescent-shaped cartilage that provides structural support to the knee — was completely torn off.

There was more. The doctors also detected preexisting ligament damage on my knee. I finally revealed that I had suffered a knee injury the last time we played the Falcons. The bottom line was that at this point I had a double-sided knee injury and multiple sites of trauma around my knee. The prognosis was not good.

"Saving the meniscus is a very big deal for the future of your knee," Dr. Dillingham told me.

Dillingham reminded me a little of Bill Walsh with his distinguished-looking white hair and his Ivy League vocabulary. Dillingham had a very personable manner that made me comfortable. He immobilized my knee with a cast and scheduled me for surgery in four days. Just like that, my season appeared to be over.

It was a lot to come to grips with. I was thirty years old and had played in well over 100 football games during thirteen college and pro seasons.

In all that time I had never been operated on. I had never broken a bone. Not even a finger or a toe. I had been knocked out a few times and sustained numerous concussions. But no broken bones or serious ligament damage.

It was pretty miraculous considering how many hits I had taken, particularly with the LA Express and at Tampa Bay. But now it looked like my luck had finally run out.

The night before the operation I went to see a religious leader from my church. I asked him for a blessing. Privately, I was hoping that when he prayed for me he'd say that I would be well enough to return to the field. But he didn't. In his prayer he said: "Lord, thy will be done."

Oh, boy, I told myself. *That sounded like God was telling me I was not going to get my wish.*

I arrived at Stanford Hospital early in the morning on November 8, 1991. An anesthesiologist gave me an epidural, enabling me to remain awake during the procedure. When Dr. Dillingham inserted a scope in my knee, I could tell something was up. He had a puzzled expression on his face. After a couple of minutes, he said the ligaments around my knee had tightened. Four days earlier they were severely separated. Plus, my meniscus had locked down. Scarring had formed over it. The meniscus had some rim damage, but overall it was healing.

"You know what?" Dillingham said. "Nature is doing its job."

"What does that mean?"

"It means we're out of here. I don't need to go forward with the surgery."

I didn't understand.

He explained that my knee looked dramatically different than it had four days earlier. It was healing on its own. And even better, it was healing fast, so he didn't think surgery was necessary.

I was speechless.

He outfitted my knee with a brace. Then we got in his car and went directly from the operating room to the airport, where we caught a flight to New Orleans to join the team for Sunday's game. We spent the flight discussing my knee and the treatment going forward. "But look," he said, "you don't need an operation."

I wanted a better understanding of what had transpired since the injury. What had changed?

My genetics, he said, played a huge role. My body was unusually strong and fit to begin with. But my genetic makeup enabled me to heal unusually fast, even in cases of serious injury. There was another factor. For my entire life, I had followed a strict health code that forbade alcohol and tobacco, while encouraging healthy eating and exercise. I always believed that I'd be healthier and stronger by living these principles.

"What's the prognosis going forward?" I asked.

"You'll wear a knee brace for a while," he said. "But it's conceivable that you could return to the field before the season ends."

I reconsidered the words of the prayer from the night before — *Thy will be done.* I told myself: *Maybe this setback is a gift from God. Maybe I need a break from football. I need to find new perspective.*

Third-string quarterback Steve Bono lost his first start, against New Orleans, and we fell to 4-6. But then the team started winning. We beat Phoenix. Then Bono had a huge game on *Monday Night Football,* and we knocked off the Rams, 33–10. The victory pulled us to 6-6 and kept our playoff hopes alive.

All I could do was watch from the sideline. And the more I watched Bono the more depressed I got. I was dying to get back out there.

After the Rams game Leigh Steinberg invited me out for dinner. We went to his favorite Chinese place in San Francisco. But I was in no mood to eat.

"I just want to tell you that I know I haven't lived up to your expectations and I know I've been a disappointment," I told him. "If you feel like you no longer want to represent me, I'll understand."

"C'mon, Steve."

"I'm probably out of a job."

"What are you talking about?"

"Have you seen the way Bono is playing?"

Leigh put down his chopsticks. "Before your injury, you had the highest completion percentage in the league," he said. He reminded me of my numbers before the injury:

Two thousand yards passing in a little over eight games.

An average of more than two touchdown passes per game.

The top-rated passer in the league.

"Steve Bono has won two games and lost one," he said. "You are not out of a job. Let's get a grip."

On an off day I flew to Utah. Sometimes I just needed to get away, and this was one of those times. I saw my brother Mike at med school. I saw Jim Herrmann. They both tried to cheer me up. But I was miserable. That night I hopped a flight back to San Francisco. My seat assignment was next to business guru Stephen Covey. His classic best-seller, *The 7 Habits of Highly Effective People,* was on my bookshelf. I had read it when it first came out.

We struck up a conversation, and it immediately turned to football. I started telling him about my situation: For four years I had played behind the greatest quarterback in NFL history. He got hurt, and I finally had a chance to start. In my eight starts we went 4-4. I would have to remind guys that Joe had actually lost a game before. He threw incompletions, even an interception or two. But it was no use saying this stuff. The idea of Joe leading a team to a 4-4 record was inconceivable. Expectations were so out of whack that the front page of the *San Francisco Chronicle* ran an op-ed titled "The Gulf War: It's Steve Young's Fault." The truth was that I was way over-invested. Maybe I should have played tennis or golf, sports where winning and losing rightly falls squarely on the shoulders of the individual. The bottom line was that the comparisons to Joe were driving me crazy. Forget talk radio. I was getting advice in the grocery store. Nothing I did was good enough. Joe had won four Super Bowls. I was in an impossible situation.

I felt like a whiner venting all of this. But Covey was patient.

"Now, Joe's still on the team, right?" he asked.

"Yeah," I said. "That's part of the problem."

"I understand," he said. "But you get to ask him questions, right? In other words, he'll mentor you?"

"Well, yeah," I said.

"And the Forty-Niners are one of the better organizations in football?"

"The gold standard," I said.

"And Mike Holmgren, your coach from BYU, is one of the best, right?"

"Best quarterback coach in the league," I said.

He paused for a moment. "I think you may be looking at your situation the wrong way," he said.

"What do you mean?"

He explained that he traveled the world in search of organizations that created opportunities for employees to become the best. "I gotta be honest with you, Steve," he said. "I don't know that I've seen an organization better than this one."

I was intrigued.

"If I understand your situation with the Forty-Niners correctly," he continued, "you are in the one place in the NFL where you can find out just how good you can get."

Now he really had my attention.

"And few people in the world get to find out how good they are at one thing," he said. "They are stuck somewhere in life where they don't have the opportunity or the platform to find out."

I had never looked at it like that. And I had completely lost track of time as I considered what he was saying. The plane touched down in San Francisco, and we were about to get off.

"So here's the question," he said. "Do you want to find out how good you can get?"

"Yeah, I do."

"I mean some people are just afraid to find out," he said.

"No. I absolutely want to find out."

"Then go do it," he said. "Good luck."

I'm a big Star Wars fan, and this was a Yoda moment. My axis had just flipped.

I was searching for a new perspective, and I had found it in my chance encounter with Covey. It was divine intervention that forced me to rethink my situation in a completely different paradigm.

I have a quest, I told myself. *My quest is to find out how good I can become. It's not about comparisons or outside expectations.*

It wasn't going to be easy. But I couldn't wait to get back on the field.

A few days later Bono had another great game, leading the team to victory over the first-place Saints 38–24. The better he played the hungrier I was to return.

On December 8 we faced the Seahawks in Seattle. Before the game I saw Dr. Dillingham. I told him I could practice without pain. My coordination was back. I had a little discomfort when I cut or ran full speed. He said he wanted to examine me in his clinic as soon as we returned to San Francisco.

Bono pulled out a 24–22 win against the Seahawks. That was four straight wins. The team was gelling around him. For the first time I started understanding what it was like for Joe to have me looking over his shoulder all the time. For the first time I understood what it was like to feel like my job was threatened. And I didn't like it.

It was as if my knee injury and the time away from the field had broken a spell that had been over my mind for four years. I had yet another conversation with myself.

Forget all that, I told myself. *Do you want to play or not?*

Of course.

Do you like the game of football?

Yeah, I do.

Can you do this?

Yeah, I can.

There was no way I was going to lose my job to Steve Bono or anybody else. I had waited too long and worked too hard for this moment. I had been given this phenomenal opportunity to play quarterback for the San Francisco 49ers. I had had four years to learn from the master. We had two games left in the '91 season. My knee was still sore. But it had healed remarkably fast. I was done waiting.

23

A RUN-PASS THREAT

DECEMBER 9, 1991. Dr. Dillingham clears me to play. Five days later we play a home game against the Chiefs. It has been only five weeks since I tore my knee ligaments. I'm still wearing a brace, and I'm not full speed. But I feel ready.

Bono throws touchdown passes to Rice and Taylor in the first half to put us up 14–0. But early in the second half he takes a late hit after throwing an incomplete pass. He's on the ground, grimacing and holding his knee. I take off my baseball cap and put on my helmet. It has never felt so good to run onto a football field. It's weird. He and I are teammates and friends. I know this is bad for him, but I also know that I really want back in. I feel like I have escaped a straitjacket. Gratitude replaces anxiety.

Knowing I'm not 100 percent, the Chiefs step up the pass rush. They start blitzing a lot more. Seifert urges me to go easy. But I'm too eager. I run the ball six times for over 30 yards. I've got a bulky knee brace, but I'm crashing into guys. I appreciate playing more than ever.

The trainer tells me I've got to be careful. He insists I should slide rather than risk taking a hit on my knee. The next time I run I slide. My toe catches the turf and I tweak my knee. I feel the ligament. I punch the ground. *Sliding is stupid, stupid, stupid. Never again!*

We win the game 28–14 to improve to 9-6. Despite the victory, we are mathematically eliminated from the playoffs on account of wins by other teams that have secured wild-card playoff berths. It's the first time in nine years that the 49ers won't play in the postseason. Still, I feel reborn. I feel young again. And I can't wait to play the final games of the regular season.

December 23, 1991. We're at Candlestick for the final game of the season against the Bears on *Monday Night Football*. Chicago is 11-4 and has to beat us to win the NFC Central. I approach the game like it's the playoffs. On the third play of the game Richard Dent hammers me after the whistle. I bounce up.

"Nice hit," I tell him.

He looks at me. "Thanks," he says.

I'm so thrilled to be on the field that even the hits feel good.

Three plays later we're on the Chicago 15-yard line. I drop back. Here comes Dent around the end again. The middle is open. I take off. Four Bears converge on me as I reach the 10-yard line. No way I'm sliding. I fake left, then lower my head and run over a defensive back before a safety drills me from the side. We land in a heap at the 2-yard line. First-and-goal.

On the next play I throw a touchdown pass to put us up 7-0. It has taken us just four minutes to go 76 yards.

On our next possession I drive us 97 yards, ending the drive with a 3-yard touchdown pass to Rice. A few minutes later I throw a 69-yard touchdown pass to Rice. By halftime we have piled up 355 yards and are up 24-0.

We believe we can beat anybody right now. Anybody. We are the hottest team in the league, and we are running all over the toughest defense in the league. Yet we aren't going to be in the playoffs. Frustrated, we put up 28 more points in the second half to crush Chicago, 52-14. It's the most points scored against the Bears in twenty-six years. I complete 21 of 32 passes for 338 yards and three touchdowns while rushing for 63 yards. The Bears lose the NFC Central Division to the Lions.

Our season was over, but I had my job back. More importantly, I had a fresh outlook on my situation. My anxiety had subsided. I realized how lucky I was to be the starting quarterback for the 49ers. Despite all of the anguish during the season, and missing seven games due to an injury,

I still finished with 2,500 yards passing and ended up with the highest quarterback rating in the NFL.

I cleaned out my locker and headed back to Provo to resume law school classes at BYU. I was getting close to obtaining my JD. But for the first time in my life I couldn't wait for training camp to open the next year.

After the '91 season, Mike Holmgren took the head coaching job with the Green Bay Packers. On January 30, 1992, the 49ers hired former Denver Broncos assistant coach Mike Shanahan as our new offensive coordinator. He brought in Gary Kubiak to be the quarterback coach.

In the spring I flew to San Francisco to meet Shanahan. It didn't take long to see that he was fanatical about preparation. During the off-season we spent some time in the film room. He showed me film of every instance when I scrambled in 1991. I scrambled sixty-six times. He knew every play. He knew exactly what I'd done. And he noticed something. Every time I pulled the ball down and scrambled I was determined to gain yardage. He wanted to change that. He was not opposed to me running the ball. But he wanted me to maintain the option of passing right up until the moment I crossed the line of scrimmage. "I just want you to take a peek before you reach the line of scrimmage," he told me. "It will make you more of a run-pass threat."

He talked about Fran Tarkenton and Roger Staubach. Both were exceptional scramblers, but neither of them, he argued, typically ran downfield. They threw on the run. Randall Cunningham, on the other hand, was an exceptional running quarterback with great speed. But once he pulled the ball down, defenses played him for the run. Mike told me that he had never seen anyone scramble like me. And he had never seen a faster quarterback. He insisted that my scrambling and running would be a much bigger threat if we added the element of throwing on the run.

I spent most of the off-season working out in Provo. I had bought an old pioneer home not far from the BYU campus. I invited my younger brother Tom to train with me. He was a fourth-string quarterback at BYU. And he was pretty discouraged about his status. He wanted to play, not be a backup. It was a situation I knew intimately.

"Remember what Dad always told us," I told him. "'Keep working hard and things will work out.'"

For six weeks we trained together under the hot Utah sun. It was a great opportunity for me to get to know my kid brother. He was only nine years old when I was a senior in high school. So my interactions with him had been pretty limited. We threw together. We worked on his technique. Every day I tried to build his confidence and pushed him to work a little harder.

"This will be the year of the Youngs," I told him.

Tom went on to be the MVP in the 1992 Aloha Bowl. I arrived at training camp in July 1992 in the best shape of my life. My knee was back to full strength. But a week into camp I developed sharp pains in my lower back. It hurt so much I couldn't sit down for more than twenty minutes at a time. An MRI on August 4 revealed a herniated disc. I received an epidural and started taking prednisone. After four days I had another MRI, confirming that the situation hadn't improved. The medical team wanted me to stop practicing.

But after sitting out five days, I insisted on getting back on the field. Joe Montana's surgically repaired elbow had not healed, and there was no way I was going to let the chance to start slip away again. Joe didn't test his arm until the last day of camp. During a morning workout he threw 15 passes and handed the ball off a few times. The team cheered when he ran a bootleg. But after practice Joe went on the injured reserve list again. He just was not ready. I was starting. Bono was backing me up.

Hours after I was named the starter, the 49ers traded Charles Haley to the Cowboys for draft picks. He had led our team with 63 sacks in six years. At the same time, he was feuding with the organization. Although I understood the trade, I wasn't in favor of it, and I certainly couldn't believe we let him go to Dallas. The Cowboys had won eleven games in '91 and made the playoffs. They were surpassing the Giants as the team to beat in the NFC East. Since taking over the Cowboys in '89, Jerry Jones and Jimmy Johnson had been building a powerhouse. They had added wide receiver Michael Irvin and running back Emmitt Smith. They had the biggest offensive line in football. And we had just sent our best defensive player to a team we would have to beat to get back to the Super Bowl.

24

MVP

SEPTEMBER 6, 1992. I'm in the locker room at Giants Stadium. For the second straight year our season opener is in the Meadowlands. I've gone over the playbook so many times that I have it memorized cover to cover. A couple of hours before kickoff, Mike Shanahan approaches me and says: "Let's go over it one more time."

"Mike, I've memorized it."

"Yeah, let's just do it one more time."

I have never worked with anyone who is so relentless about preparation. He has never coached anyone so willing to be pushed to get better and better. I nickname him "Let's Go Over It One More Time Shanahan." He nicknames me "Rain Man."

Our first possession against the Giants is like a surgical procedure. With Mike's play-calling, I methodically dissect the Giants' defense, finishing off the drive with a 3-yard touchdown pass to Tom Rathman. We go up 7–0. It's almost too easy. I am going to love playing for Shanahan.

Our defense stops the Giants and we get the ball back. Our offense is in sync. Everything is clicking. Facing a third-down situation from midfield, I drop back. The Giants blitz. I see a seam and take off up the middle. I never see Lawrence Taylor coming from my left. I cut to my left and he plants his helmet in my ear hole and drives me to the turf. I'm sure my helmet is cracked. I feel woozy, but I get up. The punt team comes on, and I go to the sideline.

Dr. Klint examines me and concludes I have a concussion. I tell him I'm playing, but he says otherwise.

I call upstairs to Shanahan. "I'm not coming out of the game," I tell him.

He tries to calm me down, but I'm hopping mad.

On our next possession Steve Bono replaces me. In the second quarter the Giants tie the game. I tell George to put me in. But the medical staff won't clear me to play. I'm forced to watch from the sideline as Steve Bono leads the team to a 31–14 victory.

On the plane ride back home I sit next to Brent Jones. I'm still angry about having to sit out the second half with a concussion.

"That sucks," he says. "But you'll be back and ready to roll next week."

"There is no way I'm losing my job," I tell him.

He tells me that won't happen. Stop worrying.

On Tuesday night Shanahan gave me the binder for our upcoming opponent—the Bills. I had it memorized by Thursday morning. Buffalo had been to two straight Super Bowls, losing both times. They had the best offense in the AFC. We had the best offense in the NFC. I expected a shootout with Jim Kelly.

There was only one play in the binder I didn't like. It was a pass play that required me to put my back to the defense. We tried the play in practice during the week. I told Shanahan I was not comfortable. He promised he wouldn't call it during the game.

September 13, 1992. In our first possession against the Bills, Jerry Rice gets knocked out with a concussion. Then Brent Jones pulls his hamstring. My two favorite targets are gone. We still march up and down the field. By halftime we're up 24–10.

Kelly throws two touchdown passes in the third quarter to put Buffalo up by three. I counter with a 54-yard bomb to Taylor to put us back up 31–27 to end the quarter.

The Bills start the final period by driving deep into our territory before Kelly is intercepted. With a chance to put the game out of reach, we drive all the way to the Bills' 39-yard line. I look to the sideline for the play call.

It's the play that Shanahan promised he wouldn't call. I don't get it. But whatever. I drop back. My back is to the defense, and I never see defensive back Nate Odomes. He intercepts me. It's my only mistake of the day.

Furious, I head to the sideline and telephone upstairs.

"Mike, I thought we weren't going to call that play," I say. "You said you weren't going to put my back to the defense. We even talked about it."

"Steve, I'm sorry."

Sorry? He gives me his word and then goes back on it? I hang up the phone. One of my teammates turns to me. "Mike didn't call that play," he says.

"What do you mean he didn't call the play? Then who did?"

"George called it."

"What?"

George isn't supposed to call the plays. Mike is. I confront George on the sideline. He doesn't respond. Now I'm really angry. But I know two things. Mike Shanahan is a guy I can trust, no matter what. And I don't want George Seifert interfering with the chemistry I have with Mike.

I throw for a career-high 449 yards and three touchdowns, but we end up losing 34–31. Still, I love where we're headed.

I told myself I didn't want to lose another game for the entire season. Not one.

The morning after the Buffalo game, I awoke before dawn and drove to the practice facility. Shanahan was already there. We were both in a foul mood. Together we worked on the game plan for our upcoming opponent — the New York Jets. He had the same mind-set as me — no more losses for the rest of the season.

September 20, 1992. It's our second trip to the Meadowlands in three weeks, and I can't wait to get this contest started. True to form, Shanahan approaches me in the locker room and insists on going over the game plan yet another time. I recite everything from memory. Then he says: "Let's put these guys away early."

Despite sustaining a concussion the week before, Jerry Rice starts. I complete my first pass to him for 23 yards. I complete my next one to

John Taylor for 19 yards. But he breaks his leg on the play. Mike Sherrard takes his place. We keep marching. On the Jets' 5-yard line I avoid a sack and find Jerry in the end zone. We go up 7–0.

In the second quarter I throw a 47-yard pass to Sherrard to put us on the Jets' 10-yard line. Shanahan calls another pass play. I end up scrambling. On the run I fake like I'm going to throw and then scamper 10 yards for a touchdown to put us up 14–0. A few minutes later I throw another touchdown pass to Jamie Williams. It's 24–0 at the half.

By the end of the third quarter it's 31–0. George Seifert sits me for the fourth quarter and plays Bono. The Jets score two meaningless touchdowns late in the game. We win 31–14. I love playing in the Meadowlands.

We have scored 31 points in each of our first three games. We lead the league in total offense, and I'm the top-rated passer among all quarterbacks. I also lead all NFL running backs with an average of 8.9 yards *rushing* per carry.

Holmgren and Shanahan are both right. Under Holmgren, I've gotten really effective at throwing blind. Under Shanahan, the new element of throwing on the run makes me a dual threat and gives our offense a new wrinkle. It creates opportunities for me to make long runs on almost a weekly basis. Against New Orleans in week four I drop back to pass from the Saints' 27-yard line. Convinced I'm throwing, the linebacker who's supposed to check me drops back into zone coverage. I sprint downfield untouched before being dragged down at the 1-yard line. We score on the next play. Overall, I rush eight times for 65 yards, enabling us to outsmart the Saints' aggressive defense.

Similarly, a week later against the Rams, the game is tied with less than four minutes to play when I drop back to pass from the Rams' 39-yard line. No one is open, and the pocket is collapsing. I pump-fake and scramble toward the line of scrimmage. As defenders approach I pump-fake again, freezing them and enabling me to run past them. I get all the way to the Rams' 20-yard line before a group of defensive backs force me toward the sideline. Expecting me to run out of bounds, they slow down and I cut back, bounce off a few would-be tacklers, and ramble all the way to the end zone, stiff-arming a final tackler at the goal line.

But it's the pump fakes at the beginning of the play that have sprung me for the long run. That's all Shanahan.

October 11, 1992. It's my thirty-first birthday, and I'm in Foxboro Stadium. The Patriots are 0-4, but they are beating us 12–10. With thirteen minutes remaining in the game, I step to the line of scrimmage at our own 25-yard line. The crowd is energized, but so am I.

All of my quarterback coaches over the years — Gillman, Walsh, Holmgren, and now Shanahan — have schooled me to dominate in the pocket. No running quarterback has ever developed into a premier pocket passer. But I am now the top-rated passer in the NFL. I have memorized every formation, studied every defensive scheme, and mastered the nuances of reading coverages and anticipating where the openings will be. I line up under center, and over the next seven plays I march us down the field with a mixture of pinpoint passes and quarterback keepers where I knife through the defense.

On the eighth play of the drive, we are on the Patriots' 2-yard line. At the line of scrimmage, I look at linebacker Andre Tippett and defensive back Maurice Hurst as I bark out the signals. They expect me to run it. Instead, I take the snap and roll out, then throw a bullet to Ricky Watters in the back of the end zone to put us up 17–12. It's almost too easy.

On our next possession I drive us the length of the field again, and we add another touchdown to close out New England 24–12 and improve to 5-1. The next day the headline in the *New York Times* reads: "Joe Who? Young Rescues 49ers Once Again."

October 18, 1992. We're playing Atlanta at Candlestick. Jerry Glanville and the Falcons gave us fits in '91. In addition to beating us twice, they knocked me out of action for six weeks. I want to hammer them.

Before the game I pull Dr. Dillingham aside. At the end of the Patriots game I landed hard on my right shoulder. All week I've been hearing a strange clicking sound when I raise my right arm. But it doesn't appear to be affecting my ability to throw. Dillingham says he'll examine me after the Falcons game.

The moment I see Glanville take the field I forget about my shoulder. He is carrying a huge trophy. It looks like something from an amateur bowling league — plastic and gawky. He sets it down on the Falcons' sideline where everyone can see it. He says it's his California trophy. The previous season the Falcons were 8-0 against California teams.

We don't need any additional motivation to beat Atlanta. But Glanville's stunt rubs salt in the wound. We take it personally.

In the first quarter we march down the field on our first two possessions for touchdowns. On our third possession I throw an 80-yard touchdown to Rice. We are up 21–7 after one quarter. In the second quarter I throw another touchdown bomb to Rice, and Ricky Watters rushes for two more touchdowns. By halftime it's 42–10 and our offense has over 400 total yards. Shanahan doesn't want to let up. Neither do I.

In the third quarter we score on our first possession to push the lead to 49–10. Seifert calls upstairs to Shanahan and tells him not to call any more pass plays.

But Shanahan doesn't share this with me.

On our next possession Shanahan calls nothing but run plays. Still, we march all the way to Atlanta's 11-yard line, where Shanahan calls another run. But at the line of scrimmage I see that Atlanta is in a defensive formation that calls for me to check off the run play and go to a pass. I change the play at the line of scrimmage and hit Brent Jones for an 11-yard touchdown pass. Up 56–10, we have 590 yards in total offense and I have thrown for 399 yards.

When I come off the field Seifert is talking to Shanahan.

"You weren't going to call any more pass plays," Seifert tells him.

"I didn't call a pass play," Shanahan says.

Seifert shakes his head.

"Coach," Shanahan jokes, "the only way we are not going to run up the score is you gotta tell Jerry Glanville to get out of that defense."

I laugh out loud.

After beating Atlanta, we had a bye week. It couldn't have come at a better time. My right shoulder was now killing me. The blow I had taken in New England a couple of weeks earlier apparently was more serious than we initially realized. An MRI on October 22 revealed fluid buildup on my tendon. I was put on prednisone in hopes of diminishing the inflammation.

There is an art to staying healthy in the NFL. Many of the younger players don't learn this before it's too late. But there are ways to reduce the odds of getting injured. There are places to get out of trouble and places to avoid. It becomes instinctual. You can get bounced around and take some hits. That's inevitable. The key, though, is to not miss games. Bill Walsh used to say: "If you're not in the huddle, you're not in the huddle."

I took that to mean you have to be smart about staying on the field. Football is the ultimate team game. But it's also a bunch of independent contractors out there trying to make careers for themselves. Staying healthy is a huge piece of the puzzle.

In week nine we flew to Phoenix to play the Cardinals. The day before the game I came down with the flu. I couldn't get out of bed. I had a fever, a bad case of the chills, and no appetite.

But I insisted on starting. The team doctor put me on an IV before the game. In the first quarter I completed six of eight passes for 76 yards. But I was so weak I just wanted to curl up in bed. Every joint ached. My head throbbed when I moved. And my fever wouldn't quit. Finally, I went to the locker room and Bono took over. The Cardinals scored 17 unanswered points and beat us 24–14, snapping our five-game winning streak.

The following week I was back to full strength. We played in Atlanta on *Monday Night Football*. We drubbed them again, 41–3, setting up a rematch with division rival New Orleans.

November 15, 1992. With the division lead on the line, we face off against the Saints. Both teams are 7-2. Game attendance is the fourth-largest in Candlestick history.

The Saints build a 10–0 second-quarter lead before I break loose for a 10-yard touchdown run to cut the lead to 3 before the half. But New Orleans adds 10 more points in the third quarter. At the start of the fourth quarter we are down 20-7.

We get the ball on our own 40-yard line. I complete four of five passes and advance us to the Saints' 14-yard line. Then I find Brent Jones over the middle for a touchdown. The entire drive takes just one minute and fifty-four seconds. We are down 20–14 with ten minutes remaining.

New Orleans chews up six minutes but is unable to convert on a critical third down. We get the ball back on our own 26-yard line. Four minutes remain on the clock. A field goal won't help us. We need a touchdown. We have 74 yards to go.

Shanahan says to go with the two-minute offense. That means I'm calling my own plays. I go with the things we do best. I complete four consecutive short passes, two to Rathman and two to Rice. Then I hit Brent Jones with a 20-yard completion, but he injures his ribs on the play and has to leave the game. We get all the way to the Saints' 30-yard line, where we face a third-and-four situation.

I know the Saints expect a pass, so I call a bootleg and run eight yards for a first down. Then I make consecutive handoffs to Watters, who runs it to the 8-yard line. Only forty-six seconds remain when Brent Jones returns to the huddle. His ribs are so bad he can't take deep breaths. "I want the ball," he says.

He runs a simple post route, and I find him in the back of the end zone. With the extra point we win 21–20.

It's bedlam in Candlestick. We've stolen the game to improve to 8-2, giving us sole possession of first place. We run off the field to a cascade of cheers. Eddie DeBartolo is at the locker room entrance, slapping hands with every player. He throws his arms around me. "Amazing, Steve! Amazing!"

"Where were you during that last drive?" I joke. "On the window ledge?"

He cracks up and hugs me again.

Then *San Francisco Examiner* columnist Art Spander approaches me at my locker.

"I know you don't want to be compared with Montana—"

"Then don't, Art. Then just don't."

He drops the subject.

Joe Montana was finally cleared to play on November 29 against the Eagles. Shanahan told me not to worry. He said there was absolutely no reason to make a change at quarterback. At 9-2 we had the best record in the league. We led the league in offense. And thanks largely to Shanahan, I was playing better than any quarterback in the league. We had a uniquely simpatico relationship. I loved his aggressive play-calling, and he loved that I could process so much information. His relentless preparation was unlike anything I had previously experienced. He embedded things in my head that enabled me to develop a reflexive recall on the field. My self-confidence was stronger than ever.

But with Joe ready to play again, the tension had returned, and it was palpable. For five years Joe had looked over his shoulder at me. Suddenly I was looking over my shoulder at him.

Then there was Jerry Rice. The previous season he had struggled with the spin on my left-handed passes. I knew that our assistant equipment manager, Ted Walsh, was also a lefty. So last year I had him start throwing passes to Jerry on the sideline during practice whenever the defense was on the field. Walsh had thrown hundreds of passes per day to Jerry over the course of last season. It had paid off.

The game against Philadelphia had big playoff implications. The Eagles were right behind Dallas in the NFC East. We were tied with Dallas for the best record in the NFC. The media billed the game as a contest to decide who was the premier running quarterback in the league: Randall Cunningham or me.

I couldn't have cared less about whether people thought I was a better runner than Cunningham. I came out throwing. In the first quarter I threw a 22-yard touchdown pass to Rice. It was his 100th touchdown reception, tying him with Steve Largent for the all-time record. Overall I had my biggest passing day of the season, completing 24 of 35 passes for 342 yards and two touchdowns. Eight of my completions were to Jerry for 133 yards. We won 20–14, becoming the first team to win ten games and clinch a playoff spot.

Jerry broke Largent's record a week later against Miami when I hit him on a 12-yard slant pattern. We routed the Dolphins to improve to 11-2. But after the game I was diagnosed with post-traumatic bursitis in my right shoulder. The doctor put me on Feldene, a nonsteroid anti-inflammatory that's commonly used to treat arthritis.

December 28, 1992. We are at home for the final game of the regular season, a *Monday Night Football* affair with the Lions. We have the best record in football at 13-2. Before the game George Seifert tells me that Joe will play the second half.

It's a chilly, wet night. Fans don rain gear. And Candlestick Park is draped in signs.

WELCOME BACK JOE

HE'S BACK

SUPER JOE

WE LOVE JOE

I have a pit in my stomach. It would be easier to just let Joe start. That's what the fans want. He hasn't played in two years, and there is a sense that this may be his final game in a 49ers uniform.

After leading us to a 10–6 halftime lead, I retire to the locker room and put a big raincoat over my pads. Chants shake the stadium like thunder when we come out for the second half.

"Joe!"

"Joe!"

"Joe!"

"Joe!"

The Lions kick off. Joe jogs onto the field, and the cheering reaches a crescendo. He has not played in two years. It's raining. It's cold. But nobody cares. Joe's back. The world is right again.

In his second possession, Joe throws a touchdown pass to Brent Jones. It's what everyone has come to see. The chants resume.

"Joe!"

"Joe!"

"Joe!"

He jogs off the field. When he reaches the sideline I slap his hand. While Joe takes in the moment I contemplate my situation. It's bizarre. Succeeding a legend is no picnic. I'm glad I didn't know what I was in for when Bill Walsh offered me the quarterback job in 1987. I never would have signed up for this. Never. It's the hardest thing I've ever done. But it's also the best thing that has ever happened to me. I love the San Francisco 49ers organization, and I cherish the opportunity to be the team's quarterback. It's the best job in football. I don't blame Joe for the way he sees the situation. I get it. Truth is, the 49ers have gotten the best out of both of us.

I finished the 1992 regular season completing 66.7 percent of my passes for 3,456 yards and 25 touchdowns, giving me the highest quarterback rating in NFL history, other than Joe's record-setting season in '89. I threw only seven interceptions. I was the first quarterback to lead the NFL in passing in consecutive seasons. I also rushed for 537 yards. On January 6, 1993, I was named the NFL's Most Valuable Player.

A year earlier I was clawing my way through the season. Then I had my encounter with Stephen Covey, followed by Mike Shanahan's arrival. In one year's time I was flying at incredible altitudes.

January 9, 1993. I am starting my first playoff game. We're playing the Redskins in San Francisco. Candlestick is a swamp, but I feel right at home in the mud. I throw early touchdown passes to John Taylor and Brent Jones to put us up 17–3 at the half. The field conditions continue to deteriorate. At the end of the third quarter the ball slips out of my hand, and I get hammered when I try to recover the fumble. The Redskins get the ball. It's my third turnover of the day.

Washington converts the turnover into a field goal to make it 17–6. We can't sustain our next drive. The Redskins open the fourth quarter with a touchdown to close to within four points. Tension mounts on our sideline. Players yell at each other. A few yell at me. Washington has the momentum. The season is slipping away.

All of my anxieties churn inside me. Inadequacy. Doubt. Loneliness. Fear. I look behind me. Montana removes his jacket and starts warming up behind the bench. The team notices. The crowd notices. Electricity sweeps through the stands.

But now my competitive nature overtakes my fears. I want back on the field. There is no way I'm losing this game. Our next drive chews up eight minutes. I scramble. I pass. I run. We march 57 yards on 13 plays. Mike Cofer kicks a field goal to put us up 20–13.

In the corner of my eye, I see Montana putting his coat back on.

Washington drives to our 24-yard line, and it looks like they will score again. But with nine minutes left, Mark Rypien fumbles and we recover. That seals the win.

The Cowboys await.

25

DALLAS

JANUARY 17, 1993. The NFC Championship game is about to start, and I'm standing at midfield with three of my teammates for the coin toss. Fog envelops Candlestick, and a misty rain is falling. It's 1:00 PM, but the lights are on. My cleats sink into the soggy sod.

Charles Haley, Troy Aikman, and Roger Staubach are standing opposite me. It figures that Cowboys head coach Jimmy Johnson would send those three. Aikman and I are the two best quarterbacks in the NFC. Staubach was my childhood hero. Haley hates the 49ers with a passion, and I'm the target.

We win the toss and elect to receive. All week Shanahan and I have been talking about the need to strike fast and strike big. On the second play of the game Jerry streaks down the left sideline and I let it fly, hitting him in stride for a 67-yard touchdown play. Jerry spikes it and Candlestick erupts.

But the euphoria is short-lived. One of our offensive linemen is called for holding. Touchdown negated. Momentum stifled.

We end up punting, and Dallas scores first to go up 3–0.

Our next drive is solid. We march 47 yards on seven plays to end up on the Cowboys' 1-yard line. I call a quarterback keeper and run right into Haley at the goal line. I keep pumping my legs, and my momentum carries me across the goal line. We go up 7–3.

With time running down in the first half, Dallas clings to a 10–7 lead. We are on the Cowboys' 15-yard line. We need to get to the 10 for a first down. I drop back, Haley beats his man, and I tuck the ball and run past him. I turn the corner, and Russell Maryland tries to tear my head off. My helmet goes flying, but I lunge for the first down. Trailing the play, Haley comes down on top of me and slams his forearm into my chest, barely missing my head.

It is my first time facing Haley since the trade, and it is pretty clear he is out to get me. The referee looks down at me. "You okay?"

I nod.

The other official takes the ball from me and signals first down.

I retrieve my helmet and walk back to the huddle. But we end up settling for a field goal. It's 10–10 at the half.

Both teams move the ball up and down the field in the third quarter. Then Dallas puts up a touchdown. We only muster a field goal. Then Dallas mounts a nine-minute drive that results in a touchdown to open the fourth quarter. With a little over twelve minutes to play, we trail 24–13.

On our next possession Ken Norton Jr. intercepts me. Dallas takes over on our 45-yard line. Aikman moves Dallas to our 7-yard line. A touchdown will put the game out of reach. On fourth-and-one, Jimmy Johnson elects to go for it. Our defense drops Emmitt for a one-yard loss. We take over on downs. We have life.

I complete eight passes and march us 93 yards in two minutes and twenty-eight seconds before throwing a 5-yard touchdown pass to Rice, cutting the Cowboys' lead to 4 with just over four minutes remaining. It's enough time if we can prevent Dallas from getting a first down.

All eyes are on our defense. On the first play after the kickoff, Alvin Harper runs a simple 8-yard slant. Aikman hits him, and our defender slips and falls, enabling Harper to run 70 yards untouched before he is knocked out of bounds at our 9-yard line. Two plays later Kelvin Martin crashes into the end zone. Dallas is up 30–20.

With less than two minutes to play, I trot onto the field. We need two scores. There isn't enough time. I know it. But I want this win more than I've ever wanted anything. I drop back. Dallas drops eight guys into pass coverage. I have to make something happen. I force it. James Washington intercepts me. While Charles Haley and the Cowboys celebrate, I retreat to the sideline. The 49ers fans behind our bench are livid.

"Seifert, you suck!" one of them shouts. "You shoulda put in Joe, you idiot!"

I'm the MVP of the league and it doesn't matter. The final two minutes feel like an eternity. The clock finally expires. Joe and I end up walking off the field together. Neither of us says a word.

Our locker room was silent. Montana cleaned out his locker and disappeared before the press entered. I wanted to disappear too. But that wasn't an option.

A pack of reporters surrounded me.

"I thought we could get the ball back and put the hammer on," I told them. "We've done it a couple of times before, and it looked like we were going to do it again, but they turned it around on us. When you get the momentum back and they go eighty yards on three plays, that's not good."

The questions kept coming. I wanted to check out. But I stayed until the last question.

"I think when you get to this point, when you know how hard it is, you just put your body and soul into it," I said. "I feel like my soul and spirit are still out on the field trying to win a ball game."

They finally left me alone. Silent, I sat in front of my locker. I was covered in mud. My body ached. I was the league MVP. But Dallas was going to the Super Bowl and we were going home. Nothing else mattered.

Shanahan approached me. "I appreciate everything you did, Steve. You had a great year."

I shrugged.

"We fell a little short," he continued. "We'll get our off-season going."

He patted me on the back.

No loss in my life felt as painful as this one.

We both knew the deal. It didn't matter how well I played during the season or how well the team did. It didn't matter how well he coached. This was San Francisco. At the end of the day there was only one goal in the 49ers organization — winning the Super Bowl. Anything less was unacceptable. Anything less was failure.

I was the last one out of the locker room. My Jeep was the only vehicle left in the players' parking lot. It was two hours after the game, but a woman in a wheelchair was waiting to have her picture taken with me. I wasn't in the best mood, but I kissed her on the cheek, and the photo was taken.

A single fan remained in the upper deck of Candlestick Park. He was bellowing: "Put Joe in. There's still time."

I shook my head, got in my Jeep, and drove off.

I've often joked for years about this moment — how it felt like the whole Bay Area was telling me to get in my Jeep and keep driving. Vallejo. Grass Valley. Reno. Good-bye. It really was Super Bowl or bust. But the quest remained, and that's what kept me motivated.

A few days after losing to Dallas, I flew to New York and appeared on *The David Letterman Show.* For fun he had me throw footballs through the window of a moving taxi on the street in front of the Ed Sullivan Theater. I then went back to Provo to resume law school. But it was hard to concentrate. My phone wouldn't stop ringing. The requests for interviews kept coming. So did opportunities to endorse products. And the amount of mail I was getting at 49ers headquarters got so out of hand that the mailroom replaced my mail slot with a bin.

The demands on my time made it nearly impossible to focus on my studies. I had barely resumed classes when I had to leave again for the Pro Bowl in Hawaii in early February. It was my first one, and I arrived in Honolulu as the MVP. I was in a new place, but it felt comfortable. I quickly discovered that a big part of the Pro Bowl weekend was the fraternity of the NFL's elite players having a chance to hang out. I spent a lot of time getting to know Troy Aikman better. But I really spent most of my time scouting for defensive players who could help us beat Aikman next year.

The guy I wanted was Cardinals All-Pro safety Tim McDonald. Besides being one of the hardest-hitting defensive backs in the league, Tim was a natural leader. He was also a free agent, and Leigh Steinberg represented him. After hanging out with Tim for three days, I called Leigh and told him to do whatever he had to do to convince Carmen Policy to sign him.

Then I went out and brought the NFC back from behind by throwing a game-tying touchdown pass on fourth-and-long with ten seconds remaining.

26

GOING DEEP

B Y MID-APRIL I was holed up at my house in Provo, studying for final exams. I turned off my phone. I got by on little sleep. I focused on my law outlines and blocked everything else out.

But on Sunday, April 18, I made the mistake of turning on my phone before church. I immediately got a call from Leigh. "I'm sorry for the intrusion," he said. "But this is urgent."

The 49ers were all set to trade Joe to the Kansas City Chiefs. But Eddie DeBartolo didn't want to part with him. Leigh told me that Joe was on his way to Eddie's house in Youngstown, Ohio, and Eddie planned to make a last-ditch effort to keep Joe in San Francisco. One of the things being discussed was the prospect of designating Joe the starter heading into training camp. Leigh told me he had just got off the phone with Carmen Policy, who wanted to know how I felt about that.

I wanted to hit something.

Instead I vented on Leigh. "Tell Carmen to trade one of us," I told Leigh sharply. "But I'm not doing that anymore."

I hung up and turned my phone off.

Later that day George Seifert named Joe the "designated starter." It was all part of the effort to get Joe to stay in San Francisco.

I started final exams the next morning. For a couple of days I cut myself off from the outside world to focus. I couldn't worry about Joe and Eddie and Carmen and George. The situation was out of my hands. I had to focus on passing my law finals.

I managed to ace them. Afterward I was in the law school parking lot when someone approached and asked if I knew that Joe Montana had been traded to Kansas City.

I got in my car and turned on my phone. My mailbox was full. There were calls from all over, including my parents, Jim Herrmann, and Brent Jones. Even Carole Burr was trying to get a hold of me. But most of the messages were from Leigh. I called him first. He confirmed it. Joe was now a Chief.

I hung up and sat in my car in silence. I should have been excited. But I was instantly emotionally exhausted. I knew what was coming.

The reaction in the Bay Area was visceral. The *San Francisco Examiner* published a poll showing that 85 percent of the fans in San Francisco overwhelmingly favored Montana over me. Season-ticket-holders vowed to shred their tickets. Bumper stickers popped up all over that said: I MISS JOE.

The following week Joe appeared on the cover of *Sports Illustrated* flashing his four Super Bowl rings. The heading read: "Kansas City, Here I Come."

Those four rings were now clearly my problem. I had to deliver a ring. I knew if I didn't, I'd get run out of town.

I retreated to Provo and went to see Carole Burr.

"I'm so tired of all this," I said.

Carole let me unload, and then she gave me her advice: it was time for me to go far away for some spiritual rejuvenation. She said she had the perfect destination — Jerusalem.

Jerusalem? I laughed.

She was serious. Carole was good friends with Truman Madsen, the director of the Brigham Young University Jerusalem Center for Near East Studies. She said she was calling him to arrange for me to spend some time with him in Israel.

Whoa, wait a second, I told her. Truman Madsen was a Harvard-trained philosopher and a prolific author. Religious leaders from faiths throughout the world respected him. He was the Mormon Church's version of Thomas Aquinas. Madsen wasn't going to want to be bothered with hosting some football player. He didn't even know me.

And despite the fact that I had read his books, I certainly didn't know him.

Carole ignored my protests and called him. It was pretty clear that Truman was reluctant. But after some back and forth, he told Carole he'd host me.

I told Carole I really didn't want to go. I just didn't feel like flying halfway around the world by myself. It was the off-season. I just wanted to lay low in Utah. Maybe another time, I told her.

It was now or never, she told me. Truman was about to step down as the center's director. In a few weeks he and his wife Ann were moving back to Provo.

"You're going, Steve," Carole said firmly.

When I landed in Tel Aviv, Truman and Ann met me outside the airport. He threw his arms around me and welcomed me to Israel. His voice made a deep impression on me. It was not loud. But it was authoritative, and his words were eloquent. He insisted on taking my bags and loading them into the trunk of his car. Then he opened the door for me. I knew right away that I was in the presence of a very unusual individual. He matched my image of Christ's disciples — spiritual yet humble, powerful but dedicated to teaching and serving others.

After I settled in, Truman showed me around the BYU Jerusalem Center. The 125,000-square-foot structure had eight levels and overlooked the Lion's Gate and the old city of Jerusalem. BYU students lived there while studying the Old and New Testaments, as well as Arabic and Hebrew. I marveled that a Christian church could be built on a campus of this size in Jerusalem.

Truman took me to meet the man who helped make it happen — Jerusalem's mayor, Teddy Kollek. Back in the early 1980s, Kollek had helped the Mormon Church secure a forty-nine-year lease on the land to construct the Jerusalem Center. But Orthodox Jewish groups in Israel vehemently opposed the idea. Kollek never wavered, however. His leadership was pivotal in seeing the project through. And much of that leadership stemmed from Kollek's friendship with Truman.

The next day was a Friday. The Jewish Sabbath officially began at sundown. We drove to Haifa to observe the Sabbath with Abraham Kaplan and his family. Abraham and Truman were close. I wore a yarmulke — a blue skullcap with a yellow embroidered border — and was invited to sit at a formal dining table covered in white linen, fine china, and silver candlesticks with tall, white candles. Before the meal, Abraham blessed each one of his children. They were grown and living elsewhere in Israel. But each child had come home for the Sabbath meal. It was a powerful example of how to strengthen family ties.

I had spent my whole life attending church services and reading scriptures about Sabbath day observance. But I learned even more about the significance and importance of the Sabbath in that one evening with Abraham Kaplan and his family. I also got an appreciation for how similar Jews and Mormons are when it comes to religious beliefs. In keeping with local custom, Mormons in Israel recognize Saturday as the Sabbath. So on Saturday morning Truman and Ann took me to Mormon services near the Sea of Galilee. Most of the congregation consisted of BYU students. Truman invited me to address them. I talked about being in the NFL and the importance of staying close to God no matter where you are.

Afterward a few of the students asked if I'd mind throwing a football with them. I couldn't help smiling at my situation. A week earlier I was embroiled in the media swirl over Joe Montana's trade to the Chiefs. Now I was in a white shirt and tie, throwing spirals to a group of students in the Holy Land. If only the football writers could see me now.

After church, Truman took me to see key places in Christ's ministry. I put on a brand-new pair of shoes that I had bought in the States especially for this trip. I figured that if I was literally going to walk where Jesus walked, I wanted to wear special shoes. This was holy ground, after all. So in a private gesture to myself and to God, I wore new shoes that I had purchased just for this occasion.

Our first stop was the Sea of Galilee. We stopped on the shore and discussed the instance when Christ stopped there and invited common fishermen to drop their nets and follow Him. Then we went to the River Jordan, where Christ was baptized. We went to Capernaum, the epicenter of Christ's ministry. At the Garden of Gethsemane we knelt among the olive trees. I prayed silently, and Truman taught me more about the betrayal that took place when Judas greeted Jesus with a kiss.

From there we went to South Jerusalem to a place called the High

Priest's Palace. It's where Jesus was imprisoned while waiting to be judged by Pilate. Truman and Ann took me to an underground dungeon. The walls were made of stone. Inside, we sang my favorite hymn, "Abide with Me; 'Tis Eventide."

Martin Lowrie Hofford, a Union soldier in the Civil War, wrote the lyrics:

> Abide with me, 'tis eventide,
> And lone will be the night
> If I cannot commune with Thee,
> Nor find in Thee my light.
> The darkness of the world, I fear,
> Would in my home abide.
>
> Oh, Savior, stay this night with me;
> Behold, 'tis eventide.

I choked up as our voices echoed off the walls.

At each stop, Truman taught me as if I were his pupil, adding richness and texture to incidents like the cleansing of lepers or the healing of the crippled boy lowered through a roof where Jesus preached. But inside the Garden we sat in silence among the olive trees, contemplating what had taken place there 2,000 years earlier.

Finally, we walked the road to Calvary. Kicking up dust in my new shoes, I visualized Jesus walking barefoot, his back bending under the weight of a heavy wooden cross beam tied to his shoulders. I visualized people spitting at him and mocking him. I wished I could have been there to help him shoulder the load. Instead, I was keenly aware of the burden I might have added with my life. I was usually very good at controlling my emotions. I almost never let anyone see me cry. But by the time we reached the spot where Jesus was nailed to the cross, I couldn't hold back. The tears flowed. Truman patted my shoulder. Then he led me to the Garden Tomb, where he deepened my understanding about the Resurrection. The NFL seemed so far away. In the big scheme of things, football and fame and all that comes with it are so transitory and trivial. The reality of my insignificance set in.

Suddenly I felt Christ's love for me, along with his grace. I have always believed in Jesus and accepted His teachings. But it had just gotten much more real. I even changed my perspective on the loss to Dallas. *What if there is a greater lesson to be learned from losing than from winning?*

What if?

I spent my last night with Truman and Ann on the beach. We talked about the Savior. We laughed. We cried. Then we said good-bye. I removed the shoes I had worn on the visit and placed them back in my suitcase. They would never be worn again.

At 1:30 AM I took a taxi to the airport. My eyes welled up in the backseat of the cab. They welled up on the plane too. I had been up for eighteen hours straight, but I forced myself to stay awake all the way to New York. I feared that if I slept I would lose the sense of spirit that I felt.

The minute I stepped off the plane at JFK I felt the change. It was noisy and hot. Thousands of people crowded the terminal. Too many of them recognized me. I was back to being the guy who replaced Joe Montana. I didn't feel like being that guy. I put on sunglasses and pulled my baseball cap down over my forehead. I walked with my head down. I didn't want to talk to anyone about football and quarterback controversies.

Plus, my emotions were too raw. I was overwhelmed by the debt I felt to my Savior. I felt like I knew Him more intimately now that I had walked where He had walked. I would have given anything to feel that close to Him every day.

From the airport I called Carole Burr in Provo.

"How was Israel?" she said.

"I loved Israel. I love the Israeli people. I want to go back."

Then I choked up.

"Steve, what's wrong?" she said.

"I didn't want to get off the plane. I'll never get that spirit again."

Three days later I attended the Cadillac-National Football League Golf Classic at the Upper Montclair Country Club in Clifton, New Jersey. Since I was the reigning MVP, the league insisted that I attend. I wore silly-looking white knickers with gold and maroon socks. I signed hundreds of autographs. And I faced blunt questions about whether I had any hard feelings over the fact that 49ers owner Eddie DeBartolo and head coach George Seifert had offered to make Joe Montana the starting quarterback in hopes of keeping him in San Francisco.

"I've been with these guys seven years," I told a writer from the *New York Times.* "The relationship has gotten better and better and better all during those years. To take that twenty-four-hour period and say it's all going backwards now is ridiculous. Let me put it this way: I have no problem playing for Eddie DeBartolo and George."

I got peppered with questions about Joe Montana too. But I was not about to get baited into saying something negative. Before going to Jerusalem, I had harbored some bitterness and resentment toward the 49ers over the whole situation with Joe. But those feelings had evaporated in Israel. After walking where Jesus walked, I realized that bruises to personal ego are pretty petty. Better to take the high road.

"I wish the best for him," I told the press. "In a lot of ways he's like Michael Jordan because the greatness gets monotonous. But you have to be careful because he continues to do things that defy the odds. That's why I would expect nothing less of Joe Montana this year."

Leigh Steinberg was a huge proponent of philanthropy. From the day I signed with him as a college student he encouraged me — and all of his clients — to use football as a means to help the less fortunate. My time in Israel with Truman Madsen prompted me to follow through in a much bigger way on Leigh's platform. One group in particular came to mind: children. Specifically, I wanted to set up a foundation capable of bringing financial resources to kids suffering from poverty, physical handicaps, and emotional challenges.

In the off-season I had some people help me research nonprofits. I met with philanthropists, and I consulted with lawyers. Leigh was a big part of the process. I never made any big decisions without his input. Finally, with the help of my Uncle Bob, I settled on a name — the Forever Young Foundation — and we were up and running within a couple of months. But I still had to figure out a way to fund it.

Leigh helped with that too. He helped me line up a number of major endorsement deals, starting with Nike. I also signed endorsement deals with four other corporations that sold consumer products from shampoo to men's apparel. But I turned down an offer from Coca-Cola. The soft drink company wanted to pay me $1 million a year to be a spokesman. However, Coke products are heavily caffeinated, and I wanted to steer clear of endorsing products that had addictive properties.

My friends thought I was crazy for turning down $1 million. They also couldn't believe the growing number of women who were approaching me. Fame had a way of prompting people to do bizarre things. I got hundreds of marriage proposals from complete strangers. They came in the mail, along with nude pictures, lingerie, bikinis, and bathing suits. I received enough risqué women's clothing to open my own boutique. My teammates liked me because I gave the stuff to them to give to their wives. I had no interest in meeting someone through the mail.

Fame made dating a complicated situation for me. There were instances when I had dated a woman during the season and she assumed we were engaged. Worse, her family would start broadcasting it. Curiously, this happened time and time again, particularly within the Mormon community.

27

SLEEPLESS IN SAN FRANCISCO

IN EARLY JULY I figured I'd better find a place to live during the up-coming season. A couple of years earlier I had formed a close friendship with Kieth and Dagny Merrill, a Mormon couple in Los Altos. Kieth was a filmmaker and a member of the Academy of Motion Picture Arts and Sciences. In 1973 he won an Academy Award for his film *The American Cowboy.* He and Dagny had eight children. They weren't football fans, but they had a connection to my family. Kieth and my mother had attended grammar school together in Utah, and the Merrills had gone to college with my parents.

The Merrills started having me over for dinner a couple of nights a week. Their home was a nice escape. The atmosphere felt a bit like Carole Burr's home when I first arrived in Provo as a college freshman. I particularly hit it off with their daughters Kamee and Kaele. I hired Kaele as my personal assistant. She handled everything from my calendar to my correspondence.

Kieth and Dagny had a new structure on their property in Los Altos that looked like a barn. The main floor was used for a musical troupe to practice and rehearse. There was a piano, other instruments, and lots of costumes. The upstairs was unfinished: no sheetrock, bare floors, and an exposed ceiling. I offered to pay for the cost to add a bedroom, a kitchen, and a bath in the loft area if I could stay there.

"There's no heat up there either," Kieth said.

"It's California. I don't need any heat," I said.

"Are you sure?"

"Yeah. I'll be fine."

Kieth said the place was mine.

On July 15, 1993, the 49ers opened training camp. The next day I signed a five-year, $26.75 million contract. The deal made me the highest-paid player in the NFL. My wish of remaining with the 49ers for the remainder of my career seemed certain. The new contract also meant that the Forever Young Foundation had a revenue stream.

As I stepped on the field for our first day of full contact at our Rocklin training facility it was immediately apparent that our defensive unit had changed. Veterans Pierce Holt and Michael Carter were gone. We had a rookie lineman, Dana Stubblefield, and my new friend Tim McDonald. We tried to convince free agent Reggie White to join us too, but he signed with Green Bay instead.

The biggest change, of course, was the absence of Joe. Everyone felt it, especially me. Talk of his departure was all over the radio and in the papers. Inevitably, the discussion turned to whether I could lead the team to another Super Bowl victory. I was asking myself the same thing.

The only way to answer the question was to get past Dallas. Meantime, the quest would begin on August 8 in our second preseason game against the Raiders in front of 84,000 fans at Stanford Stadium.

In the first quarter linebacker Aaron Wallace runs into me as I throw a pass. His helmet hits my throwing hand, sending a sharp pain through my thumb. On the next play the ball feels funny. I hand it to the ref: "This ball is flat," I tell him.

He examines it. "This ball is not flat," he says, handing it back to me.

It still feels flat to me. I look at my thumb and realize that the tip of it is folded over. I head to the sideline and find Dr. Dillingham.

"I broke my thumb," I tell him.

He looks at my hand. "You really think it's broken?"

"It's broken," I say.

· · ·

Dr. Dillingham took me to the locker room for an X-ray. But the machine was a portable one and the results were too cloudy. So he sent me to the ER at Stanford Hospital for another X-ray.

The X-rays confirmed that my thumb was fractured. The doctor put my thumb in a metal splint and said I'd be out of action for about six weeks.

He clearly had not practiced medicine in the NFL. I told myself the splint was coming off in twenty-one days or less.

September 4, 1993. We land in Pittsburgh, and as soon as we reach the hotel I take off the metal splint and try gripping a ball. I can't do it. My thumb lacks strength. I start fretting about it. Brent tells me to relax.

He always says that. And I never listen. Halfway through the night we're both still awake. He calls me the Eighth Wonder of the World because I'm a thirty-one-year-old single Mormon. I crack up. It's the first time I've laughed in days, and it takes the edge off. I don't know what I'd do without Brent.

In pregame warm-ups my thumb swells and starts throbbing. I talk to my center, Jesse Sapolu. I tell him we're going to have to alter our typical exchange. I can't take a chance of him hiking the ball and jamming my thumb. So I am going to keep my left hand back. Essentially, Jesse will be snapping the ball into my right hand. Then I will quickly rotate the ball into my left. This increases the chances of fumbling, but I have to protect my thumb.

Despite being unable to grip the ball properly, I complete nearly all of my first-half throws, including a pair of touchdowns to Jerry Rice. We're up 17–3 at halftime. But in the third quarter I throw two interceptions. After a Pittsburgh touchdown, our lead is 17–10, and I can feel the game getting away from us.

On our next possession we mount a good drive, but it's stalling when linebacker Kevin Greene hits me after I let go of the ball, slamming his forearm into my helmet and knocking me to the turf. Then he lands on me. We exchange words as we're getting up. Then my linemen start jawing with him. It's just the spark we need.

Greene's blow to my head draws a 15-yard penalty for unnecessary roughness and unsportsmanlike conduct. Determined, we are inside the

Steelers 20-yard line when I approach the line of scrimmage. Greene is lined up outside my right tackle. I know he's mad, and I know he's blitzing. So I change the snap count in hopes of drawing him offsides. Instead, my lineman moves. The referee blows his whistle and throws his flag. He's going to call a false start on my right tackle, but Greene is so frustrated he ignores the whistle and runs at me. I see him coming, but instead of ducking out of the way, I hold my ground. He wraps me up and slams me to the turf. I instantly feel my elbow swelling.

Normally I don't let defensive guys body-slam me. But this one is worth it. Rather than penalizing my lineman for a false start, the ref penalizes Greene for jumping offsides. Now he's enraged, and so is Steelers head coach Bill Cowher and the Pittsburgh fans. The penalty gives us another crucial first down. On the next play I hit Brent Jones for a touchdown, and Pittsburgh never recovers. We are 1-0.

As our team bus pulls out of the parking lot at Three Rivers Stadium, my mind flashes back to when I was a kid and I'd watch the Steelers on television. Mean Joe Greene, Jack Lambert, and Terry Bradshaw were mythical figures back then. As the stadium fades out of sight, I think to myself: *We just beat the Pittsburgh Steelers.* Sometimes there are moments in this league that take me back to being a little kid.

But I pay the price for letting Greene throw me to the turf. I have a bruise the size of a golf ball on my left elbow. Dr. Dillingham sterilizes the area and then inserts a needle and removes about 4 cubic centimeters of blood. He tells me to ice it and warns me that if I'm not careful I'll irritate the nerve that runs to the joint in my elbow.

A week later we traveled to Cleveland to play the Browns on *Monday Night Football.* Stomach problems continued to dog me. But on game day I ignored the fact that I felt miserable. I had promised to help a friend.

Karl Ricks Anderson worked in the auto industry in Cleveland. But his hobby was researching early Mormon history in nearby Kirtland, where the Church established its first headquarters in the 1830s. My great-great-great-grandfather Brigham Young resided in Kirtland before leading the Mormon migration west. In the early 1980s the Church tapped Anderson to help in the effort to acquire historically important properties in Kirtland that were once owned by Mormons.

I met Anderson in the mid-1980s when I attended the dedication of the first historic building — a general store — that the Church rebuilt in Kirtland. After the ceremony I was given a T-shirt that said: KIRTLAND, OHIO, CITY OF FAITH AND BEAUTY. I had so many T-shirts that I didn't know what to do with another one. I tossed the Kirtland shirt in a pile in my closet. Roughly five years later the Kirtland shirt was among a handful of undershirts that I grabbed and packed for training camp. One day I wore it to practice, and on that particular day a *Sports Illustrated* photographer snapped a candid shot of me walking and talking with Joe Montana. I'm in the Kirtland shirt, and Joe's in a 49ers T-shirt.

I was unaware that the photo had been taken until it appeared in the magazine a couple of years later in Peter King's profile on me that ran in the May 31, 1993, issue. By that time the Mormon Church had acquired a bunch of historic properties and was poised to reconstruct an old section of the city called "Historic Kirtland Village." But the development had hit a snag. The Church wanted to reroute two century-old roads that ran through the heart of the historic village, a request that required approval by the Kirtland City Council. Kirtland's mayor, Mario Marcopoli, supported the Church and its plan to reroute roads. But he also told Karl Ricks Anderson that it was going to take divine intervention to get the City Council to go along. "Pray to the Man Upstairs," Marcopoli told Anderson.

Weeks later the picture of me wearing the Kirtland T-shirt appeared in *Sports Illustrated.* Days later Anderson got a call from the mayor. "Thank you for arranging this with the Man Upstairs," he said.

Anderson didn't get it. He hadn't seen the magazine.

Marcopoli filled him in. Then he explained that one of the City Council members had seen the picture and had suggested that the Mormon Church purchase the photo and have it placed in the newly constructed Kirtland City Hall.

Anderson notified the Church, which responded by purchasing an enlarged version of the photograph from *Sports Illustrated.* Then the Church had it framed and presented it to the city as a gift. The framed picture was hung in the entryway to the City Council chambers. When Anderson realized I would be in Cleveland for a Monday night game, he asked if I'd meet with the City Council, and I said I would.

Early that Monday I arranged a private reception for Kirtland City

Council members and their families at the team hotel. I took individual and family photos with all of them. They had brought the framed picture from city hall for me to sign. Then I invited all of them to attend the Monday night game as my guest. The whole experience created a great deal of goodwill between the Mormon Church and city officials in Kirtland. A few months later Anderson appeared before the City Council, and it voted unanimously to permit the roads to be rerouted.

Unfortunately, the game against the Browns didn't turn out nearly as well. Early in the game I took a pretty good shot that left a deep bruise on my left thigh. Cleveland was a lousy team. But it was as if Cleveland's defense knew our plays in advance. We couldn't figure out how they were doing it. I threw three interceptions and we lost 23–13.

It was a long flight back. My left thumb, left elbow, and left thigh were all hurting. By the time I got to my loft in the Merrills' barn it was five in the morning. I was so beat I didn't bother undressing and collapsed on my bed. But I couldn't sleep. My mind wouldn't let me. Losing to Cleveland? Unacceptable. Starting the season 1-1? Unacceptable. Six interceptions in the first two games? Unacceptable.

My thumb wasn't right. My elbow was sore. My stomach was a mess. I was fatigued. I had to play better.

I tossed and turned all night. I was still awake at dawn. Panic set in. My body craved sleep, but my mind wouldn't wind down. I closed the curtains, pulled a pillow over my head, and finally dozed off. But the slightest flinch woke me.

At ten, I crawled out of bed. My thigh felt like one giant charley horse. I gazed into a mirror and saw a man buckling under the weight of the world. The 49ers had to win this year. I had to deliver.

My outlook was perplexing. On the one hand, I had incredible confidence in my ability as a quarterback. I was the MVP of the league. Yet I felt tethered to a ball and chain. I was the quarterback of a Super Bowl–caliber team. I knew what had to be done. But in the second week of the regular season I already felt the heaviness of anxiety.

I went back to my bed and dropped to my knees and pleaded with God for help. I didn't want to do this anymore. But I also didn't want to quit. I still wanted to find out how good I could become. In the aftermath of Joe

Montana, San Francisco was the hardest place in the world for a quarter-back to play. But I still wanted to know: *How far can I go?*

For now, I told myself, *You just have to survive.*

I had been repeating this same mantra since high school. It had always seemed to get me through the seasons, but for some reason it wasn't doing the trick this time. For the next couple of days I stumbled around in a fog. Finally, I called Carole Burr in Utah.

"I'm not going to make it through this season," I told her.

She stayed on the phone with me for hours. She'd been encouraging me to see a psychologist for a few years. This time she put her foot down. She said she was sending a doctor-friend to San Francisco. This time I was too mentally and physically exhausted to fight her.

Rex Kocherhans (pronounced CO-ker-hans) was a thirty-eight-year-old family therapist with a practice back in Provo. He showed up the next day at the Merrills' place, but by the time he arrived I had already left and checked into the team hotel. I was in my room with Brent Jones when Carol called and informed me that Rex was waiting at the barn.

The guy didn't even know me. Yet he had gone to the trouble of flying to the Bay Area on a weekend. I couldn't stand him up. I told the team I was sick and needed to return home for the night.

Kocherhans had an empathetic ear. We talked about my childhood, my family, my ambitions, and my fears. I told him everything. He was pretty shocked. He asked if I had ever shared this with anyone. I told him I had gone to see a psychologist two years earlier. But I hadn't done any follow-up visits.

We ended up talking through the night until Rex nodded off. By that point the sun was coming up. I told him to help himself to the couch. I had to get ready to go to the stadium.

That jolted him.

"You're going to go to the game?"

"Of course I'm going to the game."

"You haven't slept. You've been up for twenty-four hours straight."

"Well, actually, it's closer to thirty-six, but I'll see you after the game."

"So you're choosing to go to the game, huh?"

"I don't *want* to go. I *have* to."

"Well, you don't *have* to go."

I smiled. He didn't get it. "I'm the starting quarterback for the 49ers," I told him. "I can't just not show up."

"They won't arrest you for not showing up," he said. "You have a contract, and there will be implications. But you don't have to go."

"I'm going to go to the game," I told him firmly. "But I'll make you a promise. If we win today, I'll talk to the team doctor."

Then I gave him a ticket to the game and said I'd see him afterward.

September 19, 1993. It's warm and sunny at Candlestick, perfect football weather. But I'm a mess — nausea and vomiting. Plus, I'm shivering and shaking. During pregame Dr. Klint thinks I might have gastritis or a bad case of the flu. He puts me on an IV. I don't bother telling him it's anxiety. Besides, I need the fluids. I haven't slept or eaten in almost forty hours. I'm weak, tired, and yawning nonstop.

I feel like an uninvited guest at a house party when I walk onto the field. It's our first home game since Joe was traded to Kansas City. Fans hang signs of support for Joe all over the stadium. I read each one. I note that there are no signs supporting me.

Suck it up, I tell myself, and I start by completing six of my first seven passes. Then a linebacker hits me head on, planting his helmet in the crown of my helmet. I jam my neck, and there are black streaks from his helmet on mine. Under later NFL rules, he would have been penalized.

I keep going. By halftime I have two touchdown passes, but my head is throbbing and my neck hurts. In the locker room I get another IV before trying to battle back against Atlanta. With time winding down in the third quarter, we trail 20–16 and the crowd is uneasy. So am I. Desperate to make something happen, I drop back to pass from the Falcons' 8-yard line. I'm nearly sacked before scrambling free and spotting Ricky Watters in the end zone. I fire the ball. It hits defender Vinnie Clark in the chest and ricochets back toward me. The moment I see the ball in the air I run toward it, catch it, and head for the end zone before I'm dragged down at the 2-yard line. Finally, some cheers from the home crowd.

I expect a flag for catching my own pass. But the officials determine that a quarterback can complete a pass to himself. Apparently Y. A. Tittle did it once in 1959. On the next play we score to go up 23–20.

We hang on to win 37–30, but on our final play I am struck on the side of the head and I feel something pop in my neck. I walk off the field gingerly.

Despite being sleep-deprived, famished, and hampered by a jammed neck from a blow to the head, I have one of the best games of my career, completing 18 of 22 passes for 210 yards and three touchdowns. I also rush for 52 yards and catch one of my own passes.

I stagger to the training room, where I undergo a neurological exam. Dr. Klint tells me that I have a jammed neck and a mild concussion. After some electro-stimulation, he gives me an anti-inflammatory and puts a cervical soft collar on my neck.

But my neck is the least of my problems. My emotions are on the surface, and I don't want anyone to see me this way. I lie on my back on the training table until everyone except Dr. Klint is gone. Then I sit up.

"Reggie, can I talk to you?"

He looks at me. Dry sweat and grass stains coat my skin. My hair is matted from my helmet.

"You look like you haven't slept in days," he says.

"I haven't."

He closes the training room door.

"Steve, what's going on?"

I bury my face in my hands and start to shake.

"It's okay, Steve," he whispers.

"Reggie, I'm really struggling."

"Yeah, I know."

I start sobbing. "What's wrong with me, Reggie?"

He puts his arms around me.

"I'm sure this doesn't make any sense to you," I continue.

"Steve?"

"What?"

"I understand," he whispers. "I had bouts of this all throughout my days in medical school."

I look up. Reggie is crying.

"I know all about anxiety," he says. "I understand how it works."

"Is that what this is?" I ask.

I hug him and wipe my eyes.

"I watch the other guys and I know what I'm feeling is different," I say. "I don't get it."

"I know."

I stay with Reggie for nearly an hour. He says he's going to arrange for me to go back to Dr. Stanley Fischman. This time he wants me to do more than go in for a visit. Reggie wants me to start seeing Stanley on a regular basis.

I promise I will.

Outside the stadium I meet back up with Rex Kocherhans, whom I have now known for a whole twenty-four hours. Laughing, he says to me: "So let me get this straight: you have so much anxiety that you can't sleep, but then you go out and play spectacular football?"

I shrug.

"In my professional opinion, you should keep this up," he says, laughing. "This seems to work."

I thank him for flying out from Provo. He thanks me for the ticket to the game and the twenty-four hours of nonstop entertainment. Then I go back to my place and sleep for sixteen hours.

28

ONE GAME AT A TIME

O UR NEXT GAME was in New Orleans. The Saints sacked me five
times. We lost 16–13 and dropped to 2-2. Two days later I drove to
Dr. Stanley Fischman's office. It had been two years since I saw him the
first time. He had since moved to a brand-new medical building that was
primarily an OB-GYN clinic. I thought to myself — *All I need is for someone to spot me coming in or out of this place and the rumors will fly.*

Fortunately, my appointment was after hours. Still, I pulled a baseball
cap down over my eyes and slipped into an elevator unnoticed. When I
entered his office, no one was around.

This time Dr. Fischman wanted to talk about my childhood. I told
him how hard it was for me to go to school as a little boy, how I never did
sleepovers and couldn't stand to be away from home.

He said he wanted to ask me eight questions about my childhood. He
asked me to simply answer yes or no.

"Did you have recurrent excessive distress when separated from home
or your parents?"

"Yes."

"Did you have persistent and excessive worry about losing, or about
possible harm befalling, your parents?"

"Yes."

"Did you have persistent and excessive worry that an unfortunate or
untoward event would lead to separation from your parents?"

"Yes."

"Were you reluctant to go to school or elsewhere because of fear of separation?"

"Yes."

"Were you afraid to go to sleep without being near a parent?"

"Yes. I used to sometimes curl up on the floor and sleep outside my parents' bedroom door."

"Did you have repeated complaints of physical symptoms such as headaches, stomachaches, nausea, or vomiting when separated from a parent?"

"Yes."

"Have you had repeated nightmares involving the theme of separation?"

"I don't know. I never remember my dreams when I wake up. So I have no idea whether I have nightmares."

He told me there was a clinical name for my symptoms: separation anxiety disorder.

I had never heard this term, and I wanted to know more.

He said it usually manifests itself in children when they go off to kindergarten. After five years of being nurtured, fed, and cared for exclusively by parents, some children demonstrate great anxiety when they are first put in a classroom with twenty other children and a teacher who essentially functions as a new parent. "Some kids cry all day," he explained. "It's a lot of anticipatory anxiety."

Separation anxiety was what I had as a child. Anticipatory anxiety was what I had now.

He said that separation anxiety disorder and depression were often related. He treated many children who struggled with separation anxiety and depression. But the symptoms I was describing were pretty extreme. The textbook definition of separation anxiety disorder was met by answering yes to only three or more of the eight diagnostic questions. I answered yes to seven and "I don't know" to one.

"I have to be honest with you, Steve. I've been doing this for over twenty years. I see lots of adults with undiagnosed separation anxiety. Never once have I seen an adult with the kind of separation anxiety that you have."

I laughed nervously.

He added that he had never seen an adult with severe separation anxiety who wasn't self-medicating. "I usually see them after they've been to rehab or they've lost their family or their life is completely shattered."

Yet he knew I had never touched drugs or alcohol. "I don't know what to tell you," I said.

"Weren't you the NFL's MVP last year?"

"Yeah."

He paused and then said: "It's remarkable that you are able to function at the level you do. It's just remarkable."

I asked him what this all meant.

He said that many people are brought up to think that anxiety is a weakness. He corrected that notion. "It has nothing to do with weakness," he told me. "It has to do with your brain and how it was developed and what you inherited from one side of your family and what you inherited from the other side of the family."

It was so interesting to me that my anxiety was inherited. I had never heard anything like that. I had always been under the impression that anxiety stems from a traumatic event in life or from negative social settings.

He explained that anxieties could develop that way, but that many forms of anxiety are inherited. "Biology plays a humongous role," he said. "In other words, your anxiety isn't a result of you reacting to the world around you. This is just you."

For starters, Dr. Fischman prescribed Klonopin, a medication often used to treat insomnia because it tends to cause sleepiness. But it also functions as an anti-anxiety medication. I was very reluctant to fill the prescription. I was afraid of how it might affect me. But he put me on a very small dose — one tablet per day, taken in the evenings.

"Let's do this one game at a time," he told me.

I agreed to return in one week.

October 3, 1993. I am still bruised and sore when we face Minnesota at Candlestick. Jim McMahon, my predecessor at BYU, comes out throwing, and so do I. I hit Jerry Rice for an early touchdown, and we're up 21–7 midway through the second quarter.

But the Vikings are after me. Defensive tackle Henry Thomas sacks me in the end zone for a safety just before the half. Thomas sacks me two more times. But the play that nearly knocks me out of the game is an illegal hit. After I'm down, Thomas, who weighs more than 300 pounds, slams down on top of me, smacking his helmet into mine. He's flagged for spearing.

We keep scoring, and the Vikings keep up the cheap shots. Chris Doleman hits me late and gets flagged. Then Roy Barker does it. We wallop Minnesota 38–19, but I am pretty fed up by the end of the game.

In a postgame interview, Vikings lineman John Randle boasts about the attempts to take me out of the game. "We were just going at him with stuff we thought would work on him," Randle tells the press. "If you can knock the quarterback out of the game it's to your advantage. You do that by getting to him, knocking him down."

I've never shied away from rough play, but I have no patience for late hits and intentional blows to the head. Nonetheless, I don't complain when the press asks me about the late hits. "This is the kind of game where you're going to take shots," I say. "I think we're going to be okay. I just can't keep getting hit in the head."

The day after the Vikings game I saw Dr. Fischman again. I told him I had tried the Klonopin but had quit taking it because it made me feel foggy.

But having struggled for so long, I wanted to learn as much as I could about separation anxiety and anticipatory anxiety. I recounted my experience with it for Dr. Fischman: When I was a boy, anxiety seemed to be with me all the time. When I was in college, the anxiety was limited to football season, peaking in the lead-up to big games. Similarly, as an adult I was anxiety-free for the most part during the off-season. But during the season I was anxious. My anxiety was most acute in the days leading up to a game, but especially after a loss. On the night and morning before playing, it would reach a crescendo. But it always vanished the moment I got on the field.

Dr. Fischman described my situation as "episodic" bouts with anxiety triggered by my profession.

I left Dr. Fischman's office feeling that there had been a huge breakthrough. On the one hand, I resented having inherited my anxious tendencies, but on the other, this insight explained so many things. This thing had a name. That realization alone was huge. My fears were actually a by-product of my DNA. Coming to grips with that didn't necessarily solve the problem, but it did relieve some of the guilt I felt over it.

It was as if the door to a lifelong unresolved mystery had been unlocked. I began to hope that maybe I could manage the situation now that I was starting to understand the root cause.

For the first time I finally knew what I was dealing with. That knowledge gave me a powerful sense of control over a part of myself that was ever-present throughout my childhood and would still surface in my adult years.

October 17, 1993. We're in Dallas and clinging to a first-half lead when Charles Haley blindsides me and I fumble. Dallas recovers on our 18-yard line. Moments later, they score to go up 16–10 at the half. In the third quarter we regain the lead when I throw a touchdown pass to Brent Jones. But during the drive I sprain my right knee.

Aikman counters with a 36-yard touchdown strike to Irvin to put them back up 23–17. Rice is frustrated with me the entire game. With five minutes left to play, he has just two catches. Meanwhile, Irvin has 12 receptions for 168 yards and a touchdown. In the fourth quarter Jerry finally loses it. On the sideline he rips me for not getting him the ball.

On our next drive I complete five passes to Rice as we try to mount a comeback. But our drive stalls when Charles Haley sacks me again, causing us to turn the ball over on downs. Dallas wins and we fall to 3-3.

Back in San Francisco, I was outfitted for a knee brace and given anti-inflammatories to take the swelling down on my knee. I was getting my anxiety much more under control. Yes, it was present. But for the first time in my life I was able to talk about it because I finally knew what I was dealing with. In conversations with family members, I learned that many of them also had what I had. For instance, my Uncle Bob, the one who had helped me through my freshman year at BYU, revealed that he had not served a Mormon mission because he too had struggled with serious separation anxiety as a young man. Like me, he wasn't diagnosed until much later in life.

I had never known that! I had never known any of this. The sudden realization that some of my relatives were dealing with some sort of anxiety issue didn't change the fact that I also had to deal with it. But now I felt empowered to move forward with a renewed sense of confidence and determination.

Most importantly, a new line of communication opened with my dad. It had always been really difficult for him to understand what I was feeling. That's one of the challenging aspects of anxiety — it doesn't make sense to people who don't have it. When I was anxious, Dad would always say, encouragingly, "Steve, you're lucky. You're playing football. You're making money. It's every boy's dream. Just be happy and go have fun playing."

For years I'd get so frustrated because he couldn't understand what I was experiencing. Finally, I was able to explain it in a way that made sense to him. Once I was able to put a name to it and talk about anxiety's genetic roots, my dad finally had some frame of reference for how I was feeling.

By the latter part of the season, I even stopped seeing Dr. Fischman. But I was forever grateful to him, and to Dr. Klint for referring me to him. Dr. Fischman opened the door. He gave my lifelong challenge a name.

After the Dallas loss, we won six straight and every game was a blowout. During that six-game stretch we outscored opponents 211–77 and I threw ten touchdown passes to Jerry. In one of those games, a 35–10 win over the Rams, I completed a career-high 26 of 32 passes for 462 yards and four touchdowns. Eight of the completions went to Rice for 166 yards and two touchdowns. Jerry would have over 1,000 yards receiving for a league-record eighth consecutive year. It definitely felt like another MVP season.

29

KEEP THE FAITH

O UR FINAL GAME of the 1993 regular season was a *Monday Night Football* affair against the Eagles. That weekend my friends Truman and Ann Madsen were flying in from Utah for the game.

They were arriving on New Year's Day and planning to come straight to my place. The problem was that the temperatures in the hills of Los Altos had started dropping quite a bit at night. So much for my assumption that I wouldn't need heat in the barn. It got so cold that I was forced to go to the 49ers' groundskeeper, Rich Genoff, to borrow the propane-powered sideline heater. We called it "The Flamethrower." I hauled it from Candlestick to my loft. But I quickly discovered that I could run that beast for only about a minute before I'd get lightheaded from the fumes. The good news was that a minute of The Flamethrower was all I needed to warm my loft apartment. But there was no way I could use that thing when the Madsens were visiting.

The Madsens immediately started shivering. I plugged in a space heater and brought out some blankets. While they huddled on my overstuffed couch, I put on some Christmas music and opened my Christmas gifts from them. Ann had brought some of her famous Christmas pudding and needed a microwave to heat it. But I didn't have a microwave. I didn't own any dishes or silverware either. We ended up eating the pudding with our fingers. Unbelievable! Eventually I took them to a nearby hotel where I had made reservations for them.

The next morning we went to mass at St. Patrick's Seminary and University in Menlo Park. Father Raymond E. Brown, an internationally renowned biblical scholar, was close friends with Truman. Brown took us to a small chapel occupied by some French nuns who were awaiting mass. He introduced Truman and Ann to the nuns. Then Father Brown turned to me. "And this is Steve Young, who lives in this area."

The nuns smiled. They already knew my name. Turns out they were big 49ers fans.

Afterward we visited a Mormon congregation that met on the Stanford University campus. We slipped in just after services had begun and found a seat in the back row. A young woman from the Philippines was at the pulpit. She had recently converted. Suddenly she started talking about me, unaware that I was in the back of the chapel. She told the congregation that we had crossed paths and I had given her a picture inscribed with the words: "Keep the faith." She reported that she had had no faith at that point in her life. But those simple words triggered her desire to learn more about Mormonism.

Truman glanced at me. I shrugged. I was too embarrassed to tell him that I had no memory of this young woman or her story. I met so many people in so many different places and situations, and I was constantly signing and inscribing things that people shoved in front of me. I couldn't possibly keep track of everyone. But hearing her account reminded me that when you are in the limelight, you never know who is watching or how your actions might influence them.

The Monday night game turned out to be a dud. It rained most of the time, and the outcome of the game had no impact on the playoff picture. So George Seifert took me out after the third quarter in order to rest me. We ended up losing to the Eagles in overtime. But Truman and Ann didn't mind. It was their first NFL game, and they were just thrilled to see it.

Afterward we picked up pizzas and went back to my place. Before saying good-bye later that night, Truman prayed with me. I hugged him and his wife and thanked them for their love and support.

We finished the regular season 10-6 and won the division. I set franchise records for passing yards (4,023) and for consecutive passes without an interception (189). I also set an NFL record by becoming the first top-rated passer for three consecutive seasons. Statistically speaking, I had a better year in '93 than I did in '92. But in the MVP voting, I finished a few points behind Emmitt Smith.

From a personal standpoint, my career was definitely on track. I had almost won my second consecutive league MVP. But none of that mattered at the moment. My focus was on the playoffs. The media was already speculating on the prospect of the 49ers facing the Chiefs in the Super Bowl. In his first year in Kansas City, Joe had guided the Chiefs to an 11-5 record and the AFC Western Division title.

I tried to keep my mind focused on the New York Giants, our first-round opponent. On game day Coach Shanahan came up to me in the locker room and wanted to go over the game plan again.

"Mike, I've memorized it!" I said.

"I know," he said. "But let's go over it one more time."

After running through the plays yet another time, he said:

"We got this, Steve. We got this."

We play the Giants in front of a record crowd of 67,143 at Candlestick. We score on our first four possessions and lead 23–3 at the half. We add three more touchdowns in the second half. We are blowing them out. But I take a helmet-to-helmet hit that limits my ability to turn my head left. I stay in the game, though, and we win 44–3. It's the most points ever scored by the 49ers in a playoff game and the biggest margin of victory ever in an NFC playoff game. The game closes the book on the 49ers-Giants rivalry. Afterward Lawrence Taylor and Phil Simms retire.

The battle for supremacy in the NFC is now strictly between the Cowboys and us.

Sure enough, we advanced to the NFC Championship for a rematch with the Cowboys. The pressure on me was magnified by the fact that the Chiefs had advanced to the AFC Championship game. Joe and I were one step away from facing off in the Super Bowl. If Joe got his team to the Super Bowl and I didn't, I would never live it down.

The shot to the head I had taken in the Giants game had lingering effects. On the day after the game I was diagnosed with a cervical injury to my neck caused by another player's helmet. I underwent traction and was put on anti-inflammatories. But nothing was helping. By midweek I still couldn't turn my head. I looked in the mirror and realized my head was actually tilted to the right. It looked like my whole upper body was out of alignment.

With game day approaching, the team doctor injected the sore area of my neck with Decadron and lidocaine, enabling me to regain about 50 percent of my range of motion. I also wore a collar when I slept.

The day before we flew to Dallas, Cowboys head coach Jimmy Johnson called a local talk-radio program and guaranteed victory. "We will win the ball game, and you can put it in three-inch headlines," he boasted. "We will have a very, very tight game for three quarters. But before it's over, we'll wear them out. We'll beat their rear ends and go to the Super Bowl."

January 23, 1994. When we arrive at Texas Stadium, I discover that a bunch of our defensive players are wearing T-shirts that say: F*** DALLAS.

"Take those shirts off!" I demand.

The room goes silent.

"I mean it," I say. "Take 'em off!"

I usually say nothing in the locker room. But this time it's different. Charles Haley tries to kill me every time we play Dallas. He goes out of his way to try to intimidate me. The last thing I want is for Haley to have even more incentive to come after me.

Tim McDonald removes his shirt first. One by one the others follow.

But Jimmy Johnson's radio rant remains fresh in everyone's mind. All it takes is for a couple of Dallas players to bump Jerry Rice during pregame warm-ups and it's on. While both teams are waiting to be introduced, a fight breaks out in the end zone. The game hasn't even started and we're already brawling.

The problem is that all of this distracts us from what we need to do to win the game. It plays right into Jimmy Johnson's hands. Our team is so emotionally charged at the start of the game that we don't execute well. Then Cowboys tackle Erik Williams breaks the leg of our defensive lineman Ted Washington in the first quarter. It's all downhill from there. By halftime we are down 28–7.

Three touchdowns are a deep hole against any team. It's all but impossible against a team as good as Dallas. But we battle back. In the second half Troy Aikman is knocked out and taken to a hospital for treatment. Our offense gets going, and we put points on the board. But even in Aikman's absence, our defense struggles to slow down Dallas's offense. We lose 38–21.

The Chiefs lose too, which means Joe Montana isn't going to the Super Bowl either. But for the second straight year we have lost to Dallas in the NFC Championship.

30

RELOAD

I WAS FRUSTRATED. It's fair to say that everyone was fed up. But emotionally, I was in a different place at that point. Instead of getting anxious about not advancing to the Super Bowl, I was emboldened to do whatever it took to get over the mountain. For the 49ers organization, the Cowboys were the mountain. And the mountain had just gotten a little higher: they had now won two straight Super Bowls. The center of gravity in the NFL had shifted.

In the '80s when I joined the Niners, the road to the Super Bowl went through San Francisco or New York virtually every season. Between 1986 and 1990 the 49ers and Giants won four of the five Super Bowls. But the Cowboys had since pushed the Giants aside.

Right after the season I went back to Provo, finished up my final semester of law classes, and graduated from law school in the spring of '94. Being a lawyer, I figured, would at least give me options when I hung up the cleats. But as soon as I had my law degree in hand, I got busy lobbying 49ers president and general manager Carmen Policy to bring in the right personnel to help us beat Dallas.

The problem wasn't our offense. For two consecutive seasons we'd had the most potent offensive attack in the league. The reason we couldn't beat Dallas was that we couldn't stop them. They had scored touchdowns on us right from the start of each game. They had us beat by halftime. Plus, we were losing the battle at the line of scrimmage. The Cowboys' offensive line manhandled our defensive line.

With Eddie DeBartolo's support, Carmen went after a bunch of top free agents. He signed Chicago Bears defensive end Richard Dent, one of the greatest pass rushers of all time. He got New Orleans Saints defensive end Rickey Jackson, a six-time Pro Bowler. He signed linebacker Gary Plummer. He even convinced Cowboys middle linebacker Ken Norton Jr. to join the Niners.

Carmen also went after Falcons cornerback Deion Sanders. He was the one guy in the league capable of shutting down Michael Irvin. Other NFL teams were vying for Deion's services too. He said he wouldn't decide where he was going until the Major League Baseball season ended in September.

The only hole we had to fill on offense was at offensive guard. We had lost Guy McIntyre to free agency. We failed to find an adequate free agent replacement. I proposed the idea of moving center Jesse Sapolu to guard and signing New York Giants center Bart Oates, who had played with me at BYU. Sapolu was the best center in the NFC, but he agreed to change positions if we could convince Oates to leave the Giants. That was a harder sell.

Oates had spent nine years in New York and won two Super Bowls. He was a free agent, but he wanted to finish his career in New York. Regardless, I convinced Carmen and Eddie to make him an offer.

The prospect of reuniting with my center from BYU had me pretty fired up. But the Giants didn't want to see Bart leave. They offered him almost $1 million more than the Niners. I called Bart, who was struggling with the decision. In nine years with the Giants he hadn't missed a single game. His kids had great friends in their school system. Like me, Bart had a law degree, and he practiced in New Jersey during the off-season. It would be tough to uproot himself and his family.

I told him he wouldn't regret coming to the Niners. He would play on a team that was primed to go to the Super Bowl. "C'mon," I told him. "It's going to be great. You have to come."

On July 16, 1994, Bart Oates became a 49er.

When Bart moved his family to the Bay Area, I started hanging out at their place. *Forrest Gump* was released in early July. Bart and I went to see it. Bart joked that I was a lot like Forrest. Gump's charmed life took him on a journey that began when he was a college football star and led him to remarkable places ranging from the White House to *The Dick Cavett Show*. He drank Dr. Pepper and spent his life chasing an elusive love. Bart compared my unlikely journey to Gump's, from my humble beginnings as a kid who had no business playing quarterback at BYU to becoming the MVP of the NFL. And like Gump, of course, I could never seem to find love.

But the thing I loved about Bart was that he knew my life was not as idyllic as everyone on the outside thought. I was alone. I had some insecurities. And I lived with the daunting task of succeeding a legend. There were worse things in life, to be sure. But loneliness and trying to meet impossible expectations can be pretty brutal.

Bart's wife Michelle was a great sounding board. She made me dinner most nights. She cut my hair. She was a great friend. After workouts I often arrived at Bart's place before he did. I'd be in his kitchen talking to Michelle about my bachelor problems when Bart would come through the door and joke: "If you two are going to talk about Steve's love life again, I'm going to go hit golf balls."

September 5, 1994. We open the regular season at home on *Monday Night Football* against the Raiders. It's the pregame and Raiders owner Al Davis is breaking an unwritten rule. He's encroaching on our huddle by standing just off to the side while we go through our drills. He's in his trademark white sweat suit and black shoes, and his presence bothers our guys. It feels like he's scouting us up close.

Mike Shanahan is particularly agitated. He and Davis have a long running feud. Six years earlier Davis had hired Shanahan as his head coach, only to fire him after one season. It was an ugly split, and Shanahan claimed that Davis stiffed him $250,000.

Our players start complaining to Shanahan that Davis's presence is a distraction. They want Davis to get lost.

"Guys, we'll win the game," Shanahan says. "Don't worry about it. Don't let him bother you."

Then he whispers to me: "Throw a go route. If you happen to hit that guy in the white outfit, you won't make me mad."

I send Jerry on a sideline route toward Davis and let it fly. I don't intend to hit Davis, just to make him jump. At the last second he sees the ball and dives out of the way. But the ball takes a funny hop off the turf and hits Davis under the chin. Embarrassed, Davis turns and points toward our huddle. While I hide behind my linemen, our players crack up.

We roll over the Raiders that night 44–14. But we lose offensive linemen Harris Barton and Ralph Tamm to injuries. Both are out indefinitely, and the timing couldn't be worse. Our next game is at Kansas City, and the Chiefs have two of the premier pass rushers in the league, Derrick Thomas and Neil Smith — not to mention Joe Montana.

It bothered me for years that I had thrown that pass toward Al Davis. In retrospect, I felt it was disrespectful to one of the game's greats. Years later, when I was a *Monday Night Football* analyst for ESPN, I ran into Davis in the tunnel outside the Raiders' locker room. I told him how much I regretted that incident. "I appreciate you saying that," Al told me. Then he smiled and said: "I always thought you should have been a Raider."

The hype leading up to the Kansas City game was bigger than the hype for our NFC Championship games against Dallas. *Sports Illustrated* billed the game as "Joe Montana vs. Steve Young in the Vindication Bowl." The Chiefs received more than 200 requests for cameras and video credentials, whereas normally the team received only 30 or 40. I was bombarded with questions about Joe. He was bombarded with questions about me. We both said the right things about each other and played down the significance of the game.

But the truth was that we were both intensely competitive. And we were human. Days before the game, Carmen Policy put things in perspective in an interview with the *Los Angeles Times*:

> Their relationship was doomed from the beginning. Steve Young hadn't come in as a draft choice to be an understudy. He came to the 49ers in a significant trade with the obvious intent of him becoming the starting quarterback. It wasn't a case where Steve was going to learn from the master. Joe saw him as a competitor for the starting position.

• • •

September 11, 1994. I step onto the field at Arrowhead Stadium and get showered with boos and expletives. I'm pretty sure I don't have a single supporter among the 79,907 fans in attendance. As warm-ups wind down I spot Joe and run over to him. "Good to see you," I say. "Good luck."

Our exchange is brief and a little awkward. But I refuse to give credence to the idea that we are about to participate in some pay-per-view fight. It's a football game, and we are professionals. I want to act that way.

The game, however, feels like a street fight where anything goes. Early on, Derrick Thomas levels me after the whistle and draws a 15-yard unsportsmanlike conduct penalty. A few minutes later he slams me to the turf for a sack. Kansas City scores first to go up 7–0. But we add two touchdowns in the second quarter and lead 14–7. After our defense stops Kansas City, we get the ball back deep in our own territory. The crowd is so loud that my linemen can't hear me. Derrick Thomas changes his usual position and lines up to my right, where he can rush me from my blind side. I drop back in my own end zone, and Thomas nails me from behind for a safety. It's his second sack of the half. The first half ends with us leading 14–9.

Our locker room resembles a triage unit. Lineman Jesse Sapolu is down with a pulled hamstring. Right guard Derrick Deese is out with a concussion. I have bruises to my shoulder and lacerations on my back. It doesn't help that it's brutally hot on the field.

The Chiefs open the second half by scoring two touchdowns to go up 24–14. Derrick Thomas leaves the game owing to dehydration. But Neil Smith delivers another late hit on me. He blindsides me with such force that the wind is knocked out of me before I hit the ground. Gasping for air, I writhe in pain. He draws another 15-yard penalty for unsportsmanlike conduct.

As I lie on the ground I feel like someone has put a bounty on me. Hard hits are one thing, but ferocious late hits well after the whistle are just cheap. And all my veteran linemen enforcers are out of action. But I am determined not to let cheap shots drive me from the game.

We lose 24–17.

The moment the game ends I seek out Joe. It's not easy going up to him. Not after a game like this. But it's the right thing to do. I know that. I congratulate him and wish him well. He does the same.

Through all the years my relationship with Joe went as well as it could possibly go. We never had an argument. We never exchanged a cross word. When he started, I supported him. We spent thousands of hours together in meetings. Our lockers were side by side for six seasons. In the end our competition was a difficult thing for both of us. But for a couple of years now it had stopped being a big deal for me.

Unfortunately, it continued to remain a big deal for everybody else.

I was so beaten up after the game that I barely made it to the trainer's table. The medical staff determined that I had two bruised shoulders, bruised ribs, a strained pec, a bruised neck, a sprained shoulder, a deep thigh bruise, a sprain in the AC joint of my clavicle, a contusion on my left knee, and multiple contusions on my back.

Everything hurt. Kansas City had administered one of the worst beatings of my career. But for the first time I didn't feel any anguish. It actually felt good that it was only a physical beating. I could handle that.

31

THE THINGS THAT BIND

I USUALLY GOT PRETTY maniacal after a loss. The fact was that I always played hard, but never harder than when I was trying to bounce back from a defeat. Three days after losing to the Chiefs, however, I still had trouble eating. My jaw was too sore to chew. I couldn't throw a football either because something was wrong with my shoulder. I was downing anti-inflammatories. I felt like crap.

Nevertheless, days later in Anaheim, I completed 31 of 39 pass attempts for 355 yards and two touchdowns. I also rushed for two touchdowns, and we torched the Rams 34–19. If you want to get all of me, play me the week after I get beat.

There was more good news. We had signed Deion Sanders to a free agent contract. He went straight from playing outfield for the Cincinnati Reds to playing cornerback for us. In his second start for us he returned an interception 74 yards for a touchdown. In the same game I threw two more touchdown passes to Jerry, and we easily beat New Orleans to improve to 3-1.

But I was still feeling the effects of the beating I'd taken in Kansas City. The pain in my neck was now radiating into my scapula. The medical team said my treatment options were stronger anti-inflammatories, oral prednisone, or an injection. I went with option one.

The thing I really needed was better protection. I had been sacked a league-leading thirteen times in the first four games. I'd also been knocked down more than any other starter. Our next opponent was Philadelphia, and they led the NFC in sacks. Mike Shanahan was worried about my protection. Philadelphia blitzed a lot, and our offensive line was in shambles. Bart Oates was the only other starter healthy enough to play. At some positions we were now using third-string guys who had been cut from other squads.

October 2, 1994. It's my thirty-eighth consecutive start — the longest streak of any current NFL quarterback. But I'm banged up. Eagles quarterback Randall Cunningham engineers a long touchdown drive to start the game. My first pass is deflected and intercepted. Two plays later Philadelphia scores again. It's 14–0, and our offense has run a grand total of one play.

In the second quarter William Fuller sacks me in the end zone for a safety. I land hard on my bruised shoulder. A few minutes later the Eagles add another touchdown to go up 23–0.

Angry, I lead us on a 15-play drive that covers 66 yards. I run it in from one yard out. Then I throw a pass to Brent Jones for a two-point conversion. Down by 15 points, I figure we can regroup at halftime. But just before the half the Eagles score again. We go into the locker room down big, 30–8.

In our first possession of the second half I get slammed down hard, and we are forced to punt. I'm on the sideline talking to Jerry Rice when George Seifert walks over to us. "Look," he says, "it's over, boys. I'm gonna pull you guys out."

I don't like it, but I get it. We are getting blown out, and I'm taking shots left and right. But on our next offensive series Jerry and I jog back onto the field. We run one play. Then, with 4:09 remaining in the third quarter, I'm standing in the huddle about to call another play when backup quarterback Elvis Grbac appears. He tells me I'm out. Not Jerry. Not anyone else. *Just me.*

Furious, I unstrap my helmet and head for the sideline. I don't say a word until I get there, and then I explode. "You are not going to single me out!" I scream at Seifert, letting rip a string of colorful words not fit for print. I'm so hot I want to fight him. I've had it!

Deion Sanders gets between the coach and me, and I start pushing Deion. He tries to calm me down, telling me he understands my anger and encouraging me to forget it.

But I don't want to forget it. I keep going. Brent Jones tries to calm me down. Dr. Klint tries. Then quarterback coach Gary Kubiak comes over and I rip into him too.

But the guy I'm really mad at is Seifert. I keep shouting at him, and he keeps ignoring me.

"You are messing with the wrong guy!" I shout.

He says nothing.

I hate conceding defeat. I never want to give an opponent the satisfaction of knocking me out of a game. And I don't appreciate being singled out when our team is losing. If you want to pull the entire first string, fine. But don't pull me alone!

The Eagles go on to win 40–8. After the game George avoids me. I go into the training room for treatment. "Tell George I want to see him," I tell the trainer. "Now!"

The trainer returns and says George won't come in.

"Look, you tell him I'm not leaving the stadium until we at least talk it out."

An hour and a half after the game, George finally enters the training room. I'm the only one left. I'm still annoyed, but I've cooled down.

"George, this has been death by a thousand cuts," I tell him. "For years I've taken blame for so many things that are out of my control. So when you told Jerry and me that we were coming out of the game and then you only pulled me, I lost it."

He said nothing.

"I won't stand for it ever again," I continued. "And it's a good thing you didn't turn around when I was yelling at you on the sideline because I would have decked you."

He chuckled.

I didn't.

The next day I showed up at our practice facility. When Brent Jones saw me, he grinned. "Dude, you are crazy," he said.

I was still pretty fired up. "I'm sick of this crap," I told him. "Sick of it."

But I noticed my teammates were smiling. In all my years of playing football, I had never seen anyone smiling the day after a loss. But things were different after the Eagles loss. My teammates had branded my sideline outburst the "Steve Young Rant." Suddenly, everyone had decided I was the guy they wanted to rally behind. My outburst became a rallying cry for the entire team. We had the best week of practice since I had joined the Niners. Everyone was focused. Five days later we flew to Detroit to face the Lions.

October 9, 1994. We start the game by playing the way we did against the Eagles. Only worse. We trail 14–0 in the first half when I drop back to pass and Detroit blitzes. I scramble out of the pocket. Then I do something I rarely do when throwing. In an attempt to see over the defense, I elevate off my right foot, see the open receiver, and let it go. Just as I release the ball two defenders hit me. Both wrap me up as a third player — linebacker Broderick Thomas — plants his helmet in my back and knocks the three of us over. The collective weight of all three Lions defenders comes down on my right leg. Agonizing pain shoots up my leg. I'm sure I have severed a major nerve.

"No!" I shriek as Broderick Thomas takes his time getting off of me.

It's one of the few times in my career that I've been scared by an injury. Writhing in pain, I crawl GI Joe style, using my elbows, toward the sideline. My right leg drags behind. Furious, I keep crawling.

Brent Jones stands over me. "Dude, what are you doing? Get up!"

"I don't know what's wrong with me," I say. "I can't feel my leg."

My linemen wave for the doctors. Jerry Rice tries to help me. I wave him off. I wave the trainers off too. I don't want Detroit to have the satisfaction of seeing me getting helped off the field.

But I'm worried. I've endured some big hits, but this one is different. It feels like somebody hit my funny bone with a hammer. Only it's not my funny bone. It's my leg. I finally hop up onto my left foot. I can't put any weight on my right one. I get to the sideline. Feeling starts to return. Very slowly, I make my way to the bench.

George Seifert is screaming at the referees for not calling unnecessary roughness on Broderick Thomas. The medical staff starts massaging my leg. Suddenly, the feeling returns. It is like someone flipped a switch. I can stand up — I'm sore — but I can put my full weight on my leg. *What is going on?*

Dr. Dillingham says I have injured my left peroneal nerve, which controls the sensation in my leg and foot. Yes, I can walk. But the doctor is concerned I might have compressed the nerve. I don't care. I'm furious, and as long as I can walk I'm going back in. I put on my helmet.

"Steve, what are you doing?" Dillingham says.

"I'm going back in."

"Steve, if you try to go back on the field, it will be the first time a doctor tackles a player on national TV," he says.

I go past him.

"You're not going in the game," he says. "You can't run."

Two plays after crawling off the field, I jog back to the huddle. I want to destroy the Lions. I complete 17 of my next 20 passes. We score 27 straight points. We silence the Silverdome crowd and win 27–21. As I'm hobbling off the field our public relations director, Rodney Knox, says: "Nothing's easy in this league."

In the locker room I'm awarded the game ball. Usually the team is loud after a win. Not today. It's quiet.

"That was true grit," Oates says.

Jones calls me out. "Dude, you really are crazy," he says. "That was John Wayne–esque. You did the death crawl. The John Wayne death crawl."

Back in San Francisco the following day I have my knee examined. It's tender, but stable. I'm put on prednisone and instructed to rest during the week.

The Eagles game was a turning point. But it was the Lions game that saved our season. It also marked the first NFL start for rookie fullback William Floyd. He possessed a punishing running style, yet he had great hands for pass receiving. In the Lions game he rushed for two touchdowns and caught five passes out of the backfield. It was obvious to me — and everyone else — that Floyd was a potential game-changer for our offense. A lot of guys thought he could become the best fullback in the league. We nicknamed him "Bar None."

Deion "Prime Time" Sanders was also making his presence felt. He was revved up when we went to Atlanta to face the Falcons in week six. Deion talked all week about beating his former team. Despite a brief skirmish during the game with Falcons receiver Andre Rison, in which Deion lost a tooth, he could not be slowed down. In the second quarter Prime Time picked off a Jeff George pass and returned it 93 yards for a touchdown. On the way to the end zone he high-stepped past the Falcons' sideline.

On the other side of the ball I was near-perfect. I threw just one incomplete pass all day. I had four touchdown passes. We were up 42–3 when Seifert pulled me and the other starters. This time I didn't yell at him.

After the game Deion ran through the Georgia Dome tunnel shouting: "This is my house! I built this house."

We were now 5-2.

After beating Tampa Bay at home 41–16 to improve to 6-2, we had a bye week. I went to the movies with Bart Oates to see *The Shawshank Redemption*. If you recall the film, Andy Dufresne is a banker who spends nineteen years in prison for a crime he didn't commit. All the other inmates do belong there, and Dufresne is an obvious misfit. I related to the Dufresne character. I often looked around the NFL and felt different from everyone else.

I also related to Dufresne's struggle. Using a tiny rock hammer, he spends nineteen years chipping away at a tunnel that he eventually crawls through to reach freedom. It was a metaphor for my life.

After beating the Redskins 37–22 on the road to get to 7-2, we turned our attention to Dallas. They were 8-1, and we were on a collision course to meet each other in the playoffs again. But they had beaten us three straight times. It was critical that we beat them in the regular season to set the tone for the playoffs. Besides, everyone was sick of losing to those guys.

When Mike Shanahan gave me the play binder for the Cowboys game, I noticed it had some run plays for me that were specifically designed to exploit Charles Haley's aggressiveness. Instead of running away from Haley, this time we were going to run at him. And I'd be the one doing the running. But the bootlegs would be set up by ball fakes and misdirection intended to exploit Haley's overaggressiveness. I loved it.

But George Seifert didn't.

"I don't want Steve to run that," Seifert told Shanahan at our next practice.

"Coach, it's one hundred percent," Shanahan said. "Steve will be one-on-one with the free safety."

Seifert wasn't buying it.

"The ball fake is the only way we are going to slow down Haley," I said. "I have to run it."

George finally gave in. We ran the bootleg in practice all week.

Three days before the game Deion was addressing the media in our pressroom. I strolled in and appeared over his shoulder.

"This is *my* house!" I shouted.

Deion grinned, and the reporters cracked up.

The reality was that I finally felt like the 49ers were my team. So many of our top players hadn't ever been on the roster when Joe was the starter. Guys like Tim McDonald and Bart Oates and Deion Sanders were my guys. We were a new team. And we were eager to send Dallas a message.

November 13, 1994. During warm-ups at Candlestick I look across the field at the Cowboys and I know we are going to win. I just feel it.

We start the game on our own 12-yard line. I fake the handoff on a sweep to the right. Haley bites and pursues. Then I pivot and bootleg to Haley's side. He can't recover fast enough. I run around the left side and turn upfield for a 25-yard gain. Haley's mad. The next time I drop back to throw he hits me in the head with his forearm, knocking me to the ground. No flag. We end up punting.

The Cowboys' first drive ends when Deion picks off Aikman at midfield. The first quarter is a seesaw battle. Then, with two minutes to play in the quarter, Aikman throws a short dump pass to Alvin Harper, and he breaks loose for a 90-yard run after the catch. Moments later Emmitt Smith crashes into the end zone. Dallas leads 7–0.

We start the second quarter at the Dallas 40-yard line. Shanahan calls another bootleg. I fake an inside handoff. Haley bites again, and I run past him again. I get all the way to the Dallas 25-yard line before I encounter a pack of defenders. As I go down James Washington spears me and Haley, pursuing from behind, jumps on me after I'm down. He is flagged for unnecessary roughness, advancing us to the 13-yard line. Moments later I call a quarterback keeper and run right behind Bart Oates for a touchdown. It's 7–7 at halftime.

The third quarter is a defensive struggle. With 2:56 left in the quarter, we take possession at our 42-yard line. Shanahan wants me to air it out. James Washington has Jerry in single coverage. I call Jerry's number. He streaks down the left sideline. I throw it to the corner of the end zone. Jerry runs 57 yards, dives, and hauls it in. Just like that it's 14–7. The entire Candlestick crowd feels that victory is imminent. The spell has been broken.

Midway through the fourth quarter Dallas drives all the way to our goal line, but Merton Hanks intercepts for the second time. With 5:40 to play, we take over deep in our own territory. If we can string together a few first downs, the game is ours.

I connect on a short pass. Then Ricky Watters breaks loose on a run. We move the chains. With 3:24 to play, I drop back and Dallas blitzes. With no time to react, I throw the ball deep down the left sideline. I know Taylor is running a fly pattern, and I know he's in man-to-man coverage. I just have to trust my instincts. I let the ball go before Taylor looks over his shoulder. As I release I get clocked and land flat on my back. Taylor outruns his man, and the ball hits him in stride. He gets all the way to the Dallas 25-yard line. Candlestick erupts.

It's time to put the game away. Shanahan calls another bootleg. I fool Haley again, but as soon as I get past him Darren Woodson comes up and leads with his helmet, hammering me across the thighs. I feel like I've been hit with a two-by-four.

I get up slowly, call time-out, and limp to the sideline.

"You okay, Steve?"

"I'm fine. What are we running?"

Seifert is on the headset, getting the call from Shanahan. There is 2:37 to play. We're in the red zone. He wants me to run the bootleg again. Only this time I should look to throw.

I fake the handoff right and roll left. Haley isn't fooled. But everyone else is. And by the time Haley and company get to me Brent Jones is alone at the goal line. I release the ball just before Haley nails me. Jones catches the pass, scores, and spikes it! We're up 21–7 with minutes to play. The game is over.

I run around the end zone like I'm dancing on hot coals. Ricky Watters tackles me. My teammates pile on. The crowd is roaring.

Dallas scores a last-minute touchdown. But it's inconsequential. We win 21–14, and it's clear that we finally have a defense that can hold these guys down. I meet Haley at midfield.

"Good game, Steve," he says.

"I'm sure I'll see you again soon," I tell him.

32

FIERY LEADER

THE VICTORY OVER Dallas was our fifth straight win that season. It had huge ramifications. For the first time in three years we had beaten the Cowboys. There was little doubt we'd have to face them again in the playoffs. But a message had been sent. We steamrolled our next five opponents. We put up 31 against the Rams, 35 against New Orleans, 50 against Atlanta, 38 against San Diego, and 42 against Denver. During this stretch I threw 17 touchdown passes and we averaged over 39 points per game. At the same time our defense was playing with the sort of reckless abandon that we hadn't seen since Ronnie Lott left.

We finished the season 13-3. We had the number-one offense in the league. And I was named league MVP for the second time in three years. I should have felt a sense of accomplishment, but I didn't. None of us did. The first-place finish and all the awards wouldn't mean anything if we didn't win the Super Bowl. We'd have to go through Dallas. But first we had to take care of Chicago.

In the locker room following the final regular-season game, I addressed the team.

"It's thirty-four days to the Super Bowl!" I shouted. "We need to make a commitment right now!"

Everyone yelled.

"We need to commit that every day we do everything we can to put the flag on top of Everest."

More yelling.

"Will everyone make the commitment?" I yell.

A collective "*YEAH*" echoes through the locker room.

"Let's go make some history!" I shout.

Everyone roars.

January 7, 1995. I step onto the turf at Candlestick, and my cleats sink into mud. It has rained for eleven straight days in San Francisco, and it's still raining. We fumble on our first possession, and Chicago kicks a field goal to go up 3–0. Then we put up 20 unanswered points. We're driving again. It's third-and-eight. I decide to run for it. I get close to the first-down marker. I'm about to step out of bounds when 285-pound defensive lineman Alonzo Spellman goes airborne and slams into my side, sending me flying. I land hard, and it takes a few moments before I stand and jog across the field.

A few minutes later we are on the Bears' 6-yard line. I drop back. A huge hole opens, and I run through it. Linebacker Vinson Smith dives for me, but misses. I score easily. Then defensive back Shaun Gayle nails me after the play is over, sending me sprawling. I land on my back. Penalty flags fly. I jump up and spike the ball at Gayle's feet. Jerry Rice gets in Gayle's face. Brent Jones bumps him. More flags.

Alonzo Spellman starts throwing punches. My rookie fullback William Floyd grabs Spellman and flings him to the ground. Both teams are brawling.

I'm not one to advocate violence as a way to solve differences. But football follows the Code of Hammurabi. It's an eye for an eye. We crush the Bears 44–15.

For me the best thing about the game is the way my teammates come to my defense. And nobody fights harder than William Floyd. The league fines him for his role in the fight, but I promise to pay his fine.

Now it was clear. I was the leader everyone wanted to rally behind. I felt that we were more unified than any team I'd played on since coming to San Francisco. Curiously, this all started when I exploded at Seifert back in week five. That was when everyone's perception of me changed. We won ten straight games after that. Then we destroyed the Bears.

It was ironic. I had played at full throttle my entire career, but especially since arriving in San Francisco. I had two MVP seasons. I left a few pounds of flesh on the field in Kansas City in week two. But it wasn't until I screamed at my head coach that I became a fiery leader that everyone wanted to rally behind.

This taught me a vital lesson: perception *is* reality. I had worked hard my entire career to establish myself as a leader. But I wasn't a leader until I was perceived as one.

I also learned that you become a leader in times of trouble. Leaders emerge when things don't go well. When everyone else starts pointing fingers, a leader takes responsibility. My teammates saw me doing that on the sidelines when I got yanked from the Eagles game. The reality was that my sideline outburst was the result of lots of pent-up frustration stretching back years. It all just poured out in that moment on the sideline. I didn't mean for it to happen. It just happened. For me it was cathartic. But for my teammates it was revelatory. They suddenly saw me in a different light.

My leadership status was cemented a week later when I crawled off the field in Detroit and then went back out to lead the team to a come-from-behind victory.

Every week in the NFL there's a moment in the game when everyone on the team says: "This is hard. This is really hard." That moment in the Lions game came when I crawled off the field. When I returned moments later, our season changed. We changed. We were not going to be denied. We knew it. And our opponents knew it.

But the ultimate test still awaited us — once again, the Dallas Cowboys.

The day before the NFC Championship game my teammate Richard Dent collided with me in our final walk-through session. It was a freak accident, but it threatened to derail me from the biggest game of my life. Already nursing a neck injury from the Bears game, I knew I was in big trouble the moment Dent ran into the crown of my head. Less than twenty-four hours before kickoff I could not move my neck. Football players play through pain all the time. But this was different. You can't play quarterback when you can't turn your head in any direction.

Looking back, I find it sobering to contemplate how different my life might have been if I had missed the Dallas game. An injection of four milliliters of a powerful, fast-acting anti-inflammatory gave me enough mobility to play. In life, defining moments are rare. But in my case, leading the 49ers in "Dallas vs. San Francisco III" was the defining moment of my professional career.

So much was on the line. Would Dallas become the first team to go to three straight Super Bowls? Would the 49ers be the first team to go to five Super Bowls? In terms of NFL history, this game promised to be one for the ages. I wasn't just quarterbacking a team that day. I was leading the city of San Francisco. Our team set the mood for the entire Bay Area. We had come up short twice. The pressure to win this time — to avoid three straight playoff losses to Dallas — was beyond anything I had previously experienced. Yet I craved this opportunity. The moment I felt the leather football in my hands I felt peace.

It's funny. I had forgotten all about the collision with Richard Dent, the jammed neck, and the needle. It was brought back to my consciousness while working on this book. What I remember most vividly are the little things — such as the moment when we huddled as a team in the locker room right before taking the field. We were directly beneath the end-zone bleacher seats, and beer and condensation and who knows what else dripped through the ceiling. Our fans were screaming with enthusiasm. These were normal features of a game day, but that game day the dripping and the yelling seemed more pronounced. I can still smell the distinct odors and clearly hear the voices.

Then there was the play that clinched the game for us and forever changed my life.

It's the seven-minute mark of the third quarter, and we face second-and-goal from the Dallas 3-yard line. I'm in the huddle. Through the microphone in my helmet I hear Shanahan: "Steve, let's go with 'double-wing right, a right quarterback draw.' Let's go put this away."

I turn to the guys. "'Double-wing right, quarterback draw right.' Now, everybody sell the pass. Sell the pass!"

At the line of scrimmage, I survey the defense and don't like what I see. There's an extra linebacker inside. But I decide to stick with the play call. On the snap of the ball, I start backpedaling as Haley and the other defensive end both stunt inside and the tackles loop around the outside. This is a worst-case scenario, leaving me nowhere to run.

I slide outside, bounce off of a defender, and break for the goal line.

Linebacker Robert Jones lunges for me, and cornerback James Washington grabs me up high. Then Chad Hennings hits me. The four of us go down in a heap, but I land on top and my knees haven't touched the ground, giving me a second chance. I make one final lunge and break the plane of the end zone with the ball. Touchdown!

I spring up and spike the ball. I am finally on top of my personal Everest. The Cowboys are behind me.

Looking back, my life changed that January 15, 1995. And that change occurred in front of 69,000 people. Although I'm an intensely private person, I let myself go when that game ended. My relationship with the fans had been through highs and lows. At times it was strained. But beating Dallas changed everything. That run around Candlestick immediately following our win was even more exhilarating than the touchdown that sealed the game. I was now forever bonded with 49er fans.

33

SUPER

WE GOT TO Miami one week before the Super Bowl. For the next five days our practices were so precise that the ball literally never hit the ground. No dropped passes. No fumbles. No mistakes. We were totally focused.

Everything was perfect off the field too. It wasn't until the night before the game that I felt out of my routine. Unlike the regular season and the playoff games, I had my own hotel room during the week leading up to the Super Bowl. That was fine until Saturday night, when I started thinking about how much routines matter. While the team was having dinner, I contacted hotel security and had them unlock Brent's room. Then I asked them to help me remove his bed and take it to my room. On his way back from dinner, Brent spotted security outside his room and assumed his room had been burglarized. Worried that his Super Bowl gear had been stolen, he ran toward the room just as I was pulling his bed through the door.

"Bro, what is going on?" he said.

I grinned. "Bro, we've been together all season. There's no way we're going to be apart the night before the Super Bowl. It's bad luck."

Brent cracked up. Then he helped me push his bed down the hall and into my room.

Before long, he was snoring and I knew nothing could stop us from beating San Diego.

. . .

January 29, 1995. It's Super Bowl Sunday. Super Bowl XXIX. I wake up at the Miami Airport Hilton and throw on some sweats. There is a breakfast for the team at eight at the Cove Restaurant. That's where Brent is. Brent is planning to bring back my bananas and PowerBars as usual. So he's shocked when I sit down next to him and start eating a giant waffle.

"What are you doing?" he says.

I act like I don't know what he's talking about. "What do you mean what am I doing here? I'm hungry."

I'm so relaxed that it's almost eerie. My neck feels great. We're past the Cowboys. The hardest part is behind me. I eat another waffle, then a third. I'm eating like a lineman.

After breakfast I call my dad. He and my mom are staying at a nearby hotel. They're both extremely nervous for me. My dad's tone is actually solemn. For once I'm the one telling him to relax.

"By the end of today my life is going to be different," I tell him. "One way or the other it's going to be different."

The first bus heads to the stadium at 2:00 PM. On the ride there I start to feel nauseous. Suddenly I regret eating all those waffles. Kickoff is at 6:18 PM. I don't know if I'll last until then. I hide in a corner of the locker room and run through the playbook in my mind. I want perfection. No mistakes. Suddenly I feel somebody standing behind me. It's Shanahan. He has spent two weeks refining our game plan to beat the Chargers. He wants me to run through all 300 plays with him.

I rattle them off as he repeats: "Check. Check. Check."

When I finish, he says: "You know what? One more time."

"Okay. One more time."

I rattle off all 300 plays again.

"Yeah, you know it," he says.

"Let me do it one more time," I tell him.

"I don't want you to do it another time. You know it. In fact, you know it so well, I guarantee we're going to kill these guys."

"Mike, I think you're right."

This is my third trip to a Super Bowl. But this time it's on *me*. I'm not the backup anymore. This is my team. I absolutely have to win this game.

Standing in the tunnel waiting to be introduced, I notice how different I feel. For the first time since I started playing football as a boy, I have absolutely no anxiety. At the same time, I notice how nervous my teammates are. *Who knew?*

I hear my name called and run past cheerleaders with gold and red pompoms. My fist clenched and my right arm raised, I run through a gauntlet of teammates who slap my hands and my helmet. I take in the moment. Thousands of camera flashes flicker through the stands. The Goodyear blimp hovers above.

As the fireworks explode, strobe lights shoot across the stadium and jet fighter planes fly overhead. I do something I've never done before a game — I find my family in the stands and wave to them. Dad gives me the thumbs-up. He looks super-nervous. I'm totally calm. I can't wait to get started.

On the third play of the game I call "Blue right jet right Z seam." It's a play designed to open up the middle of the field for Jerry Rice. Both Chargers safeties have talked big all week that they won't let Jerry get to the middle of the field. I throw a perfect ball. Jerry catches it and races 44 yards. Eighty-four seconds into the game, we're up 7–0. It's the fastest score in Super Bowl history.

The next time we get the ball we start marching again. Linebacker Junior Seau is yelling and blitzing, anything to motivate his teammates. It's no use. After faking a handoff to William Floyd, I throw a 51-yard touchdown strike to Ricky Watters, capping a scoring drive that takes less than two minutes. We're up 14–0.

Then I throw one to Floyd, followed by another to Watters. It's not even halftime and I've thrown four touchdown passes and we're up 28–7. I'm in no mood to celebrate, though. Coming off the field, I tell our defense: "Shut 'em down again! One more time."

In the locker room at halftime, Shanahan keeps telling me: "Don't let up! This is no time to let up!"

We come out firing again. I throw a second touchdown pass to Jerry. Then Ricky runs one in. We're up 42–15 by the start of the fourth quarter. Then I throw my sixth touchdown pass of the game, connecting with

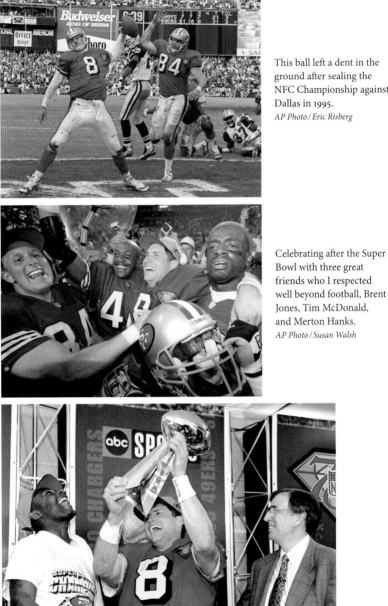

This ball left a dent in the ground after sealing the NFC Championship against Dallas in 1995.
AP Photo / Eric Risberg

Celebrating after the Super Bowl with three great friends who I respected well beyond football, Brent Jones, Tim McDonald, and Merton Hanks.
AP Photo / Susan Walsh

Hoisting the Lombardi Trophy with Jerry after defeating San Diego in Super Bowl XXIX at Joe Robbie Stadium on January 29, 1995. *AP Photo / Eric Risberg*

I was the first athlete ever
to wear the milk mustache.
Milk was my drink of choice.
Annie Leibovitz,
Trunk Archive / MilkPEP

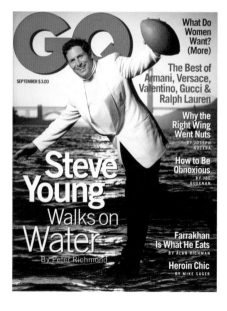

This was such a fun photo shoot with
photographer Michael O'Neill for *GQ*.
After winning the Super Bowl, I was
feeling on top of the world.
© *Michael O'Neill*

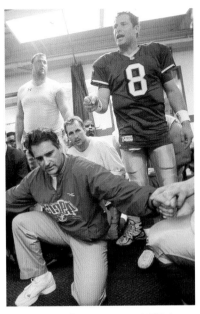

Graduating from law school at BYU in 1994 with my main man Jim Herrmann.
Courtesy of Jim Herrmann

I loved playing for Steve Mariucci. This is one of my rare postgame speeches. I was so fired up. *© Michael Zagaris*

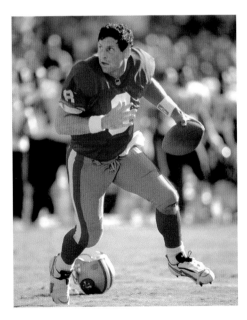

Helmet or not, there is a job to be done. Nothing could stop me from giving the game everything I had.
Mickey Pfleger / Sports Illustrated / Getty Images

After a couple months of dating, Barb and I visited my brother Tom. My niece, Sydney, dressed us up with her jewelry. If only she had a wedding ring, because I already knew I wanted to marry Barb. *Courtesy of the Young family*

HOLINESS TO THE LORD
THE HOUSE OF THE LORD

I married my soulmate Barb in Kona, Hawaii, on March 14, 2000. It was the first wedding held in the new Kona Temple. This was the beginning of the rest of my life. *Photo by Christine Johnson Photography*

I love this photo of Barb and me. It's also great because photobombing us is Tyde Tanner, who was inspired to bring us together. *Photo by Christine Johnson Photography*

Mom, Dad, Tom, and I visiting the Hall of Fame in 1973. Little did we know that we'd be taking the same picture at my induction in 2005. This time I'm not visiting, I'm staying.

Courtesy of the Young family

If you had shown me this photo when I was young, I would never have believed it was real. A very special moment with my dad, my hero.

Jonathan Daniel/Getty Images/Sculpture © Blair Buswell

Jerry and I are still having fun. Here we are in a campaign for Van Heusen. We are better friends than ever.

Photo © Daymion Mardel / Courtesy of PVH Corporation

This picture of Bill Walsh and me wearing our Hall of Fame jackets is very special. Bill always believed in me.

AP Photo / Jeff Chiu

Having my jersey retired in Candlestick brought everything together. The quest was complete. I'm next to my wife, my two sons, and my daughter, with another on the way. What you don't see here is that I'm surrounded by my teammates, my entire extended family, and 65,000 49ers fans. I will never forget it. *Jed Jacobsohn / Getty Images*

From left to right, here are Joe Montana, Eddie DeBartolo (who got his ring the next year), Charles Haley, Jerry Rice, me, Jimmy Johnson, and Ronnie Lott (Dave Wilcox was there too) all showing off our new Hall of Fame rings in September 2015.   *Courtesy of the Young family*

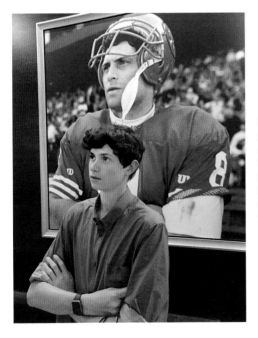

On the same day, my wife snapped this picture of my oldest son, Braedon, who happened to be standing in front of my photo at Levi's Stadium. See any resemblance?
Courtesy of the Young family /
Photo of Steve Young © Michael Zagaris

My favorite sack ever. We have so much fun together. The greatest joy of my life is my family.
Courtesy of the Young family / Photo © Chris Conroy

Jerry for the third time, putting us up 49–15. As I reach the sideline some-body tells me I've beaten Joe Montana's record and set a new all-time re-cord for touchdown passes in a Super Bowl.

But I'm not trying to set any records. I'm just trying to win. The score-board indicates that's finally going to happen. George Seifert pulls me in the final minutes. My teammates start celebrating. Linebacker Gary Plummer asks about the monkey on my back. We're all cracking up. I lean forward and pretend I'm buckling under the weight of a monkey. "Some-body take the monkey off my back," I shout.

Plummer removes the imaginary monkey. "It's gone forever!" he shouts.

My teammates cheer. So do I.

After the fact I will always regret saying that. I'm not really looking at winning the Super Bowl that way. Ever since that airplane conversation with Stephen Covey, I've always viewed the challenge of succeeding Joe as an opportunity to see how good I can become, not as a monkey on my back. The only real burden I've faced is trying to get better day after day.

Beating San Diego is nothing like beating Dallas. Still, when the final gun sounds at Joe Robbie Stadium, it's as if electricity is running through me. We are the first team in NFL history to win five Super Bowls. A cam-era crew from Disney approaches. I know what I'm supposed to do. I re-hearsed this moment with them earlier in the week.

"Steve Young, now that you've won the Super Bowl, where are you go-ing?"

"I'm going to Disneyland!"

In the locker room the players are showering each other with cham-pagne. The Lombardi Trophy is on a makeshift stage, next to Eddie De-Bartolo, Carmen Policy, and Brent Musburger.

Musburger calls me up, and Eddie DeBartolo hands me the trophy. I raise it over my head and let out a guttural yell. "Every guy in here made a commitment," I shout. "You know you did! There were times when it was dark. Really dark. But we committed to each other. We had to do it this way. It's the greatest feeling in the world."

The guys cheer, and I hoist the trophy again. "I share this with every one of you guys," I continue. "No one can *ever, EVER* take it away from us. Ever!"

The guys holler and I wrap my arms around the trophy, and hold it against my chest. The veins in my arms and neck feel like they will pop. I've never squeezed anything so tightly.

I am named Super Bowl MVP. But the sense of joy and accomplishment I feel for my team is beyond imagination. I'm especially grateful to Mike Shanahan. His offensive game plan paved the way for me to throw six touchdown passes. In the locker room he says to me: "Damn! We could have had eight!"

Everybody can't wait to celebrate. A huge after-party is planned at our hotel. But I stay and do every last press interview. I am so thirsty that I must have drunk a couple gallons of Gatorade. By the time I finish talking to the press, I feel ill. Leigh Steinberg leads me to his limousine. His prospective client Kerry Collins, a senior at Penn State, is in the backseat. I hop in. We're headed for the after-party. But as soon as we take off I know I'm in trouble. I throw up all over Collins's shoes.

Everyone laughs. I'm clearly dehydrated.

Leigh tells the driver to head to my hotel. Moments later I'm in my room, propped up in bed, hooked up to an IV. The after-party can wait. I've got a ring. And my parents and close family members and friends are surrounding my bed. For two hours we relish the moment. I'm right where I want to be.

34

FAME

After a couple of hours of sleep I boarded a plane in Miami and flew to Anaheim. By early afternoon I was on a float going down Main Street in Disneyland. The float was decked out in red and gold streamers. A sign on the side said: STEVE YOUNG: SUPER BOWL MVP.

Mickey Mouse was beside me. The Disney marching band led our float down Main Street. Thousands of people lined the parade route. They were cheering and shouting:

"Steve, you're the man!"

"Steve, you're the greatest!"

For about four minutes I lost my mind. I started to believe what people were saying. *I am the man! I am the greatest!*

Then we reached the end of the parade. The band stopped playing, and the float turned off the main road. The cheering died down. I was standing beside Mickey Mouse, waiting to get down from the float. Two little boys spotted us. They were brothers, about six and eight years old. The younger one pointed up in our direction. "There he is," he said.

I assumed he was talking about me.

"It's Mickey Mouse," the kid continued. Then he charged the float. His older brother quickly collared him. "You can't get near him," he said. "That big guy won't let you."

In a matter of minutes, I had gone from being the greatest to being Mickey Mouse's bodyguard. I literally laughed out loud. Then I thought to myself: *Well, it was fun for the four minutes that it lasted. But now it's time to get back to work.*

As soon as I finished my bit at Disneyland I boarded a flight up the coast to San Francisco. The next day was the Niners' victory parade. I rode in a big Cadillac and waved to every person I saw. I had fallen in love with the city of San Francisco years earlier. But now the city had fallen in love with me.

After the parade, Mike Shanahan pulled me aside. "I've accepted the head coaching job in Denver," he said.

"But what if you could be the head coach here?" I said. "It's not like George is going to be the head coach forever."

"Steve, we've had the best three-year run in the history of the game," he said. "But this is a great opportunity for me. Plus, you know I have a long history in Denver and Pat Bowlen is a close friend."

I drop my head.

"Steve, I have never in my life been able to coach someone like you. I'm really going to miss that."

This was a real blow, and I was not prepared for it. Mike was the best thing that had ever happened to me as a football player. My three best seasons were under him. We had something magical.

I headed to the 49ers' training facility to clean out my locker. The place was empty. Or so I thought. Then I spotted someone alone on the practice field. It was Jerry Rice. Just three days after the Super Bowl he was already training for the next season. I talked to him, but I didn't join him. No one worked out harder than Jerry and me. But we always trained alone. It was better that way — we were both way too competitive to train together.

A few hours after leaving Jerry, I started running. Now that I had won a Super Bowl, I wanted to win another one.

The Super Bowl is an American spectacle. Each year it's the most watched event on television — more than 83 million viewers tuned in to see us play San Diego. Being named MVP of the biggest sporting event in the country opens up unimaginable opportunities. After returning from Disneyland, I appeared on *Regis & Kathie Lee* in New York City. My mother was in the studio audience. After the interview, Regis insisted on catching a pass from me. So, with cameras rolling, we headed out to the street.

It was a frigid February morning in Manhattan, and the road outside the studio was under construction. With construction workers in thick hooded sweatshirts and hard hats looking on, Regis waited for the light to turn green while I blew on my hands. Then he took off, running across four lanes of traffic and past some concrete barriers before turning left and going under some scaffolding and heading toward a pile of sewer pipes. He was wearing dress shoes and a business suit. I fired a 30-yard spiral that hit him right in the hands, and he caught it in stride. Construction workers and pedestrians cheered.

I was invited to the ESPY Awards at Radio City Music Hall, where I was honored for being the Outstanding Male Athlete of the Year. Then I flew to Los Angeles for a photo shoot with American fashion photographer Herb Ritts, who was known for doing portraits of Ronald Reagan, Tom Cruise, the Dalai Lama, Michael Jackson, and Mikhail Gorbachev. Ritts photographed me for an advertising campaign I did for The Gap.

When the ad agency for the "Got Milk?" campaign discovered that I had chosen milk over beer as a high school student, I was selected as the first athlete to appear in what was one of the most successful marketing campaigns in history. I flew back to New York to be photographed by Annie Leibovitz, who dressed me in an old pair of miniature shoulder pads that looked like something out of the 1950s. Then she dirtied my face, messed up my hair, and put a milk mustache on me. It was a lot of fun.

I said yes to just about every interesting invitation that I received. When Elton John was on tour in '95, he played in the Bay Area at the Shoreline Amphitheater. A few days before the show I got word that he wanted to meet me backstage. Unfortunately, I was late. Elton held up the show until I arrived, and he insisted on taking some pictures together. We looked like quite a team: Elton in a black-and-white-checkered suit, me in blue jeans and a plaid shirt.

But there was one invitation that concerned something far more serious and important than television interviews, award ceremonies, and photo shoots. Leigh Steinberg was on a mission to change the rules in the NFL in hopes of better protecting players from head injuries. Leigh represented many of the top quarterbacks in the league, including Troy Aikman, Warren Moon, and me. In an effort to change the way the NFL looked at concussions, Leigh organized a series of brain seminars, where he brought in top neurologists and other medical experts who specialized in brain trauma research. The first seminar was held on February 18, 1995, in Newport Beach, California. I attended with Troy, Warren, and a bunch of other NFL players.

Concussions and the risks associated with repeated blows to the head were issues that had been ignored for far too long. There were active and former players who were really suffering. But nobody talked about it openly. One of the core problems was that professional football players — all of us — were accustomed to taking and dishing out hits. It was what we did. So it was a bit conflicting and counterintuitive for guys in this profession to even broach this topic.

I'd certainly had some concussions, but I was fortunate that I was not suffering from any of the adverse effects that some players were experiencing. I was in favor of making changes to the rules to better protect players, but felt that the bigger push for reform had to come from the medical community rather than the football community. So I was a big proponent of Leigh's decision to bring panels of doctors together at a symposium.

One of the big revelations that came out of the symposium was new information on the dangers of what doctors called "second concussion syndrome," which occurs when an initial concussion slows down the reaction time and makes the brain more vulnerable to a second concussion. This happens when concussed players return to the field of play too quickly. The panelists also discussed "micro-concussions," which are not as pronounced but over the long haul, because of how frequently they occur, may do far more damage.

After the conference the medical community put together a white paper for the NFL. The issue of brain injuries had now been raised.

35

REPEATING ISN'T EASY

AUGUST 13, 1995. It's the third game of the preseason, and we're playing San Diego. Although it's only an exhibition game, I want a strong showing. Instead, we come out flat. On the ninth play of the opening drive we are on the Chargers' 19-yard line. On third-and-ten I drop back to pass and safety Rodney Harrison blitzes from my blind side. I never see him, but at the last second I feel him. I duck as he goes for my head. He rips my helmet off as he zips past me. With my helmet on the turf, I start scrambling.

Occasionally, helmets come off in football. But nobody runs the ball without a helmet. Especially not quarterbacks. The Chargers expect me to go down. Instead, I turn upfield and run between the hash marks, rumbling nine yards before I'm taken down.

Why run without a helmet? It's simple. There is something known as Super Bowl hangover. It's when championship teams fall off in their performance. Well, I have never had a hangover in my life, and I'm not about to have one now. My teammates are instantly energized by the sight of me running helmetless through San Diego's defense. Ken Norton Jr. and Gary Plummer bang on my shoulder pads. The whole team responds. We dominate the Chargers.

After the game, the coaches tell me no more running downfield without a helmet.

. . .

The expectation heading into the 1995 regular season was that we were going to win back-to-back Super Bowls. One way to ensure another championship is to add good players to the roster, not subtract them. We broke that rule by letting two of our best players go during the offseason —Ricky Watters went to the Eagles and Deion Sanders went to Dallas. Losing Ricky was especially devastating. He was the perfect complement to our attacking offense. There simply was no way to replace him.

Our coaching staff had undergone an overhaul too. Not only had Mike Shanahan left, but quarterback coach Gary Kubiak had followed him to Denver. Marc Trestman, an experienced quarterback coach who had spent time in Cleveland and Minnesota, took over Shanahan's spot as offensive coordinator. He was only five years older than me, and he had big shoes to fill. But he was smart, and we hit it off right away.

We opened the 1995 regular season on the road against the Saints. Days before flying to New Orleans, I received a package in the mail from a Saints fan. It contained a voodoo doll wearing a number 8 jersey. Pins were stuck in its left arm. More motivation. In the first half I threw a 50-yard touchdown pass to Jerry to put us up 7–0. We never trailed, and I completed 21 of 27 passes on the day for 260 yards. So much for voodoo.

After beating New Orleans, we throttled the Falcons 41–10 and the Patriots 28–3 to open the season 3-0. Over those three games I completed 77 of 109 passes for 875 yards and eight touchdowns. Five of those touchdowns were to Jerry. I was also averaging 50 yards rushing per game. It was the best start of my career, and it gave me confidence that we had what it took to get back to the Super Bowl.

I was enjoying life off the field too.

Being the starting quarterback on the reigning Super Bowl championship team afforded me so many opportunities and experiences that enriched my life. I was invited to appear in an episode of *Beverly Hills 90210* — a top television drama at the time that had morphed into somewhat of a cultural phenomenon. After we beat the Giants to improve to 4-1, I flew to LA during our bye week and was on the set on October 3. We were almost done shooting when one of the directors announced that O. J. Simpson had just been acquitted of murdering his estranged wife, Nicole Brown Simpson, and her friend Ronald Goldman. The women in the cast became so upset that production was shut down for the day.

At one time, O. J. had been one of the faces of the NFL. Now I was one of the faces of the league. I always considered it a privilege that carried with it a responsibility to carry myself — both in public and in private — in a way that inspired kids to work hard and to treat people with respect. I was also very sensitive to the fact that I had so many Mormon youth looking up to me. Appearing in *Beverly Hills 90210* was a great opportunity. My parents had taught me to experience the world, not fear it. They also taught me the importance of good judgment. Before agreeing to appear on the show, I had carefully reviewed the script, and I liked the fact that it had an inspiring story line.

I was also asked to appear opposite Cameron Diaz in the movie *There's Something About Mary*. Who wouldn't want to play Cameron Diaz's boyfriend? Sign me up. But after reading the script, as funny as it was, I decided that some of the humor was a bit much for me, so I turned down the part.

October 14, 1995. It's the day before we face the Colts in week seven. I'm in an Indianapolis hotel room with a high fever and a bad case of the chills. When I stand up, the room wobbles. I have a splitting headache, and I haven't eaten in twenty-four hours. This isn't anxiety. I'm sick with a bad case of the flu. The team doctor insists that I eat chicken noodle soup, drink lots of fluids, and stay in bed. He tells George Seifert that I may not be able to play.

The next morning I arrive at the RCA Dome. I still have a splitting headache and a fever. But I have started fifty-four consecutive games. It's the longest streak for any active quarterback in the NFL, and I have no intention of letting the flu stop me. I put on my uniform and get an IV drip before taking the field.

In the second quarter I complete a touchdown pass to Jerry Rice to put us up 7–3. But on our next possession Colts defender Ray Buchanan grabs my throwing arm while I'm attempting to pass. I am already nursing an injury to that shoulder, and I feel something give when he yanks on my arm. The doctor examines me at halftime and determines that I have a mild shoulder sprain. "Mild" has a different meaning in the NFL than in ordinary life — my shoulder is on fire. And my flu symptoms feel even worse than my shoulder. But I put on my helmet and head out to the field for the second half.

I battle on, and we hold the lead until late in the fourth quarter, when the Colts kick a field goal to go up 18–17. With time running out, I drive us into field goal range. We're trying to get a little closer when I drop back and get hit as I release the ball. I land hard on my injured left shoulder. I'm unable to lift my arm, and it hangs limp at my side as our medical team walks me off the field. They begin massaging my upper arm and insist that I stay out of the game. I've been sacked six times and knocked down numerous other times.

I miss one play, and then I return to the field. I throw one more pass to get us well within range for a game-winning field goal. But our kicker misses it. We lose 18–17 and fall to 4-2.

Afterward the trainer uses big ACE bandages to wrap my shoulder in ice. He cuts the tape from my ankles and feet. I'm bruised, bloody, and dehydrated. Wearing nothing but a towel, I curl up on the training table and close my eyes.

The next day an MRI back in San Francisco revealed two injuries to my shoulder — a sprain and a deep bruise — so I went on the injured list for four weeks. My streak of consecutive starts was over at fifty-five.

While I was sidelined, we lost back-to-back games to the Saints and Panthers, two of the worst teams in the league. We scored a combined 14 points in those two games.

Worse, we lost more key players. Against New Orleans, running back William Floyd blew out his knee when 300-pound lineman Steve Wallace slipped and came down on Floyd's knee. On a separate play, Brent Jones strained his anterior cruciate ligament. Floyd, who was supposed to replace Ricky Watters, was lost for the season. Jones was out indefinitely.

November 12, 1995. We are in Dallas to face the Cowboys. They have the best record in the league at 7-1. Decimated by injuries, we are 5-4 and fading fast. Days earlier Deion Sanders mocked Jerry Rice and claimed we were a team in denial. "I want to win big — not just by seven points," Sanders said. "I want to do things in the end zone."

It's killing me to sit out this game. But my shoulder isn't healed, and I have trouble throwing more than 20 yards. I watch from the sidelines as our defense knocks Troy Aikman out of the game in the first quarter and Elvis Grbac guides our offense to a 31–7 halftime lead. But in the locker room Jerry Rice explodes, screaming at players to get serious and reminding them that we haven't won anything yet. I have never seen Jerry this intense, this animated.

We end up winning 38–20. It's our third consecutive victory over Dallas. No one expected us to win this game, and the victory galvanizes our team. Convinced that we are still the best team in the league and that we can return to the Super Bowl, I can't stand being sidelined. On the bus ride from the stadium to the airport I sit beside Dr. Dillingham and tell him I am beyond impatient. From the bus he calls Stanford Hospital and makes arrangements for me to undergo surgery the next morning.

I showed up at the ER before seven. Dr. Dillingham met me outside. He handed me a football and stepped about 20 yards away from me. He wanted me to throw it and tell him how much pain I felt.

"Throw it toward my left ear," he said.

I threw it directly at his ear. Then I described the pain.

"Now throw it to my right ear."

I repeated the process.

He had me back up and do it again. The pain was more acute from a longer distance, but my accuracy was the same. So he had me step back even farther. Eventually I was throwing directly to his left and right ears from a distance of 40 yards. He couldn't believe the accuracy.

In the operating room an anesthesiologist put me under and Dillingham scoped my shoulder. When I woke up, he told me that he had used some tiny instruments to remove some torn cartilage around the socket.

A little while later he drove me home. Two days later I met him at the practice facility and, amazingly, was able to throw without pain. The next day I practiced and began an aggressive rehab schedule. A week after my surgery, Grbac had another strong outing against Miami on *Monday Night Football* that improved our record to 7-4.

I was cleared to play six days later against the Rams. The announcement raised some eyebrows in the medical community because it had been less than two weeks since my shoulder surgery. The New York Yankees' team physician even contacted us, wanting to know how this was possible. The truth was that I should have spent more time in rehab, but my shoulder felt pretty good. The doctor said that my genetics and muscular composition had a lot to do with my rapid recovery. Mostly, though, I was determined to play.

My first pass against the Rams was intercepted. Then I threw two touchdown passes to rookie J. J. Stokes. We ripped off 35 straight points, and I completed 21 of 32 passes in the first three quarters. We won 44–13.

I had been playing with shoulder pain since week two, and it felt so good to finally be free of that pain. The next week I threw 44 passes against Buffalo. A week later I threw 45 passes against Carolina. Then 49 pass attempts against Minnesota. In four games since returning from the shoulder injury, I completed 110 of 170 throws for 1,029 yards and eight touchdowns.

We finished the season strong, winning six of our final seven games to capture another division title at 11-5. Despite missing five games, I won my fourth straight passing title, and we were once again headed for yet another showdown with Dallas on our quest to repeat as Super Bowl champions.

But first we had to deal with the upstart Green Bay Packers. Under Mike Holmgren, Green Bay's quarterback, Brett Favre, had had a breakout year that had enabled him to edge out Jerry Rice in the voting for NFL MVP.

January 6, 1996. On Green Bay's first series, Tim McDonald blocks Chris Jacke's 44-yard field goal attempt, giving us a first down on our own 34-yard line. On our first play I complete a simple swing pass to Adam Walker. He's wearing a cast to protect his broken thumb. Packers linebacker Wayne Simmons clubs Walker's hand, and he fumbles. Craig Newsome scoops up the ball and races 31 yards for a touchdown. We're down 7–0.

Green Bay kicks off, and we try to establish our running game. We run three plays and punt. Favre orchestrates a long scoring drive and puts Green Bay up 14–0.

On our third possession we try again to establish our running game. The problem is that we are going away from our strength. We are out of sync, and we go into the locker room at halftime down 21–3. This isn't supposed to happen. Candlestick is silent.

In the locker room the mood is somber. Our chances of returning to the Super Bowl are slipping away. I try to rally the team. I'm convinced we can come back.

I come out throwing, and we open the second half with a 14-play, 80-yard drive that ends when I run it into the end zone on a quarterback keeper. It's 21–10 Green Bay. We're back in it, and the crowd is ignited.

But Green Bay adjusts. They know I'm throwing on almost every down, and they drop eight guys into pass coverage. They double- and triple-team Jerry Rice. Although Green Bay rushes only three guys, Reggie White still manages to get to me. I'm sacked three times and knocked down ten times. One of the hits breaks the ring finger on my right hand.

We outplay Green Bay in the second half, and I end up setting an NFL record by attempting 65 passes for 328 yards. But it's not enough. We lose 27–17. There will be no rematch with Dallas, no return trip to the Super Bowl.

Dallas went on to beat Green Bay in the NFC Championship game. Then the Cowboys beat Pittsburgh in the Super Bowl. Having won three Super Bowls with the 49ers, I knew we had squandered a chance to get back there again. You have to play exceptional football in a playoff game. We didn't do that against Green Bay. I couldn't help looking back on the '95 season and regretting that we hadn't been able to keep together the players and coaches who had helped us win it all the year before.

36

60 MINUTES

I GOT A CALL from the head of public affairs at Mormon Church headquarters in Salt Lake City, who told me that *60 Minutes* correspondent Mike Wallace had interviewed President Gordon B. Hinckley, the leader of the Church, for a segment on Mormonism.

The prophet sat down with Mike Wallace? I was shocked. Wallace was considered the toughest interviewer in television news.

The church spokesman said that *60 Minutes* had asked for a couple of additional names of prominent Mormons Wallace could interview, and the prophet had suggested me. Days later Wallace's producer called me. I couldn't get over the fact that my church was going along with this. Millions of people tuned in to *60 Minutes* each week. This could be really good. Or it could turn out very badly.

But hey, I told myself, *if the prophet's in, I'm in.*

On a cold, wintry afternoon in March I went to Salt Lake City for the interview. President Hinckley's secretary ushered me into his private office to wait. Alone, I looked around. A leather-bound set of scriptures rested on the big wooden desk. A painting of Christ hung on the wall. The carpet was soft beneath my feet as I paced the floor, contemplating the fact that I was alone in President Hinckley's office. I was there because he had recommended me to speak to a national audience. There were 10 million Mormons in the world at that time, yet it was my name that he had given to Mike Wallace. Suddenly, losing to the Packers didn't feel so bad. The fact that a prophet felt I was fit to represent the Church meant more to me than winning another Super Bowl.

Forty-five minutes later the door opened and President Hinckley entered with a smile.

We shook hands and talked for a few moments. Then someone ducked in and said: "It's time." President Hinckley looked me in the eyes and flashed a wry smile. "Be careful," he said. "Watch your back."

I smiled. He didn't advise me on what to say or what not to say. Nor was I particularly worried about it. I was very comfortable talking to the media. I'd been doing it week in and week out since I was a sophomore in college.

I followed a producer into a conference room down the hall from President Hinckley's office, where Mike Wallace greeted me. Moments later we were sitting opposite each other, bright lights on, cameras rolling. It didn't take him long to get to the sensitive questions on topics such as the sacred undergarments that Mormons wear. To me those are an outward expression of an inward commitment, and I always felt that it was disrespectful to wear them when I was going to get sweaty and dirty. I wasn't looking forward to discussing them on national television.

"Do you think that the sacred undergarments have kept you from harm on the football field?" Wallace asked.

"I actually take them off to play football," I said. "But my teammates have enjoyed it," I continued. "When, you know, you're getting dressed and you're putting your garments on, they think they're pretty cool. A lot of them ask. 'Hey, where'd you get those?' And I'd always tell them they're way too expensive."

He smiled. Then he asked an even more personal question.

"Steve, there is a law of chastity in your church that says you shall have no sexual relations outside of marriage. You're not married, and you're a professional athlete. How do you deal with that?"

"Well, I obey it."

Wallace squinted and stared into my eyes. He knew I was thirty-four years old, and I knew exactly what he was thinking.

"You're telling me that you obey the law of chastity?" he asked.

I grinned and nodded. "Yes," I said.

• • •

On Sunday, April 7, 1996, I was in the Tabernacle on Temple Square in Salt Lake City. The Church was holding its annual General Conference. Mormons around the world watch on television and listen on the radio, but I made an effort to attend in person. When President Hinckley stood at the podium to make his customary closing remarks, he surprised the audience with an announcement:

"Months ago I was invited to be interviewed by Mike Wallace, a tough senior reporter for the CBS *60 Minutes* program, which is broadcast across America to more than twenty million listeners each week. I recognized that if I were to appear, critics and detractors of the Church would also be invited to participate. I knew we could not expect that the program would be entirely positive for us."

I was undoubtedly one of the few people in the building who had known this was coming. Still, hearing him announce it reminded me how big a moment this was for my church.

"On the other hand," he continued, "I felt that it offered the opportunity to present some affirmative aspects of our culture and message to many millions of people. I concluded that it was better to lean into the stiff wind of opportunity than to simply hunker down and do nothing."

Everyone in the Tabernacle broke out laughing. I did too.

"We have no idea what the outcome will be — that is, I don't," Hinckley said. "If it turns out favorable, I will be grateful. Otherwise, I pledge I'll never get my foot in that kind of trap again."

More laughter.

That night I watched the broadcast. As I expected, President Hinckley came off great. Mike Wallace was very fair in his portrayal of our faith.

37

PAIN

THE 49ERS' BIGGEST deficiency heading into the '96 season was still our running game. Fullback William Floyd continued to be out indefinitely with a severe knee injury, and we had no one to fill his shoes. Our other big concern was my protection. In '95 we had the highest-scoring offense in the league. But I also got sacked thirty-four times, and that was way too many times. Despite our suspect running game and depleted offensive line, we were still the preseason favorite to win the Super Bowl in '96.

I entered training camp with some physical concerns of my own. The problem originated over the summer. During the off-season I started dating someone new, a twenty-five-year-old BYU senior who was really into rollerblading. So I spent much of June and July rollerblading with her up and down Provo Canyon, which kept me in a bent-over position while speeding for miles and miles through the mountains of Utah. This posture tightened my hip flexors. As a result, I felt the strain in my groin area during camp. My elbow was also bothering me. It felt like I had torn something. Every time I threw I felt discomfort.

I didn't think much about the groin or the elbow, though. I was preoccupied with my new girlfriend. We were spending a lot of time together and eventually we decided to get married after the season. But we kept the news to ourselves.

. . .

Our season opener was at home against New Orleans. We beat them easily, 27–11. But toward the end of the game I got slammed to the turf and split my chin open. The team doctor applied something to get the bleeding to stop. Then he put a big awkward bandage on my chin. The next day a plastic surgeon sewed me up and recommended that I avoid football for a while. *Yeah, right!*

A week later we played St. Louis. Early in the second half I scrambled and felt my groin tear. It occurred when I tried to plant my foot and cut back while running. The pain was so sharp that it was all I could do to limp to the sideline. We dominated St. Louis, 34–0, to improve to 2-0. But I wondered if my season was over.

Fortunately, we had a bye week. That gave me nearly fourteen days to rest. Unfortunately, groin tears take longer than that to heal.

September 22, 1996. We're in Carolina to face the Panthers. We are both 2-0, and they are clearly challenging us for supremacy in the NFC West. Before the game the medical team asks about my groin. I tell them I'm playing. Running isn't the problem. I still have my speed. But I can't make quick stops or sudden changes of direction.

Carolina has a very young, very quick defense. When I try to scramble, my other muscles are forced to overcompensate for my compromised groin, and early in the game I pull my right quad muscle, forcing me to the sideline once again. This time I admit to the doctors that my groin is worse than I have let on. My lower abdominal area is on fire.

I sit out the rest of the game, and Carolina beats us to claim sole possession of first place in the division. Afterward I'm injected with an anti-inflammatory. The medical team warns me that groin injuries have a tendency to become chronic. If I'm not careful, I could end up missing the entire season.

At a minimum, the team doctor wants me to shut it down for two weeks.

The groin injury really bugged me. I didn't know what I'd do if I couldn't play anymore. I didn't want to think about it.

I sat out our next game against Atlanta, which we won easily. But I tried to play the following week in St. Louis. That was a big mistake. In my first series I pulled my right quadriceps and had to leave the game. My injuries were mounting. I looked on as Elvis Grbac led us to victory, boosting our record to 4-1.

The next day an MRI at Stanford University Hospital revealed fluid in the joint between my right and left pubic bones, along with some ligament strain and some fluid on the bone on the right side. My body was hurting, but the prospect of not playing bothered me more. I told our team doctor that I just had to get back on the field. He prepared a needle with a combination of anti-inflammatories and painkillers. I lay on my back on a medical table while he injected my groin area.

October 14, 1996. I have just turned thirty-five, and we are in Green Bay to face the Packers on *Monday Night Football*. We are 4-1; they are 5-1. I want nothing more than to avenge our loss to them in the playoffs back in January. But it has only been six days since my MRI and the injection in my groin area. There's no way I can play. Grbac starts, and I am forced to watch from the sidelines as Brett Favre throws a team-record 61 passes and leads Green Bay to a come-from-behind 23–20 win in overtime. We fall to 4-2.

Our next game is in six days. On the flight home from Green Bay I tell myself that I am playing the next game no matter what. My groin isn't healed, but I don't care. I am just going to stop telling the medical staff anything about how my groin hurts. I am done talking about pain.

October 21, 1996. It's a beautiful fall day in the Bay Area—sunny and warm. Perfect football weather. We're facing Cincinnati. Before the game Seifert says to me: "If it looks like you're hobbling, I'm going to take you out."

I tell myself: *Whatever I do, no hobbling. Even if it hurts, no hobbling.*

In pregame warm-ups I spot my old BYU roommate and longtime friend Lee Johnson. After ten seasons, he is still punting for Cincinnati.

"How's the groin, bro?" he asks.

"It's killing me, but don't tell your guys that."

The Bengals score on their first possession to go up 7-0. Gingerly, I trot onto the field for our first series. There is a new face in our huddle—

rookie receiver Terrell Owens. With J. J. Stokes out with a broken wrist, I know the Bengals will key on Rice. I tell Terrell: "Be ready!"

My first pass is to Owens. He catches it and immediately has the ball stripped from his hands. Cincinnati recovers. It's a rookie mistake. Five plays later, Cincinnati scores again to go up 14–0.

Things continue to go downhill. In the second quarter we trail 21–0 with eight minutes left in the first half when I get sacked and I feel my groin tear again. It feels like someone cut me with a knife. But I don't want Seifert to see that I am hurt. I get up slowly and try to walk normally. But I can't. My groin won't let me.

George pulls me, and Grbac takes over. Minutes later he throws a 17-yard touchdown pass to put us on the board 21–7.

I clench my fist and pound the bench while the doctor examines me. I tell him there is nothing to examine. I know what's wrong. And there's nothing he can do for a pulled groin.

After a few minutes I want back in. *Now!*

"It's not going to happen, Steve," the doctor tells me.

I pound the bench with my fist.

The doctor tells me I'm not just done for the day — I might be finished for the season.

I am sulking on the bench when Elvis Grbac tries running for a first down and gets slammed to the ground. He lands hard on his shoulder. We head to the locker room at halftime, and while Grbac gets X-rayed, I have the trainer stretch my groin. Grbac's X-rays show no structural damage. But he says he's in too much pain to play. My groin is feeling better. With Grbac unable to go, Seifert puts me back in for the second half.

The Bengals are double- and triple-teaming Rice. On a critical third-and-two from our 44-yard line, I keep the ball on a designed run play. I can sprint, but I can't slow down or cut without aggravating my groin injury. So instead of trying to elude oncoming tacklers, I lower my head and barrel into them at top speed. I manage to get the first down to keep the drive alive. Then I throw an interception. The physical limitations from the injury are driving me nuts.

On our next possession I throw a 39-yard touchdown pass to Ted Popson to cut the lead to 21–14. Meantime, Terrell Owens is struggling.

Heading into the fourth quarter, I pull him aside. "You have to get open," I tell him. "You have to! They are putting all their attention on Jerry. If you don't step up now, it's going to hurt the team."

On our first possession in the fourth quarter Owens goes deep and I overthrow him, killing the drive and forcing us to punt. It's my fault as much as his. Our timing is off. But he blames himself when he reaches the sideline. "We'll get it," I tell him. "We'll get it."

By the time we get the ball back only a few minutes remain and we are backed all the way up to our own 12-yard line. Plus, my groin is killing me again. Still, I complete three straight passes, advancing us to Cincinnati's 45-yard line. I call T.O.'s number again. It is the same route we messed up earlier. On the snap Owens adjusts his route to avoid the coverage. I see what he is doing and throw the ball where I think he is headed. The 45-yard pass hits him perfectly in stride. He hauls it in and scores. It's Terrell Owens's first career touchdown. Candlestick erupts. With 2:08 remaining, we're tied at 21.

I figure we are headed for overtime. But a couple of plays later Cincinnati coughs up the ball on their 32-yard line. We are practically in field goal range with 1:40 to play. After I complete a pass to Rice, he gets out of bounds at Cincinnati's 15-yard line, stopping the clock with 1:14 to play. By this point my groin is in such bad shape I can barely walk, much less run. I look to the sideline for the next play. It's a bootleg left.

I like the call. Cincinnati knows I can't run. So they'll never expect me to try it in this situation.

Owens is the only receiver lined up on the left side. On the snap our entire offense sweeps right. I fake a handoff right and the entire Bengals defense follows. I pivot and bootleg left. There is no one out there except Owens and one defender. I run 15 yards untouched. At the goal line I cut back to avoid the one defender, aggravating my groin pull. I have to practically hop across the goal line on one leg, but I don't care. The adrenaline rush eclipses the pain. My teammates mob me, and the 49ers fans are bellowing my name:

"*STEVE!*"

"*STEVE!*"

"*STEVE!*"

"STEVE!"

We have come back from 21 points down to win 28–21. It's the second-biggest comeback in franchise history. And despite being injured and missing much of the first half, I finish with 274 yards passing and 45 yards rushing. This is as good as it gets. As the final gun sounds I limp across the field and find Lee Johnson. He throws his arms around me.

"Love you, man," he says.

What a friend. I want to stay and reminisce with him. But NBC's Jim Gray approaches with a cameraman over his shoulder.

"Were you upset at being pulled in the first half?" Gray says. "It looked like it."

"Well, I've been dragging this leg for a while, and he's [Coach Seifert] trying to protect me. But I'm glad I got a chance."

"We talked in the pregame about being thirty-five years old and looking over your shoulder. Did you send a message here this afternoon that you're not quite ready to give it up?"

"Over my dead body!" I laugh.

I limp off the field. The satisfaction of the victory masks the reality of the pain. One thing about winning—it really cures a lot of ills.

I hardly practice the following week, but I start in our next game, in Houston. There's a lot of focus on my groin. On the third play of the game I stumble while backpedaling. I regain my balance and roll to my right, looking to throw downfield, when linebacker Micheal Barrow runs into me at full speed. His helmet collides with mine. Another defender takes my legs out. The next thing I know I'm lying on my back, looking up at doctors while the Astrodome lights shine down on me. Everything hurts.

This time it isn't my groin. It's my head and neck. I make my way to the sideline, where the medical team examine me and determine that I've suffered another concussion.

On our next possession I put on my helmet and head out to play. I get just past the sideline before the medical staff pull me back and inform me that I can't go. Moments after the doctors stop me, I'm in an ambulance headed to Methodist Hospital for tests. By the time I get back to the Astrodome nearly three hours have passed and only four minutes remain in the game. Terrell Owens catches a game-winning touchdown and we win 10–9 and improve to 6-2.

The next day I underwent a CT scan at Stanford Hospital. The results were negative. Still, the team doctor didn't want me to play. Leigh Steinberg didn't want me to play. George Seifert didn't want me to play. I protested, but the medical facts for the '96 season were not in my favor. I had started six games and been forced out of four of them with injuries.

I missed the next game against the Saints. It was my fourth missed game of the season. We won again, but I was miserable.

November 10, 1996. We are playing Dallas at Candlestick. The Cowboys are the defending Super Bowl champs, but this year they're struggling with a 5-4 record. We are 7-2. A victory by us would effectively kill their season and solidify our position as the top team in the NFC. I absolutely insist on starting.

In the first quarter I throw a touchdown strike to put us up 10–0. But in the second quarter linebacker Broderick Thomas blindsides me and drives me into the turf. His helmet lodges in my neck when he lands on top of me. I shake off the hit and stay in the game. Then, with 6:24 remaining in the first half, Thomas pursues me again. I try to scramble free, but my groin injury enables Thomas to get to me. He wraps me up, pinning my arms to my sides. I'm standing up and completely exposed when linebacker Jim Schwantz lowers his helmet and nails me in the head.

I'm on my back when the medical staff get to me. They escort me to the bench, where I remove my helmet and put a towel over my head. Dr. Klint squats in front of me. "I'm going to ask you some questions," he says.

I know the drill. These are the questions intended to reveal whether I have a concussion.

"Who are you?"

"Steve Young."

"What is your date of birth?"

"October 11, 1961."

"Where were you born?"

"Salt Lake City, Utah."

"Who is your father?"

"Grit Young."

"Who is the president of the United States?"

"Abraham Lincoln."

Dr. Klint's eyes widen and his eyebrows rise.

I smile. "I'm kidding!"

He flashes an uneasy smile. But he isn't taking any chances. It's my second concussion in three weeks. I'm done for the day.

This is the first time that I don't fight Dr. Klint.

I admit to myself: *I'm tired. I'm beat up. My head hurts. I want to rest.*

Elvis Grbac takes my place. In the second half I watch as we cling to a 17–10 lead. I figure the victory is in hand when Troy Aikman throws an interception on our goal line with six minutes to play. But moments later Grbac throws an interception. It's a pass that never should have been thrown. It's the kind of mistake a young quarterback makes. Especially when you're a backup trying to do everything possible to win. I've done it. Every quarterback has. Unfortunately, this one costs us the game. Minutes later Dallas scores to tie the game. In overtime they kick a field goal to knock us off 20–17.

Dallas improves to 6-4 and we fall to 7-3.

Losing at home to the Cowboys didn't sit well with the fans. The city blamed Grbac. Even San Francisco mayor Willie Brown got in the act, telling reporters: "This guy Grbac is an embarrassment to human kind." Nobody realized that earlier in the week Grbac's nine-month-old son had undergone a major operation because he had spina bifida. I gave Elvis some simple advice: "Ignore what everyone else is saying, put the Cowboys game behind you, and now focus your energies on next Sunday."

After the game the Cowboys talked about the play that forced me out with a concussion. "It was a third-and-long," one linebacker told the media. "So I came from a pretty good distance away. Broderick was just wrapping him up around the legs, and I was able to get him right in the head."

• • •

The next day I saw a neurologist in Palo Alto. After examining me, he said he didn't want me to play right away. From his office I went directly to the 49ers' practice facility, where I spoke to reporters. They wanted to know about my head, but I didn't feel like talking about it. So I changed the subject. I told them I was engaged and getting married on March 8, 1997.

The reporters didn't know what to say. Suddenly I was fielding questions about my wedding.

"We were kind of just keeping it to ourselves," I told the press. "I think a lot of guys on the team knew for a while, and our friends obviously knew — not that we were trying to keep it from anyone — but people talk. So it's out now." It had been ten years since my last engagement, so this was big news.

Later in the day my mother called. She asked if it was true that I was getting married in March. She said a reporter had just called her seeking a reaction. I apologized profusely for forgetting to tell her. But the truth was that the decision was rather rushed. I'd only been dating my fiancée for a few months when I made it. I hadn't really gone through my typical cautious deliberations over big decisions. I was consumed with football and just going through the motions of what seemed like the next logical step in our relationship.

My mother was thrilled.

November 24, 1996. We are in Washington to play the Redskins. After sitting out the previous week, I start. I feel pretty good in the first half. In the second half I get on a roll, completing 20 straight passes. Yet we still trail, 16–9. Late in the fourth quarter we get the ball deep in our own territory. I complete seven of seven passes on a 73-yard drive that ends with a touchdown. It ties the game with 1:57 remaining. In overtime we kick a field goal to win it. Despite the injuries, I have one of the finest passing games of my career, completing 33 of 41 passes for 295 yards.

The victory over Washington put us at 9-3 heading into a *Monday Night Football* game in Atlanta. A couple of days before traveling the 49ers' head of security approached me at our practice facility. "Steve, I just got a call from a psychiatric ward doctor in Atlanta," he said. "She wanted to warn us and you that a woman who had just been released from their care could be dangerous to you because she is crazy. The doctor said this patient has some fixation with you."

The situation he described sounded bizarre.

"Unfortunately," he continued, "the doctor said they had no choice but to release her. Therefore, the doctor wanted to warn us. This woman could be dangerous."

The team put extra security around me for the trip. As usual, Brent sat next to me on the flight to Atlanta. Usually we joked around a lot on flights. But this time I was preoccupied. Over my career I'd been stalked by numerous women. I had some real doozies, some who claimed they were married to me and others who followed me around for years. I ignored all of it. But this felt different.

"What's wrong?" Brent finally asked.

"Dude, I got a death threat," I told him.

"What?"

I explained the situation. When we landed in Atlanta the team asked Brent if he wanted his own hotel room. "No way," he said. "Steve and I are in it together."

In an attempt to inject a little humor into the situation, Brent started calling me Charlie to disguise my identity. But when we entered our hotel room the phone was ringing, which was very unusual. Brent answered it, and I went to the window. While staring at the building across from our room, I listened to Brent's half of the conversation:

Brent: "Who is this?"

Pause.

Brent: "Where are you?"

Pause.

Suddenly he shouted: "It's the girl! Get down!"

I hit the deck.

"Stay down!" he yelled.

"What in the world is happening?" I shouted.

"Some woman was asking for you," he said.

We crawled on our stomachs to the door. As as we reached the hallway he started yelling: "Security! Security!"

Security arrived. Our floor was searched. The building across from us was searched. Nothing turned up. At that point we were laughing so hard we were practically crying. Needless to say, we didn't sleep much that night. But when we got to the stadium the following day, I felt great. In the second quarter I rushed for a 26-yard touchdown and a 5-yard touchdown, and I ended up completing 23 of 30 passes for 254 yards. We routed Atlanta 34–10. I started calling Brent "The Bodyguard."

We finished the regular season 12-4, and I was the top-rated quarterback in the league for the sixth consecutive season. But for the first time since I arrived in San Francisco, we didn't win our division. The Carolina Panthers were also 12-4, and since they beat us twice, we were forced into the wild-card round to face the Eagles.

December 29, 1996. I have an uneasy feeling when I wake up in my room at the San Francisco Marriott.

Brent tells me to relax. "We're going to beat these guys," he tells me. "I have absolutely no doubt."

I wish I felt more sure.

It's windy and raining at game time. Despite the elements, my passes are on target and we move the ball on Philadelphia's defense. But we fail to score. Meantime, our defense shuts down the Eagles. It's late in the second quarter, and neither team has put any points on the board. Then I connect with Jerry on a deep route that puts us inside the red zone. Moments later I break loose on a 9-yard run, breaking tackles and bouncing off defenders. At the goal line I take a helmet to the ribs that propels me into the end zone. We go up 7–0.

But I'm in trouble. The pain is excruciating, and I'm laboring to breathe. I find one of the team doctors on the sideline.

"I think I broke my ribs," I tell him.

At halftime the medical team injects the cartilage around my ribs with Novocain. But the injury severely limits my throwing motion. Still, I play the entire second half.

Our running back situation is such a mess that I end up carrying the ball 11 times for 65 yards. I also throw a 36-yard touchdown pass to Jerry in the third quarter to put the game away. We win 14–0 and advance to the next round.

After the game I can't raise my left arm. It hurts to take deep breaths. X-rays appear to indicate that I have two fractured ribs.

I'm not surprised, but we face the Packers in Green Bay in six days. I have to be ready to play. We have to beat them this time.

The plan is to hold me out of practice all week and inject my ribs with painkillers on game day. That approach worked in the second half of the Eagles game. The doctor says it will work against the Packers.

January 1, 1997. It's our final practice before flying to Green Bay. I get an injection in my rib area again and try taking some snaps. But I can't throw — too much pain. I go back to the training room for a second injection. Then I return to the field and try again. My ribs are still killing me. I go to the training room and receive a third injection. It still doesn't do the trick.

"It isn't working," I tell the doctor.

"Don't worry," he says. "It will work for the game."

This makes no sense to me. *If the painkillers don't work now, why should I have faith that they will work at game time?*

I'm on the training table, peppering the doctor with questions, when Brent Jones limps in and lies on the table next to mine. He has just injured his knee. Things aren't looking good.

The next day we fly. I'm in agony the entire flight. It feels worse than a couple of broken ribs. The night before the game I'm in my hotel room with Brent. His knee is elevated. He has a sprain, but he expects to play. I'm less certain. Whenever I move it feels like I'm being stabbed in the rib cage. I can't take deep breaths.

"What is the doctor telling you?" Brent says.

"That they will shoot me up before the game and that I should be fine."

"So you have to go with that."

"But I don't know if the shot is going to work. It didn't work two days ago. I'm worried."

"Hey, buddy, you know what? You're a warrior. You gotta give it a shot. That's who we are. That's the way we approach things."

"I don't want to let the team down."

"You gotta go out there," he says. "You gotta take your shot and see if you can do it. And if you can't, you can't. But you can't take all the blame if that happens. Injuries happen. And this one's tough."

I want nothing more than to beat Brett Favre and the Packers. An hour before pregame I lie face down on the training table. I clinch the table while the doctor inserts a needle in the side of my lower back. Then I put on my pads and head out to the field to warm up.

Packers head coach Mike Holmgren is standing at midfield, watching me. I can only throw the ball 10 yards, and I'm in total agony. Holmgren looks at me, shrugs his shoulders, and walks off. He knows it's not happening for me today.

I go back inside, and the doctor shoots me up a second time. "It's not helping," I tell him. "It still hurts."

"That's impossible," the doctor says.

"I'm telling you. It did nothing."

The doctor is baffled. Novocain numbs what it hits. Period. It's not like the Novocain is faulty. The area around my ribs is injected twice within an hour. By this point I shouldn't be feeling anything in that region.

"I'm telling you!" I say.

"It just doesn't make sense," the doctor offers. "You shouldn't be able to feel *anything*."

Game time arrives. It's raining and cold. Green Bay fans are ramped up, but I feel miserable. I'm sick to my stomach and convinced that something far more serious than broken ribs is going on inside me. Wearing a flak jacket, I trot out for the first series. On my first pass play I end up scrambling for a 3-yard gain before being chased out of bounds. With each step I feel like I have daggers in my back. Running is agonizing. If I take a hit it isn't going to be pretty. Plus, I can't get warm. I play one more series and complete two of five passes for 8 yards.

I know what I have to do. For the first time in my career I remove myself from a game.

I put a raincoat on over my pads and pull the hood over my helmet. I just want to lie down. I feel like I'm going to die.

Brent Jones stands next to me. "You are still a warrior," he says. "Most guys would not have even tried to play in your condition."

I appreciate his thoughts, but it doesn't make me feel better.

By halftime the Packers go up 21–0. I feel like it's my fault. In the locker room I tell the doctors I want to give it one more try. For the fourth time I assume the position on the training table and get the injection. The area is so numb I don't feel the needle. But when I try to get up I feel sharp pain in my ribs. What is going on? I figure at this point I have enough Novocain in me to numb a horse. It's no use. I can't play.

I spend the second half on the sideline, bundled up under a coat. Favre has another big day, and the Packers hammer us 35–14. They go on to beat Dallas in the NFC Championship game and then win the Super Bowl.

38

RELIEF

I n thirteen pro seasons, I hadn't had any major injuries. In '91, I tore my ACL, but it healed without surgery and I only missed six games. In '95, I had a minor surgery to repair some shoulder strain, which forced me to sit out a few games. I had broken my thumb and split my chin open. But in the big scheme of things, all of this was pretty minor and quite remarkable, especially considering all the hits I had taken over the years. Going all the way back to the time that I fell down the stairs in my baby walker, I had always been durable and able to bounce back quickly from injuries. Like my dad, I was thick-boned. He always said we were built for a beating. Even the concussions I had sustained had never resulted in symptoms or side effects that kept me out of action.

But suddenly, for the first time in my career, I felt vulnerable. The rib injury forced me to miss a playoff game. It had been weeks since an Eagles player planted his helmet in my rib cage. Yet the pain hadn't subsided. If anything, it was sharper than ever. *What is wrong with me?*

Ten days after we lost to the Packers, George Seifert stepped down as head coach. I ran into him at our training facility when he was cleaning out his office. It was a bittersweet goodbye. "You always played better when I tortured you," he said.

I thought to myself: *You gotta be kidding me. I was the last guy who needed to be tortured as a method of motivation. As it was I tortured myself more than enough.*

But I didn't say that to George. He cared a great deal about me as a player and a person. It wasn't easy replacing Bill Walsh, and George did a great job. He had a marvelous way of poking fun at himself and he never got rattled. It was going to be different without him at the helm.

Two days later, on January 16, 1997, forty-one-year-old Steve Mariucci was introduced as the new head coach. His experience as a head coach consisted of twelve games — just one season — at Cal. He had no head coaching experience in the NFL. But his time under Mike Holmgren as quarterback coach in Green Bay had put him at the top of the 49ers' list.

I had met Mariucci at the Pro Bowl the year before, and I liked him. I was happy he was joining us. But I was also wondering if I'd ever play football again. The pain in my rib cage still hadn't subsided. I flew to Provo and met with my old friend from the LA Express, George Curtis, who was now the head trainer at BYU. After consulting with me about my ribs, he referred me to the renowned chiropractor Dr. Laney Nelson, who specialized in spinal pain and sports injuries. I didn't see how a chiropractor could help with broken ribs, but I was so desperate I was willing to try anything.

I met Dr. Nelson in his office in Salt Lake City. When I told him my symptoms, he said that the pain I was describing didn't sound like fractured ribs. "That doesn't necessarily mean you don't have a broken rib," he explained. "But I suspect that the pain you're feeling is from a dislocated rib."

He had me lie face down while he manipulated my back. I felt him moving one of my ribs. The pain was excruciating. Then suddenly the pain was gone.

"What just happened?" I said.

"Sit up," he said.

For the first time in weeks I moved without pain. I stood and started doing windmills with my left arm. It felt normal. I looked at him. "I'm healed!" I said in disbelief.

He confirmed that my ribs were indeed broken. But they were also dislocated. Basically, one of them had popped out of place, so the slightest movement triggered unbearable pain.

It felt so liberating to be pain-free. But as soon as I left his office I couldn't help getting angry. *Why couldn't I have seen Dr. Nelson two weeks earlier? I could have played pain-free against Green Bay!*

I went from one stress-filled situation to another. I was supposed to get married in March. But even before the season had ended I knew it wasn't going to work. It wasn't that I had cold feet. It was that I still hadn't found the right woman. I was searching for my soul mate. I just knew, deep down, that I had to keep searching.

Once again I called off a wedding. And I was at peace with the decision.

A month later I closed on a new house on Waverley Street in Palo Alto, three doors down from Steve Jobs's house. Mine was a two-story colonial with shutters and a balcony off the second floor. There were flower beds along the sidewalk and a large olive tree in the front yard. A rail fence wrapped the small yard. It was an ideal home to start a family. *Someday,* I told myself. *Someday.*

That summer Peter King profiled me on the cover of *Sports Illustrated.* He — and everyone else — kept asking me about marriage. But I was tired of talking about it. I wanted very badly to get married, but I wasn't going to do it until I found the one.

Meantime, I took my mother to Israel for a week, her first trip to the Middle East. I showed her the places where Jesus walked. We talked about our beliefs, and we discussed our relationship with our Heavenly Father. It had been a long time since my mother had held my hand and walked me to elementary school. Now I held her hand and we walked the dusty roads of the Holy Land together.

When we returned to the States, I spent part of the summer traveling to Indian reservations with my longtime friend Dale Tingey, the head of American Indian Services. Dale spent most of his life helping Native Americans, particularly the Navajo and the Hopi. He lived in Utah, and he had his own plane that he used to get back and forth from remote Indian reservations. For years I'd spent part of the off-season tagging along with him. He'd even given me a few flying lessons. In early July 1997, we were on our way to the Navajo Reservation and I was at the controls when the landing strip — which was nothing more than a dirt stretch — came into view. This was the time when he would take control of the plane. This time he had other plans.

"Go ahead, Steve," he said. "Land it."

"Ah, I'm not sure that's such a good idea," I said.

For one thing, I had never landed a plane. Worse, a herd of sheep were occupying the landing strip. There was a wicked crosswind too.

"You'll be fine," he said. "Just buzz low. The sheep will move."

I did as he instructed, and the sheep scattered. But I still didn't feel good about landing the plane.

"The crosswind is tipping the wing," I said. "Maybe you should take the controls now."

"You got it," he said calmly.

"No! I can't land it."

He said nothing as we approached the dirt strip.

"We're gonna crash!" I shouted. "Grab it, Dale! Grab it!"

Suddenly we hit hard, causing my upper body to thrust forward and then back. Instinctively, I applied the brakes.

"Why didn't you grab the controls?" I said. "We almost crashed!"

"I knew you could do it," he snickered.

Nothing fazed Dale. If Eddie DeBartolo had watched that scene, he would have gone over the edge.

Dale and I parked the plane and made our way to a thatched hut with a dirt floor. Inside, I addressed a bunch of high school students about scholarship opportunities. One of them knew that I was in the middle of contract negotiations with the 49ers, and he asked me how the organization was treating me. If a journalist had asked me that question, I never would have answered it. But I was out in the middle of nowhere, talking to some students, sitting cross-legged, in a thatched hut. So I spoke candidly. "Horribly," I told him. "Just horribly."

As I elaborated, I was completely unaware that the student was an aspiring journalist. He ended up writing an article about my contract situation and sending it to the *San Francisco Chronicle*. A few days later, a dispatch from the Navajo Indian Reservation appeared in the *Chronicle*. My quotes caused quite a stir in the Bay Area. Most of the acrimony was between my agents and the 49ers' front office. Normally, Leigh Steinberg would have been in the thick of it, but for the first time he was not around. He'd been arrested earlier in the summer on drunk driving charges. His legal situation had prompted him to take a leave of absence to deal with some personal matters.

I felt bad for Leigh. We had been through a lot over the previous fourteen years. But his colleagues Jeff Moorad and Dave Dunn had also worked with me for years, and they handled the negotiations. Not long after the submission from the Navajo student ran in the paper, the team offered me a six-year extension worth $45 million. The new deal once again made me the highest-paid player in the league. Far more important to me, however, was the fact that the new contract guaranteed I'd be able to finish my career in San Francisco. I had no desire to play elsewhere. The Bay Area was my home. If I managed to avoid serious injury, I'd play into my forties and retire sometime after 2002.

July 22, 1997. It was the start of another training camp. I looked forward to being back with Brent and the guys. The 49ers had a glorified golf cart that was in the shape of a giant football helmet. We called it "the helmet cart." Different personnel like the head of PR or the team trainer used it to get around camp. One night I noticed that someone had left the key in the ignition. Most of the guys had retired to bed. I turned to Brent Jones and Harris Barton: "We're taking the helmet cart and we're going to Dairy Queen."

"Are you joking?" Brent said.

"I'm serious," I said.

I hopped in the driver's seat while Brent climbed in the passenger's seat. The back of the cart had a flat bed that was used to cart injured players off the field. Harris sat there.

Once we got out to the main road, I got the cart up to 15 miles per hour. Still, cars were zipping past us. People started pointing out of their car windows at us. "Hey, that's Steve Young driving a helmet!" one guy shouted. We were a scene.

Eventually we ended up in a long line of cars at a Dairy Queen drive-up window. After shouting our order into the microphone, I couldn't get the cart to make the sharp turn toward the pick-up window. The three of us had to pick up the cart and maneuver it around the corner. Everyone in the parking lot recognized us. Kids started coming up. We invited a few to hop on. Before long, we were driving down the street with blizzards in our hands and fans hanging off the sides of the cart.

39

LET'S GO

AUGUST 31, 1997. It's Steve "Mooch" Mariucci's first game as an NFL head coach, and it's our season opener. We're in Tampa. The Buccaneers are projected to win the NFC Central Division behind a very aggressive defense led by Warren Sapp.

On the fifth play of the game I am flushed from the pocket. I scramble left, and Warren Sapp gives chase. Before I can turn the corner he drags me down from behind. Linebacker Hardy Nickerson is trailing the play, and he knees me in the head as he runs past. My helmet flies off, and my neck snaps back.

Nobody likes getting kneed in the back of the head. While I'm down, Sapp is celebrating and the fans are screaming. I roll over onto all fours. I should probably stay down, but I stagger to my feet, my right hand pressed against my forehead. A teammate hands me my helmet. I slip it on and make my way to the sideline.

While the punt team takes the field, Dr. Klint sits me down on the bench.

"Steve, how do you feel?" he says.

"Reggie, I got kicked in the head. How do you think I feel?"

To test my short-term memory he asks me about the play. I have total recall. I even recount the four plays prior to the injury. The trainer and Dr. Dillingham huddle around us. More than anything I'm angry.

"I'm all right!" I shout.

But they don't want me to play.

"I can play!"

They are convinced I have another concussion. Four minutes into the '97 season and the medical team insists I can't continue.

I have never been callous or flippant about any injury, especially ones to my head. So when I say I'm okay, I mean it. Nonetheless, the medical staff is adamant that I have a concussion.

On our next series Mariucci turns to backup quarterback Jeff Brohm. He has never started a pro game. I watch him take the field.

I go up to Mariucci. "Put me back in."

"No," he says.

"I'm fine. Put me back in."

He ignores me.

"I'm thirty-six years old, and I have been playing for a long time," I said. "I know my body. I got kneed in the head. I'm okay. I can play."

In the second quarter Brohm hands off to Jerry Rice on a reverse. Sapp is there again. This time he grabs Rice by the face mask. Jerry's toe catches in the turf, causing his leg to twist awkwardly. Sapp hauls him down, and Jerry doesn't get up. He's holding his knee. Doctors help him off the field.

After the referee assesses a 15-yard penalty against Sapp for grabbing Jerry's face mask, we have a first down inside the Buccaneers' 10-yard line. But we fail to score.

I'm furious. Five minutes remain in the first half. We are up 6–0. "C'mon," I yell at Mariucci. "Put me back in."

"No," he says.

"I'm fine."

"Go get a drink of water."

"I don't need a drink. I want in!"

At halftime I undergo a medical exam in the locker room. My blood pressure is normal. My pulse is regular. My memory is fine. The doctors tell Mariucci that I can return to the game "should it be necessary."

But Mariucci doesn't feel it's necessary. So I spend the entire third quarter lobbying him on the sideline. Tampa kicks a field goal to cut the lead to 6–3. Then, with eleven seconds remaining in the third quarter, Brohm injures his back. Our third-string quarterback isn't cleared to play. Now Mariucci has no choice.

I hustle onto the field and finish the game. But Tampa's defense is for real, and we lose, 13–6. On the sideline I stand next to Jerry Rice. He's in street clothes, hunched over crutches. We look at each other and say nothing as Tampa Bay celebrates.

We are 0–1.

The next morning I had a stiff neck when I showed up at our training facility in Santa Clara.

Jerry was already there, undergoing an MRI that revealed he had a torn lateral meniscus and a torn ACL. He had surgery hours later. The doctors said he would miss the entire season. Jerry hadn't missed a game in twelve seasons. He was the most durable player in the NFL. I had trouble imagining what it would be like without him.

My situation was much more complicated. The 49ers had reported that I had sustained a concussion and therefore would miss the next game. Yet I had played in the fourth quarter against Tampa. I felt fine, but I also sensed Mariucci's genuine concern for my health. The bottom line was that I wanted to play.

I knew that one day I'd start a family and be a father. I also knew I'd be an older dad, and I was quite serious about being there for my kids. So I always thought seriously about my long-term health, and I wasn't going to put my future as a husband and father at risk by playing when I shouldn't be. The truth was that guys were playing who couldn't remember where they had put their car keys. They couldn't taste hot or cold. They had memory losses. I never experienced anything like those things.

Nonetheless, earlier that year, the Academy of Neurology had come out with a report saying that repetitive concussions can cause brain damage. The Academy advocated that players be removed from the game if they lose consciousness or exhibit concussion symptoms. I had always had a tendency to downplay injuries and play through pain. All football players do. But I was realizing that I had to start listening to what my body — and my head — were telling me.

Dr. Klint arranged for me to see Dr. Joseph Lacy, a neurologist at the Palo Alto Medical Clinic. By the time I reached his office more than forty-eight hours had passed since I had been kneed in the head. We reviewed my history, and he reminded me that I had sustained three concussions within the past ten months. Although I appeared to be fine, he advised me not to play on Sunday. He also shared that advice with Dr. Klint, who informed Carmen Policy and Steve Mariucci.

A few days later I watched in St. Louis as our third-string quarterback, Jim Druckenmiller, got us by the Rams 15–12. On the flight back to San Francisco I sat with Dr. Klint. He and Dr. Lacy wanted me to get a second opinion before I returned to action.

The next morning I saw Dr. Gary Steinberg, Chief of Neurosurgery at Stanford. He gave me a complete neurological exam that revealed no problems, and he cleared me to play. But he spent a long time talking to me about my risks for future concussions. He made a point of saying that there was no evidence of irreversible injury at the moment, but he also said that the thing I had to be mindful of was that the repetitive nature of concussions could ultimately have significant consequences.

After a couple of days I felt fine. But quarterbacks get all the attention in this league, both good and bad. So I was in the spotlight, in the middle of a cultural change in viewing how the NFL handled concussions. Whether I liked it or not, I was a main figure in the emerging narrative. A lot of other players were dealing with much more significant issues stemming from concussions. But none of them were in the spotlight.

In week three we faced New Orleans. It was our first home game. As usual, the night before I stayed up late talking with Brent Jones in our hotel room. We were both in a sour mood. Everyone was writing us off. Even the San Francisco writers predicted we'd be lucky to finish the season 8-8.

We took our anger out on the Saints' defense. I threw two touchdown passes to Brent in the first half, and I finished the day with just three incompletions. We demolished New Orleans, 33–7. The next week we put up 34 points on Atlanta, followed by 34 points on Carolina, 30 against the Rams, and 35 against Atlanta in our second meeting. By midseason we had the best record in the league at 7-1 and our offense was ranked number one. And we had accomplished all of this without Jerry Rice. For much of this stretch we were also without Brent Jones, who had broken his leg. In their absence, Terrell Owens had now emerged as my favorite target.

After the concussion in week one, I had essentially been injury-free. As a result, I was having one of the best seasons of my career. I attributed a lot of my success to Mariucci and offensive coordinator Marty Mornhinweg, who joked that I'd win another MVP award because he was such a great coach. It actually felt like we were on our way.

November 2, 1997. We are playing Dallas at Candlestick. We have won seven straight. Dallas is 4-4. Before the game Mariucci addresses the team in the locker room. I am in the stall with the dry heaves.

"Will you keep it down in there?" Mariucci yells. "I'm trying to talk to the team!"

When I emerge from the bathroom, Mooch has a big grin on his face.

The first half doesn't go well. Early in the third quarter Dallas is up 7–0 when I throw a short pass in the flat. Deion Sanders reads the play and picks off the pass. The last thing I want is to see Deion do his touchdown dance after picking off one of my passes. I race toward him, lower my shoulder, and upend him as he tries to leap over me. My shoulder clips his knees, and he flips over before hitting the ground. No touchdown.

He jumps up and celebrates anyway.

But we outscore Dallas 17–3 in the second half to improve to 8-1. Dallas falls to 4-5.

Brent Jones played sparingly in the Dallas game. It was his first game back since injuring his leg a month earlier. After the game we limped into the training room together and underwent treatment. After everyone else had left, he said to me: "I'm going to retire."

"What? When?" I said.

"At the end of the season."

"Bro, you're just tired," I told him. "You've got three good seasons left in you. C'mon."

I gave him a big hug. I didn't want to hear him talk about retirement.

We kept rolling after Dallas, knocking off Philadelphia, Carolina, and San Diego to get to 11-1. Nobody could touch us. But a week later we lost our owner Eddie DeBartolo. He abruptly resigned and turned control of the team over to his sister after the U.S. Attorney's Office in New Orleans notified him and Louisiana governor Edwin Edwards that they were about to be indicted by a federal grand jury in Baton Rouge in connection with a gambling scandal. Eventually, Eddie pleaded guilty to failing to report an alleged extortion attempt by Edwards in connection with Eddie's application for a riverboat gambling license. A judge ordered him to pay a $2 million fine, and the NFL commissioner suspended him.

I was stunned. I loved playing for Eddie. And I remained forever grateful to him for placing the franchise in my hands in 1993. Now more than ever I wanted to deliver another Super Bowl title.

December 7, 1997. We are playing Minnesota at Candlestick. The previous week I took a helmet to the ribs, and before the game I get an injection in the nerves around my right ribs. In the first half against the Vikings, I take yet another blow to the ribs. At halftime I get a second injection in the same area. None of this slows me down. I finish the game, and we beat Minnesota 28–17, improving to 12-2.

After the game, Brent brings up retirement again. "I'm done," he says. I can tell from his voice that his mind is made up.

"My body is just too broken," he continues. "Been barreling into linebackers for twelve seasons."

Sweaty, dirty, sore, and barefoot, we wrap our arms around each other.

"We have to win it all this year," I tell him.

"We have to," he says.

Then Brent faces the media and announces publicly that this is his last season.

Afterward, I talk to Jerry. He feels the same sense of urgency about winning it all that Brent and I feel. Nobody expects Jerry to return in '97. But I know better. His knee surgery was supposed to sideline him until the spring of '98. But he has cut his cast off with a saw and begun intense training way ahead of schedule.

December 15, 1997. We are playing Denver on *Monday Night Football*. It's a home game, and Joe Montana is having his number retired at halftime. And Jerry Rice is cleared to play. People can't believe it when they see him warming up.

We have the best record in football at 12-2. Denver is tied with Kansas City for the best record in the AFC at 11-3. I am the highest-rated passer in the NFC. Denver's John Elway is the top quarterback in the AFC. I live for games like this.

Mariucci grabs me in the locker room. "C'mon, Steve Young. Just have some fun."

I grin. The truth is that I'm having more fun than ever. My anxiety has been beaten into the background. In the first half I complete three passes to Jerry. The third one is a touchdown. In the end zone Broncos defensive back Steve Atwater drills him. Jerry gets up slowly and leaves the field. He doesn't return. At halftime Dr. Dillingham tells him he's done for the night.

In the locker room, Mariucci huddles the team for a halftime pep talk. But I grab Brent, and we sneak out to see the tribute to Joe. He had retired after the '94 season. Tonight the Niners are retiring his number. A stage is erected at midfield. Bill Walsh and Joe Montana flank Eddie DeBartolo, who's at the microphone. As I take in the whole scene, I can't help flashing back over the past decade in San Francisco.

In one sense, it feels like it has flown by. In another, it feels like it's been so long. Competing with Joe brought out the best in me as a football player. It also featured jealousy, comparisons, and insecurities. All of those had to be beaten into the ground for me to become what I am today. Finding out how good I could become was not about someone else. It was about me.

We take the field again, and the second half is ugly. Broncos linebacker Bill Romanowski spits in the face of J. J. Stokes. Then he drills me with a late hit after I'm down. I don't like fools on the field. I've always admired fierce competitors who are mature enough to know the limits of that fierceness. For example, two of the fiercest I ever faced were Bruce Smith and Reggie White. They never missed an opportunity to take me down — but also never missed an opportunity to pick me back up.

We pound Denver, 34–17, to improve to 13-2 and clinch home-field advantage throughout the playoffs.

The next day Jerry undergoes an MRI that reveals his kneecap is broken. It happened when he hit the ground after being hit in the end zone. He is gone for the playoffs. And our starting running back Garrison Hearst is out too.

January 3, 1998. It's the divisional round of the playoffs, and I'm fired up to get going against the Vikings. All the guys are. Our offense clicks from the get-go. Before Minnesota has a chance to catch its breath, we're up 24–7.

But we lose Brent Jones in a violent collision at midfield. After catching a pass over the middle, he is hammered by safety Robert Griffith, who plants his helmet under Brent's chin. Brent bites his tongue and also splits his chin open. He has to get stitches in and around his mouth.

Without Jerry and Brent on the field, I complete nine passes to J. J. Stokes for over 100 yards. And I complete a 15-yard touchdown pass to Terrell Owens in the second half to put the game away. We win decisively, 38–22.

But it's no time to celebrate. We are headed back to the NFC Championship, and the Packers are coming to Candlestick. They are the defending Super Bowl champs, and we are the number-one seed in the NFC. This will be the third consecutive year that we've faced off in the playoffs.

January 11, 1998. It's raining in San Francisco, and the field is a mud hole even before the opening kickoff. Poor field conditions and bad weather promise to make this a low-scoring game. Although we have the number-one offense in the league, the game will be decided by who dominates the line of scrimmage. The question is whether we have an answer for Green Bay's front four, especially Reggie White and Gilbert Brown.

On the opening drive, Favre marches his team 76 yards before stalling at the 1-yard line. A field goal puts them up 3–0. They add another touchdown to go up by 10.

The rain picks up in the second quarter. Facing third-and-26, I hit Owens on a 48-yard bomb. We chew up the clock. But we end up settling for a field goal, making the score 10–3 with fifty-eight seconds left in the quarter. I'm happy that we're on the board, but I'm aggravated over the fact that I've thrown for almost 200 yards and all we have to show for it is three lousy points.

After the kickoff, Favre throws a bomb to Antonio Freeman. Moments later Green Bay kicks a field goal as time expires to go up 13–3.

I go into the locker room steamed. We're a better team. Our offense has run over everyone all season long. We are actually going up and down the field on Green Bay too. But we are killing ourselves with penalties. We've been flagged for 59 yards in penalties in the first half, including consecutive holding penalties that negated long completions. "C'mon, boys!" I shout in the locker room. "These mental errors are killing us!"

The second half is dominated by defense. Neither team puts any points on the board until Green Bay kicks another field goal with five minutes remaining in the game to go up 16–3. On our next possession we face fourth-and-long from our own 11-yard line. The Packers send everyone, and I get sacked. Green Bay takes over, and moments later Dorsey Levens scores from 5 yards out to put the Packers up 23–3.

We run back the ensuing kickoff 95 yards to cut the lead to 23–10. That ends up being the final score. For the third straight year Green Bay knocks us out of the playoffs.

It was a humbling and infuriating situation. All season long our offense had its way with every other defense we faced. But against Green Bay we had mustered just three points. It was the first time since my arrival in San Francisco that we had been held to a field goal. That was a testament to the fact that we had no answer for Reggie White and Gilbert Brown.

By far the most painful games of my life were the NFC Championship losses to Dallas and Green Bay. Nothing else came close.

In the locker room I put my arms around Brent Jones. My best friend on the team was hanging up his cleats. As only a brother could, he had walked with me through ten years of battles, on and off the field. I can never repay him.

40

STAYING YOUNG

IN THE OFF-SEASON it was hard to ignore the calendar. At thirty-six, I still felt young. In actual football years, I was more like thirty-two as a result of my limited playing time during my first four years in San Francisco. Still, I was now one of the oldest players in the league, and I sensed the urgency to return to the Super Bowl. After all, I had accomplished and experienced everything else the game had to offer — MVP awards, passing titles, big plays, and making money. The only thing I wanted was another Super Bowl ring. That's what drove me to keep pushing.

I spent the off-season working out, pushing myself harder than ever. I practically lived at the gym. Just before training camp opened, team president Carmen Policy resigned on July 22, 1998. That was a big blow, both to the team and to me personally. Carmen had crafted the deal that brought me to San Francisco in '87. But his relationship with the organization had soured. Although Eddie was no longer around, his family still controlled the franchise. And things were going to be different without Carmen around. Tim McDonald and I became the unofficial GMs. We even started eating lunch in Carmen's empty office to talk about what we could do to make the team better.

September 6, 1998. It's the season opener, and we're playing the Jets at Candlestick. They have a new coach — our old foe Bill Parcells. It's a wild game with eight lead changes. I throw for 363 yards, including two touchdown passes to J. J. Stokes and one to Jerry Rice. Keyshawn Johnson catches two touchdown passes for New York. The game is tied 30–30 at the end of regulation.

I'm in complete command of the game. As a quarterback, I've reached a level of ability as a passer and a leader that only comes with years of experience. Yet I still have the athleticism to scramble and run when necessary. The fact is that the game is fun for me.

We win the coin toss, and the Jets kick off. Our kicking team makes a big mistake, which puts us on our own 4-yard line. Mariucci calls "90 O," a conservative run play. I hand off to Garrison Hearst at the 4-yard line, and he runs 96 yards for a touchdown. I can't believe it. Nobody can. Candlestick erupts. I run the length of the field. I love this game. We win 36–30.

A week later we rack up 504 yards on offense and I throw three touchdown passes and run for another in a 45–10 blowout of the Redskins on *Monday Night Football*. Then we take on Atlanta at home. The Falcons are poised to challenge us for the division title. We jump out to a 31–7 halftime lead. I end up completing 28 of 39 passes for nearly 400 yards and three touchdowns. I also run the ball seven times for 50 yards. It's no contest. We win 31–20 and improve to 3-0.

I feel like there isn't anything I can't do as a quarterback.

October 18, 1998. We are hosting Indianapolis at The Stick. We are 4-1. They are 1-5. But the Colts' rookie quarterback, Peyton Manning, is generating a lot of attention. He was the number-one overall pick in the '98 draft. He comes out firing against us, the Colts go up 21–0, and we are barely in the second quarter. I am sacked four times in our first three possessions.

There is no way I am losing to a rookie. But, man, this kid seems good.

In the second quarter I throw consecutive TD passes to J. J. Stokes and Terrell Owens, cutting the deficit to 21–14 at the half. But I am winded, and I wonder why. I almost never get winded in the first half of a game. Then, during halftime, it comes to my attention that I have taken over fifty snaps in the first half. No wonder I'm tired. That's the most snaps I've ever taken in a half.

I don't know if this is related, but I also get really nauseous during half-time. It's not nerves. I'm sick to my stomach, and it comes on fast. I barely make it to the stall in time to throw up. I vomit so many times that I get to the point where I'm dry-heaving. Something is wrong with me.

Tim McDonald ducks in. "You okay?"

I am on my knees, my head over the toilet, in full pads. "Yeah. I'm okay."

I feel terrible. I just want to curl up on a bed. But I wave off the team doctor when I finally emerge from the bathroom. I drink a bunch of fluids and stagger out for the second half.

Manning picks up where he left off, opening the third quarter with a 61-yard touchdown bomb. The Colts add a field goal, and we enter the fourth quarter down 31–17.

I keep consuming fluids. Then I lead us on a long drive. I cap it off with a quarterback keeper for a touchdown. After we miss the extra point, the Colts up by 8, we get it back and start another long drive. On third-and-long I am about to get sacked. I escape. I stumble over one of my own linemen, but I keep my balance. Just before getting hit, I dump the ball to a back. He gets a first down, keeping the drive alive. But I pull something on the play. Suddenly my thigh is killing me.

A few plays later I drop back to pass from the Colts' 30-yard line. Everyone is covered. But the middle of the field is wide open. I take off. I get by a few linemen without much effort. I'm a physically ill thirty-seven-year-old quarterback with a pulled leg muscle being chased by linebackers and defensive backs in their early twenties. It's a great feeling. As I approach the Colts' 15-yard line, I have a full head of steam. But four tacklers are converging on me. There is nowhere to run. I head fake right, juke left, and cut back to the right, losing two guys and creating a lane to the outside. I have one guy to beat, a safety. He hits me up high at the 5-yard line. I bounce off him and get into the end zone. I spike the ball between my legs.

I am truly sick to my stomach, but I feel rejuvenated. I am only the second quarterback in NFL history to run for 40 touchdowns. Jack Kemp is the other.

I dash to the sideline. We have a decision to make. We're down 31–29 with 5:52 to play. The way Manning has been playing we may not get the ball back again. I want to go for two. Mooch agrees. We design a pass play. I throw to Rice. He gets it. Tie game.

Now it's Manning's turn. But our defense holds. We get the ball back with three minutes to play. I drive us into field goal range. The kick is good. We win 34–31. I end up completing 33 of 51 passes for 331 yards. It's my sixth consecutive game with over 300 yards passing, a new NFL record.

After the game Mariucci grabs me in the locker room. "Is this fun or what?" he exclaims.

I smile.

41

SHE IS OUT THERE

Heading into the eleventh week of the season we were 7-3 and I felt really good about the way we were playing as a team. Our offense, in particular, was really rolling. The season was also yielding some nice personal achievements. A week earlier Jerry Rice and I had connected on a touchdown pass that established us as the top-scoring duo in NFL history. In the same game I scored my forty-first rushing touchdown as a quarterback, breaking the all-time record previously held by Jack Kemp. Steve Mariucci's motto was "Just have fun." Well, I had never had so much fun as a quarterback.

When I wasn't on the field, my mind kept drifting back to a spiritual experience I'd had earlier in the year. During the off-season I had gone to Utah to meet with Apostle Richard G. Scott. I confided in him my concern that I had missed my opportunity to meet my wife. He told me not to worry, and he assured me that I was right where I was supposed to be. Then he placed his hands on my head and offered me a blessing, promising me that God was mindful of my situation.

Not long after the Falcons game, I called my close friend Tyde Tanner and told him about the blessing I had received from Elder Scott. It wasn't the sort of thing I shared lightly. But I trusted Tyde. We were quite close, and we often talked about spiritual things. So after telling him about my meeting with an apostle, I said that I had gotten a strong impression.

"This is going to sound a little strange," I told Tyde. "But you're supposed to help me find my wife."

Tyde and I joked around about a lot of things. But he knew instantly that I wasn't joking about this. I was looking for some guidance from him — some inspiration — that would help me find my soul mate.

He asked if he could have the night to pray about it.

The next morning he called me back and said he'd been up most of the night, and he'd spent a lot of that time on his knees before finally nodding off. When he awoke, he said, he had an unmistakable impression that he knew who I was supposed to marry.

"What? Who?"

"Her name is Barbara Graham," he told me. "She's a model from Scottsdale. She goes by Barb."

I'd never heard of her, and I had no interest in dating a model. So this conversation was going nowhere as far as I was concerned.

"Just hold on, Steve. There's something I need to tell you."

He proceeded to explain that ten years earlier — back in 1989 — he had attempted to set me up with Barb. At the time Barb was nineteen and working for the same modeling agency as Tyde's fiancée, who was also a model. They knew each other, although not well. Then one Sunday Barb showed up with some friends at the Mormon church Tyde and his fiancée attended. Barb wasn't Mormon, but she had friends who were. Tyde claimed that the moment Barb entered the chapel he turned to his fiancée and said, "That's Steve Young's future wife."

His pronouncement seemed so random. His fiancée told him he was crazy.

Nonetheless, he tried to convince Barb to go on a blind date with me. She told him forget it. She had zero interest in dating a professional athlete because of all of the horrible things she had heard about them, especially with respect to the way they mistreated women. Tyde insisted that I was different, but she wasn't interested. So he dropped the subject and never told me about it.

The story was intriguing, but I couldn't see why in the world Tyde had tried to set me up with someone he barely knew and who wasn't a Mormon. He, of all people, knew how important it was to me to marry within our faith.

Anyway, that had been ten years ago. I didn't see what any of this had to do with my current situation.

Tyde said he knew she was the one back then. And he knew it now. So he wanted me to trust him.

"I'm on my way to find her now," he told me. "I need to find out if she's still single."

"What? Where are you going?"

"Just trust me," he said.

Later that night Tyde called back and told me he had just gotten back from the Phoenician, a luxury resort in Scottsdale that was hosting a fashion show. Tyde had gone in hopes that Barb might be there.

"You'll never believe this," he told me, "but I arrived a little late, and when I walked in Barb was walking down the runway. And she was wearing a floor-length, white beaded gown. It's a sign. I'm telling you."

I couldn't believe what I was hearing.

"Steve, she's still single!" he said.

"How do you know that?"

He recounted a rather awkward conversation in which he straight up asked if she was still single. "There's only one problem," he said. "She still doesn't want to go out with you."

I'd heard enough. This was embarrassing. I told him to just forget about it. I didn't want to discuss the situation any further.

December 27, 1998. The day of the final game of the regular season. We were at home to face the Rams. A lot was riding on the outcome. At 11-4, we had already clinched a wild-card berth. We also knew that our opponent would be the Packers. But there was still the question of whether the wild-card game would be in San Francisco or Green Bay. We would control our own destiny. If we beat the Rams, Green Bay would have to come to Candlestick the following week.

Around midday Tyde Tanner called. A month had passed since I'd told him to stop pursuing Barb Graham. Suddenly, he informed me that he had big news: Barb had agreed to go out with me. I couldn't believe what I was hearing. I guess the date that was ten years in the making was finally going to happen.

What he failed to explain, however, was that the only reason Barb had agreed to go on a blind date with me was to appease Tyde. He'd been harassing her every day for a solid month. Her roommates had convinced her that if she'd just go out with me once, Tyde would leave her alone. In the meantime, Tyde had been talking to Barb about Mormonism, and she had indicated a genuine interest in learning more about it.

Tyde insisted that I had to get to Phoenix as soon as the season ended.

I told him that I couldn't talk about any of that right now. I had to focus on the Rams.

We rolled to a 38–19 victory over the Rams. It was an emphatic ending to one of the most prolific seasons in NFL history, in which we became the first team to lead the league in rushing and passing. Garrison Hearst had rushed for 1,570 yards, and I had set a team record by passing for 4,170 yards. I had also run for 454 yards and six touchdowns. Overall, we led the league in total offense with 6,800 yards.

The fact was that at thirty-seven I had turned in the most productive season of my career, throwing 36 touchdown passes, attempting a record 517 passes, and passing for 300-plus yards in a record six straight games. I was playing the best football of my life, and I wasn't feeling any of the effects of age. On the contrary, I was healthy, and my experience was really paying off. It felt like my anxiety was fading in the rearview mirror.

After such a stellar season, I couldn't live with losing another playoff game to Green Bay. It just couldn't happen.

42

THE CATCH II

IN EIGHT STARTS against Green Bay — four times as quarterback of the Buccaneers and four times as a 49er — I was flat-out winless. The three playoff losses were the most frustrating:

In '95, I threw 65 passes and we lost.

In '96, I had broken ribs and had to leave after taking just nine snaps. We lost again.

In '97, we made way too many mistakes. Another loss.

I was beyond fed up with losing to Favre and the Packers. Mariucci felt the same way. It had become personal for us.

One chief concern was pass protection. Reggie White led the league in sacks and was hands-down the best defensive player in the league. I had been sacked forty-eight times during the regular season, which was the most in any season in my career. This didn't bode well for us. We had to figure out a way to slow down Reggie.

Reggie and I had been friends since we both went to the USFL in '84. He would hit you hard, but he was a true spiritual athlete. He was fierce and would throw people out of the way to get to me. But when he wrapped me up on a sack, he would always slightly turn so he didn't drive me into the ground. Then he'd immediately reach down and offer a hand up and say: "Steve, it's been too long. How you doing?"

"It hasn't been long enough, Reggie," I'd joke. "I don't want to see you again until after the game."

Our defensive line was so banged up that we were afraid we'd be unable to put any pressure on Favre. Two key starters, including All-Pro Bryant Young, were out. And All-Pro Chris Doleman was questionable. If we didn't get pressure on Favre, he'd pick us apart.

A few days before the game Mariucci called me into his office, along with eleven other veterans, including Jerry Rice, Tim McDonald, Harris Barton, Garrison Hearst, Kevin Gogan, Merton Hanks, and Chris Doleman. Mooch called us his "Dirty Dozen."

We filed in, and Mooch closed the door.

"All right, here's the deal, guys," he said quietly. "We have a chance to sign a defensive lineman who is out there."

Nobody said anything.

"It's Charles Haley," he continued.

Nobody said a word. Everyone in the room knew that Haley had a history with the Niners. He also had a history with me. He'd been out of football for a couple of years, but Mariucci thought he could help us get past Green Bay.

"But I want to hear your opinion," Mariucci said. "Then we're gonna vote."

Everyone looked at me.

"Steve, if you think this will cause a distraction, or if you don't want him on our team, then I will completely understand."

"Coach, if he's gonna help us win, I'm all for it," I immediately said.

"Let's vote," Mariucci said. "How many are in favor of bringing Haley back?"

I raised my hand. Everyone followed. The vote was 12–0.

Two days before the game Haley showed up at our practice facility. He was out of shape, but we only needed him to play on third-and-long situations.

January 3, 1999. Green Bay opens the scoring with a field goal to go up 3–0. But on the Packers' next possession, Haley pressures Favre, causing him to throw an interception. We capitalize. Moments later I throw a touchdown to Greg Clark to put us up 7–3.

But Green Bay responds with two touchdowns. We counter with a field goal. We're down 17–10 at the half.

We dominate the third quarter. I throw my second touchdown pass to

Greg Clark, and we retake the lead, 20–17. Green Bay opens the fourth quarter with a field goal, tying the game at 20. We respond with a long drive consisting mostly of running plays. With ten minutes to play, we kick a field goal to go up 23–20. Then I watch impatiently as Favre engineers a nine-play, 76-yard drive. With 1:56 left, he throws a 15-yard touchdown to Antonio Freeman to put Green Bay back on top 27–23.

Favre did his part. Now it's my turn. Mariucci turns to me on the sideline. "We're going to stick with what we do best," he says. That means we're sticking with our base offense — two running backs, one tight end, and two receivers. "Let's start with 'Fox 3 Protection,'" he says.

I go to the huddle. The play calls for maximum protection. We are sending just two receivers downfield — J. J. Stokes and Jerry Rice. I hit Stokes for a 17-yard gain.

On the next play I hit Stokes again for a 9-yard gain. It's second-and-one from the 50-yard line. One minute and six seconds remain.

I drop back. Rice and Stokes are covered, and Reggie White is coming hard. I scramble and dump the ball off to fullback Marc Edwards well behind the line of scrimmage. Hit immediately, he breaks free, then sheds two more tackles, fighting his way for a 3-yard gain. First down. I call time-out and head to the sideline.

"Two time-outs left," Mariucci says. "Fifty-two seconds. We need a score."

The Packers are in a prevent defense. They are dropping eight guys into pass coverage and only rushing three guys.

"Let's go with 'zebra,'" he says.

"Zebra" takes us out of our base offense and switches to one running back and three receivers. Terrell Owens joins Stokes and Rice.

On the snap I see that no one is open, and I quickly throw the ball away, stopping the clock.

On the next play I hit Jerry on a slant pattern, and he fumbles as he goes down. The moment I see the ball on the ground my heart sinks. Green Bay recovers. I can't believe this is happening. But the officials rule that Jerry was down. The Packers are livid. We still have life.

It's third-and-four from Green Bay's 41-yard line. We use our second time-out.

"They are going to blitz," I tell Mooch on the sideline.

"Let's get a quick throw to the backside," he says. "'Two hundred-jet-dragon.' We gotta get out of bounds."

It works. I complete a 9-yard pass to Terry Kirby out of the backfield. He gets out of bounds, stopping the clock with twenty-one seconds left. First down.

Next, I complete a 7-yard pass to Garrison Hearst. He gets to Green Bay's 25-yard line, but his hamstring cramps up to the point where he can't walk. I call our final time-out. Only fourteen seconds remain.

Over 66,000 people in the stadium are on the edge of their seats. Millions more are watching from home. It's simple. Either we score or Green Bay beats us for the fourth straight year. Mariucci is talking faster than machine-gun fire. I live for moments like this. Our backs are against the wall, and everyone is looking to me to win it.

"We need to throw it to the end zone, or we have to throw it out of bounds," Mariucci shouts.

"You want to run 'three-jet-all-go'?" I ask.

"Yes. Let's run it twice."

I like the call. "Three-jet-all-go" is four receivers running vertical routes. Running it twice means that if it doesn't work the first time we line up and run the same exact play again. Green Bay won't expect that.

My first attempt is nearly intercepted when I try to loft it to J. J. Stokes at the goal line. The clock stops with eight second left. We're down to our last play.

Approaching the line of scrimmage, I survey the field. We're on the 25-yard line. Green Bay has eight guys in coverage. They expect me to go to Jerry. I want to create a hole in the middle of the field for Terrell. He has been dropping balls all day. But I have confidence in him. He's lined up in the slot to my right, and he's running a skinny post, meaning he's basically going straight downfield and making a little bend toward the goalpost. Packers safety Darren Sharper is the guy I'm worried about. He's standing right where Owens is headed. I want to move him out of there. I plan to do that with my eyes by looking at Jerry, who is lined up to my left and will be running straight down the sideline toward the corner of the end zone.

I take the snap and look in Jerry's direction as I backpedal, but my center, Chris Dalman, steps on my foot. I trip and almost go down. Meanwhile, Sharper moves toward Jerry. Reggie White is coming hard from my right. Owens makes his cut. Five Packers surround him. But there's a razor-thin opening.

I step up and let it fly. If my calculation is right, the ball should meet Terrell in a fast-closing space among five defenders.

Owens leaps, and the ball lands in the crook of his arm. This time he holds as he gets sandwiched by Packers.

Candlestick erupts. It's the loudest collective roar I've heard in my career. It's not just the miraculous play. It's also that time has expired. And the Packers are beaten! The atmosphere is sheer delirium. Chin strap dangling, I pump my fist in the air. As a boy on the playgrounds of Greenwich, I dreamed of making plays like this. Today my playground is Candlestick Park and 66,000 fans are screaming with unbridled approval. This feels as good as anything I've ever experienced as a pro.

When I reach the end zone, my teammates are mobbing Owens. He's crying. It's total pandemonium. Mariucci stops me as I reach the sideline. He can't believe the ball got through five defenders and ended up in Owens's hands.

"He was open!" I shout. "He was open!"

Mooch smacks my helmet with joy.

T.O. throws his arms around Mooch and sobs on his shoulder. The fans won't let up. I'm covered in goose bumps. There are plenty of last-second shots in basketball and walk-off home runs in baseball. But football games almost never end with the game-winning score coming as time runs out. To end a playoff game that way is the ultimate thrill.

T.O. turns to me.

"Thank you for staying with me," he says through tears.

"Nice job," I tell him. "Good job."

After the extra point is kicked, we win, 30–27. At midfield I meet Mike Holmgren, my old coach.

"Nice play," he says. "Real good play."

I smile broadly and shake Mike's hand.

Then I find Favre, the ultimate competitor.

"Good luck to you," he says. "Helluva job!"

"You too."

"You did a helluva job," he continues. "They'll be talking about this for a long time."

The atmosphere in the locker room is reminiscent of when we won the Super Bowl against San Diego.

"Everybody come down here!" Mooch yells. His voice is so hoarse nobody hears him.

"Get 'em down here," he orders one of the players.

I'm in the training room.

"Where the hell is Steve?" Mooch yells.

Guys keep shouting.

"Be quiet, dammit!" Mooch says.

I enter the room and casually walk past Mooch.

"Hey," he says nonchalantly, "nice throw."

Everybody roars with laughter.

I stand next to Mooch, and guys finally quiet down and form a big circle in the center of the locker room.

"T.O.," Mooch says.

Owens steps forward. "I want to apologize for the way I played in the second half," he says. "But the group of guys who were with me stayed with me on the sideline . . . They told me I was going to have to make a big play. Steve gave me a chance. I appreciate every teammate I got in here."

Everyone claps.

"Guys," Mooch says, "if we stick together, through thick and thin, nobody can beat us!"

More applause.

"Steve and T.O.," Mooch continues, "you have both the throw . . . and the catch. Awesome play! That's going to go down as one of the big ones. But protection was awesome. Everybody did it."

Guys are yelling and clapping.

"Everybody did their job against a great football team," Mooch says. "They were healthy as hell, and that's a helluva football team you just beat. Congratulations to every man in this room!"

More whooping and hollering.

"Now listen," he continues. "We play on Saturday at Atlanta. We owe 'em one."

Everybody celebrates. The shouts echo off the walls.

I seldom say anything in the locker room. But on this occasion I feel I must.

"Hold up!" I shout. "Hold up."

Everyone stops.

"Hey, I wanna say something to the defense. The defense kept us in that ball game all day long."

Everyone yells.

"Defense kept us in that ball game *ALL . . . DAY . . . LONG!*" I shout. "You guys were shorthanded. We knew it. And you guys were awesome. Tim McDonald. Nort. Roy. Chris. The guys who were hurt and weren't supposed to be able to play. Pete. Every time we needed the ball back, you gave it back to us.

"Special teams, it seemed like every time we were nailing them. We were making great punts. We were giving no yardage away. No yardage away!"

Everyone yells again.

"Now listen," I shout. "This is great. But it makes it greater next week. We got a short week and a *LONG . . . ASS . . . TRIP.* Right? So do all you can to get rested up. Because if we want to make this one count, to make it worth something, we gotta win this game this coming Saturday. All right?"

The team lets out a collective: "*YEAH!*"

We all take a knee and hold hands. "Our Father, who art in heaven . . ."

43

THE ONE

JANUARY 9, 1999. We take the field at the Georgia Dome, and nearly 80,000 fans are already on their feet. Atlanta has never had so much to cheer about. The Falcons have had their best season in franchise history. At 14-2, they have the best record in the NFC. We split our series with them during the regular season. But they were 8-0 at home.

I can't wait to get this thing started. We have the best offense in the league, and we're ready to bring it to the Falcons. Our game plan is to establish the run with Garrison Hearst. On the first play from scrimmage I hand off to him. It's a simple dive play. But Hearst goes to cut and catches his toe in the turf. Nobody touches him. His left leg twists, and his fibula snaps. Everybody stops, and the Dome goes silent as medics rush out and a stretcher is summoned. Garrison is a tremendous competitor and a huge part of our offense. He has rushed for over 1,500 yards on the season. Minutes later he leaves the stadium in an ambulance, and Terry Kirby replaces him in the backfield.

A few minutes later Kirby is helped off the field with a leg injury. He's finished too. Now we're in deep trouble. We end up using fourth-string receiver Chuck Levy as a running back.

With our running game in shambles, we go three-and-out on our first three possessions while the Falcons put up two early touchdowns to go up 14–0. If we don't do something fast, the game is going to get completely away from us. The problem is that Atlanta knows we can't run. So they are doubling down on our receivers and blitzing often.

The crowd, sensing a blowout, ramps up their noise even more. In the huddle I tell the guys we have to respond. We have to dig deep. On a critical third-and-23 situation, the protection holds and I hit Chuck Levy out of the backfield for a 34-yard completion. Then I connect with Jerry Rice for a 17-yard touchdown play. Atlanta's lead is cut in half, 14–7.

In the second quarter our defense settles down. Neither team scores. With 1:10 remaining in the half, Atlanta has possession and I expect them to just run out the clock. But Chris Chandler attempts a pass, and Charles Haley deflects it into the hands of Junior Bryant, who returns it to the Falcons' 36-yard line. On the final play of the half we kick a field goal, cutting Atlanta's lead to 14–10. We're right back in it.

In the locker room I tell our guys we can win this game. We have claimed the momentum. We just have to sustain it.

In the third quarter we string together a long drive that chews up the clock and puts us on Atlanta's 3-yard line. A score here and we take the lead and put Atlanta's back against the wall. But Eugene Robinson intercepts me in the end zone and runs it back 77 yards. I'm so mad I could put my fist through something. Our defense holds, forcing Atlanta to settle for a field goal. But instead of being up 17–14, we are down 17–10.

Atlanta adds another field goal in the fourth quarter to go up 20–10. Time is running out when we get the ball back on our own 13-yard line. We need two scores. I cap off an 87-yard drive by running it in from eight yards out with 2:57 remaining. After a botched snap on the extra point, Ty Detmer, who was my backup and who held the ball for extra point attempts, recovers an errant snap and throws into the end zone for a two-point conversion. It is 20–18.

After we kick off, our defense forces Atlanta to punt, but not before the Falcons eat up nearly all of the remaining time. Only thirty-three seconds remain when we get the ball back on our own 4-yard line. And we have no time-outs left.

I still believe we can get into field goal range and get a shot at winning.

My first pass is a 23-yard completion to Chuck Levy. But it chews up almost all of the remaining time. There's time for only one more play. Everyone in the building knows we have no choice but to throw a 73-yard Hail Mary. Atlanta intercepts it. Our season ends in Atlanta.

· · ·

As soon as we got back to the Bay Area, my attention turned to Barb Graham. Despite my protests, Tyde had continued to talk with her about me and about Mormonism. And the more I learned about her through Tyde the more I started warming up to the idea of meeting her. Finally, Tyde convinced both of us to go on a blind date in Scottsdale on January 21, 1999. I had some business in Los Angeles earlier that week. My plan was to rent a car and drive from LA to Phoenix. But while I was in LA, I started having second thoughts. I called Tyde and told him I had changed my mind. I wasn't coming.

After all the effort he had spent arranging this date, he wasn't pleased. *"Are you kidding me, Steve?"*

"Just tell her we'll do it when she's in Utah next time."

"Steve, she's not going to fly up there to meet you like some girls would."

The call ended without resolution. In short, he refused to call Barb and break the date. And I refused to go.

Instead, I drove to Palm Springs. I owed a visit to my old friend Jack Lambert. Even though Eddie DeBartolo no longer owned the 49ers, Jack still worked for the DeBartolo family. He had moved to Palm Springs, where the DeBartolos owned a hotel. Ever since that first day when Jack befriended me in the buffet line at the 49ers training camp in 1987, I felt comfortable talking to him the way I would talk to my dad.

I met him in Palm Springs, and we spent an afternoon on an outdoor patio, talking about my situation. He was well aware of my long search to find my soul mate. I explained that I had just broken a blind date in Scottsdale. My biggest reason for walking away from it was that Barb Graham wasn't a Mormon. I just didn't see the point in dating someone who I knew I wasn't going to marry.

Jack was Jewish, and he fully understood my desire to marry within my own faith. He also knew that I had dated plenty of Mormon women over the years.

"Maybe what you have been looking for all this time is someone who is outside the box," he told me.

Then he asked me what the downsides were to going on the date in Phoenix.

I couldn't think of any.

So he asked me what the upsides were. I told him that my good friend

Tyde was absolutely convinced that Barb Graham was the woman that I was supposed to marry.

"It sounds to me," Lambert said, "that maybe you need to go to Arizona and find out."

I left Jack's place and drove all night to Phoenix. I never told Tyde I was coming before I arrived at his doorstep at about eight the next morning and rang his doorbell. He was stunned when he opened the door and saw me.

I smiled. "I'm home."

The next day was the big date. Tyde and his wife Linda had made reservations for four at Houston's, a restaurant in Scottsdale. A few hours beforehand, I telephoned Barb in hopes of speaking with her briefly before showing up at her door. But my call went to voice mail: "Hi, this is Barb. Sorry I can't come to the phone right now. Go ahead and leave a message and I'll get back to you as soon as I can. Thanks and have a nice day."

This will sound incredible. But the moment I heard her voice I knew that she was my wife. It's hard to explain how I could feel so sure about a woman I'd never met. But I knew.

A couple of hours later Tyde and I pulled up in front of her townhouse. As we did, my cell phone buzzed. It was my old buddy Lee Johnson calling from Utah. I told him I couldn't talk because I was about to go on my long-anticipated blind date. Typical guy, he wanted to know how good she looked. I didn't have time for LJ's zaniness, but he insisted on knowing.

So I handed my phone to Tyde and told him that when I returned to the car with Barb, he should ask me how the stock performed today. If I said it was a ten, that would be code.

Tyde kept LJ on the line while I approached the doorstep. When Barb emerged, I nearly fell off the step. I'd seen plenty of attractive women in my life, but she was the most naturally beautiful woman I'd ever laid eyes on.

As soon as we got in the backseat, Tyde says: "Hey, LJ wants to know where the stock ended up today."

"Tell him it went all the way to twenty," I said.

Tyde's wife met us at the restaurant. Afterward they went home, leaving me the extra car so I could drive Barb home. We ended up staying out until after two. She was so different from what I had expected. She had a business degree from Arizona State University, where she graduated summa cum laude. She'd spent four years on and off working in Europe as a model to put herself through college. She wasn't just a gorgeous woman. She was independent and had a strong work ethic. She also had serious views about religion, politics, and a wide range of social issues.

There was so much to talk about. But the one thing I really liked was that she knew very little about football. It meant nothing to her that I was a famous player. She was much more interested in what I thought about the world.

I couldn't believe that someone so stunning and so smart was still single at age twenty-nine. Barb informed me that she had made herself a promise not to get married before age thirty, based on her mother's advice. Turns out she was turning thirty in three weeks. The more I learned about her the more my mind raced.

It was 3:00 AM by the time I dropped her off and got back to Tyde's place. He was waiting up for me. The minute I saw him I unloaded: "What have you gotten me into? She's amazing!"

I had originally planned to head back to San Francisco the next day. But Barb had a fashion show that night. I stayed on in Phoenix and went to it. Then I took her out to eat again. Only we never made it inside the restaurant. We were so wrapped up in our conversation that we never made it out of the car. Three and a half hours later the restaurant had closed and we hadn't even noticed. This became typical of our dates.

I liked Barb so much that I didn't go back to San Francisco. I moved into Tyde's place and slept on his floor. He and his wife had five kids, so there was no bed for me. I didn't care. I got to see Barb every day.

But I did have to leave Phoenix briefly to attend the Pro Bowl in Hawaii on February 7, 1999, because I was starting for the NFC. I tried to convince Barb to come with me so she could see me play, but she insisted that we hadn't been together long enough to travel together. That response only made me admire her more.

I'd played in many Pro Bowls, but this one felt different. Times were changing. John Elway started for the AFC, and it was his last game as a pro. It was also Barry Sanders's last game. A lot of the players I'd come up with were now retiring.

I felt my life was changing too. I had never fallen so hard and so fast for anyone. I'd known her only a few weeks, but I already knew Barb was the one. As soon as the game ended I flew back to Arizona.

A couple of weeks later, at Tyde's invitation, Barb started meeting with the Mormon missionaries at Tyde's home. I sat in on these sessions, but I didn't say much. The last thing I wanted was to pressure her to change churches for me. It had to be her decision.

Barb was a Christian, and Mormons are Christians, so she had no trouble accepting Mormonism's basic teachings on Christ. Those were familiar to her. Plus, she had grown up around Mormons in Mesa, and many of her best friends belonged to the faith. Her hesitation about Mormonism had more to do with some of the Church's policies. Barb believed strongly that true religion is rooted in unconditional love, acceptance, and inclusion. As far as I was concerned, her heart was in the right place and her questions were thoughtful.

Over the spring our romance really took off and she continued to explore Mormonism. Each month, on the anniversary of our first date, I gave her a dozen giant sterling silver roses and a box of chocolate turtles. I kept thinking back to the blessing I had received from Apostle Richard G. Scott, when he had told me that God was mindful of me and I was right where I needed to be. At the same time I grew increasingly grateful to Jack Lambert for giving me the extra push I needed to think outside the box. After years of searching for my soul mate, it was all coming together in a most unexpected way.

In a private service attended by our friends and family, I baptized Barb into the Mormon faith in Arizona in April 1999.

A couple of weeks later Visa began airing a TV commercial that played off my famous bachelorhood. The commercial portrays me as lost without the one I long for. The ad shows me sitting alone in a café while two lovers kiss. In the next scene I'm at a bar telling the bartender — played by actor Jack McGee — to pour me another. He rolls his eyes and pours me a glass of milk. Then the ad shows me walking alone on a beach. Finally, I use my Visa card to purchase flowers for someone.

The narrator then says: "There are certain things you can't live without."

Jerry Rice walks into the locker room, where I'm alone. "Okay," he says. "I'm back."

The narrator says: "A good receiver is one of them. Visa's the other."

As we exit the locker room together I say: "Jerry, don't tell the guys about the flowers."

That commercial was one of Visa's most popular. But behind the scenes I was pretty sure that my life as a bachelor was finally coming to an end. In May I took Barb to Israel for nine days. There we spent our time with Truman and Ann Madsen. In sharing powerful spiritual experiences in the Holy Land, Barb and I fell deeper in love.

Training camp would open on July 29, 1999. A couple of days before I reported to camp, Barb and I were in Utah. We hiked to the top of Mount Baldy, and on the way up I picked a bunch of wildflowers. When we reached the summit, we sat on stones near a big fire pit. No one else was around except one guy who was writing in a journal. I kept waiting for him to leave. But he never did.

All right, I thought to myself. *Everything needs a witness. I'm just going to do this.*

I handed her the bouquet of wildflowers. Then I dropped to one knee and looked up at her.

"I want to confess my love to you. I want and need you to be my wife, friend, lover, partner, and soul mate. You are heaven sent to me, and I have brought you here to the highest mountain, which is as high as we can go as mere mortals. Together, I want our marriage to help us reach the heavens, to be greater together than humanly possible. I want the simple arithmetic of one plus one to equal eternity."

I pulled the ring from my pocket.

"Will you be my wife? Will you marry me?"

She threw her arms around me and said yes. I was overjoyed! We were engaged!

We said a prayer, and by the time we looked up we noticed that the guy with the journal was gone. We both smiled.

44

OVER AND OUT

I ARRIVED AT TRAINING CAMP with a bounce in my step. I was heading into my sixteenth season. I was thirty-seven. Jerry Rice was thirty-six. We were two of the oldest guys in the league. But neither of us felt old. We still trained harder than anyone. Yet our increasing age led other teams around the league to view the 49ers as a team in decline.

Bill Walsh had returned as the general manager. One of the first things he had to deal with was our running back situation. Garrison Hearst was still recovering from his broken leg. We were so desperate that Bill signed Lawrence Phillips, who had a string of prior arrests and had been released by the Dolphins after a woman accused him of striking her at a nightclub. Commissioner Paul Tagliabue made Phillips pay a fine for violating the league's violent crime policy before he was cleared to enter training camp.

But we had bigger problems. The salary cap had depleted our roster. From 1997 to 1998 we lost thirty-two veterans. From 1998 to 1999 we lost another thirty veterans. Heading into training camp this year, we were a very different team. We'd had a window of opportunity to get back to the Super Bowl in 1997 and 1998, but we'd missed it. I knew it. Jerry knew it. Mariucci knew it.

Nonetheless, I couldn't have been happier. I had finally found my soul mate and we were getting married.

Barb flew up for training camp, and she went to the first couple of preseason games. We won both games, but barely.

And for the first time in my career, I felt our team was very vulnerable.

August 30, 1999. It's our third exhibition game. We're playing at Oakland, and NFL Films has asked me to wear a wire for the game. They have also designated a camera to shadow my every move. The minute I emerge from the tunnel the Raiders' fans are on me.

"Hey, there's crybaby Young," one of them yells. "Hey, Steve, I got your diaper."

A bunch of them get in the act, booing and screaming expletives at me. I jog onto the field, grab a ball, and start warming up. Guns N' Roses's "Welcome to the Jungle" is blaring. It's fitting. The fans act like they belong in a jungle.

"No wonder it's insanity," I say to a teammate. "They actually encourage it here."

Before the starting lineups are announced, a gong starts banging over the stadium sound system. I recognize it as the opening to AC/DC's "Hells Bells." The crowd is in a frenzy. I'm standing in the end zone, my back to the crowd. A police officer now approaches and stands beside me. The fans behind me are out of control, shouting obscenities and promising violence. They hold up a pole with my effigy attached. There is a noose around my neck. A guy is tugging on it, and people are cheering him on. AC/DC is barking:

You're only young but you're gonna die.

I turn to the cop. "This is crazy."

"It is."

"It's just a matter of whether I'm gonna get shot."

"That's why *we're* here," he says.

By this point the Raiders fans are shouting the lyrics: *I got my bell I'm gonna take ya to hell . . . Hell's bells.* They are giving me the finger. And the guy with my effigy is tightening the noose around the neck. My teammates are getting flipped off too.

I walk over to Tim McDonald. "This is messed up," I tell him.

· · ·

Our first possession is rough. After a quick first-down pass to J. J. Stokes, I throw two incomplete passes and get popped both times just as I release the ball. We end up punting.

Our second possession is worse. After a botched run play and a false start, three Raiders sack me. Then, on third-and-long, they blitz and I scramble around in my own end zone before getting body-slammed just as I release the ball. I land hard on my shoulder. The crowd loves it.

I'm fuming when I reach the sideline.

Mariucci tries to calm me down, but I'm fed up. We're disorganized. We're out of sync. Guys look lethargic. And I'm getting hammered.

On our third possession I lose my cool in the huddle.

"Let's make something happen! We gotta get going. We gotta get going!" I shout.

One of my linemen is looking at the crowd instead of at me.

"Get in the huddle!" I yell. "Listen close. Get your ear into my face. You know what I mean? Let's go! 'Red left, 19-5' on one."

After each play guys walk back to the huddle. They aren't into it.

"Let's go!" I scream. "Let's go! C'mon."

Two plays later guys are still listless.

"Hey! Hey! Let's go! Let's put it together. What are you guys doing? Don't wander around!"

My linemen don't appreciate my angry outburst.

"C'mon, man," one of them says.

"Back off a bit," another says.

When I'm on the field, I don't care if it's the preseason or the playoffs, I don't back off. I want to win. I run the ball and nearly pick up a first down before getting pounded to the ground. Then I call a pass play. Oakland blitzes. I throw on the run and get intercepted. I rip off my chin strap and walk off the field.

The offensive coordinator grabs me. "Steve, that's enough, pal. That was a good drive. We've seen enough from you."

I remove my helmet. I'm done for the day. But I'm in for a long season.

September 12, 1999. We open on the road against the Jacksonville Jaguars, one of the youngest teams in the league. After torrential rains, the field is a swamp by game time. Early on, running back Lawrence Phillips leaves the game with a concussion. Our other running back, Charlie Garner, can't find the holes. With our running game in shambles, Jacksonville knows we are going to pass and they start blitzing. Even on quick three-step drops, I am getting hit as I release.

Under extreme pressure all afternoon, I complete just nine of 26 passes for 96 yards. I throw two interceptions. It's one of my worst games in thirteen years as a 49er. Jerry has one of his worst games too, catching just one pass for 17 yards. I am sacked four times and knocked down I don't know how many times. We lose 41–3. It's the team's worst regular-season loss since 1980.

The Jacksonville game exposed what I already knew. The effects from the change in ownership and the big changes in personnel were really starting to show. We no longer had the players for the championship brand of football that was synonymous with the 49ers. That was particularly obvious when I was in the pocket. I was getting pressured from all directions on virtually every play. A quarterback can't operate that way.

After the game I called Barb in Scottsdale. She had watched me play on TV, and all she could talk about was the hits.

"How do you stand in the pocket knowing you are going to get hit like that?"

"The second you flinch you can't play."

"That's . . ." she paused, ". . . remarkable."

"I don't have a choice."

It was hard for her to understand. The mind-set of a quarterback in the NFL is hard for anybody to understand. Even the other players don't know what it's like to stand in the pocket and look for receivers while opponents with superior strength and size come at you full speed with the intention of knocking you down or even out. Some defenses even put bounties on quarterbacks' heads. But the quarterbacks who think about that stuff don't play quarterback for very long.

Eager to see me play live, Barb would be coming to San Francisco for our home opener against New Orleans, and more than anything I wanted to play well for her. But as the weekend approached the more anxious I became. I knew our team was in trouble. I knew I was vulnerable. I even started contemplating retirement. But I wasn't about to mention that to anyone.

Two days before the game I went to see a religious leader at the Mormon Church and received a blessing. Usually something like that would help. Not this time. The next night at the team hotel I tossed and turned much of the night. For so many years I'd longed to have my wife watch me play. Ironically, now that it was finally happening, the urge to walk away from the game was getting stronger by the day. I wanted to be with Barb and start a family more than I wanted to play football.

September 19, 1999. There are nearly 68,000 fans on hand for the Saints game. But my thoughts are only on one. Barb is sitting ten rows behind our bench. We score first when I connect with Terrell Owens on a 5-yard touchdown pass. The Saints stay with us, though, and it's 14–14 at halftime and I'm taking another beating.

The Saints open the third quarter with a long scoring drive that puts them up 7. Then I take a blow to the head while getting sacked, and I'm knocked out of the game. While I'm sidelined, our offense stalls. We can't get anything going.

With five minutes left in the game and New Orleans still leading by 7, I return in hopes of mounting a game-tying drive. On a crucial fourth down I throw an incomplete pass. That would end the game, but Chris Hewitt hits me late, ramming the crown of his helmet into my face mask. Cheap shots hurt the most. Instead of New Orleans taking over, the late hit penalty gives us an automatic first down and a new chance. My neck is wrenched, and I'm a little woozy. But moments later I throw another touchdown pass to Terrell Owens, tying the game at 21 with 2:03 remaining.

Thirty seconds later our defense intercepts a New Orleans pass and returns it 64 yards for a touchdown. We win 28–21, and our fans go crazy.

But I'm in rough shape. I've been sacked five times, and I've endured 21 hits. I have bruises everywhere. Twenty-one hits would be a lot for a running back. It's far too many for a quarterback.

Barb waits for me in an area reserved for family members and friends.

When I limp out of the locker room with a collar on my neck, a huge ice bag taped to my shoulder, and bruises all over, she gets her first true taste of life in the NFL.

"Oh my gosh!" she says.

I try to reassure her. "It's normal."

But the truth is that I've gotten the crap beaten out of me worse than I've had it in a long, long time.

I wished she could stay with me. But she had to get back to Arizona for a modeling shoot. It was her busy season too.

The next day I was in so much pain that I could barely move. The NFL announced a $7,500 fine on Chris Hewitt for his helmet-to-helmet hit on me.

I can't keep taking these hits, I told myself. In the first two games I'd been sacked nine times and hit more than thirty times. I felt more unprotected than I'd ever felt in my career. At this point, the only reason I wanted to keep playing was to win another Super Bowl. It was looking more and more like we lacked the personnel to get back there.

September 27, 1999. It's Sunday night, and I'm in my hotel room in Phoenix. We are scheduled to play the Cardinals on *Monday Night Football* in twenty-four hours. I have a bad feeling, and it isn't the typical pregame anxiety. My thoughts are much more ominous, like something bad is about to happen to me. I can feel it, and the closer the game gets the more it wears on me.

I telephone Barb from my hotel. She has her whole family coming to the game, along with some friends. She's so excited about it. But I suddenly unload on her.

"I don't know about this game . . . I'm not getting the protection I need . . . I'm getting killed out there . . . I don't want to keep doing this if we can't win a championship. And if we can't win a championship, maybe this should be my last year."

All of this blindsides her. This part of my world is all new to her.

I keep her on the phone for three solid hours. She keeps saying: "Don't worry. You're going to do great."

It was strange. I was worried about the game and my health, and she was confident. I didn't want to hang up.

Once I get on the field my outlook changes. It happens the moment I have a ball in my hand and I see Barb in the stands with her family. I can't wait to escape with her after the game.

Despite all of my pregame dread, the game is fun from the moment it starts. In the first half I complete 13 of 23 passes for 92 yards, including a touchdown pass to Jerry Rice. We're actually playing pretty well. As the first half winds down we're up 17–0.

Only thirty seconds remain in the second quarter when I approach the line of scrimmage. It looks like Phoenix is planning to blitz. On the snap I see cornerback J. J. McCleskey coming hard around the left side. I'm not worried. I take three steps back and get into my throwing motion.

What happened next I honestly don't remember.

Arizona cornerback Aeneas Williams, one of the hardest hitters in the league, was blitzing from my blind side. On the snap he sprinted toward me. Lawrence Phillips was supposed to pick up any blitz from my blind side, but he missed his assignment. Williams was untouched, and I never saw him coming. He got to me in 1.2 seconds. His helmet hit me first. Then the rest of his body went through me. Williams happened to be wearing a hidden microphone for NFL Films. I'm told that the sound of his crashing into me sounded like a man getting hit by a car. On the way down my head smashed into my lineman's thigh. As I said, I don't recall any of this.

But I clearly remember lying on the ground, flat on my back, motionless, with my eyes closed. I knew I had taken a brutal hit, and I feared my neck was broken. I was more worried about that than being knocked out. I knew doctors and Coach Mariucci were hovering over me. I could hear them. But when I finally opened my eyes, the stadium was silent. It's a weird sensation to be amid 60,000 spectators and hear quiet.

The doctors asked me a couple of questions. I don't remember if I responded. The first thing I do recall saying was "no" when they called for a stretcher. I was adamant — I would off on my own. By this point I was confident that my neck wasn't broken. I just wanted a few more minutes to lie on the ground.

Eventually I sat up. Then I stood. The crowd cheered as I groggily made my way to the sideline, where I took a seat on our bench.

We ran one more play, and the half ended. I stood up and somehow jogged off the field.

As soon as I reached the locker room the medical team led me to the training room, where I was examined. I sat on a table until Mariucci entered. I had a towel around my neck.

"Put me back in," I told him.

He looked at the doctors. They shook their heads no.

"Coach, I'm fine! I'm fine!"

Mariucci looked at me.

"I can play," I insisted.

"I can't, Steve," Mooch said firmly.

"C'mon. We have to win this game."

The trainer took my helmet.

"C'mon. Let's go. I'm ready to go," I insisted.

"Steve," Mariucci finally said, "I've got to make a decision here. I know you want to play. But I'm not going to put you back in."

"Coach, you gotta put me back in. The team is counting on me."

"Steve, you're not going back in. I love you too much to play you right now."

As he turned to leave his eyes welled up and I buried my face in my hands.

We won the game 24–10. But I never returned in the second half. After the game I spoke to the press and admitted for the first time that I was concerned about the ramifications of repeated concussions. Barb waited for me outside the locker room. All her friends and family wanted to see me. But I only wanted to see her. More than anything, I wanted to get out of there. We had previously arranged for me to stay behind the team for a night in Phoenix so Barb and I could have some time alone. I had cleared it with the team. But Mariucci was now having second thoughts.

"Coach, I'm fine."

"Steve, you're not fine."

"C'mon, coach. I don't have a headache. You can let me stay."

"I think you should come back with us."

"I just want to be with Barb for a little bit. Then I'll be right back."

"Steve, I think you better come back with the team."

Barb was disappointed, and I was miffed. I glumly said good-bye to her at the stadium and got on the bus to the airport with the team.

45

THE LONG GOOD-BYE

THE NEXT DAY I underwent an MRI at Stanford Hospital. The results were inconclusive. In other words, the scans showed no visible signs of injury or trauma to the brain area. But I was very sore and in need of rest. I was told that, as a precautionary measure, I shouldn't return to action for a couple of weeks. Initially, I interpreted that to mean I'd miss a couple of games.

But controversy over the timeline of my return quickly escalated into a national debate over whether I should ever play again. Outlets from sports talk radio to newspaper editorial pages weighed in on my situation. The NFL was already attracting a spotlight from the growing awareness about the dangers of concussions. On one level it wasn't surprising that so many voices were weighing in and that most of them were saying I should retire. The fact was that I had taken a brutal hit in front of a national audience on *Monday Night Football*. Although I never watched the replay, I am told that it aired over and over again on television news broadcasts, on ESPN, and on the Internet. The more people saw the image of me lying motionless on the ground the more politicized the entire situation became.

All this being said, the fact was that the symptoms from my concussion in the Cardinals game — some dizziness, being groggy, headache — were completely gone within forty-eight hours of the hit. My neck was sore for a little more than a week. But after sitting out for two weeks, I felt great. I underwent a thorough medical exam and passed with flying colors. I went to see Mariucci and told him I was feeling better and couldn't wait to get back on the field. He told me he wasn't prepared to play me.

Internally, I was having a tug-of-war. Part of me felt duty-bound to help my team. But part of me wasn't sure I wanted to keep playing football. I talked with Barb. She was behind me either way. But while I sat out, the team kept losing. Two in a row. Three in a row. Four in a row. It got worse each week. The team ended up losing eight straight and ten of the last eleven games. The 49ers' run was over.

I was still conflicted by the time November rolled around. From a career standpoint, I knew I was still at the top of my game as a quarterback. I also knew that physically I had a clean bill of health. At the same time I knew that the team was in free fall and the organization didn't want to put me back in uniform. Yet the neurologists could point to nothing that suggested I was injured or unfit to play. All of the focus was on future risks.

Eventually, Leigh Steinberg called the lead neurologist on whom the 49ers were relying for a medical opinion about my fitness to play, and the doctor told him that there was no way he could clear me to play.

Shortly after that, I went back to the neurologist for another checkup. Brent Jones came with me. I had been through a battery of tests, MRIs, and consultations. The bottom line was that I was healthy and the imaging around my brain looked ideal. The entire consultation focused on the future risks to my health. The doctor wasn't prepared to clear me to play.

When we left his office, Brent stopped on the sidewalk outside the clinic and said: "Look around, Steve. How does it feel?"

"How does what feel?"

"Retirement," he said. "It's a beautiful thing."

The 49ers finished the season 3-13, and I never returned to the playing field. At the end of the regular season I agreed to work as a television analyst during the playoffs.

It was the first time in a decade that I wasn't playing in the NFL playoffs myself. On January 8, 2000, I was in a suit and tie in a television studio. Television work came fairly naturally to me. I liked it. But I still wasn't ready to walk away from playing. I figured I'd use the off-season to figure out my football future.

But that could wait. My immediate focus was my wedding.

Barb and I got married in Kona, Hawaii, on March 14, 2000. It was the first marriage ceremony in the newly opened LDS Kona Temple. The wedding was as joyful as I had hoped. Many of my teammates and coaches attended. Even my number-one fan — my ailing eighty-year-old grandfather Gorin Steed — made the trip. Brent Jones and Harris Barton threw a party to kick off the week. We had five days of golf, volleyball, more parties, and a luau before the big day. It was a celebration. During all of this excitement I had kept Barb's wedding ring in a safe behind the desk in the hotel's main lobby. On the afternoon of the wedding I realized I had lost the key. In a panic, I turned to Brent Jones: "Bro, I'm leaving you in charge. You've got to get the ring out of the safe and get it to me by sunset."

"Bro, you gotta be kidding me!" he said.

While I dashed off to the ceremony, Brent dealt with hotel security. They were going to bring in a locksmith, but Brent said there was no time for that. "You gotta break it open," he demanded.

They used a motorized hacksaw, which set off the hotel alarm system for fifteen minutes.

Meanwhile, the ring ceremony had already started. Barb and I were standing in front of everyone while her uncle sang "The Lord's Prayer." I was sweating because I still didn't have the ring. It was third-and-ten when all of a sudden Brent came running in, passing all the seated guests and giving me a giant bear hug while slipping the ring into my pocket. Nobody noticed the handoff. Moments later, I slipped the ring on Barb's finger.

Once again, it was Brent to the rescue. *What would I do without him?*

After the wedding, Barb and I left on our honeymoon. We planned to travel the globe for six weeks. But we had to cut the trip two weeks short to attend my grandfather's funeral. The sad loss of my grandfather was soon offset by the great news that Barb was pregnant.

· · ·

For the rest of the spring I didn't think much about football. The realization that I was now a husband and soon-to-be father really tilted the scales for me. My life was filling in, and I could feel my priorities shifting.

In May I got a call from Denver Broncos head coach Mike Shanahan. After winning back-to-back Super Bowls in '98 and '99, Denver desperately needed a starting quarterback. John Elway had retired, and Shanahan was looking for someone to lead the team back to a third Super Bowl. He asked if I was interested.

Deep down I knew I could still play at a very high level. My skills were as good as ever. I was in exceptional shape too. And unlike San Francisco, the Broncos had a solid offensive line and a team that was loaded with talent. Really, all they needed was a quarterback to take them back to the Super Bowl. Another tempting factor was that three of my best years as a quarterback had been under Shanahan.

There was one more factor. We were about to have a child. I really wanted my child to see me play. But the 49ers had made it clear that they were not going to let me play again. Suddenly I had a dilemma: *Do I play for Denver or retire?*

I agreed to meet Mike Shanahan in Denver. Barb went with me. But she was still having morning sickness, and it was so bad that she couldn't leave the hotel room. Mike and I met alone in a restaurant. Over lunch he asked me about my health. I told him I was fine. Then he told me about how close Denver was to returning to the Super Bowl. In many ways it was an ideal situation for me.

"It would be great to reunite and do this again," he said.

"It would," I told him. Then I paused. "But, Mike, I can't."

I did want to keep playing, but now that I was in Denver I knew I could never play there. It was certainly nothing against Denver. But I had realized that I couldn't play anywhere but San Francisco. It was my town. I would have felt disloyal to leave and finish my career elsewhere. As the song says, I left my heart in San Francisco. I wanted to retire a San Francisco 49er.

There was a long pause.

"Steve, I understand completely," Mike said.

"I'm going to miss this," I told him. "I'm really going to miss this."

· · ·

June 12, 2000. Barb is three months along now and looks stunning. I am in love with this woman. I can't believe how lucky I am.

We leave our home in Palo Alto and drive to the 49ers' training facility. In one hour I am scheduled to announce my retirement. This will be no ordinary announcement. It will be televised live. Hundreds of people are coming. And we're doing it in the locker room.

When we arrive, I get Barb comfortable in a conference room — a soft chair, beverages, whatever she needs. Then I duck into Mariucci's office. He looks up from his desk.

"Got the speech all written out?" he says. "Is this like a lengthy deal?"

I laugh. "It's gonna go on forever."

We hug each other. Mooch is one of the people I've asked to speak, along with Brent Jones and Jerry Rice.

"Anything else you want me to do?" he says.

"Nah. Just go for it."

"You want me to announce you're the starting quarterback next season?"

We both laugh.

"Is this great or what?" I tell him.

Then we hear a familiar voice coming down the hall. It's Eddie DeBartolo. He has a big smile on his face.

"Hello, Steven."

"Mr. D."

He hugs me.

"Thanks for coming to this," I say.

"Are you kidding me? I wouldn't miss this."

"Can you imagine? After all these years, I'm going to end up with a kid."

"It's wonderful. You're doing it the way you wanted to do it."

I hear another familiar voice coming down the hallway. It's the sportscaster Chris Berman. He has a huge grin on his face.

"Boomer!"

"Just wanted to say hello and offer my congratulations . . . on everything," he says.

I have to go check on Barb. On my way to find her I bump into LaVell Edwards and his wife. They have flown in from Provo.

"Coach, so good to see you."

He hugs me. Then his wife hugs me.

"Let me go get Barb. She'll want to say hello."

I dart out and find her. Every time I look at her I pinch myself. *Is this really happening? Can life be this good?*

It's 9:30 AM. Time to get this going. I duck into the training room and remove my speech from my pocket. Using the training table as a desk, I make some last-minute edits. The noise from the adjacent locker room draws my attention. I part the curtain and take a peek. The place is jammed. My parents are in the front row. Barb sits next to them. My brothers and their wives are one row back. I see Jim Herrmann and Lee Johnson. Leigh Steinberg is next to them. Mike Shanahan is seated next to Carmen Policy. Harris Barton is in a suit. Terrell Owens is in practice attire.

I step into the shower area to be alone. I've spent the last fifteen years here in this locker room, playing for San Francisco. This is my last time. It's bittersweet. I've been through so much here. This is where I was racked with anxiety. And it's where I finally surmounted that anxiety. This is where I suffered defeat, injury, and pain. And it's where I celebrated the glorious taste of victory. I reached the top of Everest here. It's the place where I finally answered the question, *How good can I become?*

Suddenly the retirement ceremony begins. I'm still in the shower waiting. But I can hear Steve Sabol's voice. He's narrating a special film about my career that's been put together by the folks at NFL Films for my retirement. Everyone in the locker room is watching it. I can't see it, but I can hear it. And when the film gets to my famous run against the Minnesota Vikings in 1988, I instantly go back in time. "Cuts back at the forty. Gets away again!"

I reach back into my pocket, remove my speech, and make one final edit. Then I step through the curtain and enter the locker room.

Everyone breaks into applause. Nearly 200 seats are packed with former teammates, friends, and family. The media occupy the seats directly in front of a makeshift stage. The walls are lined with people standing. I step to the microphone and spot my dad. He's somber. My mother is pleased. They are holding hands. Barb is beaming.

I welcome everyone, and then I introduce Brent Jones. He steps to the microphone. "This is a sad time for the Bay Area," he says. "It's truly an end of an era. But it is also a happy day for people who care about Steve Young."

Brent was my roommate and moral support for more than a decade. The bond between us is thicker than blood. As he speaks I have trouble keeping my emotions in check.

"He's desperate to win," Jones says. "He needs to win. And he always has. That puts him on a different plane than most people."

Brent sits down, and Denise DeBartolo York gets up. She is Eddie De-Bartolo's sister, and she took control of the team when Eddie stepped down. She has tears in her eyes when she takes the podium and thanks me. Steve Mariucci gets up after her. Through each of these speeches I manage to control myself.

Then Jerry Rice gets up. As usual, he's dressed to the nines. He pulls out a poem he's penned for me. But he chokes up when he tries to read it. I'm not used to seeing Jerry cry. Nobody is.

Finally, he gathers himself.

But then I start crying. I've been blessed to play quarterback for the 49ers and throw footballs to Jerry Rice. Jerry and I teamed up for eighty-three touchdowns. We set an NFL record.

When Jerry sits down, I take the microphone to give my speech.

"I think many probably wondered what we're doing here in a locker room," I say. "When they asked me where I wanted to hold my retirement announcement, I thought, where else? This is the most intimate place for a player. This is the place where you make all the big decisions, where all the sweat and the toil are. This is where the relationships are forged. In a way, this is where football happens away from the crowd."

I pause.

"In a way, I guess, I wanted to show up for work one more day."

The reporters smile. The cameras click and flash. My teammates are all looking up at me. I want to get off the stage, walk over to my locker, put on my uniform, and head out to the practice field. I want to warm up with Brent. I want to joke with Mooch. I want to huddle up the team. I want to throw one more touchdown to Jerry.

"Retiring at thirty-eight . . . in some ways it sucks," I say.

Everyone laughs. I smile. But I mean it.

But when I look at Barb, I want a family more than I want to keep playing.

I smile through the rest of my speech. I have so many memories. And all the people who helped me along the way — from high school to college to the pros — are on hand to share them with me. I'm in the 49ers' locker room, and it's full of people who care about me. I love these people. And today, as I leave this locker room for the last time, I go with my wife who is carrying our child.

I go with no regrets, only gratitude.

EPILOGUE

MARCH 28, 2015. Gripping a football, I'm wearing leather dress shoes, blue slacks, and a checkered shirt. It's sunny and warm, and I'm in Candlestick Park, standing almost exactly where I stood when I threw the last-second touchdown pass to Terrell Owens to beat Green Bay in the '98 playoffs. I can still remember how loud it felt at that moment. It was as though the entire Bay Area let out a collective yell. What a wonderful memory!

Today is different. The Stick is being demolished to make way for a new mall and housing units. I'm here with a crew from NFL Films to shoot a documentary about my football life. I'm supposed to throw some passes while the cameras roll.

But first, I look around and take it all in. I loved playing here. So many memories. The Run. Beating Dallas. The Catch II. My jersey being retired. To this day I run into people in the Bay Area who give me a high-five or a hug and tell me the seat number they were in for these moments. These fans are like family. It's sobering to realize that this place where I grew up as a player and a man is disappearing.

After I finish throwing passes for NFL Films, I exit Candlestick for the last time, passing through the dark tunnel that leads to where our locker room used to be. I recall standing in that space before every game, feeling the enormity of the moment. I take one last look around.

Then I emerge into the sunlit parking lot. A few construction workers in hard hats and steel-toe boots want to take pictures. One of them has his teenage son with him. He hands me a jersey with number 8. "Thanks for all the great memories," he says. He also lets me know I am the last Niner to leave The Stick before it's torn down. I cherish the moment.

After a few minutes, I get in my Toyota minivan. It's filled with my kids' things — baseball mitts, gymnastics gear, sneakers, tap shoes, and backpacks. Driving away, I look in the rearview mirror at Candlestick. *This place is history,* I tell myself. *I am so grateful to have been part of it.*

February 7, 2016. I'm with my family outside Levi's Stadium, the San Francisco 49ers' new home in Santa Clara. Today is Super Bowl 50 between the Denver Broncos and Carolina Panthers. The NFL has invited the MVPs from the previous forty-nine Super Bowls to be on hand for a pregame ceremony. The halls of the new stadium are lined with life-size pictures of all the legends who ever played for the 49ers. My kids stop at every picture of me. We pass by the stadium's EDWARD J. DEBARTOLO SR. 49ERS HALL OF FAME. It has a new exhibit featuring life-size bronze statues of 49er greats. Mine shows me running out of the pocket, pointing to my intended receiver before I throw.

Just before kick off, I am ushered into a waiting room and instantly start reconnecting with old friends Joe Namath, Roger Staubach, Brett Favre, Troy Aikman, Tom Brady, Aaron Rodgers, and my former teammates Jerry Rice and Joe Montana. It's a great moment that's made even greater by the fact that my wife and children are on hand to witness it. I'm reminded that I have actually lived two lives — my football life and the one I live now. Barb and I have been married for sixteen years. We have four children — fifteen-year-old Braedon, a six-three freshman who loves singing, the arts, computers, and comedy; sensitive and tough Jackson, who is almost thirteen, likes to play every sport, and loves animals; nine-year-old Summer, our tenacious gymnast who could dribble a ball at two, fills our house with song; and sweet seven-year-old Laila, our aspiring dancer, keeps us all full of love. My life used to revolve around being a quarterback. Today it centers on being a husband and a father.

These days my life is pretty sublime. I spend a lot of time in my minivan, carpooling kids to school and activities. I love coming home from work and throwing balls in the backyard with my kids. I've also discovered I'm a pretty good cook. Each week I teach Sunday school at my local congregation. When I was in the NFL, my life always felt like third-and-ten. That feeling is never to be replicated, nor should it be. But a few years ago, right around the time I turned fifty, it hit me that my kids never actually saw me play. A big part of my past is a mystery to them. That's what motivated me to write this book. I wanted my kids to learn about the life I had before I had a family.

The process of writing about my life as a football player has enriched my appreciation for the life I have now. It's a wonderful life. I have the two things I always wanted when I was in the league — marriage to my soul mate and children. I help Barb run the Forever Young Foundation, which won the Charity Navigator Award for best children's and family charity for its efficient and positive work. Our foundation focuses on the development, strength, and education of children. Barb founded Sophie's Place, which is making homes for music therapy inside children's hospitals. Barb also continues to be a strong advocate for human rights. That is her passion. She was honored with the Human Rights Campaign's Ally award for her incredible work. Together we have spoken at events to help raise awareness and create a better world for LGBT youth and families.

When pro athletes retire, it's like falling off a cliff. One day you are the best in the world at one thing; the next day you wake up and realize you're not very good at anything else. I didn't want to feel that way. So I immediately traded my helmet and pads for Silicon Valley slacks and button-down shirts. With three partners I started a private equity firm in the Bay Area. I've now been in private equity for as long as I played professional football. HGGC, where I'm a managing director, has grown into a global firm with companies in the United States and Europe. But my office is close to home. I'm also an on-air analyst for *Monday Night Football* on ESPN, which allows me to remain connected to the game I love.

My dad is eighty and still keeps his workout routine. He is all smiles these days. He has found he loves growing a vegetable garden and golfing with friends. My mom is seventy-seven and still as beautiful as ever with the energy of a twenty-year-old. She writes a monthly column in a Utah paper. When Dad retired fourteen years ago, they sold our family home in Greenwich and moved west to be closer to their five children and twenty-six grandchildren (my amazing nieces and nephews). My parents split time between Utah and Arizona. I am so grateful for their example in my life. My three brothers are doctors and my sister works at my foundation. I have so much admiration for each of them.

One of the highlights of my life was having Dad introduce me when I was inducted into the Hall of Fame in 2005. I actually invited Mom to give the introduction speech — she would have been the first woman to do so. But she insisted that Dad be the one. With Barb and our two boys looking on, I reflected on the time when I visited Canton with my parents at age twelve. Dreams do come true. I was the tenth quarterback in history to be inducted on the first ballot. I was also the first lefty. When I arrived at BYU as a freshman and the quarterback coach told me I'd never make it there as a quarterback, he tried to prove it by showing me there were no lefty QBs in the Hall of Fame. This year, 2016, there will be two in the Hall, Ken Stabler and myself.

When I was inducted, my fellow inductee was Dan Marino, the Pitt freshman who I watched in awe when I was a high school senior recruit at Army. Who would have imagined that Dan and I would enter the Hall of Fame together?

I'm still close to my friends from my BYU days — Jim Herrmann, Lee Johnson, Tyde Tanner, and Greg Madsen. We talk all the time. Our focus these days is helping Greg beat cancer. I also remain close to my 49er teammates. Shortly after retirement I formed a company with Brent Jones. I owe him so much. Jerry Rice is an even closer friend today than when we played together. We have teamed up to raise a lot of money for our 8 to 80 Zones and the Forever Young Foundation. We've also been fortunate to pair up again for many commercial campaigns. Toward the end of 2015, Jerry and I went to Los Angeles to film a commercial for AT&T with Joe Montana, Bo Jackson, and Emmitt Smith. It aired during the college football championship in January 2016. Titled "Awkward," the ad featured Joe and me trying to shake hands and high-five each other. It was great being together with Joe again, and critics called it one of the best commercials of the year.

I've also got my health. I either outgrew my anxiety or football beat it out of me. Since retirement it really hasn't been around. I guess playing in front of 65,000 people over and over again has its positive effects. Everyone who has anxiety experiences it in a unique way. Similarly, there are plenty of ways to deal with anxiety, including medication. I avoided medication for the simple reason that it made me feel foggy, like being under a blanket. There are obviously many situations where medication is a lifesaver for others who struggle with anxiety. In addition, epigenetics, nutrigenetics, and nutrigenomics are new frontiers that will change the way anxiety is treated in the future.

The NFL has continued to make strides when it comes to head injuries. As I finished writing these pages, the NFL's top health and safety official admitted for the first time that there is a link between football and chronic traumatic encephalopathy (CTE), a brain disease found in dozens of retired players. CTE is real. A lot of guys who played in my era are really struggling. We need to get some real clarity surrounding the potential dangers from Pee Wee football all the way to the pros so that players, coaches, and parents fully understand the assumption of the risk, take preventive measures, and continue to play the greatest team sport.

When I sustained concussions as a player, I did not experience any lingering effects. I can honestly say that to this day I have had no effects from concussions. Maybe it is the way I kept my body/mind healthy or my genetics, but I can only hope and pray that it remains that way throughout my years.

At this stage of my life, I'm most grateful for two things: my family and my faith. The way I met Barb has a storybook quality. We've gone on to raise the kind of family I always dreamed of having. But my life before retirement was filled with moments where things didn't go so well or turn out the way I had planned. Looking back, I'm grateful for those experiences. They were defining moments that made me a better person. I'm also grateful to the individuals and families who came into my life at critical times, all of whom spent years at my side; too many to mention in one book. And I'm thankful for the angels who still remind me what's most important in life.

Playing in the NFL was a great life. But the life I have today is even better. Much better.

ACKNOWLEDGMENTS

This book couldn't have been written without all the wonderful people who comprised the chapters of my life.

Thank you to all of my surrogate families through the years. I hold you all so very close to my heart. The Burrs, Merrills, Peerys, Lynn and Gene Bennion, Barbara and Doug Schaerrer, and Greg and Danette Williams.

Carole, thanks for listening to thousands of hours of all of my worries. You are my second mom and one of my spiritual mentors.

Truman and Ann, thank you for your spiritual guidance and friendship. Many of the bedrock testimonies that I hold dear were solidified as we walked the dusty roads in Israel together.

Uncle Bob, I am so grateful for your unwavering belief in me way before I believed in myself.

Bonkus, I know you don't miss *City Slickers* but I know we both miss our long talks in room 9043. What would I have done without you? Brothers forever.

Tyde, how is it such a goofball was so inspired, tenacious, faithful, and funny? You helped make our family possible. We are forever grateful to you.

RQ Jones (LJ) and Herm, my best friends for life. You helped a shy, timid kid find his legs and propped me up through everything. Lake Powell to 111 Yacht Club to The Rosa. My best memories are with you two. Now that you both have Gold cards, lunch is on you.

Mad Dog, master of the eternal perspective. Nothing was too complex. Your ability to take real life issues and overlay the Gospel was invaluable. Now we fight for you.

Dave and Linda Bradford, thanks for taking us in and providing everything we could ever need those first years. We love you.

Harris and Johnny. Football was just the vehicle we rode as we grew deep roots of friendship. The Jewish-Mormon mafia.

And Turk (D. van Blerkom), thanks for being such a great friend all these years.

Along the way I made great friends who seasoned me with the good things in life. Mark Belini, Lake Powell forever. Scott and Tammy Runia, Johnny Miller, Ken Leister, Shirley, Chad Lewis, The Duke, Ryan Tibbits, George Curtis, Ollie, Floyd, Gordy, among so many. My boys back in the mean streets of Greenwich, Eddie Sheehan, Dan and Mike Gas, Bobby Haidinger, Randy Caravella, Paul Perry, Marc Gangi, Steve Gebhardt, Frankie Parelli, Nick LeRose, Jim Gannon, Randy Pace, and so many more.

Thanks to all of my teammates and coaches from beginning to end.

Mike Holmgren, Mike Shanahan, Marc Trestman, Mooch, Marty, Jimmy, Greg Knapp, Gary Kubiak, Sid Gillman, Ted Tollner, the best QB coaches anyone has ever had.

Coach LaVell, how did you ever think the wishbone kid could throw? You made faith and football be friends. I loved you as my coach and love you even more now.

Jimmy Mac and Joe, thanks, I learned from the best.

Jerry, thanks for all of the inspiration and friendship.

Mike Cofer, Mark Harris, Greg Clark, Billy Musgrave, Tim McDonald, Merton Hanks, Bryant Young, Derrick Deese, Jesse Sapolu, Steve Wallace, Junior Bryant, Ray Tufts, Bart Oates, Ted Walsh, Steve Bono, Dave Rahn (we miss you), Rodney Knox, Bronco, Fred, Kirk Reynolds, geez I could go on forever the number of 49er family that I owe so much.

There is no way to mention everyone let alone the hundreds of stories that go along with our time together. Football is the ultimate team game and I'm so blessed to have played with you all.

Eddie and Candy DeBartolo, thank you for being the first to make a franchise a family. Honored to be in the Hall of Fame with you.

Carmen Policy, grateful you kept rowing against the current to make it happen.

Thank you Denise, John, and Jed York for treating me so well.

Jack Lambert, the Jewish uncle I never had. Thanks for sending me to Phoenix for the date. Your wisdom was priceless.

I couldn't do it without the experts. Leigh Steinberg, Jeff Moorad, and Dave Dunn, I know your secret was to negotiate after midnight. Russ Speilman and Frank Vuono, my marketing geniuses, thank you. Thanks Kaele and Stef for assisting me.

Thanks to my sister and sisters-in-law for handling all of the fan mail: Melissa, Stacy, and Shamberlin.

Doctors Dillingham, Fanton, Gamburd, Brodie, and Millard, thank you for keeping me upright.

Ira, Art, Ann, Cam, Murph, Matt, Silver, Mark, Clark, Packer, Dennis, Eric, Lowell, you were sometimes tough but always fair. Thanks for writing it all down.

Seth Markman thanks for keeping me close to the game I love.

Thank you to our Forever Young Foundation family led by Sterling Tanner and Michelle Knox. Thanks to all our board members past and present Bob Gay, Junior Bryant, Gayla Compton, Mike Merchant, Bob Steed, and Mike Leavitt, as well as the hundreds of like-minded givers of self who are counted among us, thank you from the bottom of my heart for all you do and all that you are.

Roger, Kelli, Mick, Marie, John, and Joe. Loving the thirty-three years together helping the kids at Children's Miracle Network Hospitals. One of the best chapters of my life.

Thanks to all those friends who dropped everything and took the time to proofread the manuscript in only three days. Every one of you made it better. Greg Madsen, Brent Jones, Herm, LJ, Kim Mazinter, Raina Scribner, May Herr, Tanya Dargel, Chad and Sophie Christensen, Dallas Lloyd, Tom McCook, Derek Anderson, Ann Madsen, and all of my family. I want to thank Katie Jepsen for all of the See's chocolates and candid opinions. Also thanks to Stacy Young and Kathryn Macleod for their expert opinions. Thanks to Eric Borelli and Barb for the title.

I am indebted to those who agreed to read portions of the manuscript and provide comments: My mom and dad, Bob Gay, John Frank, Harris Barton, Carole Burr, Bart Oates, Kay Rasmussen, Harv Barenz, Chris Barlow, and my brothers and sister, Mike, Tom, Melissa, and Jimmy.

NFL Films's Chris Barlow spent hundreds of hours getting NFL Films's *A Football Life* ready with the book. I can't wait to see it.

My personal assistant Joy Hayame and all my colleagues at HGGC, especially my longtime business partner Rich Lawson, were incredibly supportive of this project.

A very special thanks to my trusted friend and collaborator, Jeff Benedict, who I met through a mutual dear friend, Bob Gay. Bob suggested that Jeff could help me write the part of my story my children never got to see. I liked the idea of having a chance to tell it to them in my words and not have them glean it from articles and secondhand stories. I had no intent of publishing this book. As Jeff worked tirelessly to finish his many interviews of friends, family, former teammates, coaches, and went through boxes and boxes of journals, scrapbooks, documents, articles, and film, the book came to life and he encouraged me to publish it. I declined twice. I guess the third time is a charm. Jeff's perseverance was the key.

Jeff then introduced me to literary agent Richard Pine, and I'm grateful for his guidance and expertise.

Thanks to my old friend Rick Wolff, who acquired and edited the book. Rick, you were so very patient with us and we will always be grateful to you. I'm also indebted to all the wonderful folks at Houghton Mifflin Harcourt: Bruce Nichols, Rosemary McGuinness, Chloe Foster, Margaret Anne Miles, Rachael DeShano, Cindy Buck, Simone Payment, Sara Thomas, Kate Mills, Katrina Kruse, Laurie Brown, Maire Gorman, Becky Saikia-Wilson, Heather Gray, Emily Andrukaitis, Crystal Paquette, Carla Gray, Lori Glazer, Megan Swartz Gellert, and Ron Hussey. Plus a special tip of my cap to Brian Moore, who worked so diligently and patiently on making the cover perfect. I'm also grateful to Dorothea Halliday, a friend of Jeff's, who helped us on the narrative.

Of course, my favorite editor was Barb. Thank you, my love, for spending endless hours going through drafts of the manuscript and carefully fact-checking and making sure the context, tone, and voice was right. This book had no chance without you.

I'm grateful for the way my children supported me in this process.

Braedon and Jackson, thank you for fending for yourselves many nights, doing your homework without help while Mom and I worked on the book. Summer and Laila, you were so patient. I loved when you would read or do a project nearby while we worked. I know you're glad to have your captive audience back for all your daily choreographed trampoline routines. This book has always been for the four of you, my greatest gifts.

INDEX